D1473980

WE SHALL DIE TOGETHER

And Forty-Four Other Stories
Of Turmoil, Tragedy & Triumph in Georgia

Co-Edited by R. Olin Jackson and Daniel M. Roper

Published by Legacy Communications, Inc.
P.O. Box 585
Armuchee, GA 30105-0585
1-800-547-1625
www.georgiabackroads.com

I

International Standard Book Number (ISBN):
978-1-880816-23-7

Library of Congress Control Number:
2008934194

For Additional Copies:
Legacy Communications, Inc.
Post Office Box 585
Armuchee, Georgia 30105-0585
1-800-547-1625
www.georgiabackroads.com

Dedication

For twenty years from 1985 to 2005, R. Olin Jackson manned the helm of *North Georgia Journal* magazine, which became *Georgia Backroads* magazine in 2002. Many other regional magazines devoted to Georgia were born and died during this period, but under Olin's steady leadership, *North Georgia Journal/Georgia Backroads* thrived.

Through the years, Olin encouraged and nurtured the careers of dozens of freelance writers. Some of these writers were professionals who wrote for leading publications and wire-services including Associated Press, Reuters, and Knight-Ridder. They had opportunities to visit and write about far-flung, exotic locales, but always returned home to write about their first love – Georgia.

Many of these writers proudly referred to themselves as amateurs. They loved nothing more than discovering a fascinating story about some little-known person, location, or event in their "neck of the woods," researching the story, and writing for publication in *North Georgia Journal* or *Georgia Backroads*. Olin always encouraged them in their endeavors, and the satisfaction of seeing their work in print frequently encouraged them to pursue new stories.

As a result of Olin's commitment to the magazine, hundreds of fascinating stories about Georgia's history, natural environment, lifestyles, and travel destinations have been preserved for posterity.

After twenty years at the helm of Legacy Communications, Inc. – twenty years of deadlines and details; of publishing eighty issues of the magazine and eight books; and of managing a small but complicated and demanding business – Olin retired from the publishing world in 2005. He and his wife Judy reside in Roswell, Georgia, where Olin now spends as much time as possible singing in the choir at Mt. Pisgah United Methodist Church when he's not working on his beloved cabin "on a peak in Polk" near Rockmart, Georgia.

DANIEL M. ROPER
SEPTEMBER 2008
ROME, GEORGIA

Acknowledgements

The articles, facts, and photographs on the pages that follow are a compilation of information carefully researched and painstakingly collected over a period of approximately six years, from 2002 to 2008. Each chapter represents an article that appeared in *Georgia Backroads* magazine during that period. R. Olin Jackson served as editor and publisher of the magazine through the first half of 2005, and upon his retirement Daniel M. Roper assumed that position.

All research involved in the preparations of the stories included in this book was conducted by skilled historians – whether professional or dedicated amateur. Each story represents countless hours of careful research and writing. Thanks to their efforts, many fascinating stories from Georgia history have been preserved for posterity and for the enjoyment of others.

Grateful appreciation is hereby extended to these writers and researchers without whose assistance this book would not have been possible:

Mary Ann Anderson
Bob Andrew
William E. Bray
C. Ray Chandler
Jean A. Curran
Robert S. Davis, Jr.
Gary Elam
Hugh T. Harrington
Nathan S. Hipps
Robert Latimer Hurst
Leslie Johnston
Jackie Kennedy
Michael Kirton
Joyce Kramer
Brandon Lowe
Eileen Babb McAdams

Michael H. McDougald
W. Pate McMichael
Maylinda McRae
Deborah Malone
Alexander Kathryn Mosca
Joshua Owens
Dwayne Keith Petty
Martin Register
Daniel M. Roper
Robert D. Temple
Carol Thompson
Jane Walker
Kathleen Walls
R. Allen Wilburn
Michael Williams

Book cover and design by Clifford Johnson Design
cj.design@mindspring.com

Table of Contents

We Shall Die Together

Like an Old Testament prophet, Talbotton, Georgia's Isidor Straus rose from the ashes of the U.S. Civil War, journeyed through a wilderness and began life anew for himself and his family. He prospered, rising to become the owner of R.H. Macy & Company in New York City. In the end, he lost his life in the icy waters of the North Atlantic on an ill-fated ocean liner called Titanic, but even death could not conquer the love Isador shared with his wife Ida.

DANIEL M. ROPER

The silence awakened Archibald Gracie at midnight. The ship had grown quiet. Too quiet. For four days, Colonel Gracie had been a passenger on board the R.M.S. *Titanic* and now, for the first time, he no longer detected the constant, almost imperceptible vibration of the huge ocean liner as its great engines drove it through the waters of the North Atlantic.

Archibald Gracie

The 54-year-old retired U.S. army officer and historian figured that the problem – if there was one – had to be minor. He got out of bed, checked his watch, and opened his stateroom door. The passageway outside was silent and empty but he heard the eerie sound of steam escaping somewhere on the otherwise silent ship.

In his wildest dreams, Gracie could not have imagined the magnitude of the crisis that had suddenly and calamitously befallen the ship that he considered "perfect."[1] After all, wasn't *Titanic* all but unsinkable? How could there be anything seriously amiss on a liner that was a marvel of modern technology, commanded by an experienced captain of the esteemed White Star Line, steaming in peacetime through the unusually placid North Atlantic?

Under these conditions, only a madman could envision a nightmare scenario in which *Titanic* might be imperiled. Yet, even as Archibald Gracie calmly surveyed the quiet passageway outside his stateroom, seamen quite likely were already dying in the bowels of the ship where an iceberg had ripped open the hull and icy water was pouring through the gaping wounds.

Until that moment, Gracie had enjoyed an idyllic voyage. He was celebrating his completion of "The Truth about Chickamauga," a book seven years in writing. He had an abiding interest in the Battle of Chickamauga because his father, the scion of one of New York City's most prominent families, had commanded a brigade of Confederate infantry in the battle. Archibald felt that he had finally set the record straight about the northwest Georgia engagement, revealing "how the history of Chickamauga [had] ever since the day it was fought been made a conspiracy for the silencing and suppression of the truth."[2]

Isidor Straus

Earlier in the voyage, Gracie had loaned a copy of his book to Isidor Straus, another New Yorker with roots in the South and ties to the Confederacy. Straus, an owner of R.H. Macy & Co., had been raised in Talbotton, Georgia, volunteered to serve in the Confederate army at the start of the Civil War, and later in the conflict had gone abroad to work in a blockade running enterprise. This unorthodox background of one of New York City's foremost businessmen and philanthropists fascinated Archibald Gracie.

Isidor Straus traveled a remarkable and unlikely road to become one of New York City's leading citizens. He was born in Bavaria in 1845. His father, Lazarus Straus, fled Germany after the Revolution of 1848, and in 1852, immigrated to America. Lazarus eventually ended up in Georgia in the peddling business "selling an assortment of dry goods and Yankee notions." This seems like a modest start, but notes Joan Adler, Straus Historical Society's executive director, "pushcart peddlers at that time were highly regarded in the South because they brought necessary goods as well as news from plantation to plantation."

Lazarus Straus found success and soon made enough money to open a dry goods store in the west Georgia town of Talbotton. "By 1854," Adler explains, "he was sufficiently established to send for his wife and four young children, Isidor, Hermine, Nathan and Oscar." It would be many years before the family recognized the irony in the fact that the ship that brought them to America – the S.S. *St. Louis* – was celebrating its maiden voyage.

The family settled in Talbotton and became a respected part of the community. They owned a succession of nice homes in town (the last one still stands today on U.S. Highway 80 just south of Talbotton) and enrolled Isidor and Nathan in the prestigious Collinsworth Institute school. Although the Strauses were Jews, the children even attended a Baptist Sunday school because there was not a synagogue in the area. "The minister was a close family friend," Joan Adler notes. "He read to them only from the Old Testament in deference to their religion."

An unfortunate sequence of events during the Civil War prompted the Straus family to leave Talbotton and later the state of Georgia. First, in 1862, a Talbot County grand jury issued a presentment that excoriated local businesses for charging exorbitant prices, contributing to harmful wartime inflation. "The spirit of speculation and extortion is rife in every department of trade, and has become an evil of such alarming extent as, in our opinion, to seriously threaten the peace of the country," the jurors grumbled. "We do no injustice to that class of our population known as Jews," they continued rancorously, "when we assert that the responsibility for much of this evil is directly chargeable to them."

The grand jury's allegations outraged many members of the community who quickly rallied around the Straus family in a show of support. A letter published in the Columbus *Enquirer* newspaper condemned the presentment as "unjust and uncalled for." The letter writers pointed out that many Jews from Talbotton and throughout the South were serving in the Confederate armed forces. As for the grand jurors' suggestion that people ought to have as little as possible to do with Jews, the writers hoped that "an enlightened people will treat it with its deserved contempt, and as for the jurors themselves, we are perfectly willing to dispense with their intercourse."

Despite the outpouring of support, nothing could undo the hurt caused by the venomous grand jury presentment. The Straus family shortly thereafter moved to nearby Columbus, Georgia, a larger town that offered greater commercial opportunities and, they hoped, a more tolerant populace. Again, the family seems to have done well. "Although the Lazarus Straus house in Columbus is no longer standing today and we

A model of *Titanic* sinking is displayed at Savannah, Georgia's Ships of the Sea Maritime Museum.

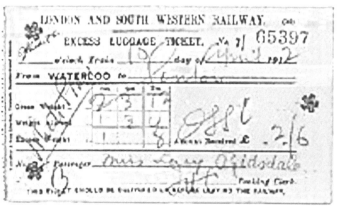

Luggage ticket from the Titanic

have no photographs of it, based on the neighboring houses Lazarus Straus must have done much better financially in Columbus," Joan Adler deduces.

Shortly after the outbreak of hostilities in 1861, Isidor Straus and other young men from Talbotton had formed an infantry unit and volunteered their services to Georgia Governor Joseph E. Brown. The governor rejected the offer, however, because at the time the state lacked the arms with which to equip any additional men. Therefore, Isidor found another way to serve in the cause of Southern independence. The Straus family invested in a blockade running enterprise and Isidor served as secretary to the head of the company. In 1863, he departed Georgia, bound for England on a ship that successfully slipped through the Federal blockade. For the remainder of the war, he bought and sold Confederate bonds.

Like his father, Isidor was a gifted businessman anxious to improve the family's prospects. Both kept their fingers on the pulse of commerce and when Union troops burned Columbus just before the end of the Civil War, they realized that it would take years for the South to recover. Shortly thereafter, Lazarus Straus decided that the family ought to leave Georgia for better opportunities in the northeastern United States, a decision fully supported by young Isidor.

"Twenty-year-old Isidor returned from Europe after the war with $12,000 in gold – an enormous sum in those days," Adler points out. "He bought his mother a three-story house in New York City for $10,000 and probably used the rest of his money to help his father repay antebellum debts. One merchant was so impressed by Lazarus Straus's integrity and determination to pay his obligations that he offered to sell him his business."

Lazarus and Isidor established L. Straus & Son, a china and glassware business in New York City. "When Nathan Straus later joined the family firm," Adler continues, "he convinced Rowland H. Macy to allow the Strauses to set up a small consignment shop in the basement of the Macy's Department Store on 14th street. This shop thrived and eventually accounted for almost one-fifth of Macy's sales, returning the establishment's highest profit."

Socially and financially, the Straus family flourished in New York City. By the turn-of-the-century, they owned R.H. Macy & Co. and Isidor had married, fathered seven children, served a term in the U.S. Congress, and was on the board of directors of many civic and philanthropic organizations. Nothing in his life, however, could have

4

prepared him for what lay ahead shortly after he and his wife Ida encountered Archibald Gracie on *Titanic's* A-deck shortly after midnight on April 15, 1912.

The unnatural quiet that had awakened Colonel Gracie at midnight descended over the ship some time after the collision with the iceberg. Contrary to most published accounts of the tragedy, Captain Edward J. Smith did not immediately order the engines shut down. He knew that the great ship had been gravely wounded – despite *Titanic's* reputation as an all but unsinkable vessel - and therefore continued steaming for some time, perhaps as much as a half-hour, in order to position her closer to the main sea-lane to increase the odds that passing ships would see *Titanic's* distress rockets.

The few passengers awake shortly before midnight simply did not recognize the gravity of the situation. "The actual accident was of such slight impact that few people realized what had happened," notes *Titanic* historian David G. Brown.

"Nobody had any fear at that time at all," Archibald Gracie later confirmed in testimony·before a U.S. Senate committee investigating the disaster. "I looked on deck outside to see if there was any indication of a list. I could not distinguish any." A lighthearted passenger even handed Gracie some ice shaved off from the berg saying, "We had better take this home for souvenirs."

The calm demonstrated by Gracie and the other passengers at that point was understandable. *Titanic* actually had been constructed to be virtually unsinkable due in part to its state-of-the-art design featuring bulkheads that could be closed off by automatic watertight doors, isolating any damaged area and therefore limiting flood-

One of *Titanic's* canvas-sided lifeboats.

"...however much, in a flattering future, that science and skill may augment; yet for ever and for ever, to the crack of doom, the sea will insult and murder him, and pulverize the stateliest, stiffest frigate he can make; nevertheless, by the continual repetition of these very impressions, man has lost that sense of the full awfulness of the sea which aboriginally belongs to it."
— from Herman Melville's *Moby-Dick*

ing. Even in the event of a catastrophic failure, this design supposedly ensured that the ship would stay afloat long enough to allow other vessels to come to its rescue. "Unfortunately," notes Brown, "Captain Smith and First Officer Murdoch found a way to sink the ship faster than help could arrive."

The sad fact is that a sequence of human errors – perhaps amounting to gross negligence – caused the fatal collision. In the first place, *Titanic* was steaming at more than 21 knots – nearly full speed – through ice-choked waters. Although it is not true the ship was trying to set a new speed record for the trip from England to New York City, there is no doubt the intention was for the fastest possible maiden crossing. This imprudent haste reduced the reaction time necessary for the ship to avoid disaster.

Second and perhaps most importantly, there were not enough eyes probing the ocean waters ahead for hazards. At night, it was more difficult for lookouts perched high above the ship to spot icebergs than it was for officers or crewmen on the bridge. "Antarctic explorer Earnest Shackeleton noted this phenomenon," observes David Brown, "as did Arthur Rostron, captain of the *Carpathia*."

After *Titanic* had stopped for the second and last time that night, the appearance of what seemed to be another steamer just a few miles away reassured many passengers. Archie Gracie calmed some acquaintances by pointing out the light of what he took to be a ship about six miles away.

"It did not seem to be a star," Gracie noted, "and that is what we all thought it was - the light of some steamer." This hope, too, proved stillborn and it soon became clear to the officers that no help would arrive until after *Titanic* had foundered. Finally, at about 12:40 a.m., Captain Smith gave the orders for passengers to board the lifeboats.

Things were about to get dicey. There were approximately 2,222 people aboard *Titanic* but only 20 lifeboats with a total capacity of 1,178. The widespread belief that *Titanic* did not have enough boats due to sheer negligence is wrong, Brown observes. "The boats were not intended to hold survivors after the ship sank. The idea was that *Titanic* would float long enough to be 'its own lifeboat.' Then, after rescue ships arrived, the lifeboats would be used to shuttle passengers to safety."

For several reasons, many of the lifeboats departed well short of capacity. Some passengers still believed that rescue was likely and that they were far safer on *Titanic* than in a little boat adrift in the vast Atlantic Ocean. Others simply refused to leave loved ones.

Gracie encountered one such couple on A-deck. "I saw Mr. and Mrs. Straus," he later recalled. "I had heard them discussing that if they were going to die, they would die together. We tried to persuade Mrs. Straus to go alone, without her husband, and she said 'No.'" Gracie wanted to make an exception to the "women and children first" edict for Isidor Straus, given his age, but he too refused stating that he would "share his fate with the rest of the men." Gracie gave up and left Mr. and Mrs. Straus there while he went elsewhere to be of assistance.

Macy's employee John Badenoch, heading to Europe on business, happened to be a passenger on *Carpathia*, the ship that rescued the *Titanic* survivors at dawn. He searched in vain for the Strauses, interviewed some of the survivors, pieced together a more complete picture of the fate of Isidor and Ida, and sent a detailed letter to their son Percy:

> "Your Mother was asked by the officer in charge and urged by your Father to get into one of the lifeboats. She refused to do so...They stood by while other boats were being filled, all the while your Father continuously urging your Mother to enter one of them. Finally when it became apparent that there was no hope of the Titanic staying afloat, your Father insisted that your Mother enter the second from the last boat that was being launched from the side they were on. She still refused, saying she would not go without him and when the officer in charge, again urged her to enter, and, in fact, attempted force, aided by the urging of your Father, she placed her foot in the boat, thinking at that time that your Father would accompany her. Just then, some demonstration seems to have been made by the men standing around and the officer in charge ordered all the men back. Mr. Isidor, thinking that your Mother was safe in the lifeboat, stepped back with the other men. Your Mother, looking

Titanic at Queenstown, England, shortly after departure.

around and seeing that your Father was not with her, got out of the boat, went to where your Father was standing and put her arms around him...Your Father and Mother then walked to the opposite side of the ship and when last seen were standing, clasped in each other's arms, calmly waiting for any help that might come."[3]

Help did not arrive until too late for Isidor and Ida Straus and some 1,500 other unfortunate passengers and crew. Shortly after 2 a.m., *Titanic's* bow slipped beneath the surface, and due to the incredible force of the weight of the water inside the monstrous craft, the liner broke in two. The front section plunged to the bottom while the stern remained afloat for a few more minutes as so stunningly depicted in the 1997 blockbuster movie, *Titanic*.

Archibald Gracie should have died then. He worked on the boat deck, loading passengers on lifeboats until all the davits were empty. "Soon after that," he said, "the water came up on the boat deck." Freezing water swept over him and he clung tenaciously to an iron railing. "I was taken down with the ship," Gracie recalled, "and hanging on to that railing, but I soon let go. I felt myself swirled around, swam under water, fearful that the hot water that came up from the boilers might boil me up." He fought desperately against the suction "and succeeded finally in reaching the surface and in getting a good distance away from the ship."

When Gracie surfaced, all the people who had been near to him when he went under were gone. "All around me was wreckage," he recalled with obvious dismay weeks after the tragedy. "I saw what seemed to be bodies all around." Completely exhausted, Gracie said he managed somehow to drag himself onto the wooden bottom of an overturned canvas-sided collapsible lifeboat.

Survivors in the lifeboats and water had a spectacular view of *Titanic's* death throes. "After she got to a certain angle she exploded, broke in half, and it seemed to me as if all the engines and everything that was in the after part slid out into the forward part, and the after part came upright again, and as soon as it came upright, down it went again," seaman Frank Osman testified at the U.S. Senate hearing on April 25, 1912.

Less than three hours after the collision, *Titanic's* maiden voyage had come to an incomprehensible end in the frigid waters of the North Atlantic.

Isidor Straus's body was recovered several days later and today his remains are entombed in a replica of a galley ship in Woodlawn Cemetery in the Bronx. Ida Straus's remains were not recovered but her name is etched beside her husband's near an inscription: "Many waters cannot quench love – neither can the floods drown it."

The *Carpathia* finally steamed into New York harbor on April 18 carrying *Titanic's* survivors. Archibald Gracie was one of the fortunate ones although he had suffered many cuts and bruises. Less than eight months later and shortly after completing The Truth About The *Titanic*, Archibald Gracie died. Appropriately, his grave is not far from that of his friend Isidor Straus in Woodlawn Cemetery.

Endnotes

1. Archibald Gracie, U.S. Senate Inquiry, Day 11. All quotations attributed to Gracie are from his testimony before the Senate committee investigating the sinking of the *Titanic*.

2. Gracie, Archibald, 1911. *The Truth About Chickamauga*, Houghton Mifflin Company, Boston, p. ix.

3. April 24, 1912 letter from John A Badenoch to Percy Straus in possession of the Straus Historical Socity, Inc., Smithtown, New York.

POSTER COURTESY NEVA OWENS, ROME, GEORGIA

Courageous Georgian Rode Into History On Ill-Fated Titanic

Though little-known today, one courageous Georgian had a knack for organization and pluck, and calmly helped women and children into life-boats as the ocean liner on which he was a passenger was sinking. So impressive was his character that he has subsequently been portrayed in a number of major motion pictures, calmly playing cards as the great H.M.S. Titanic slipped beneath the cold waters of the North Atlantic.

ROBERT S. DAVIS, JR.

The preceding chapter described the dramatic exploits of Colonel Archibald Gracie IV and Isidor Straus (owner of R.H Macy & Co. in New York), both of whom hailed from the South and were passengers on the ill-fated maiden voyage of the ocean liner R.M.S. *Titanic*. Interestingly, the most famous Georgian on board *Titanic* was not mentioned in the story, and has been largely forgotten in history. His courage and subsequent notoriety, however, have caused him to be portrayed in one of the most dramatically filmed scenes in motion picture history, yet even there he is almost never identified.

Archibald "Archie" Willingham deGrafferreid Butt was born in Augusta, Georgia on September 26, 1865, the third son of Confederate veteran Joshua Willingham and Pamela Robertson Butt. His family genealogy extended for generations back in Georgia history and his mother's family includes a Moseley line back to Massachusetts. The famous federal Admiral Farragut of Civil War fame was a cousin.

Archibald lost his father at age fourteen, and therefore left the Summerville Academy in Augusta, Georgia, in order that he might work to support his family. However, after three years, his mother and several family friends were able to raise funds enough to send him to the University of the South in Sewanee, Tennessee, where he completed his education.

As a student, young Archibald actively participated in the drama and military programs, while authoring the first book on the Mayan civilization. With the encouragement of his writer mother, Butt initially chose journalism as a career, working first for the Louisville (Kentucky) *Courier-Journal* and later, briefly, for the *Macon* (Georgia) *Telegraph* before becoming a Washington, D.C. correspondent for a group of Southern newspapers. His articles won him widespread and high praise, and ultimately led to his employment as secretary to General Matt Ransom, ambassador to Mexico.

Archibald's connections also earned him a commission as a second lieutenant when the Spanish American War broke out in 1898. As an assistant quartermaster, he was promoted to captain on January 2, 1900. No less a personage than President William McKinley himself commissioned Archibald as a captain in the regular army shortly thereafter, and assigned him to the newly captured Philippine Islands. During his four-year stint there, Archibald successfully organized the Army's unprecedented supply lines within the continental United States which had grown to immense proportions and become ensnarled in confusion. As usual, he won high praise for his efforts. He was so successful and efficient at shipping horses across the ocean that his strategy was later studied and duplicated by the British government in the Boer War.

Returning to America in 1904, Butt's talents were next put to work organizing the supply logistics for the American occupation army of Cuba. He continued in this capacity until his successes caused him to be recalled to Washington to serve as a military aide to President Theodore Roosevelt. The president and Butt became fast friends, in no small part because the captain was one of the few individuals in the Presidential circle who seemed to be able to keep up with the often physically demanding Roosevelt in sports, hunting, and horse-back riding.

Archibald "Archie" Willingham deGrafferreid Butt

Interestingly, Butt had met future President William Howard Taft when Taft served as occupation governor of the Philippines. The two men later renewed their friendship and, in 1908, Butt became not only a military aide to President Taft – Roosevelt's successor – but, in effect, guardian of access to the President of the United States.

While Butt himself did not care for Washington social events, he successfully managed these for the White House, and at one reception for the judiciary, Butt smoothly and successfully presented 1,275 people to the President in only one hour! No member of Taft's staff enjoyed a closer relationship to the President than did Butt, who was promoted to major in March of 1911.

This monument dedicated to Archibald Butt was erected near the White House.

President Taft, however, lacked the social skills of the ever-popular Theodore Roosevelt, and public animosity toward him steadily mounted during his term. In order to avoid embarrassment to the President during Taft's 1912 New Year's Eve party, Butt surreptitiously increased the Secret Service counting machine by 1,000 names, so that the President would not know how few people had actually attended his gala event.

Due in part to Taft's decreasing popularity, rumors that Roosevelt would challenge Taft for the White House began circulating in earnest. Butt personally visited the former president – his old friend – at Roosevelt's home at Sagamore Hill in January of 1912. Biographers of these two presidents have frequently mentioned that meeting which occurred in freezing winter weather. Butt never revealed the details of the meeting, but he reportedly did come away convinced unfortunately that the struggle for the Republican nomination would take place between two men he regarded almost as brothers. As a result of the stress of the situation, Butt reluctantly took Taft's advice to depart on a European vacation in March of 1912. During the trip, he served as special emissary to the Pope.

Butt, however, was only able to endure his separation from the activities at the White House for a month before deciding to return to the United States and, with great reluctance, throw his support to Taft over his devoted friend Teddy Roosevelt. In what can only be described as a dark omen of things to come, Butt wrote cryptically that should his ship sink, he had his will in order.

With his friend artist Frank Millet, Butt booked passage on the "unsinkable" wonder of the age – the R.M.S. *Titanic*. At 11:40 p.m. on the night of April 16, 1912, the monstrous ocean liner struck an iceberg, rending the great vessel along one side. Captain Edward J. Smith, realizing that his proud ship was sinking, began the process of manning the life boats – some of which, disastrously, were far from filled with passengers. Smith, however, sensed that he desperately needed to get as many passengers and crew as possible off the *Titanic* before word got out that the ship had far too few life-boats to save everyone. He suspected, correctly, that once that fact became known, chaos would reign supreme.

Shortly after the worst became known, Captain Smith began searching in earnest for Major Butt, no doubt due to the latter's renowned skills of organization in the face of disaster. He eventually located him calmly playing whist (a card game) with Clarence Moore of Washington, Millet, and Arthur Ryerson. This calm card-playing scene – on-going in the face of disaster – has been included in almost every motion picture ever made of the *Titanic* disaster, and it is one of the most often reproduced scenes in motion picture history.

Ironically, Butt's next actions – as remembered later by survivors – were some of the most dramatic, and yet have never been portrayed in any media. While Captain Smith returned to the ship's bridge, Butt took charge of the protection of the women and children on deck, at one point using an iron bar as a weapon to fend off cowardly males who attempted to overtake empty seats in the lifeboats. One of the survivors

Archibald Butt was a close friend of President Theodore Roosevelt.

later remarked that Butt acted as if he were running a White House function, smoothly and efficiently organizing the life-boat launchings while offering words of encouragement to frightened passengers.

According to other reports from survivors, Butt – true to his nature – was also prepared when chaos threatened once again. When the cables of one boat-load of hysterical women became snarled, he directed the seamen in solving the problem, all the while calming the panic-stricken females. When a man tried to jump into a boat already loaded with women, Butt pulled him back roughly by the neck, and threatened to break every bone in the coward's body. America's newspapers would later carry accounts of numerous incidents – as revealed by the *Titanic* survivors – of the major's heroism.

Butt and Millet courageously made no effort whatsoever to save themselves. When the boats were gone, the major attempted to calm the steerage passengers. He also instructed the ship's orchestra to begin playing, summoning all his skills in a final effort to provide whatever calming effect was possible. Somehow, in the midst of this maelstrom, Butt had also found time to dress in his finest tuxedo which he wore as he joined the captain on the bridge of the mortally-stricken *Titanic*.

As the great ship was in its final throes, the courageous Major Archibald Willingham deGrafferreid Butt – advisor and confidant to Presidents of the United States and dignitaries abroad – was last seen arm-in-arm with multi-millionaire John Jacob Astor. According to folklore of the incident, Butt reportedly yelled to the passengers on one life-boat to "remember me to the folks back home" as the great liner began its awesome descent beneath the strangely-calm waters of the North Atlantic.

Unlike Astor, Butt's body was never recovered. President Taft, upon learning of the fate of the *Titanic*, immediately sent a warship to intercept the survivors in the forelorn hope that his friend Archie had somehow managed to cheat death. The president later wrote however, that upon hearing of the sinking, he knew the major would not have left the ship in place of anyone else.

The struggle between Taft and Roosevelt ultimately split the vote of the Republican party, opening the way for the election of Woodrow Wilson to the Presidency. One can only wonder today what the outcome of the election might have been had Archibald Butt survived to put his skills to work in the re-election efforts for President Taft.

Despite his demise, Butt was later immortalized in the well-known play "Backstairs to the White House," which includes a scene in which the major hurries back to America from Europe to persuade Roosevelt not to challenge Taft in the upcoming campaign.

Interestingly, Butt and the office of the President of the United States are associated with the state of Georgia in a number of odd instances. Theodore Roosevelt's mother – Mittie Bulloch – was a Georgian whose family hailed from Roswell, Georgia. Roosevelt himself journeyed with his wife to Bulloch Hall in Roswell on at least one occasion (and possibly several others). President Woodrow Wilson was raised in Butt's native Augusta, Georgia, and practiced law in Atlanta and Gainesville, Georgia, before moving on to prominence in New Jersey. Wilson also married a Georgian and his political heir apparent was also a Georgian.

The death of Archibald Butt drew a great deal of national attention. President Howard Taft traveled to Augusta to a special memorial service for the major on May 2. The ceremony drew a crowd of approximately 1,500 mourners. Today, a bridge and a monument in Augusta honor Archibald Butt and monuments to his memory were also erected near the White House and at Arlington National Cemetery.

Butt's autobiography, *Both Sides of the Shield* was published in 1912, with a foreword by President Taft. Major Archibald Butt's private writings were published by Lawrence F. Abbott as *The Letters of Archie Butt* (1924). This publication has become a classic source of information on the White House and Washington D.C. during Roosevelt's presidency.

Archibald Butt was never married – Taft claimed – because of his close attachment to his mother who passed away in 1910. He reportedly was engaged to be married in the autumn of 1912. In later years, a scam to claim an illegitimate child was Butt's progeny created a national sensation until it was exposed as fraud. This, however, could in no way tarnish or diminish the image of one of the most courageous passengers – if not the most courageous passsenger – on board a tragic ship called *Titanic*.

They Leapt to Their Deaths from the Burning Winecoff

On December 7, 1946 – the fifth anniversary of the Japanese attack on Pearl Harbor – happy guests packed Atlanta's Winecoff Hotel for holiday season festivities. When a fire raged through the structure early that morning, the appalling death toll was seared into the memory of a heartbroken city and state. For the second time that decade, December 7 became a date that would live in infamy.

Jane Walker

Perhaps nothing is more terrible than being trapped in a burning building with no means of escape, as happened to 119 people who perished in Atlanta's Winecoff Hotel on December 7, 1946. A 1937 postcard and even the hotel's lovely stationery claimed that the hotel was "absolutely fireproof," an assertion eerily similar to boasts that the *Titanic* was unsinkable. The Winecoff was indeed an engineering marvel for its time, but just like the Titanic and the Hindenburg, human error and the vagaries of chance worked together to create an unforgettable disaster.

Atlanta's Winecoff Hotel ablaze.

At fifteen stories – 155 feet – the Winecoff was Atlanta's tallest hotel. The "fireproof" boast meant that the brick-covered concrete and steel structure would remain standing, even if gutted with fire, long enough for its guests to escape. While the hotel did remain standing, many guests were unable to escape and as a result the fire was then – and remains today – the deadliest hotel fire in U. S. history.

A Magnificent Accommodation

New York City's William L. Stoddard designed the Winecoff. Constructed in 1913 and named for builder William Fleming Winecoff, it featured two elevators run by operators and a central staircase. Its most famous room was the lovely baby-blue bridal

With his last flashbulb, Georgia Tech student Arnold Hardy took this Pulitzer Prize-winning photograph of a woman who had leaped from the burning Winecoff. Amazingly, she survived the fall.

suite decorated with Harrison Fisher's drawings portraying the joyous journey from courtship to marriage.

Despite its lavishness, the hotel lacked many of today's rudimentary safety features like fire escapes, fire-proof doors, and a sprinkler system. Such safeguards simply weren't required in that era. To make matters worse, the Atlanta Fire Department's ladders only reached the eighth floor.

There were 280 guests at the Winecoff on December 7, 1946. Its 195 rooms were filled to capacity with people in town for the holidays, for the premier of "Song of the South," soldiers recently discharged from military duty, and forty teenagers from high schools throughout Georgia attending a YMCA youth assembly at the capitol building. The Winecoff must have had a festive air that evening, but the celebrations soon became nightmares.

The Candy Kid

Even today, the cause of the fire remains a mystery. In *The Winecoff Fire – The Untold Story of America's Deadliest Hotel Fire*, authors Sam Heys and Allen B. Goodwin raised the possibility of arson. Goodwin, the son of a reporter who covered the fire for an Atlanta newspaper, and Heys mention several suspects in their book, but give particular attention to an Atlantan known as the "Candy Kid."

The Candy Kid earned his nickname in 1926 when he and several other youths burglarized the Sophie Mae Candy Corporation near Georgia Tech, stealing 100 pounds of candy. The Candy Kid associated with a group of criminals known as the "Georgia Boys" and spent decades on chain gangs and in Georgia prisons.

Another member of the Georgia Boys, Ray Maddox, later became a born-again Christian and a deacon at Atlanta's First Baptist Church. In his 1981 autobiography *In This Corner*, coauthored by Atlanta clergyman Gene Moffatt, Maddox names the Candy Kid as the arsonist who started the Winecoff fire. Maddox related that the Candy Kid "remembered one of the men in a gambling game [at the Winecoff] as the one who had ratted on him in another prison experience." There was never sufficient proof to indict the Candy Kid for the Winecoff fire, but he spent the rest of his life in prison on various unrelated charges including drunkenness, robbery, and attempted murder.

The Christmas Shoppers

Dr. Robert Cox, today a pediatrician in Hays, Kansas, was a three-year-old child at the time of the fire. His parents, Bob and Billie Cox, brought him and his babysitter,

Delilah Chambers (now Hulsey), to Atlanta for Christmas shopping. They occupied adjoining rooms on the Winecoff's tenth floor. The parents stayed in one while their son and babysitter occupied the other.

When fire broke out on the floors beneath them, Delilah took Robert from his bed, dressed him, and carried him to his parents' room. As the fire and smoke drove them to the window for fresh air, Bob Cox ripped the sheets from the beds and made a rope ladder in hopes that they could descend two floors to the nearest fire department ladder. With the smoke swirling and the flames literally licking at their backs, Bob Cox told Delilah Chambers to go first. She had worked on a farm milking cows and carrying heavy jugs of milk and had enough strength to climb down to the relative safety of a nearby ladder.

Then it was Billie Cox's turn. She had suffered a miscarriage several weeks earlier and was still mentally and physically exhausted, unable to hang on to a rope seventy feet above the street. With her husband and child watching, Billie Cox lost her grip on the sheet rope and plummeted to her death, nearly knocking Delilah Chambers off the ladder as she fell.

Ambulances and rescue vehicles at the Winecoff. The dark vehicle in the center is marked "Medical Department U.S. Army." A number of recently discharged veterans were guests at the Winecoff on the eve of the fire.

Bob Cox saw his wife's fall and undoubtedly knew that she could not have survived. He clutched little Robert to his chest, climbed through the window, and paused momentarily. Desperate to escape the flames, he intended to jump to the ladder two floors below, but it had been moved.

His only alternative was to jump through the dense, swirling smoke to a rescue net set up seventy feet below. He held Robert tightly and jumped. Although father and son both landed on the net, Bob Cox struck his head on the metal rim and died an hour later. Robert landed safely and survived the ordeal unscathed.

When asked whether he remembered any of this tragedy, Dr. Cox replied that he had no memory of it, though he's heard the story many times from other people. After his parents' deaths, he was raised by an aunt in Kansas. Through the years, he kept in touch with Delilah, who is now in her 80s and lives in Cleveland, Georgia.

The Soldiers

As the fire raged through the hotel, the windows became terrifying frames of guests silhouetted against the advancing orange flames. Screaming and pleading for help, some guests did like the Cox family, making ropes of bed sheets. Others panicked and leapt to their deaths, landing and dying below on Peachtree Street and the intersecting alley. In Room 1416, Ashley John Burns, a newly discharged soldier, attached his U.S. Army discharge pin to the lapel of his pajamas before suffocating in the noxious smoke.

James D. Cahill, another former soldier, took lodging at the Winecoff while he applied to re-enter Georgia Tech. Cahill managed to exit the building and run around back to attempt to reach his mother's room.

Cahill entered an adjacent building and maneuvered a board across a ten-foot alley to his mother's sixth-floor room. Then, crawling across the board (which sloped downward at a thirty-degree angle) sixty feet above the alley, he reached his frantic mother. Then he crawled back up to safety with his mother clinging to him.

Firemen quickly adopted this hazardous yet effective strategy and, with Cahill's help, rescued many guests who had no other means of escape. Their perilous trips across the board were accomplished amid the pandemonium of wailing sirens and screaming people, as pocketbooks, window screens, and bodies were falling around them.

The Movie Goers

Ed Kiker Williams of Cordele was seventeen when he, his mother, his nine-year-old sister, an aunt and her three children, went to Atlanta to shop and see the premier of Song of the South. Truth be told, Ed admitted in a recent interview, the primary reason he went along was to drive his aunt's new Buick.

Their rooms were on the Winecoff's 15th floor, a breathtaking 155 feet above street level. His aunt and cousins were down the hall from Ed, his mother, and sister. As the fire swept into their room and the smoke became unbearable, he held his mother and sister as they leaned out the window, straining for every breath, hoping and praying that help would come. Due to the darkness and dense smoke, he couldn't see anything below. Every once in awhile, he remembers, a refreshing drop of water from a fireman's hose sprinkled his face.

Ed counted twelve drops as he held his mother and sister at the window. Eventually, he realized both were dead and that he didn't have much time left either. He leaned out of the hotel window as far as he could and lost consciousness. He plunged from the fifteenth floor but landed on a ladder twenty-five feet below (the ladder extended horizontally across the alley the Mortgage Guarantee Building the Winecoff). A fire fighter helped him back into the hotel. From there he made it to the ground floor and took a taxi to St. Joseph's Hospital.

Amazingly, Ed Williams suffered only a cut on his head and a broken ankle. The rest of his family - his mother and sister, his Aunt Dot and his three first cousins - perished in the fire. His aunt reportedly told her three children to lie down on one of the room's double beds. She lay down with them so that they might draw strength from one another. In this way, they all suffocated.

The Students

Those injured or killed in the fire came from all across Georgia and throughout the United States, but several small towns - including Bainbridge, Thomaston, Douglas, Fitzgerald, Donalsonville, Rome, Gainesville, and Clay City, Illinois - were hit particularly hard. Joe Goodson, a 35-year-old geologist for Pure Oil Company, was en route with his family from Clay City to Florida hoping that the warm air would cure his pneumonia. The entire family expired in the conflagration.

Bainbridge, Georgia lost Miss Mary Davis, a teacher, and seven of her high school students who were in Atlanta for the youth assembly. The Bainbridge delegation had rooms on Winecoff's ninth floor. Two of the girls jumped to their deaths and the others, along with their teacher, died from smoke inhalation. One of the students was 14-year-old Patsy Griffin, the daughter of Marvin Griffin, who later became governor of Georgia.

Most of the thirty students killed in the fire were identified by their class rings. Dental records, clothing, and jewelry also aided in the grim forensic task.

In 1954, the Decatur County Memorial Association unveiled a striking marble monument in memory of the teacher and students from Bainbridge who lost their lives in the Winecoff. Located in Bainbridge's Willis Park, the names of the victims are inscribed, followed by a verse from the Book of Matthew: "Blessed are the pure in heart: for they shall see God."

The Photographer

Arnold Hardy became the first amateur photographer to win the Pulitzer Prize for his photo of a woman jumping from the smoke-shrouded Winecoff. A 26-year-old Georgia Tech graduate student at the time, Hardy was still awake during the early morning hours of December 7, 1946.

When he heard the shrill sirens he called the fire department and learned that the

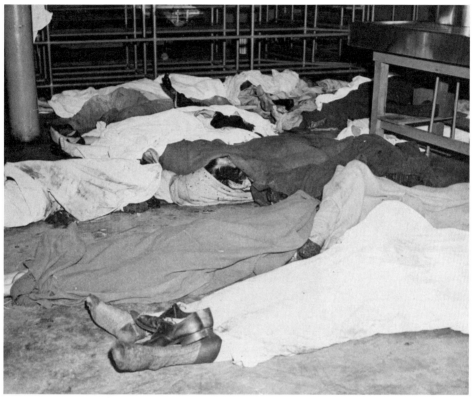

Some of the 119 victims in the deadliest hotel fire in U.S. history.

grand old hotel was ablaze. Grabbing his Speed Graphic camera and five flashbulbs, he hailed a taxi and raced to the scene.

After snapping several photographs of terrified guests huddled at the hotel's fiery windows, Hardy had just one flashbulb left. Looking up through his camera's viewfinder, he photographed Daisy McCumber, a 41-year-old Atlanta secretary, leaping in mid-air from an eleventh-story room, her skirt billowing up around her neck.

Miraculously, she survived but was critically injured by the terrible fall. She broke her back, pelvis, and both legs. She underwent seven subsequent operations over ten years and eventually one leg was amputated. Even so, she was able to work until retirement. She died in 1992 in Jacksonville, Florida having never admitted to anyone that she was the woman in Hardy's Pulitzer Prize-winning photo. Based upon their research, however, Heys and Goodwin concluded that she was indeed the woman in the photo.

While Arnold Hardy was snapping photographs, he heard a fireman and police officer discussing the need to get medication from a nearby drugstore. Hardy raced across the street and kicked the door open, only to be arrested by the same officer. Hardy was released on his own recognizance and shortly thereafter developed his stunning photo.

The Associated Press paid Hardy $300 for exclusive rights to his pictures and a $200 bonus. Although his photo of the jumping woman was reprinted around the world and on magazine covers numerous times, he hasn't received another dime for his work. In fact, realizing that his later photos would always be measured against his Pulitzer Prize-winning one, Hardy promptly retired from amateur photography.

The Firemen

It is difficult to imagine standing on the street outside the Winecoff in the early morning hours and witnessing people leaping to their deaths, falling from flimsy sheet ropes, and screaming in fear. Many firemen risked their lives in the fire, rushing into the hotel's smoke-filled interior only to be forced back outside for quick gulps of air before rushing in again with their heavy fire hoses.

These large fire hoses became snarled in the inky darkness of the narrow hallways of the hotel, causing further chaos and anguish as terrified guests stumbled and fell. Some firemen became disoriented in the smoke-filled hallways and had trouble finding their way back outside to fresh air. Miraculously, no firemen lost their lives fighting the fire.

During the blaze, which officially lasted from 3:42 A.M. until 6:04 A.M., fireman Newton Elmer (Red) Pittman was carried to the hospital three times for smoke inhalation. The first time he left and returned to the fire. The second time, hospital staff kept his boots to deter him from leaving again. The third time, they held his clothing and undergarments.

The heavily damaged Winecoff Hotel the day after the fire (December 8, 1946).

According to his granddaughter, Peggy McClure, Pittman returned to the scene and continued to climb the ladders and fight the fire "in a borrowed fireman's raincoat with nothing underneath. He will always be my hero!" she says with a note of pride in a review she wrote for Heys' and Goodwin's book.

T.H. (Rick) Roberts of Peachtree City retired from the Atlanta Fire Department in 1976. He was on duty the night of the Winecoff fire and has given many interviews about the experience over the years. He recalls carrying a smiling baby girl down a ladder, and he remembers meeting her nearly fifty years later. "Her name

LEFT: Ed Kiker Williams of Cordele was 17 at the time of the fire, he fell from a 15th story window to a ladder 25 feet below, suffering nothing more serious than a broken ankle. His mother, 9-year-old sister, an aunt and three cousins perished in the fire. RIGHT: T.H. "Rick" Roberts was a firefighter for the Atlanta Fire Department from 1942 until his retirement in 1976. At a reunion event fifty years after the Winecoff blaze, he met some of those he rescued.

was Connie," he recalled recently. "I told her I'd have known that smile anywhere." He added that the Winecoff tragedy did "prove an impetus for building code revisions."

The Survivors

Of those who escaped the burning building, many suffered lifelong health problems associated with the fire, smoke, falls, and shock. Rudolph Ogilvie's vocal cords actually melted together, resulting in speech problems. Furman Anderson, a fire captain, led in the rescue of more than forty people, then suffered a heart attack at home. His health continued to decline until his death several years later. John Turk, who managed to escape from Room 1018, had nightmares and would awaken screaming long after the fire.

Some survivors had to recover from major burns. Some endured nightmares and other sleep problems for years afterwards, while a few succumbed to alcoholism or drug dependencies. Others battled depression, anxiety, and what would now be recognized as post-traumatic stress disorder. At least one grieving mother committed suicide.

The Reunion

Coinciding with the publication of *The Winecoff Fire – The Untold Story of America's Deadliest Hotel Fire*, a memorial event was held in front of the Winecoff Hotel in December 1994. The event began with the dedication of a Georgia Historical Marker by A. D. Bell, assistant chief of the Atlanta Fire Department at time, and remarks by several prominent speakers. The ceremony then moved to the Atlanta Public Library, where Heys and Goodwin recounted the events of that fateful night.

Firefighters and survivors of the tragedy met at this poignant reunion. A retired Grady Hospital nurse who cared for a young female burn victim hugged the now elderly woman she had become. A retired Atlanta fireman, wearing his uniform for the occasion, embraced Dr. Bob Cox, who survived only because his father shielded him as they made the terrifying plunge from the tenth floor to a safety net. It was a memorable occasion that brought a sense of closure to the victims, the firefighters, and their families.

The Winecoff Today

The Winecoff Hotel building still stands today at the intersection of Peachtree and Ellis streets. It remained vacant until 1951 when it re-opened – this time equipped with a fire escape – as the Peachtree on Peachtree Hotel. In the 1960s, the grand old hotel became a retirement home. During the '80s and '90s, various restaurants and other small businesses occupied the ground floor, but the upper floors were unused. Vacant, dilapidated, and boarded up for many years, the Winecoff Hotel building recently underwent renovations and reopened as the luxurious Ellis Hotel.

Acknowledgements

The author and *Georgia Backroads* wish to thank Sam Heys and Allen B. Goodwin, co-authors of *The Winecoff Fire – The Untold Story of America's Deadliest Hotel Fire*, for their gracious assistance in the preparation of this article. Visit their website at www.winecoff.org or email Allen Goodwin at allenbgoodwin@yahoo.com or Sam Heys at SRHEYS@southernco.com.

TERRIBLE DAY IN VALDOSTA:

The Rampage of Gypsy the Elephant

Most circus spectators are constantly in awe of the performing animals, particularly the elephants with their huge bulk and exceptional intelligence. All too often however, these poor beasts have been trained through the use of brutally abusive treatment, and occasionally, the trauma becomes too great, causing one of the great animals to snap. The 1902 incident with Gypsy in Valdosta, Georgia quite possibly is a good example.

MARTIN REGISTER

O n the chilly evening of November 22, 1902, Gypsy, "the largest elephant in the world," looked down at her trainer, James "Whiskey Red" O'Rourke, as he lay comatose on a Valdosta, Georgia street. The man did not know it at the time, but this was the last road he would ever travel.

As was his habit, O'Rourke had once again had too much to drink and, from most accounts, had simply passed out and fallen awkwardly from his seat astride Gypsy's neck. He flopped in an ignoble heap at the intersection of Central Avenue and Toombs Street.

According to an account of the incident published the next day in the Valdosta *Times*, Gypsy, to the great pachyderm's credit, tenderly attempted to lift O'Rourke

The Harris Nickel Plate Shows paraded through Valdosta in 1902.

25

back to his place atop her neck, but her trainer was unresponsive. She reportedly prodded him a few more times and, still getting no response, proceeded to lower her five-ton bulk onto the trainer, crushing him into a bloody mish-mash of teeth, hair and bones.

With that simple act, a night of terror had begun for the city of Valdosta. Before it ended – miles away on the following day – a circus clown had been maimed for life and at least three other circus employees had been injured in a rampage that sent terrified Valdostans scrambling for their lives.

Obviously distressed by all the turmoil she had suddenly created, Gypsy shrieked and screamed up and down city streets, chasing those in her path, climbing the steps of buildings and wreaking general havoc before finally trumpeting loudly and lumbering on a generally northward path beyond the limits of the shocked town. As these huge wild beasts have been semi-domesticated and trained in the West over the past several centuries, deadly outbursts such as this have been well-documented. Sadly, more often than not, these incidents have occurred because a trainer or owner has consistently abused the elephant, or because an injury (such as severe tooth decay) or some other physical trauma was left untreated.

When the tragedy with Gypsy ended, a much-beloved elephant lay dead, and a local legend – which would be told and retold for over a century – was born.

A Home For The Circus
Valdosta's growing population and moderate climate made it a prime choice as the home of the Georgia State Fair in the early part of the 20th century. The fairgrounds were located at the edge of town, east of the property which today comprises Valdosta State University.

The site made a good winter home for what was known as The Harris Nickel Plate Shows. This circus was never the size of a Ringling Bros & Barnum Bailey outfit, but was nevertheless a well-known attraction.

E.D. Ferrell, who wrote about the infamous incident involving Gypsy in the Lowndes County Historical Society's newsletter in 1973 said Valdostans had a long relationship with the elephant, billed by the circus as "the biggest-born of brutes." Albert S. Pendleton, Jr., secretary of the Lowndes County Historical Society, quotes a female by the name of Corinthia Morgan who had moved from Troupville to Valdosta in the 1860s and witnessed the huge wild animal:

"Did you ever hear of Gypsy, the elephant, and how she ran away?" Morgan reportedly said. "John Robinson's circus used to come to Troupville back in the old days, traveling over the dirt road with one elephant, the only animal with ivory tusks which the circus possessed at that time. The pacyderm (sic) was called Gypsy, a name she lived up to only too well. She will never be forgotten by the old inhabitants around here."

In his article, Mr. Pendleton explained that Ms. Morgan's memory of Gypsy appearing with the circus at Troupville means the elephant probably had been known to Valdostans for over 40 years. Indeed, at the time of her death, circus employees estimated Gypsy's age to be between 65 and 67 years, claiming she had been bought by circus management in India around 1847.

Other records document Gypsy's odyssey from circus to circus beginning in 1867. Pendleton says he believes the Gypsy referred to by Ms. Morgan in Troupville is definitely the same Gypsy who carried out her last outrageous performance on the streets of Valdosta in 1902.

As things turned out, Ms. Morgan's assessment of Gypsy's days in Troupville was quite an understatement. As long as there are modern-day residents in Valdosta, that town and Gypsy no doubt will be forever linked in folklore.

A Final Performance
Valdosta's railroads ran more than a mile south of the fairgrounds and the circus' winter home. Every year, as The Harris Nickel Plate Shows returned to their cold-weather retreat, the circus would hold a pair of evening performances in front of the hometown crowd.

As the railroad cars loaded with tents and cages and carriages and animals rolled to a stop in Valdosta's downtown in late 1902, nothing seemed amiss. The circus unloaded in front of its fans and set up shop for a night of fun before heading northward afterwards, back to the fairgrounds.

"Gypsy was the last elephant that night to leave the grounds," wrote E.D. Ferrell, "as she was used in the dismantling of the tents with her trainer, O'Rourke. The long caravan of animals, wagons and various types of circus conveyances proceeded from the East Hill (circus) grounds to Patterson Street and turned north to the Fair Grounds.

"This continued most of the night after the closing about 11 p.m.," Ferrell added. "O'Rourke was mounted on Gypsy's head. . . . the two were seen by many people quite late as far north on Patterson Street to present Gordon Street. However, no one could remember seeing Gypsy and O'Rourke north of there, so it was decided that he must have fallen asleep because Gypsy was seen walking south on the road which is now Toombs Street..."

Although it wasn't widely known at the time, Whiskey Red O'Rourke's crushed and broken body was already lying in the street as Gypsy meandered southward. What some say pushed Gypsy's bad mood into an all-out bloodbath was the fact that she apparently had broken a tusk at the same time, for the broken ivory appendage was later found near O'Rourke. A broken tusk would be no different than a broken tooth in a human, though the pain and suffering of the animal would obviously be magnified many times that of the human.

Ferrell wrote that Gypsy had rolled O'Rourke's body to the granite curbside in front of the First Baptist Church, where a collision of ivory against granite apparently broke off the huge tusk.

"The pain of the [shattered] tusk must have enraged her terribly and she started running like wildfire back to Patterson Street," Ferrell continued. "By that time some of the circus people became aware of her being loose, and they rushed to the scene with large pitchforks. When they could get close enough, two of the men with pistols fired into her body, one shot after another."

The rounds from the handguns, however, had little effect on the huge elephant. "Gypsy was roaring in a high screaming voice and shook the town," Ferrell said. "While the circus people were trying to subdue her, the local citizens, who were still up, were running from her, frightened to death."

Battling The Beast

The center of the ensuing battle moved to the Valdes Hotel, a grand, three-story structure which occupied an entire city block in downtown Valdosta, and was owned by Ferrell's father. Twenty-year-old James Madison Pearson – Ferrell's cousin – was on night desk duty that night.

It was at the Valdes that circus personnel managed to corner the raging Gypsy, holding her at bay with pitchforks while firing a continuous rain of bullets into her. Despite the bloodbath and horror of the situation, it soon became obvious that it was going to take more than small bullets to bring down a brute the size of Gypsy.

With a growing crowd of pistol-packing pursuers dogging her every step, Gypsy's rage increased steadily. Suddenly, without warning, she reportedly looked toward the hotel and, to the horror of those present, ascended the steps of the structure in an apparent attempt to enter the structure. Suddenly, there seemed to be a very real possibility that the panicked elephant might literally burst through the side of the hotel.

Doing the only thing he could think of on such short notice, the night clerk Pearson raced to the electrical switchboard of the hotel and turned off the lights, leaving the area in darkness. This tactic somehow changed Gypsy's course and she reversed herself and quickly moved back out into the street.

For more than two hours, "Gypsy took control of the whole street," wrote a reporter for The Valdosta *Times*. "She would charge at the crowd, then hurl loose bricks and timbers into the air and all the while she was emitting a blood-chilling elephant cry."

Panic swept through the streets. Women and children were herded to relative safety behind strong walls, but Gypsy's rage did not seem to be aimed at women and children. According to all reports, she very deliberately attacked only the men who worked for the circus.

Though they enraged her, the continuous shower of bullets piercing Gypsy's flesh did not slow her down, and certainly did not kill her. At one point, she wrapped her long leathery trunk around a light pole, shook it, and shattered the lights.

At the First Christian Church – then under construction – she suddenly grabbed a backpedaling circus clown and tossed him more than 30 feet according to newspaper accounts. Three other circus employees, cornered and attacked by the on-rushing giant in full wrath mode, were saved only by massive pitchfork and pistol attacks on Gypsy from both sides and behind.

In the electrical blackout brought on by Gypsy's onslaught, Valdostans and circus personnel alike held their breath and listened for elephant shrieks and crashing debris in an effort to locate the danger.

"It was an eerie sight," the newspaper reported, "the huge elephant thundering up and down the streets past the street lights, then into the shadows, no one knowing where she would strike next."

The Valdes Hotel, Valdosta, Georgia around the turn of the 20th century.

Then Came The Police

Valdosta Police Chief Calvin Dampier was on the scene, but in the pitch darkness described by the newspaper, it was almost altogether impossible to guess from whence the thundering bulk of Gypsy would next appear. Facing the seemingly impossible turn of events caused by a berserk five-ton elephant in a city's downtown, local citizens and lawmen began organizing themselves and gathering firearms of a heavier caliber.

"There was a group going from house to house in an area of [shotgun houses]," Pendleton said. Someone in the group finally asked a group of people if they had seen an elephant thundering past. Had not the situation been so dangerous, some of the responses might almost have been comical.

"I don't know who it was," one man reported, "but whoever it was stole a bunch of cabbages from the garden, put them under his arm and went running that way."

In a dilemma perhaps unique in American history, Chief Dampier spent a troubled night under bizarre circumstances. Just how does one stop an

The grave of James "Whiskey Red" O'Rourke.

attack by something as large and uncontrollable as Gypsy in 1902?

Finally, a resident whose name is lost to history reported that he had a Krag-Jorgensen rifle, a large caliber weapon from the Spanish-American War. It was most likely the one gun in the county capable of bringing down an elephant. However, there was a problem even with this solution. The gun was 10 miles away in Clyattville.

A unit was immediately dispatched to Clyattville to retrieve the weapon. It was about this time that Gypsy suddenly raced away to the north, reportedly crashing through the board fences surrounding the circus's winter home, and disappearing into the darkness and dense woodlands.

A Mortal Wound

At some point during the night, the Krag-Jorgensen rifle was finally brought to Chief Dampier, who, along with an enormous unofficial posse, set off after Gypsy once again. With an animal that large, the trail couldn't have been very difficult to follow.

Various reports differ in the details involving Gypsy's ultimate fate, but the end result of all the stories is the same: Dampier and hundreds of followers finally found the runaway elephant the following morning, lying in tall grass near Cherry Creek, miles to the north on the Nashville Road.

One report maintains Gypsy's execution consisted of a single, well-placed Dampier shot. The Valdosta *Times* however, reported the elephant stood up, was brought to her knees by one shot, and finished off by another. Ferrell's version of the story maintained Dampier "pumped several shots into her body."

An estimated 3,000 people made the trip to see the dead elephant amid an atmosphere that has been described as a mixture of relief and sadness. Certainly, the execution of a huge, regal beast such as Gypsy was a traumatic experience for all involved.

Today, the exact site of Gypsy's remains is unknown, other than the fact they were buried in the vicinity of Cherry Creek, an area being overtaken today by subdivisions as Valdosta sprawls northward. The carcass was so massive that, even utilizing teams of horses, Gypsy's remains had to be hacked to pieces with axes and dragged by the horses to several graves.

On the same afternoon, James O'Rourke, the 44-year-old trainer whose untimely slide off Gypsy's head had started the whole nightmare, was buried in Sunset Hill Cemetery, transported there by a carriage pulled by six "beautiful white horses," Albert Pendleton wrote. The body was placed in what Pendleton described as "a very fine casket, bought by Mrs. Harris, owner of The Nickel Plate Circus." Today, O'Rourke's tall, narrow grave marker sits about 50 yards behind the sexton's office at the cemetery.

As might be imagined, various newspapers widely reported the incident for days – some accounts carrying a critical evaluation of the way the incident had been handled. The Valdosta *Times* scoffed at criticisms pouring in from distant locales accusing Valdostans of mob violence leading to the tragic end to the animal. The newspaper stood behind the Valdosta residents stating it was circus personnel who began shooting first.

Shortly after the incident, Valdosta *Times* Editor C.C. Brantley wrote "Generations unborn will be told about things that happened the day the mad elephant was killed near Valdosta." His words turned out to be prophetic. More than a century later, Gypsy may be as much a local legend as is Valdosta High School football and the many state championships and renowned athletes produced by the school over the years.

Notches On Her Tusk

Interestingly, the tragic story of Gypsy might have ended right there, had not Renate Milner, director of the Lowndes County Historical Society museum, begun corresponding in 2001 with Kenton Cornish who was collecting information on infamous circus elephants.

Through their correspondence, Milner uncovered a new and shocking truth which turned the familiar story of Gypsy on its head. Milner discovered, much to her surprise, that Gypsy had always been considered a highly-trained animal (it was claimed the huge pachyderm could even play the harmonica), but that she was also considered a very dangerous and formidable performer as well. In fact, she had killed humans – on several different occasions – prior to the day she ended the life of Whiskey Red O'Rourke.

Seeking information on Gypsy, Cornish cited sources in *Bandwagon*, a circus periodical which labeled Valdosta's famous Gypsy a temperamental murderess. "Before coming to Valdosta, she was evidently already a notorious elephant and had killed a number of people over the years," Cornish wrote to Milner. "They carved notches on her tusks each time she killed someone."

An article in *Bandwagon*, written in 1993 by the late Bill Johnston and entitled "Tough Circus Elephants," chronicles the stories of several circus elephants which eventually turned violent. Johnston's article describes "one of the toughest elephants ever imported to this country...an Asian female named Gypsy."

Johnston wrote that by the time The Harris Nickel Plate Shows bought Gypsy in 1888, she had killed at least four men associated with circuses in which she had performed. "Gypsy never bothered women and children, but apparently only went after people connected with the show," Johnston wrote. This bit of information lends more credence to the possibility that Gypsy was regularly abused by her trainers and other circus personnel over the years. She knew who was abusing her, and when the moment arrived, she apparently exacted her revenge upon her tormentors.

Among the murderous deeds committed by Gypsy after joining the Valdosta-based Nickel Plate Shows were the following:

An unluckily cold circus employee emerged from his tent in the middle of the night one evening in Ronceford, Virginia, to take some of Gypsy's hay in an effort to keep warm. That simple act proved to be his undoing, for Gypsy broke loose from her chains, grabbed the employee from his tent and slammed him to the ground, killing him instantly.

In 1896, ignoring warnings from Bernard Shea, Gypsy's trainer at that time, circus worker Frank Scott decided to exercise the temperamental elephant. For his efforts, Scott was rewarded by being thrown to the ground in a Chicago alley and stomped to death by the elephant's front feet.

Bernard Shea ultimately turned Gypsy's reins over to O'Rourke in 1896 after an incident in which Gypsy almost killed Shea. According to a description of the incident in Johnston's article, Shea and Gypsy were soaking up the cool water of a stream in Smith's Grove, Kentucky, when Gypsy suddenly grabbed Shea with her trunk and forced him under the water. He fought to the top several times, only to be shoved

Valdosta Police Chief Calvin Dampier brought an end to Gypsy's rampage with a large caliber rifle from the Spanish-American War. It was likely the only weapon in the county capable of doing so.

back under by the determined Gypsy. He eventually managed to escape, but immediately quit the show, because he knew then that it was only a matter of time before the elephant added him as another notch on her tusk.

Legends Never Die

It's just like the old saying – Legends never die. They just keep getting bigger, which in Gypsy's case is saying quite a lot. Her place in history is secured in the Historical Museum in Valdosta, and with each new generation, the story is passed along anew.

Milner, who frequently gives tours of the museum to school groups, says many of the children already know parts of the Gypsy story. And those who don't already know the details of Gypsy's wild final night on earth ask so many questions that they leave knowing at least most of the legend.

"Children love the story," Milner says. "I try to be a little careful about [explaining the part about] Gypsy being hacked to pieces, but they want to know all about that too."

Of even more interest to the children is the fact that one or more of them may even be living right over the scattered remains of Gypsy today, since quite soon, the entire area in the vicinity of her grave will be completely occupied by the new subdivisions being built in the area.

The Great 1898 Hurricane

JANE WALKER

*The United States has recently experienced a series of staggering hurricanes. Hugo,
Andrew, Fran, Charley, Ivan and Katrina are just some of the more memorable storms that
have wreaked havoc. Georgia has not suffered a direct hit during this rash of hurricanes,
leading some to postulate that the curvature of the coastline shields the state. Those who
lived through the Great 1898 Hurricane – the "Big Flow of '98" as it was called – would
fervently disagree.*

Very few natural disasters strike terror in the heart of man like a hurricane, for
it not only brings devastating wind and drowning water, but also spawns
powerful inland tornadoes that kill and destroy. The horrible aftermath of
Hurricane Katrina is the most recent example of the might of these storms.

The recovery from Katrina is still ongoing and will undoubtedly last many years.
New Orleans, Biloxi and other coastal towns are rebuilding, but they will never be the
same. Many landmark structures are gone forever, wiped from the face of the earth.

For many days before Katrina struck the Gulf Coast with howling winds and a
deadly storm surge, residents were informed of the dangers and some were under
mandatory evacuation orders. Some chose to stay, either hoping that they could ride
out the storm or unable to afford the cost of leaving.

Such forewarning was not possible during the late 19th century when one of the
most powerful hurricanes of the past two centuries actually did strike Georgia's coast,
causing immense damage and leaving 179 dead. Horace Gould, a resident of St.
Simons Island during this period, chronicled this terrible incident for posterity in a
letter to a relative.

> *"I went over [to St. Simons Island] from Brunswick Saturday afternoon. The next
> morning there was much rain and while at breakfast the wind began rising. There
> was nothing, however, to cause alarm..."*
>
> Horace Gould
> St. Simon's Island, GA
> October 10, 1898

Although early reports indicated that this fierce storm made landfall on Sapelo
Island, meteorologists now believe it first struck the northern end of Cumberland
Island. There the pilot boat *Maud Helen* – destined to be one of the storm's first U.S.
targets – ultimately came to rest upon the bluff at High Point, more than twenty feet
above sea level.

35

Newcastle Street immediately after the hurricane (either October 2 or 3, 1898).

This hurricane hit long before storms were assigned names and scientifically measured. It would be decades before meteorologists developed the now familiar Saffir-Simpson Scale which categorizes hurricanes from "1" (least dangerous, winds of 74-95 miles per hour) to "5" (catastrophic, winds over 155 mph and storm surge exceeding 18 feet).

"I took the opportunity between the showers to run down to the landing and secure the boat...We were sometime at the breakfast table and when we came out, the water was in the lower part of the peafield...For the first time I felt uneasy and hurried back to the house..." —Horace Gould

Since storm surge is an indication of a hurricane's intensity, meteorologists evaluate high water marks to determine the severity of the storms that occurred before modern times. Storm surge data from the distant past is compared to that of more recent storms. This, coupled with computer analysis, enables the National Weather Service to determine with accuracy the size and strength of the older storms. Using these techniques, meteorologists recently estimated that the 1898 Hurricane reached Category 4 strength with winds of 131-155 mph and a thirteen to eighteen-foot storm surge.

In a National Weather Service ranking of the most destructive U.S. hurricanes between 1851 and 2004, the one that hit Georgia in 1898 ranked 14th out of 65. Only three hurricanes - Andrew (1992), Camille (1969), and the Labor Day Hurricane that struck the Florida Keys in 1935 – reached Category 5 intensity at landfall. The 1898 storm was comparable to Hugo, a Category 4 hurricane that rav-

This photograph of Newcastle Street (taken from the Oglethorpe Bank) shortly after the hurricane hit shows the devastating storm surge that inundated downtown Brunswick.

aged South Carolina in September, 1989.

"Up to this time, though blowing a brisk gale, the wind was not causing any uneasiness, but the puffs became more frequent and each puff seemed stronger than the one preceding it..." —Horace Gould

The islands of the West Indies – especially St. Vincent and Barbados – were directly in the path of the 1898 Hurricane and were among the first to experience the storm's wrath. From *Fifty Years in Western Africa*, by A. H. Barrow, written in 1900, the following excerpt of a letter from the commander of Her Majesty's ship Intrepid to the Admiralty addresses the effects of the hurricane disaster on St. Vincent:

"It is impossible to overstate the damage done to every town and village in the island, and to crops and works. The whole island has the appearance of having been fired through; utter desolation prevails everywhere. Hardly a green spot is to be seen where before all was verdant and beautiful to look upon; the towns and villages, as viewed from the sea, have the appearance of having churches, houses and public buildings mostly leveled to the ground, and those that are still standing will have to come down and be rebuilt. The inhabitants are in a state of destitution, with no roofs over their heads, excepting the shelters that have been hastily raised for their protection from the weather, which are not by any means adequate to the number of the population, and that if it had not been for the very prompt assistance of the Government, and of the ships ordered to their relief, the inhabitants would for the

A sailing vessel marooned in the "marshes of Glynn."

most part have starved."

The devastation in the West Indies was a portent of things to come. Brunswick, Georgia, has the lowest elevation of any city in the state at just fourteen feet above sea level. It is therefore the most susceptible to damage from tidal surges. The 1898 Hurricane left downtown Brunswick under sixteen feet of water.

Photographs taken shortly afterwards show citizens struggling through town on horseback with floodwater up to their horses' haunches. The city hall on Newcastle Street survived relatively intact, but many of that neighborhood's stately Victorian houses incurred substantial damage.

"The water was now to my knees and still rising. Going into the dining room, I put everything eatable out of the safe...I saw the sideboard with its load go over, the table and its load floating around, dashing against the wall, first on one side and then on the other, bringing up each time with a crash that would topple over a chair or two and as each fell it would join the mad dance of the waves..."

—Horace Gould

Brunswick's Bill Brown, an 86-year-old realtor and owner of Bill Brown Company, remembers family stories about the terrible storm. His ancestral home at 4 Glynn Avenue (presently occupied by the Brunswick-Golden Isles Chamber of Commerce) withstood the hurricane, but his grandfather spoke of the nightmare of trying to live through its fury.

"My mother was a six-year-old girl at the time, and she told us that the water rose to six inches over the window sills. It covered the keys of the piano in the front parlor. The cellar was filled with marsh mud and was never dug out. My grandfather carried my mother to the back of the lot and told her to stay where he put her. Being an obedient child, she didn't move, though her father had inadvertently placed her in a prickly pear bush." He chuckled about this before continuing with his recollections.

"Some of the windows of our house were blown out, and we lost some shingles, but no one was hurt. I've also heard about the man who owned a livery stable in town. He took his five or six horses and mules to the First Baptist Church and put them in the sanctuary there. They chewed up the hymnals and the backs of the pews of the church, and someone said, 'It wasn't the first time there was a jackass in the pulpit.'"

Just offshore, the Golden Isles suffered widespread devastation. At Gould's Inlet on

St. Simons Island, fourteen feet of water covered the marshes. Grazing livestock were trapped and had no chance at survival. More than 100 cattle on General's Island met a similar fate, their carcasses later washing up in the woods. An aerial photograph of Jekyll Island showed only one pine tree left standing. Nearly the entire island was under water.

"Grasping my tin with food, I made my way to the hall door as best I could, the water up to my arm pits. The door was jammed and for some time I could not open it. I succeeded at last, standing on the sill...mother called to us to come in her room as the shed rooms were going up and down like bucking horses and the waves were striking the sides of that room like a battering ram..." —Horace Gould

Damage reports from nearby communities were likewise extensive. Fernandina Beach, Florida, reported a twelve-foot storm surge. The tug *Gladiator* was deposited there in the middle of town and four feet of water stood in the office of the *Mirror* newspaper.

On Georgia's St. Catherines Island, just one person – a man who climbed a tree and waited for the tide to recede – reportedly survived the wall of water that struck that locale. The captain of the coastal steamer Hesse said that eighty bodies were found on Butler's Island. On Campbell Island, fifty drowned and the island was completely washed away. The Champneys Island mills were devastated by the storm, which carried pieces of the structure miles away to the upper end of Butler's Island.

"Just as we entered [the parlor], Herbert gave a shout and running to the window we saw the south piazza with the roof separate from the main body of the house and disappear. At this time the wind was blowing a hurricane, the yard looked like the ocean, great waves chasing each other across from East to West and striking the trees; the spray was thrown high in the air..." —Horace Gould

A few miles north of Brunswick, tiny Darien took a hard hit as well. One old inhabitant described the Altamaha River as a "roaring sea" spreading over rice fields and wharves. The water level, he recollected, rose five feet in twenty minutes and, at its crest, was about twelve feet higher than the previous record.

The cataclysm obliterated nearly every raft of lumber in the river near Darien scattering millions of board feet of timber in every direction. Two weeks later, a local newspaper reported that "a view of the river last storm day was a better illustration of Noah's flood than book pictures ever will be."

"I saw something that I have often read of, but never saw before. Frequently the crest of a wave was taken off clean, as though cut with a knife and the mass of water was sent flying through the air, like a great sheet..." —Horace Gould

A poignant letter from A.C. McKinley to his nephew in Atlanta provides insight into what coastal residents experienced during the frightening storm. It was written from Inverness, Georgia, on November 4, 1898, as follows:

"Dear Willie: Your kind letter of Oct. 13th recd. & I would have replied sooner, but we have been exceedingly busy trying to patch up the damage done us by the terrible hurricane and tidal wave of Oct. 2d. For four weary hours we stood (your aunt & myself) waist deep in water. The waves coming across the island – direct from the ocean, covered the tops of our windows. In the house the water was nearly 3 feet deep – in the yard, nearly 6 feet on a level. The waves in our yard were fully 12 feet high. Your Aunt S. was in bed with fever, but when her bed began to float, she had to get up & stand waist deep in water for hours. We lost most of our possessions – either outright or from damage by salt water. All our furniture is dropping to pieces, and my Bibles – my own, my fathers & my grandfathers with all the family records for three generations, were ruined, as the Bibles were under water for hours...."

The *Brunswick News* ran an article in its July 13, 1998, issue about the 1898 hurricane, almost exactly one hundred years after it occurred. In the article, Frances Burns of St. Simons Island, now deceased, gave her recollections of the storm from hearing her father, Clifford Postell, talk about it. She recalled hearing her father tell of all that he endured in 1898, trying to rescue his mother and brother from drowning in the chaotic floodwaters. As a young man in his twenties at the time, he placed his invalid mother on his shoulders and struck out into the fury, hoping to carry her to a friend's cabin and return for his mentally impaired brother.

Uprooted trees and howling winds thwarted his plan, so he secured his mother in the fork of a tree and left her to retrieve his brother. He remembered seeing a rabbit and a rattlesnake side-by-side on a floating log, too busy trying to survive to think of their natural roles as predator and prey. Frances related that this was the one thing her father was able to laugh about in re-telling of his trials during the hurricane

"The pig, still clinging to its perch, passed out of sight on the crest of a wave. For a time we could see fowls and turkeys in all stages of drowning, but poor things, it was soon all over with them..." —Horace Gould

A touching anecdote from the Coastal Georgia Historical Society circulates about Horace Gould's brother and sister-in-law, who lived near Black Banks. Mrs. Gould placed their two toddlers in a washtub as a precaution, so they would have their own little lifeboat. Fortunately, they didn't experience any flooding at their house.

Many lighthouses in the storm's path were either demolished or crippled. Tides were reported to be eighteen feet above normal at the Sapelo Island lighthouse where water covered the floor of the dwelling's second story and submerged the oil house's roof. The beacon suffered damage to the extent that the government deactivated it and also the lighthouse on Wolf Island.

"When the water began to thump against the floor of the parlor I feared we would have to get on the roof as the safest place in case the walls fell. Much to our relief the water began falling about 3 o'clock..."
—Horace Gould

As quoted in Buddy Sullivan's book, *Early Days on the Georgia Tidewater*, "Mr. William Cromley, keeper of the Sapelo light, had a very narrow escape. [One] man tied him to the boat and he was safely landed but unconscious. He lost everything but his life...."

The tidal surge scattered lumber and other goods across Brunswick's docks.

Also from Sullivan's book is the following account: "A little three-year old...boy was rescued from a limb while floating in the river on Monday morning. It is said that he drifted over from Champneys Island. Report says that his father and mother drowned."

Some distance to the north, the lighthouse at Hilton Head, South Carolina (which had been built just seven years before the hurricane struck) shone brightly in the midst of the tumult. The stalwart keeper, Adam Fripp, endeavored to keep the light burning regardless of weather or danger. At some point, the raw power of the elements became too much and a violent wind gust shattered the glass protecting the lantern room, extinguishing the light. Fripp suffered a fatal heart attack during the turbulence and urged his daughter to relight the lantern and keep it burning. She was able to obey the request, but the stress was such that just three weeks later she also, at the tender age of 21, joined her father in death.

These tragedies inspired ghost stories that have become part of the folklore of the Hilton Head lighthouse. Today, visitors and residents alike report sightings of a young girl in a long blue dress, walking the grounds, wailing and sobbing in grief.

Georgia has thus far escaped the recent onslaught of storms striking the U.S., but statistics suggest that this is merely an aberration. While no major hurricanes made landfall along the Georgia coastline in the 20th century, at least fifteen did

Years later, residents who survived the "Great Flow of '98" still remembered the awful slaughter of livestock trapped in Glynn County's marshes.

so during the previous century. As Al Sandrik, warning coordination meteorologist for the National Weather Service in Jacksonville, Florida, notes, "We have seen in the 19th century that major hurricanes can strike the Georgia coastline. Certainly, if we were struck in the 19th century, there's absolutely no reason why we can't be struck in the 21st century."

"The water fell rapidly and before night it was possible to walk out, the wind having moderated to a gentle breeze. Tis hard to convey an idea of the destruction wrought by this storm. Every house on this place, except the dwelling, is either washed from its foundations, or down, and the yard one scene of devastation and ruin..." —Horace Gould

These are ominous warnings considering the Georgia coast's tremendous population growth during the past few decades. From luxurious housing developments near Cumberland Sound to high-rise condos and hotels on Jekyll, St. Simons and Tybee Islands, it is just a matter of time before Georgia's preparedness is tested.

With coastal landowners perhaps lulled by the calm of a century with no major hurricanes, meteorologists are delving deeper into Georgia's past and finding that monster hurricanes with winds well over 100 mph and storm surges of fourteen feet or more were frequent occurrences in the past and may be once again in the future.

One such storm arrived on August 27, 1893. This tempest hit Tybee Island, Georgia, and adjacent areas of South Carolina, bringing a twenty-foot wall of water topped with waves cresting at 25 feet. Though this storm was not as powerful as the storm of 1898, it exacted a far greater toll – more than 2,000 perished. From Savannah to Charleston, many victims were washed out to sea, their bodies never recovered.

"Old oaks that were prominent in my childhood's recollection are flat. Indiscriminately they lie, their limbs crossed and re-crossed in every direction, while mingled with them are the remnants of chairs, tables, linen, crockery, everything broken into bits..." —Horace Gould

Despite the ominous forebodings for the future, we can learn lessons from recent hurricanes. When Hurricane Floyd brushed the Georgia coast in September, 1999, for instance, approximately 350,000 Georgians evacuated, including 60,000 from Brunswick and Glynn County alone. They joined more than two million people from Florida, North Carolina, and South Carolina as part of the largest peacetime evacuation in U. S. history. Many evacuees were stranded for hours in traffic gridlock, and this resulted in new measures such as the dedication of all lanes of I-16 to west-bound traffic during hurricane evacuations.

After sweeping past the Georgia coast, Floyd hit North Carolina, Virginia, and coastal New England, causing seventy deaths and $6 billion in damage. Just two weeks earlier, Hurricane Dennis had skirted Georgia before striking North Carolina in late August, 1999. Dennis resulted in eight deaths and more than $40 million in damage.

The dead animals, both wild and domestic, lie plentifully scattered around. Many birds came in from the ocean during the storm. Pelicans by the score sheltered themselves about the house and after the storm waddled feebly to the river, unable to fly. Fruits from the tropics, quite fresh, were found in the yard showing evidently that vessels were lost near the coast..." —Horace Gould

Since more than sixty percent of the U.S. population lives on or near the coast today, the threat posed by hurricanes is substantial. The principal concern is the copious rainfall accompanying many storms. In fact, inland flooding has killed more people during the last thirty years than coastal storm surges and high winds.

Ironically, some of the greatest rainfall results from weaker storms that stall over an area and produce terrible flooding (the havoc caused by the slow-moving, meandering remnants of Tropical Storm Alberto in southwest Georgia in 1994 is one example).

"The storm was very destructive to the sea shore. The hotel was flooded and verandas washed away, the parlor furniture, including the piano, strewed over the beach. All the pretty cottages, bath houses, etc., are piled in one inextricable mass next to the woods..." —Horace Gould

Weather forecasters warn that the Georgia coast should expect a hurricane every ten years and a major hurricane every fifty years. They also refute the long-held theory that a major hurricane cannot hit the Georgia coast because of its shape. Meteorologists, in fact, now suspect that the configuration of the coastline actually makes Georgia even more susceptible to deadly storm surges.

"One man, with his wife, who lived on Egg Island, took refuge on his roof when his house blew down, but soon were washed off. With a desperate effort he reached a tree, with his wife in his arms...he clung to a limb, holding fast to his wife until she died; then giving up hope he let go of her and the limb...he clung [to driftwood], more dead than alive, for three days, when he was seen and picked up by the crew of a steamer. He had drifted 60 miles!..." —Horace Gould

Hurricane season begins in June and lasts through November. According to weather prognosticators, when the first two-thirds of the season are active, October and November tend to be, as well. Perhaps the Peach State will once again escape a hurricane of the magnitude of Hugo, Andrew and Katrina, but the bad news is that the sand in the hourglass of chance is running out. There will come a day when the Georgia coast once again experiences a storm of the magnitude of the Great Flow of '98.

Source

1. Sullivan, Buddy. *Early Days on the Georgia Tidewater: The Story of McIntosh County and Sapelo*, 1990, *The Darien News*, Darien, Georgia.

Quiet Valor

REV. ALLEN WILBURN

A country boy who enjoyed fishing and hunting in west Georgia later received the Medal of Honor for selfless gallantry in the steaming jungles of Vietnam. His hometown has done its best to ensure he wasn't forgotten, yet today there is surprisingly little known about the life of this brave man.

How is valor quiet when boldly demonstrated in the chaos of combat? How is courage hushed when recognized with a Congressional Medal of Honor? How is a hero forgotten when a hometown highway bears his name? Such contradictions do not seem possible.

I've made many trips to the Haralson County courthouse in west Georgia over the years, but I do not recall ever seeing anyone reading the plaque that honors Sergeant Ray McKibben. When I read it for the first time I marveled at the bravery of the young soldier whose exploits it describes. I learned that he acted with "intrepidity, conspicuous gallantry, indomitable courage, and

Ray McKibben on the left.

extraordinary heroism; that he came under heavy automatic weapons fire; that bullets were striking all around him; that he undertook single-handed assaults on enemy emplacements; and that he disregarded his own safety to pull a wounded comrade out of the line of fire."

The citation accompanying McKibben's Medal of Honor is inscribed on the plaque. It begins: The President of the United States of America, authorized by Act of congress, March 3, 1863, has awarded in the name of The Congress the Medal of Honor posthumously to Sergeant Ray McKibben United States Army for conspicuous gallantry and intrepidity in action at the risk of his life above and beyond the call of duty.

While the plaque provides details about what Ray McKibben did, it reveals little about who he was. I wanted to know more about the courageous young man, but I soon discovered that while it is simple enough to find out why he received the Medal of Honor, it is much harder to get to know Ray McKibben the brother, friend, schoolmate, and comrade.

From a researcher's standpoint, that seemed odd. When historians examine events in the distant past, they can expect their only sources of information to be musty books and yellowed archival papers. But this young man resided in Haralson County less than forty years ago – it should have been easy to find residents in this rural area who remember him.

Sergeant Ray McKibben distinguished himself by conspicuous gallantry and intrepidity in action above and beyond the call of duty while serving as team leader of the point element of a reconnaissance patrol of Troop B, 7th Squadron (Airmobile), 17th Cavalry operating in enemy territory near Song Mao in the Republic of Vietnam on 6 December 1968.

There are still, though, a number of locals whose roots trace back to the day Ray McKibben was laid to rest in the Center Primitive Baptist Church cemetery. His December 14, 1968 funeral fell on "the coldest day – the wind was blowing and it was gray," recalls McKibben's childhood friend Amos Sparks. "It occurred to me that just a few days before he was in the jungles of Vietnam, and then he came home to the coldest weather you've ever seen."

Due to the frigid weather and lack of news coverage, there was sparse public attendance. He had died a little more than a week earlier, half a world away, and perhaps word of his accomplishments had not reached home in time to generate the kind of outpouring of affection one expects from such a small and tight-knit community.

Sergeant McKibben was leading his point element in a movement to contact along a well-traveled trail when the lead element came under heavy automatic weapons fire from a fortified bunker position, forcing the patrol to take cover. Sergeant McKibben, appraising the situation and without regard for his own safety, charged through bamboo and heavy brush to the fortified position, killed the enemy gunner, secured the weapon and directed his patrol element forward.

Memories of Ray McKibben seem to have faded from the consciousness of this quiet community like ground fog dissipated under a hot summer sun. Even his relatives have little to offer. "His immediate family is dead or moved away; can't find anyone who knows much about him," one distant relative recently wrote. "I don't have anything but questions myself," another family member sighed.

Only snippets of information are left – sketchy memories of those who knew him.

"As a small boy," remembers Charles Partridge, another boyhood friend, "he had to take baths in a large round wash tub. He was so big he did not fit and had to pull his knees to his chest to sit in the wash tub." He was nicknamed "Bear" because he was so much larger than his peers, but he was always easygoing. "He loved to play army and wore a World War II vintage steel helmet," Partridge reminisces. He was also an avid fisherman and hunter who knew how to use a rifle and a shotgun.

As the patrol moved out, Sergeant McKibben observed enemy movement to the flank of the patrol. Fire support from helicopter gunships was requested and the area was effectively neutralized. The patrol again continued its mission and as the lead element rounded the bend of a river it came under heavy automatic weapons fire from camouflaged bunkers. As Sergeant McKibben was deploying his men to covered positions, he observed one of his men fall wounded. Although bullets were hitting all around the wounded man, Sergeant McKibben, with complete disregard for his own safety, sprang to his comrade's side and under heavy enemy fire pulled him to safety behind the cover of a rock emplacement where he administered hasty first aid. Sergeant McKibben, seeing that his comrades were pinned down and were unable to deliver effective fire against the enemy bunkers, again undertook a single-handed assault of the enemy defenses. He charged through the brush and hail of automatic weapons fire closing on the first bunker, killing the enemy with accurate rifle fire and securing the enemy's weapon.

"Ray McKibben grew up in the community of Felton," U.S. District Court Judge Harold Murphy recently recalled. "I remember him having flaming red hair. From my very early youth I knew his grandfather and grandmother, Tom and Janie McKibben. They lived in a rented house and Tom did a little farming and some plowing for other people. He earned a meager living."

Like his grandparents, Ray did not have much growing up. "I would see him walking by my parent's home on his way home from school," Murphy noted. "His father, Dean, was a truck driver and was frequently away from home for long periods." Another friend recalls that McKibben's family did not own a car, and on Saturdays he and his mother would take a taxi to Cedartown. Ray would often go to the picture show while she shopped.

He continued his assault against the next bunker, firing his rifle as he charged. As he approached the second bunker his rifle ran out of ammunition; however, he used the captured enemy weapon until it too was empty, at which time he silenced the bunker with well-placed hand grenades. He reloaded his weapon and covered the advance of his men as they moved forward. Observing the fire of another bunker impeding the patrol's advance, Sergeant McKibben again single-handedly assaulted the new position.

Information about Ray's military service proved similarly elusive. Richard J. Hefferman of Pennsylvania, who served in the same unit (Troop B, 7th Squadron, 17th Cavalry), offered assistance, but with little luck. "Like you," he wrote, "I have

had difficulty in contacting members of Ray McKibben's family…I have a passing memory of Ray, but I was in the Scout Platoon and didn't cross paths often with the ground troops. I've tried to make contact with others, but the Blue Team is very guarded about [things]. I can't really explain it, but it's there."

He explained that B Troop, 7/17th Air Cavalry was employing a new tactic. Troop B was divided into three components: Red Team used scout OH6A helicopters to locate the enemy; White Team consisted of Cobra gunship helicopters, and Blue Team utilized Lift Hueys (Slicks) that carried in the Aero-Rifle Platoon Blue Team, the infantry, to engage the enemy. A command and control helicopter flew overhead and directed the mission.

Ray McKibben was part of the Blue Team, an outfit of sixteen men that "was on patrol," Hefferman explains, "inserted into a known area of enemy personnel and equipment." The Blues were maneuvering down a trail through dense vegetation along a river when they encountered a large enemy force, perhaps company size (approximately 125 men). In the intense firefight that ensued, the GIs fought tenaciously. "Of the sixteen engaged," Hefferman, "one received the Silver Star, three others the Bronze Star with a V [or Valor], and McKibben the Medal of Honor. What he did was pretty amazing, pretty tough stuff."

As he neared the bunker he was mortally wounded but was able to fire a final burst from his weapon killing the enemy and enabling the patrol to continue the assault. Sergeant McKibben's indomitable courage, extraordinary heroism, profound concern for the welfare of his fellow soldiers and disregard for his own personal safety saved the lives of his comrades and enabled the patrol to accomplish its mission. Sergeant McKibben's conspicuous gallantry and intrepidity in action at the cost of his life above and beyond the call of duty are in the highest traditions of the military service and reflect great credit upon himself, his unit, and the United States Army.

On Independence Day in 1994, rain fell while Tom Murphy, Speaker of the Georgia General Assembly, read a resolution naming Georgia Hwy. 120 from Tallapoosa to Buchanan the Ray McKibben Medal of Honor Highway. Judge Harold

McKibben's memorial service.

Murphy spoke at the dedication and asked the penetrating question: "What have I ever done, what am I doing now, to deserve having Ray McKibben die for me?" Then he asked the audience, "What have you ever done, what are you doing now, to deserve having Ray McKibben die for you?"

We may never know whether Ray McKibben's uncommon strength of character was innate or a product of his environment and military training, but his sacrificial actions are testaments to a young man instinctively stalwart, vigilant, and valiant – and we ought to remember valor like that.

Note: Ray McKibben was an SP4(E4) at the time of his death. He was promoted posthumously to the rank of sergeant (E5).

The Toccoa Falls Flood

BRANDON LOWE

It began as just another wet late-autumn evening in Stephens County in northeast Georgia, but ultimately became a night of horror for the students and faculty of Toccoa Falls College.

On the night of November 5, 1977, Toccoa Falls College student Bill Anderson and his family went to bed at 10:00 p.m. They lived in a mobile home on the campus of the conservative Bible college in the mountains of northeast Georgia. Though he didn't know it at the time, Bill was about to experience a terror-filled ride into history which he and many other students and faculty at the college would never forget for the rest of their lives.

Before he could even close his eyes, Bill heard a knock on his door. Answering the knock, he discovered he was needed at a small bridge over Toccoa Creek. A large tree had fallen and was jammed against the bridge. This came as no surprise to Bill. It had rained steadily in Stephens County for the past nine days. Aside from his scholarly pursuits, he was employed as the school's maintenance man, and was a logical resource during times of need at the college.

Amazingly Toccoa Falls – Georgia's highest waterfall – is over 20 feet higher than Niagara Falls.

A large truck – itself carried away by an even more powerful force – lies downstream from the flood.

Almost everyone in the area knew Bill had a chainsaw. He made short work of the downed tree and the bridge was soon put back into service. The creek was high, just as it always was when it rained heavily, and Bill had urged a number of people on the college campus to move out for the night – until the weather could clear and the water level could drop. He sensed the danger, but had little luck convincing others.

His task on the bridge completed, Bill returned home just before 11:00 p.m. He slipped off his boots and returned to bed. Three hours later at approximately 2:00 a.m., his sleep was interrupted yet again. This time, however, it was the excited voice of a young female student that roused him from his slumbers.

"Get out! The dam has broken," the young woman shrieked. Stunned by the statement, Anderson hesitated a few moments before reacting. He went to the deck of his mobile home to gaze up the valley toward the vicinity of the dam. As he did, he realized to his horror that a wall of water four feet high was rushing towards him. He didn't know it at the time, but that initial wave of water was the least of his worries.

"I was trying to figure out what to do next," Anderson explained in a recent interview. "I was basically mesmerized."

Bill watched as the wall of water swept down the valley and then rolled over his deck, flooding the interior of his home. Arrested from his stupor, he ran back inside and slammed the door shut in a futile effort to evade the onslaught. This, however, did little to stop the quickly rising tide. Unbeknownst to him, a crashing, devastating wall of water many feet higher was yet on the way.

"Trailerville" at Toccoa Falls College after the flood. Toccoa Creek – still quite high – flows along the bottom foreground. Notice the area between the creek and the top of this photo which has been swept clean. It was ihere that the 35-foot-high wall of water initially crashed into the campus.

Beginnings

Toccoa Falls College is nestled in the northeast Georgia mountains in rural Stephens County, a short drive down Highway 17 off Interstate 85. The campus of the Bible college is quite humble, as is its enrollment of approximately 800 students and faculty. It basically is composed of a series of small buildings set against a backdrop of the rolling foothills typical of that region.

The college derives its name from a substantial waterfall which exists at the edge of the campus. The waterfall, however, is not as humble as the college. At 186 feet, it is over 20 feet higher than Niagara Falls in upstate New York – a little-known fact that reveals the actual immenseness of the Toccoa falls.

Even more impressive is the fact that the water from Toccoa Falls drops such a long distance that one can see the water actually separating several times before it hits the large pool below. Behind the falls are peach-colored clay rocks off which sunlight reflects dramatically on a bright day.

In 1911, Dr. R.A. Forrest purchased the property containing the waterfall, as well as the land on which the college exists for a $10 down-payment to a Toccoa banker. Twelve years earlier, a stone dam had been constructed above the falls to impound much of the water of robust Toccoa Creek, so that it could be used to generate hydroelectric power for the college.

A short time later, the trustees of Toccoa Falls College took control of the stone dam, demolishing it and constructing a larger earthen dam to replace it. This large impoundment of water continued to be used for hydroelectric power for a number of years until the generator was no longer necessary. In the ensuing years, the dam was

Rescue workers carry a victim on a stretcher over the Highway 17 bridge.

– for all intents and purposes – abandoned.

In the summer of 1977, Bill Anderson asked his boss if he could move his mobile home onto the college campus to be nearer his work and studies. Though space for such residences was at a premium on the college campus, Bill was able to find a spot in an area known locally as "Trailerville" where married students resided. The spot to which he moved his mobile-home was right beside Toccoa Creek. Bill didn't think about it much at the time, but his home was located in such a precarious spot that his two sons could literally drop a line and fish in the creek from their bedroom window. It was a location which would come back to haunt him.

That autumn was very wet, particularly in the latter portions of October and early November. On November 4 and 5, there were torrential storms. Though the dam above Toccoa Falls was steadily being extended beyond its capacity, no action was taken to evacuate the campus. Many of the college's 400 students, faculty and staff lived on campus in the area downstream from the falls, either in mobile homes or dormitories.

By the early morning hours of November 6, the dam had begun to leak. If the dam failed, Kelly Barnes Lake – with its nearly 130 million gallons of water – would come rushing over the falls in a cataclysmic 35-foot-high wall of water.

On-rushing Disaster

As the on-rushing water struck the side of the Anderson mobile home, the powerful surge immediately ripped away the 12 x 24-foot section Bill had recently built as an additional bedroom and office. He knew that if the current was powerful enough to destroy that room, then it could move the entire mobile home.

With the side ripped off, more water immediately flooded the interior of the house. Dishes fell from the cupboard. The children began to panic and scream. Though their circumstances were perilous and getting worse by the moment, Bill tried to remain calm, telling his family to "hold on," as he offered up a quick prayer that his family be spared.

Just as Bill had suspected, the strong current easily lifted the mobile home off its supports and then began moving it out into the main portion of Toccoa Creek – which by this time was a torrent. Still intact for the moment, the house quickly floated downstream.

As the structure – with Bill and his panic-stricken family still inside – drifted, a sudden powerful force crashed into it, breaking off two more rooms. The roof also was now torn off so that the terrified family could see the night sky. Today, Bill says he believes that sudden force which struck his house at this point was the horrendous 35-foot-high main wave of water which crashed through the valley after plummeting the 186 feet from the top of the falls.

Amazingly, the Andersons were still all together at this point. With the interior of the home flooded, they struggled to stay as high as possible as the house sank lower and lower in the water. They could feel the home grinding horribly against the debris and the earth below. Both ends of the house were now broken off, and it swayed crazily back and forth as it was carried away. Bill knew that the wildly bobbing building would be crushed into kindling wood when it struck the opening of a bridge or other obstruction through which it would be sucked downstream.

As it floated along, the remnant of the Anderson mobile home suddenly turned in an odd direction, and temporarily slowed somewhat. "I knew at that point that we had an opportunity and we had to get out quick," Bill later explained. As the house floated toward the tops of a clump of trees, Bill put a chair on top of the couch and began to pull his children to the highest point in the room. He then lifted them – with one arm – into one of the trees.

At this point, Bill became separated from his wife, four-year-old son, Joey, and 22-month-old daughter, Becky, all of whom were on the other side of the room. As he struggled to reach them to help them to safety, he suddenly saw to his horror that the wall above them was collapsing.

"My wife started to respond to me," Anderson later sadly remembered, "but then she said 'Come on kids, let's go with Jesus.' It was like she was going to say, 'Let's go with daddy,' but she realized in

On the day of the flood, this aerial view shows Toccoa Falls (top left) and the path of the waters which were released from Kelly Barnes Lake. The area known as "Trailerville" begins at the lower right.

time to say Jesus." Suddenly, the wall fell and buried Karen, Joey, and Becky. Bill never saw them alive again.

As the wall fell, the house suddenly disintegrated. Though he struggled mightily, Bill was unable re-locate his wife and two youngest children. Wracked with grief, he knew he had to concentrate on the safety of his oldest children. Twelve-year-old Lisa and six-year-old Billy

were perched precariously 12 feet up in the tree, but they were safe for the time being. Bill's other daughter – 9-year-old Susie – had been carried away into the inky darkness on a large piece of tin.

Grasping a string of barbed wire around the tree, Bill was able to climb up to his two surviving children. Grief-stricken and horrified, Lisa and Billy cried "Where's Mommy, Becky and Joey?" Bill later related that it almost seemed like someone else talking when he softly replied, "They went with Jesus."

"It stunned me how I said it so positively, so absolutely," he added. "I felt the grace of God flood over me. It sustained me completely. It gave me peace and seemed to do something for my children too."

For many of the other families and students at Toccoa Falls College, the damage would be just as devastating. The enormity of the disaster would not be known until the light of dawn illuminated the campus the following morning.

The Devastation

Though the flood would prove to be one of the worst in the state's history, the rescue effort by state and federal forces was almost as dramatic. Hundreds of rescue personnel from all over the Southeast rushed to respond. Joe Anderson (no relation to Bill), director of the Emergency Management Agency for Stephens County today, was a member of the rescuers, and among the first to arrive at the disaster. He reached the site within 25 minutes after the dam failed.

"When we got there, it was sort of like, well, 'What are we going to do now?'" he related. "Most of the victims didn't have a stitch of clothing on. It was wet and rain-

TOP: A view of the debris which became wedged beneath the Highway 17 bridge, causing the wall of water to slow, sparing other lives downstream. ABOVE: A small home – one of many uprooted and washed away by the flood – came to rest in the debris field.

ing and cold."

Worse, the disaster had dumped huge amounts of emulsified mud throughout the college campus and beyond. Anderson said it was up to his chest in some places.

Other hazards existed as well. Broken propane tanks spewed gas into the air. "You could hear them spewing," Anderson added, "but there isn't much you can do in the pitch dark."

Rescue workers shed their own clothing to help survivors. Other people in the area began to respond as well. The Red Cross arrived on the scene and immediately began to distribute food and clothing, while the First Baptist Church of Toccoa collected food and made room for survivors in the church.

"I remember the manager of (the local) McDonald's bringing her car – with a trunk full of free food for survivors and rescue workers," Anderson smiled.

As morning dawned and the new day began, most of the survivors had been located, and the grim task of recovering the victims began. "That was the first time I was exposed to a dead body," Anderson continued. "It was stunning. It was the next day before we even found many of the bodies. There was no light."

Troy Douglas, commander of the local Civil Air Patrol, flew above the scene and helped to locate bodies of the victims. Flying in his Cessna 206, he and other members of the Patrol ultimately located six bodies from the air, including the 39th and final victim discovered nearly a month later.

"We just happened to see two knees sticking up out of the sand," he said. "It was the

An overturned car is pulled from the mucky debris of Toccoa Creek.

body of Paul Williams, a 74-year-old man who lived on the campus."

In the midst of the disaster, the next grim task became the identification of the bodies. For the most part, this job fell to Ken Sanders, dean of students and athletic director at the college. After assisting in the rescue, Sanders went to the Stephens County Hospital for identification proceedings. He remained there for the next 24 hours.

"I saw 38 dead," he said. "A lot of them were swollen and they didn't look the same. You had to picture them as they had been in life."

Today, Sanders says he has been able to block out the horrific images of the victims and the devastation wrought by the flood. "If I couldn't block them out of my mind, I wouldn't be able to sleep at night. I couldn't handle it. There's just no way."

Sanders, now the vice president of Student Affairs and the women's basketball coach, says the flood was a demonstration of the school's strong faith, a characteristic which has played a strong role in attracting new students to the college.

The college itself had suffered damages estimated at over 2.5 million dollars. Much of this destruction occurred in three buildings which had been most in the path of the wall of water which rushed down the Toccoa Creek corridor on that terrible night.

Two dormitories were damaged. The worst of these was Forrest Hall where four freshman students were killed after becoming trapped on the first floor of the building. This four-story tall brick structure still stands today, but has been renovated and improved with $300,000 in federal funds.

Also in the Toccoa Creek corridor, eleven houses and 25 mobile homes – including that of Bill Anderson – were a complete loss. Most of the victims of the flood had been sleeping in the homes in Trailerville.

Fortunately for Toccoa Falls College, the majority of the school buildings on the campus – both then and now – stand on the crest of a hill above Toccoa Creek. This fact minimized damages to the school physical property, but did very little to curtail the loss of human lives.

The Anderson Family

For Bill Anderson, the flood was a tragic turning point in his life. His two oldest children – Lisa and Billy – had survived the flood by hanging on in the trees until the torrent passed. Miraculously, nine-year-old Susie survived as well. She somehow had ridden the piece of tin until the rushing water subsided. She was found the next morning – shaken and cold – but alive.

Bill and his children – particularly little Susie – struggled for years to deal with their loss. It took seven years – until she was 16 years old – before Susie was able to visit the gravesites of her lost family members.

Immediately following the flood, the Andersons were taken in by friends, and then provided with housing by the federal government. To be certain, it was a different lifestyle from that prior to the flood.

Marks on this tree created by the on-rushing waters from Kelly Barnes Lake offer an impression of the height of the terrible torrent.

"It truly was difficult," Bill said. "I prepared the kids for school, then would go to college and work. When they got out of school, someone had to take care of them."

Bill says he decided to get his children a babysitter, and little did he know the one they chose would later become his new wife. Liz Tenay had taught the children swimming lessons the previous summer, and was a student at the college. The kids liked her and gradually became determined to make her a permanent fixture in the family. Every family outing turned into a date, and Liz and Bill were married the following August, less than a year after the flood.

Bill himself did not adjust well to the permanent separation from his first wife. Karen had been his high school sweetheart. They had come to Toccoa Falls College as a family. Now she and their two youngest children were gone.

Despite his mourning, Bill completed his studies at Toccoa Falls College and departed the town with his new wife.

After working as a pastor at two different churches in New York from 1979 to 1986, Bill finally decided to leave the ministry. "I never actually had anyone counsel me," he said, "but it was coming back and haunting me. I didn't know how to deal with it. I resigned from the ministry for that very reason."

Anderson's resignation from the ministry finally brought him back to the site of his torment – Toccoa, Georgia. He returned with his children and wife Liz – along with their new child – in 1987. That same year, Bill bought a carpet and upholstery franchise in Toccoa, and his business moved along, but fate once again awaited him.

In February of 1989, while driving in his Dodge van in nearby Habersham County, a dump truck suddenly pulled out in front of Bill. In the resulting collision, the lower bone in his left leg was smashed through his knee and up into the bone in his upper leg, splitting his femur seven inches. For the next seven years, Bill struggled to recuperate, but the injury was too terrible. It ultimately required that the leg be amputated.

Postscript

November 5th of 2003 was a normal day in Stephens County. At the monument erected at the base of Toccoa Falls, there are no flowers, and no gatherings. There is only a fading, artificial floral arrangement with yellow and white roses, set off by a silver bow. The frame of the floral arrangement is rusted now, and it was probably put there by a loved one of the deceased, months, perhaps even years, earlier. On the monument above the arrangement, the large stone has been engraved to read "As is true here in the park, recovery is not complete, but is progressing." The words are now as outdated as the flowers themselves, for Toccoa Falls College is strong and prospering once again.

The impact of the flood on the college was almost total devastation initially, but in the end, it had the effect of actually helping the school to grow. Prior to the flood, Toccoa Falls College was almost overwhelmed in a large mortgage, and was hemorrhaging red ink. For the next 17 years after the flood, however, it functioned smoothly in the black.

A special federal grant through the Federal Disaster Assistance program amounted to some $2 million, and still more money poured in from around the world as good people opened up their hearts and wallets to the school. Since that time, the college has been completely re-built and has grown tremendously.

Also as a result of the flood, the safety of dams has become a paramount issue in Georgia. Ed Fiegle has been the program manager for the Georgia Safe Dams Program since February of 1979.

"The Toccoa flood caused the Safe Dams Act," he explained, describing legislation which has mandated the monitoring and safe management of all dams in the state of Georgia. It forced the draining and elimination of a number of unsafe impoundments in the state, including one atop Amicalola Falls in Dawson County similar in nature

Bill Anderson survived the terrible 1977 flood but lost his wife and two youngest children to the torrent. He stands with a monument – dedicated to the victims of the flood – which was erected below the falls.

to the disastrous Toccoa Falls impoundment.

Today, nearly 30 years after the Toccoa disaster, only two dam failures have occurred in Georgia, both of which occurred in 1994 as a result of Tropical Storm Alberto. No one was injured in either event.

As for Bill Anderson, November 6 comes and goes each year now. Despite his losses in the tragedy, his spirits no longer are downcast. In his office today at the college, cluttered with computer monitors, laptops and ink cartridges, he talks about his life.

"I just love helping people," he says, as he leans back in his wheelchair. As the director of Technical Support for the college, he oversees various computer problems, and even teaches a class on Tuesdays and Thursdays. "Like they say, we've been through the fire. We've been through the flood. God put us out there," he smiles.

Today, Bill Anderson has recovered. Life goes on. He has been fitted with a new prosthetic leg and is working on a book. It's a non-fiction account of his life. The story is one of faith. It's his life story, and in a small way, the story of Toccoa Falls College. His title? *The Experience of Clay.*

The Lost City of Etowah

Article & Photography Bob Andrew

The remnants of a pre-Civil War town and industry sleep today beneath the quiet waters of Lake Allatoona in Bartow County.

The loud roar of the blast furnace fills the air on this hot summer day. Spectators back away to a safe distance to avoid the fiery sparks dancing in the heat-blurred cauldron of molten iron. "Mary Anne," the name given this heaving furnace, produces a 2,800-degree heat that gnaws away at the ingredients – limestone, charcoal, and iron ore – poured in at the top and now melting in the super-heated belly. It is the start of the awe-inspiring "Hills of Iron" celebration at Red Top Mountain State Park in north Georgia which is attracting more and more visitors each season.

This scheduled event observes iron pourings from March through September each year. It is the brainchild of James Hamilton, former superintendent of the park who demonstrates the art of producing "pig iron." But why have an "iron pour?" Why to demonstrate to the public the 200-year-old art of producing iron of course!

To understand fully, one must peer back through the mists of time. Back to the fiery beginnings of our continent, when the hills of north Georgia were being formed and great mineral deposits were being laid down.

Mineral Madness

Gold, silver, manganese, bauxite, copper and high quality iron ore are all found in northwest Georgia today – some in abundance. Even the journals of early Spanish explorer Hernando De Soto in 1540 described the area as being "rich in Indian culture and natural resources."

Copper was the metal mined by the Indians, and later gold was discovered in Cherokee country. A volatile mineral that enriched some and ruined others, the precious yellow metal proved the source of much angst and despair before most of it was mined out of north Georgia.

Today, there is still an ancient Indian grave in a cemetery at Red Top Mountain which contains the last remains of Young Deer (1790-1828). Legend maintains he was a Cherokee killed by white men in a dispute over a mining claim in the area. The killers were never brought to justice.

Shortly after Young Deer's death, the lust for gold and the early state land lottery in 1832 ultimately decimated the remaining Cherokees in the area, forcing them out of the Southeast and changing their way of life forever. Iron, however, was a much more basic metal, nowhere near as valuable pound for pound as gold, but infinitely useful nonetheless. But contrary to gold – which is usually found in nuggets and pure veins in the earth, iron must be produced – smelted – from iron ore.

First Furnaces

In 1803, there were three furnaces operating in Warren, Elbert, and Chatham counties in Georgia producing pig iron for local use. The chief products made from this pig iron were pots, knives, picks and shovels – and a most precious item at that time, nails. Stories relate how the early settlers, when moving to a new location, would sacrifice their abandoned homes – burning them to the ground – in order to

Immense size for immense heat: Visitors to Cooper Furnace obtain a first-hand perspective of the massiveness of the historic furnace structure once owned and operated by early industrialist Mark Anthony Cooper to create iron from the ore in the area.

Just beneath the surface of Lake Allatoona, in this vicinity, the pioneer industrial community of Etowah once existed.

retrieve the scarce nails from the ashes for future construction needs. Such was the value of the iron in those days.

The abundance and high quality of the iron ore in the Etowah River area and the surrounding "red hills" began to lure investors and business entrepreneurs from other parts of the country in the early 19th century. The attraction was further fueled by a report in the early 1800s by a noted geologist, J.T. Hodge, who toured the Etowah River valley and stated, "...the quantity of the ore in this area is incalculable. I have visited almost all the great iron deposits in the United States, but have never been so impressed afore as by the mines of the Etowah district."

The potential of the valley area eventually attracted Master Furnace builder and Iron-Master Jacob Stroup, who was an important figure in the establishment of early iron works in South Carolina. Stroup, whose knowledge and family background can be traced back to the iron-rich Ruhr Valley of Germany, had been trained in the skills of the trade by his father and grandfather, pioneers in Pennsylvania and Maryland prior to moving to South Carolina.

In 1832, when the area was still inhabited by Indians, Stroup built his first furnace and bloomery forge in Georgia on the Soque River, three miles south of present-day Clarkesville. Four years later, in 1836, perhaps motivated by the notoriously mineral-rich territory in northwest Georgia, Stroup sold his operation and moved to Cass (present-day Bartow) County.

Entrepreneurial Stroups

According to hand-written records still in existence, he purchased "land lot #298," a beautiful wooded area along Stamp Creek which flowed into the Etowah (now Lake Allatoona) north of the present-day Allatoona Dam. Within a year, Stroup had built his first blast furnace on the creek and erected a bloomery forge about 100 yards above the furnace which produced hollowware and castings.

At this same general time, Stroup also built a gristmill and saw mill. The start of the Etowah River Valley industrial era had begun. This original complex was located just north of the present-day Wilderness Camp Marina at Lake Allatoona.

Jacob's son, Moses, arrived in Cass County in the early 1840s, after having sold his

This early woodcut of the Etowah Rolling Mill and village was published circa 1850s.

own extensive holdings in the South Carolina iron industry. Within a year, he had bought out his father's Stamp Creek complex.

A true technician of the trade and shrewd businessman, Moses enlarged the business by adding a rolling mill, a flour mill and then later, partnering with other investors for more furnaces.

During the middle 1800s, there were as many as eleven furnaces operating in the Etowah River Valley area. A number of the ruins of the furnaces can still be seen today.

Stroup's successes – and his own entrepreneurial flair – ultimately attracted Mark Anthony Cooper as an investor. As he once quoted from the Iron Masters Guide, "This country alone... has concentrated in its limits as much iron ore as all of Pennsylvania together, and is of superior quality." The ready availability of water power and timber (for charcoal needed in the process) made the iron ore deposits here even more valuable.

Mark Anthony Cooper

Born in 1800, Cooper was an attorney by trade, and had served as a state legislator from Putnam County, a U.S. Congressman and Senator, a bank founder in Columbus, Georgia, an Indian fighter in the Seminole wars, and advocate for railroad development, and one who saw the potential of the iron industry in north Georgia to be, as he put it, "a replacement for King Cotton."

Cooper had met the Stroups while campaigning for his unsuccessful gubernatorial bid in Georgia in 1843. He had decided to settle in the Cass County area.

Cooper first partnered with Moses Stroup and a John Wiley in 1845, to form the

COURTESY BARTOW HISTORY CENTER, CARTERSVILLE, GA

Last remains: Photographed circa 1940s, the remnants of Cooper's Iron Mill stand forlornly prior to the construction of Lake Allatoona. These factories were burned by contingents of Union Gen. William T. Sherman's troops during the U.S. Civil War

Etowah Manufacturing and Mining Company, the mighty backbone for the thriving enterprises to be spawned over the next 15 years. Its assets ultimately included:

- A rolling mill which turned out wheels, axels and rails for the railroad.
- The River (Cooper) Furnace, which still stands today just below the present-day dam at Allatoona.
- The Etowah (Stroup) Furnace on Stamp Creek.
- A 250-barrel-per-day flour mill in a five-story building.
- The Etowah Railroad Company, designed and built by Cooper.

In the meantime, Jacob Stroup packed up and moved on to Alabama in 1842, where he began furnace building there. In 1844, at the age of 73, he returned to Cass County and built yet another furnace on the banks of Allatoona Creek near the community of Allatoona, Georgia. All are now buried beneath the earth bridge supports at the west end of the Bethany Bridge over Lake Allatoona at the entrance to Red Top Mountain State Park.

Two years later, in 1846, Stroup died while still operating his furnace and foundry. His gravesite and furnace shaped grave marker can still be seen today in the old Furnace Cemetery near his former home site off Stamp Creek Road.

City Of Etowah

Meanwhile, Mark Anthony Cooper was designing and incorporating the city of "Etowah" on the banks of the Etowah River, located today beneath the deep waters

Viewed from the Interpretive Center and circled in the photo is the small island which is the tip of Glen Holly hilltop where Mark Anthony Cooper's home once stood.

just behind the Allatoona Dam. The site of the town had been selected because it was at a point where the river was 600 feet wide and could accommodate a dam to provide waterpower for industries that needed it.

Cooper carefully planned the layout of each street and the location of each building in order to take maximum advantage of the narrow flat space along the river's edge and preserve the natural beauty of the area.

In the words of Mrs. Roe Knight, the last remaining citizen of the town in 1930, "the selected land was laid off into streets, lots and localities. A few more important structures which immediately went up were the church, school house, president's office, bank, boarding house, and several large stores. The chief boasts of the town, however, were the railroad turn-table, and the post office where mail was distributed daily for twenty years."[1]

On the west side of the present-day dam on what then was Allatoona Creek, a large spacious hotel was built on the mountain side. There was also a nail factory, two corn mills, and two saw mills.

"Pig iron" was shipped to foundry markets in Atlanta, Macon, and Augusta. The $20 a ton offering by the New York markets at the time was considered "unprofitable" because of transportation costs.

And just what is "pig iron?" When molten iron accumulated in a "hearth," a dam was removed and it was allowed to flow into a long trough excavated in the sand. The long trough then fed into smaller side troughs. To the iron workers, it looked like a

Though almost camouflaged against a rust-brown hillside of dead leaves and pine needles, the many outcroppings of iron ore show why the Stroups and Mark Anthony Cooper developed iron works in this vicinity.

mother pig feeding her young – and thus the name.

"There also was even a brewery," Mrs. Knight continued. "The proprietors gave their consent...for making lager beer...on behalf of the German workers of the barrel factory."

There also was a tavern in the town, once run by a Cherokee woman called Laughing Gal. Though Indian businesses were usually not tolerated, and few remained after the removal in 1838, "Laughing Gal's Tavern" was a most popular place for the workers.

Cooper's Trials

"Cooper's Iron Works" as the locals called Etowah, prospered, and began to attract workers from all over. From North and South Carolina and Virginia and even as far away as Germany they came.

Cooper himself built a spacious home he called Glen Holly on a hill overlooking the Etowah River, away from the hustle and bustle of his new town. Today, while most of the actual site is now beneath the waters near the dam at Lake Allatoona, a small island can still be seen from the present-day dam overlook. It is the hilltop of Glen Holly, and when the waters are low in the winter, the 150-year-old foundations of Cooper's old home can still be seen.

In 1849, Moses Stroup, unable to meet his share of the debts of the business, sold his share and moved to Alabama. Cooper's industrial complex continued to do well, but during the economic banking crisis of the mid-1850s, he found himself $200,000 in debt.

Strapped for cash, Cooper called upon 38 friends in Georgia to help satisfy the debt. By the end of the decade, he had repaid all the debts, and to show his gratitude to those who had come to his aid, he had a marble obelisk made and on it inscribed a message of thanks and the names of all 38 friends. The "Friendship Monument" as it came to be known, was originally erected near the Cooper furnace in the old town, but was removed and today stands near the old train depot and Visitors Center in downtown Cartersville.

The outbreak of the U.S. Civil War initially appeared to bring more prosperity to the area when a $1,000,000.00 contract was signed with the Confederate government for "cannons and other weapons." Unfortunately, the war also brought disaster in its wake.

On May 21 and 22, 1864, Union General William T. Sherman ordered the town of Etowah destroyed. While no actual fighting occurred there, the city was leveled and never rebuilt.

Sparks shower into the darkened night as the dam in the furnace is removed at the "Hills Of Iron" Iron Pour at Red Top Mountain State Park. And at 2,800 degrees Fahrenheit, that's some hot sparks!

A Forgotten Ghost Town

As people moved away to find work, only the ruins of the buildings remained. The bank, flour mill, the hotel, and other remnants which Mrs. Knight once called "The Switzerland of the South," became a ghost town.

After the war, the iron industry never fully recovered, primarily for financial reasons, but also because of the limited availability of coal for charcoal which was abundant in competing sites such as Birmingham, Alabama and Pennsylvania.

Though the roaring blast furnace fires of the 19th century complex have been extinguished forever and the clamor of life has faded into the ages, one can still visit remnants of the pre-Civil War industrial complex once known as Etowah. The immense Cooper Furnace still stands on the banks of the Etowah River below Allatoona Dam. One can also visit the U.S. Army Corps of Engineers Interpretive Center museum which provides a good description of the historic site. From there, on a clear blue sky day, one can also look down on the green waters of Lake Allatoona and know that below the surface still exists the Lost City of Etowah.

Endnote

1. Frances Adair interview, 1930, Bartow History Center, Cartersville, GA

Grateful appreciation is hereby extended by the author and Georgia Backroads to the Etowah Valley Historical Society, Cartersville, Georgia, for its assistance with the information necessary for this article. The Society is a co-sponsor of the annual "Hills of Iron" Celebration.

River of Fire

A day of fun and frolic at a popular South Georgia picnic area and swimming hole turns into a nightmare of suffering, death, and grief when propane leaking from derailed tank cars erupts in a sea of flame.

Daniel M. Roper

The day was already uncomfortably hot and humid in Americus, Georgia, shortly after sunrise on June 28, 1959. The morning had begun badly for the crew of Seaboard Air Line Railroad Train 82. They were more than four hours behind schedule leaving town and were fated to endure an interminable afternoon under a scorching summer sun while the heavily laden freight train made its way toward Savannah.

When it finally departed Americus at 7 a.m., Number 82 consisted of 123 freight cars and a caboose pulled by three diesel-electric engines. At the forward end of the one-and-a-half-mile long procession, an engineer and brakeman occupied the first engine's control compartment, two student brakemen occupied the second engine's control compartment, and a fireman occupied the third.

At the rear, a conductor and a flagman took station in the caboose. From its cupola, they looked out on the long chain of cars stretching ahead. The ninth and tenth cars forward were tankers - 35-foot-long metal cylinders, each containing 11,000 gal-

COURTESY SAVANNAH MORNING NEWS

In January of this year, Nathan Creasy returned to the site of the derailment for the first time since 1959.

lons of highly pressurized liquefied petroleum gas.

As the train traveled east that sunny Sunday morning, many residents in towns along the railroad were preparing to go to church. There was a new preacher at the Methodist church in Meldrim where L.B. Slater and his wife Helen normally worshiped. They didn't attend that day, however, because they went shopping in nearby Bloomingdale for home canning supplies.

Nathan Creasy and his wife Vera, who was eight months pregnant, drove to Claxton that morning to visit Vera's mother. From their Port Wentworth home, the Creasy's drove west on U.S. 80. As they crossed the Ogeechee River bridge near Dasher's Landing, Nathan glanced downstream, as was his habit, to enjoy the view of the pristine black water river flowing serenely between densely forested banks.

In Meldrim, 17-year-old C.R. Saturday's family had out-of-town company, but his thoughts were also on the Ogeechee. The sultry conditions were perfect for a refreshing swim, but it didn't require warm weather to entice him to take a dip in the river. "I used to go down there to swim at least once every day of the year – Thanksgiving, Christmas, New Years Day, whenever," Saturday recalled in a recent interview.

Behind Schedule

At noon, Number 82 arrived in Vidalia five hours and five minutes after leaving Americus. As late as they were, things only continued to go downhill for the crew members. They coupled a fourth diesel-electric engine to the train and consequently fell an additional forty minutes behind schedule before departing at 1:30 p.m. Then, just 19 miles from town, they made yet another stop to uncouple the twenty-first car which had developed an overheated wheel assembly.

Because of these delays, Number 82 was still fifteen miles west of Savannah at 3:40 p.m. Traveling at or near the maximum permissible speed of 49 mph, the freight train clattered onto the half-mile long Ogeechee River trestle bridge and rumbled towards Meldrim.

From a sand bar twenty-five feet below the tracks, C.R. Saturday paused to watch Number 82 cross. He had already been at the river for hours, swimming and sunbathing with George "Topper" Hodges and Topper's wife, Nealtha (who, like Vera

DAN ROPER

Creasy, was eight months pregnant). The sand bar was a perfect vantage point to observe the four powerful engines and lengthy string of cars roar by.

Saturday and the Hodges were not alone. The temperature was 98 degrees that day, hot enough to persuade more than 75 others to crowd the popular riverside picnic and swimming area near the trestle. That number was far less than usual on such a steamy weekend afternoon. "A lot of the boys and men were playing in a baseball league game," recalls Saturday. "It kept about half the community from being there."

The First Sign of Trouble

As Number 82 crossed the trestle, something went terribly wrong, although seconds or perhaps even minutes passed before anyone realized it. A flaw in how the rails were secured to the trestle allowed them to slide forward just a bit in the direction in which the train was traveling. This movement exerted tremendous pressure on the rails nearest the end of the bridge. They butted up against the tracks on the bank, which were properly secured and did not budge. This pressure, combined with the intense heat of the summer day which caused the metal to expand, forced a section of rail about 117 feet from the end of the bridge to bow outwards slightly. The railroad tracks were no longer in gauge.

The distortion of the tracks allowed the right rear wheels of the 107th car to drop just inside the rail. The wheels continued moving forward, scraping along the inner side of the rail, exerting still more outward pressure. Soon the wheels began to slice deeply into the rail, shearing off a steel splinter two feet long and one-and-a-half inches thick.

The overstressed, badly damaged rail could no longer withstand the enormous strain. The result, which would prove to be catastrophic, was that at a point 75 feet

from the east end of the trestle, the rail inevitably – and tragically – snapped. One by one, the last fifteen cars of the train hurtled toward the rupture. The seventh and eighth cars in this progression were the tankers loaded with propane gas.

From his location on the sand bar, C.R. Saturday knew there was a problem. "We were sitting on the sand bar watching the train go by. The first sign of trouble was when I saw parts of the trestle fall."

The wheels of the freight cars tore apart the trestle's wooden decking and ripped out a 75-foot section of bridge. The 107th car slewed violently, straddled the tracks, and skidded for some distance, eventually halting with the front wheels on one side of the rails and the back wheels on the other.

The next car in line derailed to the right, crashed down the embankment, and came to a stop near the river. The following eleven cars tumbled off the trestle one by one, some landing in the woods on the east bank while others plunged into the Ogeechee. The last two cars and the caboose did not derail but came safely to a stop on the bridge.

The tankers were among the cars that fell into the river. In the process, the coupler of the second tank car punched through the tank head of the first. Thousands of gallons of liquefied petroleum gas immediately spewed out of the punctured tanker.

No Present Danger

When the derailed cars finally came to rest, the amazed onlookers gaped at the wreckage. Some of the picnickers and swimmers approached the train out of curiosity, others to see if they could be of assistance. Nobody had been hurt to that point, and to C.R. Saturday it seemed like the crisis had passed. "I just stood there captivated," he recalls. "We didn't realize there was any present danger."

COURTESY POOLER FIRE DEPARTMENT

Saturday watched as gas from the ruptured tank car "spread out in a fog covering the water." He had no idea what it was. "I was just standing there watching it. Some people scattered. Others were just curious. I didn't think about it being dangerous."

At least one person recognized the peril. From his position on the sand bar, Saturday saw a man - most likely the train's flagman - standing on the trestle in the vicinity of the caboose. From this man's actions, it was apparent that he fully understood what would happen if the propane gas ignited.

Shortly after the caboose had come to a halt on the bridge, both the flagman and conductor spotted the gas from the damaged tanker blanketing the area. They dashed to the caboose's rear platform, where, to their horror, they observed people in the water. The flagman stepped down to the bridge deck; and then both he and the conductor, who remained on the platform, "shouted warnings to the people in the river and the adjacent area."

Some people heeded the alarm while others, including the Hodges, fled of their own volition. "I was scared," remembers Saturday, who nevertheless remained on the sand bar for some time. "I didn't know what it was. Topper (Hodges) thought it might be poison and was worried about his wife and the baby. They jumped into a deep part of the river at the end of the sand bar and started to swim."

Hodges had his hands full looking after his pregnant wife. "He got real tired – it nearly drowned him," Saturday says, "and he called me to come and help. If he hadn't called me, I probably would have died that day."

Like Looking into an Oven

By that point, an eerie white vapor formed by the escaping liquefied petroleum gas

had covered an area a thousand feet wide and four hundred feet deep. The bulk of the cloud was north of the trestle (the wind blew from the south that day) where most of the people present were picnicking and swimming. Since propane is heavier than air, the gas spread at ground level, enveloping everything in its path.

Some onlookers continued to watch in amazement while others scrambled to escape the oncoming fumes. Mothers called for their toddlers. A father grabbed his two children, leapt into the river, and held their heads just above the surface of the water as the cloud of gas spread overhead. Others made for their cars in a desperate effort to save themselves.

Then, just three or four minutes after the accident, something sparked the volatile expanse of gas – it might have been a cigarette, a charcoal grill, or a car engine turning over. A tremendous explosion suddenly rocked an area greater than five acres. In an instant, a sea of searing flame (propane burns at 1200-1400 degrees) engulfed the trestle, the derailed freight cars, a cabin, twenty automobiles, and over two dozen people.

Meldrim is on Fire!

When the gas exploded, the flagman jumped from the trestle into the river, sustaining minor injuries. The conductor sought refuge in the caboose and closed its windows and doors. He was fortunate to survive, because even though both freight cars coupled to the caboose were consumed by flames, the caboose did not burn.

The crew in the forward part of the train was unaware that there was anything amiss until the emergency brakes engaged. The engines halted 560 feet east of the train station in Meldrim, well over a mile from the trestle. The engineer thought a broken air hose had caused the brakes to employ until he noticed smoke rising some

In its official report on the derailment, the Interstate Commerce Commission concluded that the two propane tank cars would have remained on the trestle had it been equipped with guardrails. Forty-seven years after the tragic derailment they were still absent.

DAN ROPER

distance behind.

Nathan Creasy noticed the smoke from a different vantage point as he crossed the Ogeechee on the drive home from Claxton. When he saw the enormous ball of smoke boiling up just downstream, he wondered, "What in the world?" He turned to his wife and said, "Vera, I think Meldrim is on fire."

Creasy proceeded toward Meldrim and pulled over beside a man standing in the road flagging down traffic. When Creasy stopped, the man yelled, "There's a train wreck. People are in the water burning. We need people with trucks to drive down there and carry the injured out. All the vehicles are burning. We just want anybody with a pickup truck to get down there."

Creasy parked his truck near the railroad tracks, asked his wife to remain in the vehicle, and sprinted down the tracks to the river. He arrived upon a scene of utter mayhem: "I saw trucks and box-cars laying all down there and fires everywhere."

The first person Creasy encountered was an acquaintance who was both crying and retching. The acquaintance warned, "Mr. Creasy, I don't believe you can stand it. I ran as hard as I could when the gas started spewing. When it ignited, I stayed for about two minutes. I saw people running around in all directions, some with their backs on fire."

Total Chaos

When the gas ignited, C.R. Saturday was several hundred yards downstream help-ing Topper Hodges extricate his wife from the water. The trio started back to the pic-nic area, but the carnage and wall of flame brought them to a standstill.

"You could see it was total chaos," Saturday recounts. "Everything was burning; people burning; not much left. We met a woman on the riverbank. She was burnt completely up. She was totally charred – just black. She was looking for her baby. She

74

went back up the bank hunting. We went back down to the river."

Topper Hodges returned to the blast zone to do what he could, but Saturday had seen more than he could stand. "I never did go back down there. You could walk around and see pieces of flesh." He had to walk back to Meldrim on foot since Hodges' '57 Ford convertible had been incinerated in the blaze.

Bodies Everywhere

Nathan Creasy estimates that he arrived at the scene roughly eight minutes after the explosion. What he saw as he approached the river was appalling.

"I couldn't believe my eyes when I came through there," he recalled earlier this year when he visited the scene for the first time since 1959. "Just so much burnt – corpses everywhere; their hair, flesh, everything burnt off. Cars, trucks, everything was burned. The freight cars and wheels were scattered for blocks.

"You had people out there throwing up. They couldn't stand the smell. There were bodies everywhere. I saw a dead man on a blanket. His sunglasses had melted down into his eyes and on his face. I walked a little further and there was a dead woman. She was pregnant and had been burned very badly. We tried to move her but her skin came off in our hands.

The picnic area once seared by the explosion has recovered and is once again a peaceful, but largely forsaken, locale.

"Cars were still burning – mainly the seats. There was a pickup truck over by a cabin. I opened the door and smoke billowed out. There was a little baby in there. I closed the door," Creasy said, pausing momentarily to maintain his composure. "Then I opened it again and the bones fell right down between the springs in the seat.

"One of the saddest things I saw was Mr. Beasley. He had four in his family down there. He came down to identify them. He'd say, 'Yes, that's her; yes, that's him….' He was crying. It was terrible."

Creasy assisted with the

75

dreadful job of removing the bodies. "I helped get the last few – they were burned. We carried them out and lined them up, laying towels or whatever we could find over their faces. We put four to a stretcher and took them to the hearse. We asked how many did they want us to put inside; they told us, 'As many as you can get.' We put five or six bodies in."

It Looked Like a War

The Slaters had the top down on their '56 Ford convertible that afternoon and were enjoying the drive back to Meldrim when L.B. pointed ahead and, exactly as Creasy had done earlier, exclaimed to his wife, "Helen, looka yonder. Meldrim is on fire!"

Slater had endured six months of combat in the Korean War and was no stranger to death, but the tableau in the vicinity of the trestle bridge was beyond belief. "I never saw anything like it. The gas had saturated the trees. The leaves had all burned off to just bare twigs. Not a leaf was left."

He was horrified by the condition of the numerous victims. "I saw people I knew lying on the ground," he said with much sadness in his voice. "It looked like a war." The strewn bodies reminded him of something he had once seen on a farm: "It was just like this herd of pigs wiped out by cholera – two here, three there, five over there."

Three of the victims Slater initially encountered belonged to one family. "Mr. Frank Dixon was over by the trestle just about two feet from one of the propane cars and was dead. Mrs. Dixon and her eighteen-month-old grandson Ted Barnes had got tripped up. He was lying about two feet away from her. Their clothes were burned off. They were dead."

A short distance away, Slater discovered someone he knew well: Ted's mother, Elizabeth Barnes. Her injuries were frightful, but she was still alive. "She was not much more than four feet tall and cute as a picture. My father-in-law and I picked her up and got her to a helicopter" (a rescue helicopter had landed on the railroad tracks to evacuate the wounded).

The next day, L.B. Slater tried to visit Elizabeth at a Savannah hospital, but the staff would not allow him into her room. From the hallway, he heard her labored breathing. She died a short while later.

I Hate to See Them Forgotten

Elizabeth Dixon Barnes was laid to rest in the Meldrim Cemetery with her little boy in her arms. Her parents, Mr. and Mrs. Frank Dixon, were buried beside them. "We went to fourteen funerals in one day," recalls Helen Slater in a quiet, sorrow-stricken voice. "There were so many people at the Methodist church that some were standing outside the fence."

The Meldrim derailment and explosion resulted in twenty-three fatalities and unfathomable misery and pain. Nearly everyone in the community lost a relative or a friend. "Everybody in Meldrim was like family back then," Saturday notes wistfully. "Everyone looked out for everybody. So we pulled together and leaned on each other."

Some of the survivors are haunted even today by memories of friends and loved ones who died in agony in the freakish accident on that scorching June day. Many did not return to the once-popular picnic and swimming area for years, if ever. C.R. Saturday, who as a young boy swam there every day of the year, didn't go back for a decade.

The people of Meldrim affected by the tragedy still cherish the memories of the twenty-three victims. There was 14-year-old Barbara Hales, who C.R. Saturday remembers well. "She was pretty," he sighs. "I was sweet on her."

Barbara Hales died that day near the trestle, as did her sister Margie Hales Smith who, Saturday notes, "looked like a movie star." Margie's husband James Smith and their sons Timothy and Wayne also perished.

"I hate to see them forgotten," Saturday says quietly, referring to all who lost their lives. "I hate to see them forgotten."

In memory of those who died in the Meldrim derailment:

Jimmy Anderson	Barbara Hales
Elizabeth Dixon Barnes	Claudia Johnson
Ted Barnes	L.B. Lamb
Julian Beasley	Terry Lane
Linda Jean Beasley	Elbie Lane
Reba Lamb Beasley	Florence Lane
Michael Bland	Leslie Lee
Charles Carpenter	James Smith
Billy Dent	Margie Hales Smith
Joan Dent	Timothy Smith
Edna Dixon	Wayne Smith
Frank Dixon	

Georgia Backroads wishes to express its gratitude to Stephen Newsome of Meldrim for his invaluable assistance in arranging interviews and in the preparation of this article.

*Details regarding the derailment are found in the official Interstate Commerce Commission Report (Ex Porte No. 21) issued August 15, 1959.

MOUNTAIN LAWMAN MURDERED IN 1940

The Brief Life and Death of Lumpkin County's Sheriff Jack Gillespie

DEBORAH MALONE

"Where's my friends? I'm cut. I'm cut to the heart."
— Sheriff Jack Gillespie following his stabbing.

On the evening of March 20, 1940, the knife wounds suffered by Lumpkin County Sheriff Jack L. Gillespie changed the lives of his two children, wife and the community of Dahlonega, Georgia, forever. Today, some details surrounding this murder are still a mystery, despite the fact that it occurred in broad daylight on the public square in the little mountain town. It is believed this is the only instance in history in which a sheriff was murdered in this county.

To fully appreciate the circumstances of this incident, one must go back to earlier days of Sheriff Gillespie's residence in Dahlonega. The town, located in the foothills of the Appalachian Mountains approximately 60 miles north of Atlanta, is a captivating area highly coveted by those lucky enough to enjoy its confines. Each autumn, "leaf watchers" travel from afar just to glimpse the breathtaking leaf colors painted upon the mountain landscape in this area by Mother Nature. It was a beauty often enjoyed by Sheriff Gillespie.

Early Law Enforcement

At the center of Lumpkin's history is the fact that it was the location of the first major goldrush in America. As a result, Dahlonega and Lumpkin County have witnessed the comings and goings of a variety of citizens and transients since 1828 when the precious yellow metal was first discovered in the vicinity. Sometimes the individuals were courteous and law-abiding, and sometimes they were criminals in dire need of incarceration. Law enforcement in Lumpkin is a role that has been very capably filled by a number of individuals over the years – including Sheriff Jack Gillespie.

From 1833 to the latter portion of the 19th century, a variety of jails have been built in Lumpkin to house and confine the county's criminals and accused. On May 10, 1884, the county contracted with local builders Alonzo C. Johnson and Henry Ramsaur to build a new jail – the fifth such in the history of the county. It was in this jail, which still stands today, that Sheriff Jack Gillespie lived and kept watch over prisoners from January 1, 1937, until his death in 1940.

Today, many individuals are surprised to learn that early sheriffs such as Mr.

COURTESY JIMMY ANDERSON

Sheriff Gillespie was photographed here in a lighter moment during his tenure as sheriff of Lumpkin County.

Gillespie lived with their families in the jails themselves – usually on the first floor – with the prisoners housed in the upper floor(s). It was a time-honored practice, and one that served the law enforcement community well until more stable prison systems with more personnel came into use in later years.

Today, the old 1884 Lumpkin County Jail still stands a short distance from the Dahlonega town square and has been preserved as one of the county's most historic sites. Visitors may view all aspects of the old jail, including the stairs leading to the prisoners' cells. These stairs are located in the room once used as a bedroom by Sheriff Gillespie and his wife. To reach or exit a cell in the jail, prisoners were marched right through the sheriff's bedroom each time. No prisoner ever left that jail without exiting through the Gillespie's bedroom – the most sensitive room in the entire building.

Over the years, several infamous criminals walked through this room and up these stairs in the old Lumpkin County Jail, including one of the most notorious bandits in American history – Bill Miner. Also known as "the gentleman bandit," Miner was deceptive in his demeanor, since he had also been responsible for more than one murder during his years of outlawry. After robbing stagecoaches, trains and banks from California to Georgia in the latter portion of the 19th century, Miner finally was captured in Lumpkin County in 1911, and housed temporarily in the old Lumpkin County Jail prior to his trial in Gainesville, Georgia that same year. (Readers please see, A North Georgia Journal of History, Volume I, "The Capture and Last Days Of Old West Bandit Bill Miner," Legacy Communications, Inc. (2002)

Upstairs in the old Lumpkin County Jail, there are four cells and a hallway which extends around the block of cells. A main door leading to the cells is constructed of thick iron plating. A master control for the cell doors is located outside this main door.

Along with the routine parade of prisoners through their bedroom, the Gillespies (Mrs. Gillespie at least) provided the meals for those incarcerated during her husband's tenure as sheriff. This practice was still in use in Lumpkin County as late as 1964 when the old jail was last used.

Enroute To The Hospital

Charles H. Phillips, 21 years of age at the time, drove the car in which Sheriff

Photographed circa 1931, this view of the south side of the Dahlonega Public Square shows the general vicinity (far left foreground) in which Sheriff Gillespie was stabbed on the evening of March 20, 1940.

Gillespie was a passenger enroute to Downey Hospital. Today, at 85 years of age, he still remembers that fateful night.

"I had been at the square where everyone was waiting for the election returns," Phillips explained. "I was on my way home when I noticed a commotion on the steps of the local clinic close to where I lived. I knew Dr. Lancaster wasn't home. They were knocking on the door and yelling for him. I shouted that he was out of town.

"'Buckshot' (Robert) Welch and Ralph Fitts yelled back to me that Sheriff Gillespie had been stabbed," Phillips continued. "'Gotta get him to a hospital or he's going to die,' they told me. I went and got my car. It was a brand new 1940 Ford, and I drove them to Gainesville.

"Buckshot and Ralph sat in the back seat with Gillespie," Phillips said. "We picked up Willard (Gillespie's son) on the way out of town and he sat up front with me. I could hear Jack in the back seat. He'd sing awhile, cuss awhile, and then pray awhile. I drove as fast as I could. We made it to Gainesville in 19 minutes." (Author's Note: According to the Internet program "MapQuest," it is approximately 30 miles from Dahlonega to Gainesville on modern-day roads.)

"When we got to the hospital, the intern on duty examined the wounds and said Sheriff Gillespie would be alright," Phillips added.

Though he did not know it at the time, Sheriff Gillespie's wounds were much more serious than originally diagnosed by the intern at Downey Hospital. The two small cuts beneath his arm looked somewhat innocent, and therefore had been misdiagnosed. In reality, the two cuts were deep stab wounds that had severed major blood vessels causing Sheriff Gillespie to die slowly from blood hemorrhaged into his abdomen over the span of several days.

Sheriff Jack L. Gillespie and his young wife, Amanda Kanaday Gillespie.

Election Evening Troubles

Mr. Phillips went on to tell me what he later learned had happened on the town square that fateful night. As was often the case in those days on election day, spirits were high – and not just the emotional kind of "high." "Moonshine" liquor was easy to find if one wanted it in Lumpkin. Everyone was in a frenzy waiting for the returns.

"Sheriff Gillespie was running (for reelection) behind Joe Davis with most of the returns already in," Phillips continued once again. "Several people told him to 'go on home' [since the outcome was obvious by then], but he wasn't going to give up – not yet – cause he was still sheriff.

Phillips explained that there was a flatbed truck parked at the Pure Oil Station near where the Dahlonega-Lumpkin County Welcome Center is located today. "They were playing and buck dancing on that truck," he said. "Fearing things were getting out of hand, Sheriff Gillespie went over to the truck and tried to pull some of the people off. That's when he was stabbed. That's when they took him over to Dr. Lancaster's clinic and I became involved."

Area resident Bonnie Minish who was a nurse in Dr. Lancaster's medical clinic in Dahlonega at the time also remembers that night. "From my apartment upstairs at the Clinic, I could hear the loud talking of the people milling around the square, and it seemed that violence could easily erupt anytime," Ms. Minish said. "When the mass of people got to the door, yelling and hollering for Dr. Lancaster, I raised the window and told them the doctor was out of town for the night...The crowd was so thick that people were backed across the street to Henry Moore's garage and partly up the street toward the Square."

Today, the blue granite building on West Main Street which housed Dr. Lancaster's practice still stands on the block between the historic Holly Theater and the commercial buildings known as Chestatee Village in downtown Dahlonega. It was built in 1939 as Dahlonega's first medical facility, and is used as a dentist's office as of this writing.

"It was officially known as "The Dahlonega Medical Center," Ms. Minish added. "North Georgia College students and people from Lumpkin and surrounding counties were grateful to have what was one of the finest medical facilities of its day."

Ms. Minish described how Dr. Lancaster was the first doctor to occupy the Center. "When he and his family moved from Clermont, I came also...I moved into the two-room apartment on the top floor of the three-story building. The doctor and his family moved into living quarters on the lower level.

"The front door of the Medical Center faced West Main, and opened into a large waiting room which extended across the entire front of the building," Ms. Minish continued. "I was receptionist as well as nurse and greeted patients as they entered. Just outside the front door was an old millstone from a gristmill that Mr. John Moore had embedded in the cement as a stepping stone. The blue granite rock used to construct the building came from a quarry on Wimpy Mill Road."

COURTESY LIFE MAGAZINE

Joe Davis, a candidate in the 1940 race for the sheriff of Lumpkin County was photographed here in 1942, two years after the murder of his opposition in the race, Jack Gillespie.

Remembering Dahlonega

Willard Gillespie, the son of the late sheriff who lives today in Florida, was 17 years of age at the time his father was murdered. He was interviewed for this article in 2004 during a visit to his old hometown. He explained how he rode in the automobile to the hospital in Gainesville with his wounded father in 1940, and how he and his family dealt with the trauma of the incident.

Though he did not know it at the time, Willard Gillespie was taking the last ride he would ever take with his dad on that cold night of March 20, 1940, when he rode with his injured father to the hospital. Though the initial prognosis for Sheriff Gillespie was good, he never left Downy Hospital after that night, and died two days later.

What must it have been like to be inside the car that night as it sped around the curves taking Sheriff Gillespie to Downey Hospital. What was it like to be the son, holding onto every hope that your father would make it to the hospital and survive? Willard Gillespie provided not only a full account of those circumstances, but an inside view of the Gillespie family as well.

"We always had a big garden while growing up in Dahlonega," he smiled in remembrance. "We lived about a half-mile from the Square (where their family home was located). The first big curve on the left was where we lived. The house has been

The Davis family was active in law enforcement in Lumpkin County for many years. Photographed here circa 1916 outside the old Lumpkin County Jail in Dahlonega are (l-r): James Davis, Gordon Davis, Joe Davis, Bill Davis, C.C. Davis, and Rufe Davis. James Davis served two terms as sheriff, and his son, Joe, who opposed Jack Gillespie in the 1940 election, also served two terms.

moved now; they just moved the whole house out of there. I went back to see it one time in the fifties or sixties.

"We grew corn, beans, peas and okra," he explained. "When I was ten or twelve years old, I had a little red wagon, and I had a regular route where I delivered. I would go and find out how much corn or peas someone wanted. . . The roads weren't paved back then...they were mostly gravel.

Gillespie For Sheriff

"The first time my dad ran for sheriff, the citizens of the county around here had asked him to run," Willard explained further. He ran against and beat Joe Davis. I was fifteen then.

"He treated everybody alike – rich or poor or what have you – while he was sheriff. He didn't have any specials or people like that," Willard noted. "Most people I know of around here said he was the best sheriff they ever had in the county.

"I remember living in the jail too. It was like living in a regular home to us. My mother cooked for the prisoners. We had a maid – Ethel Elrod – that helped sometimes. She used to work at the hotel too. She was a good cook; she made the best biscuits.

DEBBIE MALONE

Sallie Sorohan, president of the Lumpkin County Historical Society, stands on the staircase leading to the jail cells in the old Lumpkin County Jail in Dahlonega. Sheriff Gillespie and his wife used this room as their bedroom. Though this jail is quite small by today's standards, it, at different times, confined not only Sheriff Gillespie's murderer, but also one of the most famous outlaws of all time – Bill Miner. After robbing stagecoaches, trains and banks for many years from California to Georgia, Miner was finally captured in Nimblewill outside Dahlonega in 1911.

"We rented out our house during this time (while Gillespie was sheriff). We lived on the bottom floor of the jail. There was a college boy (from North Georgia College) that rented a room too.

"I remember one of the prisoners from the west side of the county," Willard smiled again. "About once or twice a week he would get me to go to the store on the corner and get him the biggest onion I could find. He liked onions I tell you. He'd eat them like apples.

Moonshiners

"Dad told me when he went in (into office) that people were complaining about "stills" (moonshine distilleries) in this county. He told them, 'All you have to do is write me a card and tell me where it's at and it will be shut down.' And that's what happened. He would raid them, then arrest them and put 'em in jail.

"I remember several (moonshine stills) during the time he served," Willard went on. "I even went with him on one or two. There's one raid I remember in particular – the first one I ever went to. Dad said 'You stay right here.' It was cold that night and he told me to stay back and that if anyone tried to run by me, to grab them by their coat and hold them until he got there.

"I could see them around the still. Daddy and the other lawmen had it surrounded. I don't remember the names of the other guys. I grabbed one when he ran by, but my hands were so cold I couldn't hold onto him.

"I remember [another raid] where the whole still was underground," Willard added. "It was off a farm road on the edge of the woods. It was covered and would be hard to see if someone was walking through the woods. Dad caught two or three that night. They had to pour kerosene in there and put up poison signs so people wouldn't mess with or drink it. That was the last raid I went on.

Remembering The Ride

"It was a cool evening the night of the election in 1940," Willard said, more serious now. "He was running against Joe Davis again. Right about dusky-dark, all the votes were in except those from Nimberwill (a tiny voting district approximately five miles northwest of Dahlonega). Roy Calhoun and Mr. Dowdy decided to go and get the votes. I rode out there with them.

"We got back around 8:30, and just south of the courthouse there was a big crowd. Some guy opened the door and said, 'Jack's been cut.' Best I can remember now they carried him down to the Clinic and then put him in Charles Phillips' car. They told me to get in, and we all went to Gainesville.

"Going up that hill on the other side of Yahoola Creek, Charles was driving as fast as he could go. Dad told me, 'Take care of your mother and your sister, and I'll see y'all in heaven.'

"A little further on down, Dad told Charles, 'Don't drive too fast. You'll kill us all.' Charles then cut the light down on the speedometer so you couldn't see how fast he was going. It was the fastest ride I've ever taken.

"It seems to me (Dahlonega businessman) Henry Moore had a wood-bodied station wagon back then. Might have been a '39 or '40 model," Willard said. "I'm just not sure. They brought my mother down that night.

"They already had Dad on the operating table when [my mother] got there. The doctor working that night, [however,] said everything would be alright. [But] . . . about two days later, he died. There wasn't really much they could do in them days. He was cut right under the rib. He bled to death. It's still hard to think about.

"I remember it was raining really hard the day of the funeral. There were more than 40 cars in the procession. They estimated there were about 1,200 people that day. He was buried at Wahoo Baptist Church up on Highway 52."

The Perpetrator

"Paul Lance is the one who cut my dad," Willard continued. "I've been told they were friends long before Dad was sheriff. Then he (Lance) moved away from here and had come back that night.

"The best I can remember, there was a ton-and-a-half truck backed up on the square. They were out there talking about the election and they were raising cane. Dad went out there to arrest somebody. The guy jumped out and cut him in the side. After he cut him, Dad threw him down and handcuffed him. If he hadn't done that, he might have lived.

"'Fayte' (Lafayette) Duff was working at the jail that night. He didn't usually work, but he was guarding the prisoners that night. He was sitting at the bottom of the steps with a shotgun when they brought in Paul Lance and put him in jail. He later told me, 'If I had known he had killed your dad, I would have shot him before he ever got up the stairs to the jail.'

"They had his trial right here in this old courthouse on the square at Dahlonega,"

Willard added. "They found him 'Guilty' and sentenced him to five to seven years. I don't know if he served the whole sentence or not, because I was in school at the time.

Post Mortem

"It was hard getting our lives back to normal. My sister finished college in Dahlonega and moved away when she got married. My mother died of cancer five years later in 1945.

"A few months after my dad's funeral, we moved back into our old homeplace. When it was summer, (Dahlonega businessman) John Moore told someone he wanted to see me. He asked me if I wanted a job, and I told him 'Yes.' He said he knew a guy that needed someone to tote water for a road gang building a road to Amicalola Falls.

I started off at ten cents an hour, and after three weeks they raised it to fifteen cents. We worked thirteen hours a day, and I was making $1.30 a day. After that I went to trade school in Clarkesville, and after a year, they started huntin' you a job.

"They had some applications for Pensacola, Florida, and I filled one out. About five or six weeks later, I was at the service station (in Dahlonega) where a bunch of us would go and eat crackers and drink a coke. That's when I found out that I had a government letter waiting for me. I went back to school and found out I had the job. I left the next day for Pensacola on November 7, and I've been there ever since."

Special appreciation is hereby extended to Dahlonega Postmaster and historian Jimmy Anderson, and Dahlonega resident Sallie Sorohan for their assistance with the materials necessary for this article.

Massacred by the Cheyennes

Following the close of the U.S. Civil War, many Southern families sought a better life out West. Enroute, however, untold numbers of them encountered horrors even worse than the depredations they had left behind.

Robert S. Davis, Jr.

In 1927, Catherine German dictated her memoirs – later entitled *The Girl Captives Of The Cheyennes* – to her niece, Grace E. Meredith. These memories, much of which focus upon historic accounts involving north Georgia, were so captivating that the book was praised by acclaimed writer Zane Grey himself as a classic of the Old West.

This startling book describes the harrowing adventures of four sisters held captive for months by the Cheyenne Indians after the remainder of their family had been brutally executed. It also includes an extremely rare life study of Georgia's Fannin County prior to the U.S. Civil War.

The book features the German family with roots in the South. John German was born in Wilkes County, Georgia on September 3, 1830. By March 3, 1853, he had settled in what today is northwest Georgia where he married Lydia Cox, born October 8, 1929.

Lydia was the daughter of William and Elizabeth Bradley Cox. William had been sheriff of Wilkes County and would be a justice of the inferior court of newly created Fannin County.

John and Lydia began their lives together in a one-room cabin on William's farm. John eventually prepared to build a house of his own on the 580-acre farm of his father, Thomas.

In their daughter Catherine's descriptive prose, a classic account of pioneer life in north Georgia is depicted. She explains in her memoirs how neighbors came from far and wide for the raising of the cabin. Hunters along the way brought squirrels for the noon meal, supplemented with cornbread, chicken, vegetables, and fruit.

Catherine details the intricacies of building a cabin and life in general during pioneer days in north Georgia. In building the cabin, points out how notched logs were carefully put in place, with four men setting each corner. When the walls of the "pen" had been built as high as a man could reach, poles with spikes were then used to set more logs still higher.

Small boards held mud in the cracks between the logs. Rough hewn boards were used to add a second floor to the cabin. More logs were raised to this second floor on skids. Joists were finally added to make a roof, with a "ridge log" added along the

COURTESY ROBERT S. DAVIS, JR.

Catherine and Sophia German after their rescue. Like her older sister, Sophia was raped and scalped as well.

peaks of the joists. Hewn boards were then laid across the joists for the three-foot-long overlapping wood shingles which kept the elements from entering the enclosure.

The finished home had two windows and two doors on the first floor, with a ladder to the second floor. A single fireplace provided the only heat in the building. It measured an impressive twenty feet wide by twenty-four feet long.

Fresh water for the cabin was obtained from a spring located approximately 200 feet to the rear. John German closed that distance by using logs he hollowed out as "pipes" to bring the fresh water from the spring's rock basin right up to the rear of the house. A spring-house provided refrigeration for the food of the growing family. Here, cold water flowed past jugs of milk and other perishables, then out the opposite side of the spring-house and through the orchard before finally rejoining the creek.

John added a lean-to kitchen to the rear of the cabin and a bedroom and porch to the front. With the erection of a barn, he had completed his farm.

In this snug cabin above the Toccoa River, the Germans produced their first four children prior to the U.S. Civil War. They were: Rebecca Jane (1854), Stephen W. (1855), Catherine E. (1857), and Joanna C. (1859). Morganton, the nearest settlement, was five difficult mountainous miles away, and the children had to walk three miles to reach the school for the three months of education they received each winter. They lived in a vast forest of pine, oak, elm, maple, fir, beech, poplar, and ash trees. American chestnut trees, now almost extinct, proliferated in the region at that time as well.

The distances and isolation necessitated self-sufficiency among the Germans. They raised flax, vegetables, and cotton supplemented with cattle, hogs, chickens and even sheep. Lydia made clothing for her family by spinning cotton and flax, while John tanned cowhides.

Cheyenne Indians in ceremonial dance, photographed in the 1890s.

Just as with most families in Georgia in the 1860s, the war years were extremely harsh. John joined the 65th Georgia Infantry (formerly Smith's Legion) and served in some of the worst fighting in Georgia and Tennessee until his capture at Ringgold, Georgia on November 28, 1863.

Despite numerous attempts at escape, John remained a federal prisoner until the last days of the fighting when he was released after he took an oath to remain north of the Ohio River until the end of the war. He thus was able to leave the brutal conditions of the federal prison at Rock Island, Illinois.

When he finally made his way back to Fannin County, John was in exceedingly poor health. The war had been very hard on his family too. As a result of a trip home which he had made prior to his capture, he had spread measles throughout his household. This and other diseases took a heavy toll on the family.

When the war began, the Germans had two cows, a yoke of oxen, a flock of sheep, a hundred hogs, a team of black horses, and thirty or forty chickens. Lydia and the children had eaten the oxen to keep them from being stolen. Guerrillas and deserters had decimated the remainder of the family's livestock, leaving the Germans with only two hogs which were too wild to be caught, one heifer, one cow, nine sheep, and a few poultry. Even their faithful watchdog had disappeared – no doubt in search of food.

John, still physically ill, had heard of a healthy land in the West known as Colorado. He and Lydia decided to set out for there to start a new life. However, five long years would pass before they were able to scrape together enough resources to begin this odyssey. Little did they know that it would all be in vain and end in a terrible ordeal.

By the time they began this trip, the family was composed of seven children, having added Sophia L. (1862), Julianne Arminda (1867), and Nancy Adelaide (1869) to the group. It must have been somewhat difficult for them to leave behind their land and the hard work they had invested in the construction of their home and barn and fields back in Georgia. However, during the Reconstruction years, the South was a devastated land, with a lifestyle literally gone with the wind and virtually no opportunities remaining for a livelihood.

The Germans initially settled in Howell County, Missouri. Later, they joined John's uncle, Rufus Burton Brown near Hurley, Missouri. Rufus had

The German cabin, in what today is Fannin County, was photographed a few years prior to the time it was demolished. No remnant of it exists today.

COURTESY ROBERT S. DAVIS, JR.

received a military bounty land there for his service in the Cherokee removal of 1838.

By the spring of 1874, John decided to move the family again, this time to Elgin, Kansas. He worked for a time on the nearby Osage Indian Reservation.

In the late summer of 1874, the German family resumed its journey to Colorado. Along the way, the family inadvertently rode into the midst of a brutal war between the Cheyenne Indians and the U.S. government. It proved to be a fateful mishap.

Many of the Indians at that time were not ready to submit to virtual prison on a reservation, and they fought back viciously against the U.S. government. Time, however, was not on their side. The influx of large numbers of white settlers threatened them from all sides, and the progression of the railroad hastened this growth. Worse yet, the U.S. Army pursued a policy of exterminating the buffalo in order to force the Plains Indians into a choice of starvation or submission to life on a reservation.

It was into the very teeth of this conflict that the German family walked. On September 11, 1874, they were driving their wagon and cattle along the Smoky Hill River. John anticipated that they would reach the safety of Fort Wallace, Kansas the

COURTESY ROBERT S. DAVIS, JR.

Catherine German, shown here later in life, was scalped and raped by Cheyenne Indians, but managed to survive. From this view it is difficult to tell she was scalped at all.

following day, and was feeling somewhat relieved.

In her memoirs, Catherine said she would remember the morning light that day forever as dawn broke, the color of the clouds changing from pink to gold to purple, amidst the millions of sparkling dew drops and the sounds of the crickets. John walked ahead of the wagon in search of game, while son Stephen and Catherine herded the cattle.

Suddenly, the Cheyenne attacked on horseback with lightning speed. The settlers in John's group included seventeen men and two women, and they were all caught in a maelstrom of confusion. Stephen, who had his musket, tried to run, but was quickly overtaken and cut down. Catherine took an arrow in the thigh. A warrior pulled it out, but then began violently kicking her to force her to submit to him.

John had avoided killing anyone during the Civil War, but according to Catherine's notes, he now realized he had no choice but to fire on his family's attackers. His face turned a ghastly black in panic, and in his hesitation, a bullet through the back suddenly felled him, and then a tomahawk through his skull freed his spirit forever.

Lydia, though heavily pregnant, tried to defend her husband and died from a similar blow to the head. Both of them were then scalped. Even more traumatic, Lydia's unborn baby was torn from her body in retribution.

When daughter Rebecca Jane resisted, the Indians stripped her of her clothing and forced her to submit to them before wrapping her in sheets and horribly burning her to death. Physically handicapped, daughter Joanna was also raped, and then killed by a bullet in the head. The warriors had selected her scalp because they prized her long hair.

Of the four remaining sisters, the older two – Catherine and Sophia – amazingly survived, but were raped and scalped as well. Eventually, they were claimed by two braves. Addie and Julia were somewhat luckier, having been protected by a sympathetic Indian couple, the wife of whom had saved the crying Addie from being silenced with a bullet during the raid.

COURTESY CATHOLIC UNIVERSITY OF AMERICA

Forced into submission at Fort Keogh, Montana, Cheyenne Indians perform a ceremonial dance.

The Cheyennes rode their horses bareback during a raid. Following this carnage, they carried off the four girls to the place where they had left their saddles and other trappings. They then killed and ate the Germans' cattle. Catherine described in her memoirs how they all then rode through the rain and lightning across the vast plains.

Catherine discovered that her captors, in their rage, would kill or cripple any cattle they found. They consumed roasted skunk as a delicacy, but would not eat prairie chicken. When buffalo were not available, the Cheyennes would eat their horses as a substitute.

On one day, Julia rode behind a warrior who had shot a buffalo in the neck with an arrow. Though wounded and struggling, the great animal had not completely expired. As he rode past the animal, the Indian killed the beast by forcing the arrow deeper inside the animal with his foot.

Catherine described in detail how her captors would often threaten to kill their hostages. Addie (age five) and Julia (age seven) were useless to the Indians, and eventually abandoned. They struggled to find food wherever they could, while being stalked by wolves. They eventually were picked up by a Cheyenne scouting party and, amazingly, were briefly reunited with Catherine before finally being rescued at the Battle of McClellan Creek, Texas, on November 8, 1874, by United States cavalrymen under the command of Lieutenant Frank D. Baldwin. He would receive the Medal of Honor for rescuing the German girls. (Sophia had also been in the camp on McClellan Creek during the attack, but was unable to escape.)

According to Catherine's notes, following the raid, the Indians decked themselves out in their best finery – shirt, leggings, blue cloth belt, face paint, and moccasins – for their grand entrance back into their main camp. Catherine (age eighteen) and Sophia (age twelve) were brought in as booty, while the scalps of their dead family members dangled horribly from the Indians' rifles.

Catherine and Julia were then stripped naked, beaten, and chased by suitors. The brave who was able to tag them from horseback would be rewarded with them as a wife. Fortunately, a sympathetic family adopted Catherine, but twelve-year-old

Sophia was soon traded to a warrior as his wife.

For several months thereafter, the two German sisters were separated, and traveled with different bands of Cheyennes. Catherine said she learned the language, but Sophia refused to cooperate in that manner. For the most part, they both had lost hope after the horror of seeing their family slaughtered. Neither of them believed they would live to see freedom again.

The Cheyennes were a generous society among themselves. Anything they had would be given to a visiting native upon the asking. The men took care of the horses and the hunting, and the women did the cooking, clothing, and wood gathering. They all lived in lodges that family members assembled and took down with each camp. The tribe, in a nomadic existence, lived almost exclusively on an all-meat diet, served raw or almost raw.

General Nelson A. Miles even-

Lieutenant Frank D. Baldwin and cavalrymen under his command rescued Addie and Julia German at the Battle of McClellan Creek on November 8, 1874. Baldwin, received his second Medal of Honor – the U.S. military's highest award for bravery. He received the first for his service as a captain in the Michigan Volunteer Infantry at the Battle of Peachtree Creek north of Atlanta, Georgia during the U.S. Civil War.

tually learned of the two senior German sisters from their siblings who were rescued at the Battle of McClellan Creek. The two little girls had been tortured by their captors with flaming splints placed between their fingernails and around their eyes. For some time, they would not talk to their rescuers but would only cower together in fear in a corner.

The deaths and captivity of the members of the German family eventually received national coverage in the news media – such as it was at that time. One news report even reached the girls' grandparents back in Fannin County, Georgia.

General Miles began negotiations through Kiowa Indian intermediaries to ransom the girls. A letter from Miles, and later a photograph of the rescued sisters, reached Catherine in New Mexico, delivered no doubt by Indians who were working for the U.S. Army. The federal cavalry had been relentlessly pushing the Cheyenne into barren lands where starvation would force them into submission.

During this time, some of the warriors wanted to kill the girls, but the great peace chief, Stone Calf, wanted the girls returned as a step toward bringing an end to the carnage. Many of the Cheyennes, however, feared white retribution. Meanwhile, in the freezing winter in New Mexico, the old and the very young among the Cheyenne slowly starved and froze to death.

Finally, on February 28, 1876 – almost 18 months after their unbelievable ordeal had begun – Catherine and Sophia were released to federal authorities in Darlington, Oklahoma. Despite her experiences with them, Catherine, strangely, refused to hate the Indians for what had happened to her and her family. During the girls' stay at the Indian agency, they saw how the Native American culture and identity were being completely erased by the school there.

In a show of loyalty, the girls were even able to save Stone Calf from prosecution, but they did help identify some of the Indians responsible for the slaughter of their family.

In the end, the sisters never returned to Georgia. That part of their lives was over forever. For a time, they lived at Fort Leavenworth, Kansas. Catherine, reunited with her other sisters, steadfastly held them together as a family unit.

All the sisters eventually married and raised families. Catherine, Sophia, and Julia moved to California, while Addie and her family remained in Kansas. All of them became minor celebrities as well – a living testimony to the last days of the pioneers in north Georgia and in the old West.

Much of the information on the ordeal of the German sisters comes from *The Moccasin Speaks: Living as Captives of the Dog Soldier Warriors, Red River War, 1874-1874* (1998) by Arlene Feldmann Jauken. Ms. Jauken is the great-granddaughter of Sophia German.

In the Paw of a Lion

During their struggle to remain in Georgia, the Cherokee people had powerful allies in church and government and even prevailed in a landmark case before the United States Supreme Court. But in the end, not church, politics, or the law could keep the Cherokees in their native land.

Leslie Johnston

While the story of the infamous 1838-1839 Trail of Tears is well known, few today are familiar with the legal battle to prevent the removal from taking place and the story of the Christian missionary who was at the center of the legal proceedings.

Cherokee migration westward from Georgia actually began in the early 1800s as the people of the Cherokee Nation became increasingly wary of their white neighbors. In 1828, the discovery of gold in the north Georgia mountains raised tensions as whites encroached on Cherokee territory and came to resent Native American dominion over the valuable, fertile, and sparsely populated land.

Under pressure from the white community, the U.S. government determined that the Cherokees must leave their homeland and move west to the Indian Territory. In 1830, President Andrew Jackson signed the Indian Removal Act. The Reverend Samuel Worcester, a missionary to the Cherokees at New Echota, mounted a challenge that went to the U.S. Supreme Court to establish the Indians' title to the land, but it would ultimately prove to be "a white man's court."

President Andrew Jackson refused to enforce the decision of the U.S. Supreme Court confirming the rights of the Cherokee Nation. In this manner, he was able to stave off the secessionist tendencies arising within the Southern states.

A Young Missionary Comes South

Samuel A. Worcester was the seventh generation of pastors from the Worcester family. When Samuel was born in 1798, his father, Rev. Leonard Worcester, was a minister and printer in Peacham, Vermont. As a student, the young Samuel Worcester found that he had an aptitude for foreign languages. He met and became close friends

Just like the apostles Peter and Paul, Moravian Missionary Samuel Worcester was willing to go to jail for that in which he believed.

with Buck Oowatie, a Cherokee Indian from Georgia who attended school in New England and took the name Elias Boudinot.

In 1825 Worcester was ordained as a Congregationalist minister after graduating from Andover Theological Seminary in Massachusetts. When Worcester joined the American Board of Commissioners for Foreign Missions, he requested an assignment to a Cherokee village that Boudinot said was particularly needy. In August of that year, Worcester left Boston with his new wife, Ann Orr Worcester, for the Brainerd Mission, which had been founded in 1817 by the Rev. Cyrus Kingsbury.

Brainerd Mission was located just east of Chattanooga, Tennessee. Today, the last remnants of the mission – a wrought iron fence cemetery with dozens of graves of both Cherokee students and their white instructors who passed away while serving at the mission – are found near the northeastern edge of the Eastgate Mall parking lot, between the lot and the Brainerd Village Shopping Center.

Within a matter of days after arriving in the community, Worcester was not only preaching, but also working as a blacksmith, carpenter, translator, and doctor.

Christianity Spreads among the Cherokees

When Worcester moved further south to the Cherokee capital at New Echota, he worked with Sequoyah, who had developed the Cherokee syllabary a few years earlier, to make the new syllabary suitable for printing.

Then Worcester teamed with Elias Boudinot to establish a Cherokee language newspaper. Worcester saw the newspaper as an important tool in the development of Cherokee literacy and as a means to unify the Cherokee Nation. He secured funds from the Mission Board and built a printing office, bought a printing press and ink, and cast the alphabet's characters into type.

The first edition of the *Cherokee Phoenix* came off the press at New Echota, near present-day Calhoun, Georgia, in 1828. Boudinot served as the editor for four years and Worcester always had a voice in the newspaper and most other Cherokee publications. (It has been noted that, although Worcester was quite adept at using the Cherokee language in conversation and in translating Scripture and hymns, he was never very good at preaching in Cherokee.)

A replica of the building that housed the Cherokee Phoenix newspaper was built at New Echota in the 1950s.

The Cherokees had largely resisted giving up their traditional religion and converting to Christianity until the beginning of the19th century, when dramatic changes developed. The establishment of schools played a large part in the Cherokees' embracing Christianity.

While the earliest missionaries to the Cherokees were Scottish Protestants, other denominations soon followed. Arriving in the area around 1799, Moravian missionaries had established a mission school at Spring Place (near present-day Chatsworth) by 1801, and the Rev. Gideon Blackburn had founded a Presbyterian mission school at Tellico, Tennessee. Baptist missionaries arrived in 1819, and Methodists in 1824. By the mid-1820s, it was not unusual to find Cherokee men who were becoming preachers.

In 1826, John Ridge wrote a description of the Cherokee Nation which included a report on the work of the missionaries: "The Standard of Religion is advancing with a steady march in different parts of the Nation – and the Gospel is preached in eight organized churches by Presbyterians, Baptists, Moravians, and Methodists."

Yet Ridge noted that all was not well: "It is true, we enjoy self-government, but we live in fear, and uncertainty foretells our Fall. Strangers urge our removal to make room for their settlements, they point to the west and there they say we can be happy. Our National Existence is suspended on the faith and honor of the United States alone. We are in the paw of a Lion – convenience may induce him to crush, and with a faint Struggle we may cease to be!"[1]

American Opposition to Removal

In his book *The Politics of Revelation and Reason: Religion and Civic Life in the New Nation* (1996), author John G. West, Jr. observes that many Americans today are under the impression that Indian removal proceeded with little or no opposition from whites, but that was not the case. He contends that many Americans of that time, especially those in the north, were uneasy at the prospect of Indian removal in the same way that they were opposed to slavery, and such eloquent speakers as Henry Clay and Daniel Webster spoke against removal on the floor of Congress. Removal was nearly defeated - it passed by a single vote.

U.S. Supreme Court Chief Justice John Marshall argued in favor of the sovereign rights of the Cherokees in Cherokee Nation vs. Georgia (the Corn Tassels case) and in Worcester v. Georgia. Marshall, according to some sources, did so to help President Andrew Jackson's efforts to stop state secessionism in the Nullification Crisis, and he reportedly did it in a manner which would spare the president from enforcement of federal laws in favor of the Indians

Using the pen name of William Penn, Jeremiah Evarts, an evangelical missionary who spent time among the Cherokees and served as corresponding secretary for the American Board, composed a series of 24 essays published in newspapers and journals, and later as a pamphlet, opposing removal. West describes this collection of essays as the "most celebrated piece of political journalism since The Federalist," and notes, "Chief Justice John Marshall called the essays the 'most conclusive argument that he ever read on any subject whatever.'"[2]

West writes that in spite of the justness of the cause and the persuasiveness of the advocate, "the fact remained that many Americans were not prepared to treat the Cherokees as equals. In Evarts's mind, this raised a terrible question about America's identity. In the end what defined America – a common racial identity or devotion to a common ideal?"[3]

In his book *Religion, Race, and the American Ideas of Freedom: From the 17th Century to the Present*, Paul Harvey, professor at the University of Colorado, presents a related thesis. Harvey, who has written widely on religion, human and civil rights and racism in America, says that Native Americans, especially the Cherokees, had a "tortured relationship" with Christianity.

98

As U.S. Attorney General, William Wirt made some decisions which favored Cherokee Indian sovereignty, and others which did not. As attorney for the Cherokee Nation, he fought for George Corn Tassels and for the right of the Cherokees to keep their nation in Georgia.

For Native Americans, Christianity was the religion of the colonizers and the exploiters, yet missionaries made important contributions to the defense of Native American rights and advances in education, government, and culture. However, Christianity - and this is Harvey's most significant point, especially in regard to the Cherokees - did not become the ally of the Native Americans in the way that it would eventually prove to be an ally for African-Americans.[4]

The Mission Board Formulates a Plan

Worcester and his benefactor, the American Board, formulated a plan to fight the encroachment of white settlers in north Georgia in court, their last hope; no other civil authorities would support the Cherokees' right to remain on the land that they had been promised in the Treaty of Hopewell in 1785.

The first step in Georgia's campaign to subjugate the Cherokees came in the fall of 1830 after state officials arrested, tried, and sentenced Corn Tassel for the murder of another Cherokee in what is now Hall County. The crime took place in Cherokee territory and the Nation therefore protested that Corn Tassel was subject to Cherokee laws and courts.

The American Board hired former U.S. Attorney General William Wirt to defend Tassel and challenge the state, taking the case to the U.S. Supreme Court. Chief Justice John Marshall rejected the suit on technical grounds. (Later, however, Marshall intimated to an acquaintance that he sympathized with the Cherokee position). Pending an appeal, Marshall signed a writ of habeas corpus, but Georgia authorities defiantly hung Corn Tassel in Gainesville before the writ could be enforced.

A New England Yankee in Justice Marshall's Court

Lawyers for the Cherokee Nation soon brought another case before the Supreme Court as an independent foreign nation contending that the state of Georgia had broken treaties with the federal government. In 1831, in the Cherokee Nation vs. Georgia, the Supreme Court ruled that the Cherokees could not bring suit as an independent foreign nation because it was a "domestic, dependent nation."[5]

Shortly afterwards, Georgia Governor George Gilmer and the Georgia legislature officially adopted a policy of forcible Indian removal. Worcester and 11 other missionaries met at New Echota and published a resolution to protest a law that required whites to obtain a license to work on Native American land and take an oath of allegiance to obey the laws of the state. Those who refused to do so either had to leave the state or face imprisonment.

The new Georgia law was aimed, without a doubt, at the 32 missionaries

In 1827, a mission house was erected at New Echota through the leadership of Rev. Samuel Worcester. He was known among the Cherokee as "The Messenger." This is the only structure which still stands from the era when New Echota served as the Cherokee Nation's capital.

then residing in the Cherokee Nation. Worcester believed that obeying the law would mean yielding the sovereignty of the Cherokee Nation. The missionaries' opposition to removal was, by this time, well known, even reaching national publications such as *The Christian Advocate.*

Governor Gilmer ordered the militia to arrest Worcester, Dr. Elizur Butler (a minister and physician at the Haweis Mission near present day Rome) and the others who signed the resolution. They were quickly moved to Lawrenceville and tried, convicted, and sentenced to four years of hard labor in the state penitentiary in Milledgeville. Governor Gilmer offered a pardon if they would leave Georgia, but the missionaries stood firm, choosing instead to go to prison. Under guard, they walked some 35 miles a day to reach the penitentiary in Milledgeville.

Lawyers for the missionaries appealed immediately and, once again, William Wirt argued the case. In late 1832, the U.S. Supreme Court held in *Worcester v. Georgia* that the Cherokee Nation was an independent, sovereign nation, and that all dealings with them fell under federal, rather than state, jurisdiction: "The Cherokee Nation is a distinct community occupying its own territory…in which the law of Georgia can have no right to enter but with the assent of the Cherokees."[6]

A Supreme Court Ruling Ignored

The ruling was ignored by Governor Gilmer and President Andrew Jackson, who were embroiled in the larger crisis engulfing the country over whether states could nullify, that is, ignore, any disagreeable laws or rulings by a branch of the federal government. Jackson

The Council House at New Echota State Historic Site near Calhoun, Georgia, is a replica of the original structure based upon descriptions and valuations made at the time of the Cherokee removal in 1838.

is reputed to have commented: "John Marshall has made his decision; let him enforce it now if he can." Thus, despite their legal victory, the missionaries continued to languish in prison.

Wilson Lumpkin became Georgia's governor early the next year and, faced with the Nullification Crisis in neighboring South Carolina, he decided to set Worcester and the others free if they agreed to minor concessions. For months, Worcester refused to cooperate, but eventually decided that the missionaries had achieved their objective with the Supreme Court victory. He concluded that he would be more effective serving the Cherokees out of prison, but following his release he realized that the battle had been lost because white settlers refused to abide by the ruling of the court.

The Move Westward

Although the Supreme Court had confirmed the Cherokees' rights as a sovereign nation, the Cherokee people could not prevail against "the greed of gold seekers, land speculators and politicians."[4] Within three years, the Ridge Party, a small cadre within the Cherokee Nation led by Major Ridge, signed the Treaty of New Echota, surrendering Cherokee land without the consent of the entire Nation. The treaty was ratified by Congress in 1836, giving the Cherokees two years to move to Oklahoma. Principal Chief John Ross and his allies vigorously resisted the treaty and the removal, but to no avail.

Worcester left for Oklahoma in 1835 to prepare for the arrival of the Cherokees that he deemed inevitable at that point. He established the Park Hill Mission near Tahlequah, Oklahoma which became the largest mission in Indian Territory and a well known educational center referred to as the "Athens of the Southwest." Worcester died in Oklahoma in April 1859.

While both religion and the law failed the Cherokees in Georgia 170 years ago, *Worcester v. Georgia* became the basis for several 20th century court rulings and laws which recognized Native American tribes' inherent national sovereignty and their right of self-determination. But by then it was far too late for the people who suffered in the paw of a lion.

Sources

1. Barbara R. Duncan and Brett H. Riggs, Cherokee Heritage Trails Guidebook. Chapel Hill, North Carolina: The University of North Carolina Press, 2003.

2. John Wilson, "Books & Culture Corner: Why Evangelicals Can't Opt Out of Political Engagement—Remembering Jeremiah Evarts and Samuel Worcester." http://www.christianitytoday.com/ct/2002/127/11.0.html. 7/15/2002

3. Paul Harvey, *Project Statement for Religion, Race, and American Ideas of Freedom: From the 17th Century to the Present.* http://web.uccs.edu/pharvey/relracecivilrights.htm.

We are but Humble Caretakers

For decades, a beautiful old house in Gordon County was known simply as Daffodil Farm.
Then an owner discovered evidence linking it to leaders of the Cherokee Nation. Was
Daffodil Farm in fact the birthplace of Elias Boudinot and Stand Watie?

WILLIAM E. BRAY

During my senior year in high school I took my girlfriend on a drive to Lily Pond, near Calhoun, to show her the home places of my ancestors. On that beautiful, warm Sunday afternoon in May 1955, we visited the cemetery where my grandfather's first wife is buried. Nearby, I had enjoyed childhood fishing trips to Oothcaloga Creek and family picnics. Then, my girlfriend and I drove by the homes of my grandfather, great-grandfather, and cousin Minnie.

Back in the 1930s and '40s, Minnie had planted 25 acres of daffodils and shipped the bulbs and flowers to northern markets from the train station at Lily Pond. Everybody called Minnie's place Daffodil Farm and for years we thought that was its main claim to fame.

When we drove by Minnie's house that day, I was horrified to see that the front porch was falling in. The house was in disrepair, and I feared that it might be gone within a few years. Upon returning home to Dalton, I asked my father what had happened. He didn't know, but we soon learned that Minnie had passed away and that the farm had been sold at public auction. For the next year, I crusaded to try to get my father to buy back a farm he didn't want in order to save it from ruin.

Back in the Family

That fall, I enrolled at the University of Georgia and spent countless nights in the basement archives of

Daffodil Farm 1958

the University library, diligently researching Daffodil Farm's history. I learned that Cousin Minnie had inherited the farm from her father who, in turn, had inherited it from his father. This would have been my father's great-grandfather who owned the farm by 1840.

My persistent plea became, "You have to buy it – as an obligation to your ancestors." My campaign was successful. On May 17, 1956 – 92 years from the day General Sherman's troops passed through on their way south – my father, James Wellborn Bray, Sr., relented and acquired Daffodil Farm, becoming the fourth generation in the Bray family to own it.

Having achieved my goal – saving the farm from imminent destruction – I was satisfied that my mission was accomplished. I soon stopped digging through musty old records, but not before discovering that my great-great-grandfather, Reverend Bannister R. Bray, sold his home in Henry County in 1837 and next appeared in the 1840 census in Gordon County, where he owned the property that later became Daffodil Farm.

A Methodist minister, Bray left Gordon County in 1847 and moved to what was to become Atlanta, where he "preached from the stumps of Marthasville" before the first church was built there. William A. Bray, Rev. Bray's eldest son and Minnie's father, was the next Bray to own the farm. That proved to be the extent of my knowledge about the history of the property for many years to come.

Off to Experience the World

My father's enthusiasm for the farm increased once he took title to the property, and we moved there as soon as he had renovated the main house. Summers and weekends spent on the farm convinced me that its acres of daffodils, century-old oaks surrounding the glen, and antebellum house combined to make it an ideal location for an arts center or arts school. Upon graduating from the University of Georgia, I decided I would go to the cultural centers of the world, get the best education I could, and return, using my education and the farm as resources to try to make this a better world for the next generation.

My educational odyssey lasted 15 years. Finally, in 1975, I returned with graduate degrees from Yale and Johns Hopkins and independent study at Oxford. After I founded the Georgia Fine Arts Academy, more than 1,000 students studied at the farm during the 1980s and '90s, just as I had hoped.

Hinting at History

During my research into the history of Daffodil Farm, I had concluded that Bannister R. Bray built the house when he moved to Gordon County from Henry County in 1837. When historian Jewell B. Reeve visited the farm in 1959, while she was writing *Climb the Hills of Gordon*, my parents suggested she contact me. I wasted no time in enthusiastically sharing my research, as she records in her book: "I received a special delivery, air mail package from William E. Bray, Yale University,

New Haven, Conn. He had sent me his entire script with generous permission to use it all." Thus my early conclusions about the house's origins were repeated in at least one history book.

Over the years I continued to tell my story based on the historical research I had done, but when I would tell historians, "My great-great-grandfather built the main house in 1837," some disagreed and claimed, "It is much older than that. I think it was built in the 1790s." Over the ensuing years, knowledgeable historians insisted that the structure dated from the 1790s, some forty years before the first white settlers reached this part of Georgia.

One memorable visit was by a man who lived in Dalton. He bought and tore down old houses in Tennessee and Kentucky and used the logs to build new houses. When he looked at Daffodil Farm's chimney, he exclaimed, "This is the oldest chimney I've ever seen."

Finally, Dan Biggers, then director of the Oak Hill Museum at Berry College in nearby Rome, visited the

A member of the Treaty Party, Stand Watie (1806-1871) escaped death by a stroke of luck. He was absent from his home the day Major Ridge, John Ridge, and Buck Watie (Elias Boudinot) were assassinated. As a young man, he attended the Moravian Mission School at Spring Place, Georgia, and later served as a clerk of the Cherokee Supreme Court and Speaker of the Cherokee National Council prior to removal. During the Civil War, he reached the rank of brigadier general in the Confederate army.

house and joined the chorus proclaiming that Daffodil Farm dated from the late 18th century. I decided it was time to take these comments seriously, so the following day I drove to New Echota State Historic Site, the restored capital of the Cherokee Nation just nine miles up the road.

The historic site staff informed me that during the 1830s all Cherokee property had been itemized, described, and valued. Since Daffodil Farm is located in the area known as the Oothcaloga District, which whites renamed Lily Pond in 1850, I looked through the records for houses that matched the dimensions and description of the house my great-great-grandfather acquired in 1837. What I found came as quite a surprise.

Humble Caretakers

Three Cherokee houses seemed to fit the details of the Daffodil Farm residence: those belonging to Archy Rowe, Isabella Hicks, and Stand Watie. None of those names meant anything to me at the time, so I dutifully transcribed notes on each property to scrutinize at home that evening.

Long after darkness settled over Daffodil Farm, I was sitting in my den reading the ancient descriptions of outbuildings, pastures, and other features of these Cherokee estates. Those of Rowe and Hicks did not seem to fit, but when I got to Stand Watie's property

The Oothcaloga Moravian Mission building disappeared, sadly, years ago. The date of this photograph of the structure is unknown.

and read "Yard and spring Lot 2 Acres," I jumped to my feet. It was a perfect account of Daffodil Farm. In the dark, I ran outside the house and walked off two acres (each 210 feet square) encompassing the house, glen, and springs. Could this indeed be the home of Stand Watie?

The next day, I eagerly phoned Dan Biggers to report my discovery. "Dan," I said, "I believe the house was owned by some Cherokee named Stand Watie." There was a long pause on the other end of the line. Then Dan said slowly and emphatically, "Bill, your ancestors were but humble caretakers compared to the Cherokees who lived there."

That surprised me since I didn't know anything about Stand Watie, and it spurred me to further research. I soon learned that Stand Watie's father, Oo-watie, came to Oothcaloga with his brother The Ridge at exactly the time historians estimated that the house was built. One historian explained that it would have been standard for Stand's name to appear on property originally owned by his father.

If so, then Daffodil Farm has a remarkable lineage. Not only would Stand Watie have been born there, but so would his brother Buck (who later changed his name to Elias Boudinot). These discoveries led me to appreciate all the more the significance of Dan Biggers' remark.

Suddenly, the pyramid-shaped rock piles on both sides of the front and back entrances to the property had new meaning. These were grand entrance gates more than 200 years ago. I also discovered that the original driveway curved around behind the place so that visitors would have enjoyed a remarkable view as they approached the house.

The giant boxwoods surrounding the house – some 10 to 15 feet high – which

Buck Watie (Elias Boudinot) (1802-1839) was the brother of Stand Watie and editor of the *Cherokee Phoenix* newspaper. His support for the Removal Treaty caused him to be replaced as editor of the paper and, later, to be brutally murdered at his new home in Park Hill, Oklahoma.

grow at the rate of an inch a year are links to events that took place on the grounds two generations earlier than I previously believed. Not only were the fireplace stones old, they also matched those at Elias Boudinot's house at New Echota. Then I scraped off paint in the front room, examined the woodwork, and discovered that it matched the design of the har in Spring Place and that the paint was consistent with colors favored by the Cherokee – red, green, and blue.

It is hard to believe that the existence of Oo-watie's home remained unknown for more than a century. It took the good sense and perseverance of Betty Snyder, a director of the Milledgeville-Baldwin Arts Council and a historian in her own right, to first point out to me that the house dated to the 1790s. She recognized that the fireplace mantels were distinctive, matching only a few others in Georgia, and were built long before the Civil War.

Her insistence, along with input from other historians, including Dan Biggers, started me on my quest. With the assistance of Jeff Stancil, then the manager at New Echota, I consulted the historic site's library where I found the real estate description that linked Stand Watie's property and Daffodil Farm. Then, upon discovering that the front room was originally painted in colors favored by the Cherokee – similar to those at the Vann House in Spring Place – I decided to seek as much authoritative verification as possible.

So I telephoned Don L. Shadburn, a leading authority on Cherokee history in Georgia. For nearly two hours, he listened while I related the evidence I had accumulated pointing to Oo-watie as the builder of the house. Shadburn, the author of *Cherokee Planters in Georgia*, then stated: "Bill, with all this evidence you would be derelict not to make this claim."

A Noble Line

The field just beyond the 15-acre daffodil field may have been the one described in Thurman Wilkins's book *Cherokee Tragedy:* "That summer [1825] a national ball-play had been held near the home of Boudinot's parents in Oothcaloga." I sought more information about this event thinking it might confirm mounting evidence that this was the site and read that Moody Hall, a Moravian missionary, had been extremely upset with Elias Boudinot for participating. Stickball games, it seems, were riotous events that lasted several days and nights. The missionaries believed they were sinful and Hall scolded his wayward pupil.

As I continued piece by piece to put together my findings what emerged was this:

In the 1790s, The Ridge moved to Oothcaloga from Pine Log, perhaps to be closer to his political allies James Vann and Charles Hicks. Oothcaloga was described as a "garden spot" where many of the chiefs built homes to be close to the Cherokee capital city, New Echota. The Ridge built his house near Oothcaloga Creek and, shortly thereafter, his brother Oo-watie built a

John Ross (1790-1866), principal chief of the Cherokee Nation from 1828 until his death, was an eighth-blood Cherokee. He unflinchingly opposed the treaty which ceded Cherokee lands to the whites.

house two miles to the west, just over the rise from the creek. Oo-watie's residence was obviously modeled after his brother's and was virtually identical except for The Ridge's original log rooms. Oo-Watie's house was built of cut lumber.

Oo-watie farmed more intensively and developed his property more elaborately than The Ridge, who soon moved to Rome where he built a fine house (today's Chieftain's Museum) and operated a ferry on the Oostanaula River. Oo-watie added the boxwoods, elaborate entrance pyramids of rocks, and the graceful grand entrance drive to the house. The columns on the south façade were made from hand-hewn lumber, and garden walkways led down to several springs which bubbled from the ground in the glen.

Children of Kings

As the story continued to unfold with each historical document unearthed, I began to see the farm as a seat of this royal family of the Cherokee Nation, a virtual wilderness palace of Native American nobility.

The Ridge (He Who Walks on the Mountaintops) and his brother Oo-watie (The Ancient One) traced their lineage in direct descent from King Attakullakulla, the solon of the Cherokees, who with Cherokee leaders visited King George II in England in 1730. Their family tree included virtually every major leader in Cherokee history

Major Ridge was speaker of the lower house in the Cherokee Council. He was also chief of the Cherokee police, and a close advisor to Chief John Ross. Once he realized that hope for keeping the Cherokee land in Georgia was futile, he supported the treaty for removal. His support for this treaty eventually cost him his life.

including Old Hop, Dragging Canoe, Nancy Ward, Doublehead, and Old Tassel, as well as Sequoyah, who achieved fame by inventing the Cherokee syllabary.

Buck Watie was born here in 1802 and Stand Watie in 1806. As boys, they would have enjoyed playing the fields, fishing in the creek, and drinking the cold spring water on a warm day just as I did a century-and-a-half later. As young men, they would have marveled when visiting chiefs and other dignitaries from throughout the Cherokee Nation attended national council meetings at New Echota.

Seeking the best education for their children as future leaders of the nation, The Ridge sent his son John and Oo-watie sent his son Buck to the finest Moravian School in the United States at Cornwall, Connecticut. So impressed were the Moravians with the intelligence of 16-year-old Buck Watie that on his way north he was taken to meet three U.S. presidents – Thomas Jefferson at Monticello, James Madison at Montpelier, and James Monroe at the White House in Washington, D.C.

In New Jersey, Buck Watie met Elias Boudinot, former president of the Continental Congress and president of the American Bible Society, who was so taken with the young Cherokee that he asked Buck to assume his name, which Buck did once he arrived in Cornwall. Later, the Cherokee Elias Boudinot became editor of the national newspaper the Cherokee *Phoenix* and worked beside Moravian missionary Rev. Samuel A. Worcester to translate Christian hymns into the Cherokee language and to begin translating the Gospel of Matthew.

Cherokee Civil War

A near civil war erupted in the Cherokee Nation when Georgia sought to seize the Cherokees' land after the discovery of gold in 1829. A split developed between the John Ross faction, which opposed removal, and the Ridge-Watie faction, which advocated moving west. Intent on leading the Cherokee people out of harm's way to a land where they could live unmolested, the Ridge-Watie family departed Georgia in

March, 1837 for Oklahoma, where they joined earlier "old settlers" who had preceded them.

Some Cherokees despised the Ridge and Watie families for the part they played in the removal. After the horrendous Trail of Tears in 1838-39, John Ross' allies formed assassination teams to murder the Ridge/Watie leaders. A group of twenty-five assassins were assigned to kill John Ridge. He was awakened from sleep at his home on Honey Creek, Oklahoma. He was dragged from his bed into the yard and stabbed 25 times, once by each assassin. Then they threw his body as high as possible into the air and, when it hit the ground, each assassin took turns stomping on his corpse. All the while, Ridge's wife and children looked on in horror.

John Ridge was awakened from sleep at his home on Honey Creek, Oklahoma. He was dragged from his bed into the yard and stabbed 25 times, once by each assassin. Then they threw his body as high as possible into the air and, when it hit the ground, each assassin took turns stomping on his corpse. All the while, Ridge's wife and children looked on in horror.

John Ridge's father, Major Ridge, fell victim too. He was shot five times in the back of his head and body, while riding his horse.

Another group went after Elias Boudinot. He and his wife were staying with Samuel Worcester while their house was under construction. While at the site of his new home, Boudinot was called aside by assassins disguised as men in need of medical help. One stabbed Boudinot in the back. After he fell, another split his skull. The carpenters came to his assistance, but seeing it was too late, sent word to Worcester. "Worcester called to a Choctaw Indian working nearby, told him to mount bareback Worcester's own swift horse, Comet…and ride to the store where Stand Watie worked, to warn him of possible danger to his life."

Stand Watie escaped the assassins. He became a Cherokee ruler in his own right, and much later a general in the Confederate Army, commanding the last organized Confederate force to surrender at the end of the Civil War. He has been described by some as the "foremost soldier ever produced by the North American Indians."

Living with History

At the height of my research into Cherokee history, I awoke at the farm one night with the full moon casting rays of light across my bed. I turned and looked at the moon through the open window. I was awed by the sudden realization that in that same room and through that same window others who looked at that same moon included Oo-watie, Buck Watie, Stand Watie, my great-great-grandfather, and my great-grandfather. Countless children would have been born in the room while others were mourned as they lay on their deathbeds. The sweep of history seemed to march through the room that night and through my mind.

This was the home of the Watie family and many, if not all, of the principal Cherokee rulers during that momentous time in history likely visited here. A century after they departed for the last time, their presence here had been forgotten and the place was known simply as the Daffodil Farm. But for the persistence of a few knowledgeable historians, the house's remarkable Cherokee history might have been lost forever.

Note: Today, Daffodil Farm is privately owned.

Sources

Wilkins, Thurman, 1986. *Cherokee Tragedy: The Ridge Family and Decimation of a People*, 2nd Edition, Revised. University of Oklahoma Press, Norman, Oklahoma, p. 192.

Ehle, John, 1988. *Trail of Tears: The Rise and Fall of the Cherokee Nation*, Doubleday, New York, p. 377.

DEATH ON THE GEORGIA FRONTIER

Wildes Massacre and the Okefenokee Indian Wars

MARTIN REGISTER

Though places like New Mexico, Arizona, and Texas are commonly considered to have been the "western frontier" in U.S. history today, the southern and western extremes of Georgia once held that title. One particularly grisly Indian attack in the Okefenokee Swamp in 1838 emphasized just how wild that area actually was.

At sunrise on the morning of July 22, 1838, the Maxemilian Wildes family awoke at their homestead northwest of the Okefenokee Swamp to find themselves in the midst of what had become the greatest nightmare on the Okefenokee frontier: an attack by hostile Indians.

In retrospect, the Wildes may well have anticipated the impending ambush. Legend persists today that they had spent the previous night peering into the darkness outside their house, listening to unfamiliar and eerie sounds, sleeping little, trying to reassure themselves that Seminoles thought to be in the area would perhaps steal their food then leave.

History variously records Mrs. Wildes' given name as Elizabeth or Mary, and tradition has it that she herself was part Creek, one of the reasons the family had not followed other frontier families into the safety of a U.S. Army fort not more than four miles away.

Local historian Luther Thrift, who lives in the Boggy Bay community near the site of the ultimately bloody massacre, says that Maxey Wildes felt the Indians might show mercy on one of their own; he also says there was reliable information through surviving family members that the homesteaders had made plans to head for the safety of the nearby fort after eating breakfast on that very morning.

It was most likely Mrs. Wildes who first saw the charging warriors as she walked out the door to prepare breakfast over an open fire. Thrift says most accounts maintain she made it back inside the security of the house, then screamed a warning to her husband, their children, and her nieces and nephews who had spent the previous night there.

Her terrified screams would be among her last acts: In a matter of moments, the family emerged to face the warriors, the father and oldest son firing guns at the intruders; the children "scattering like partridges," as they had been instructed to do by their father. Mrs. Wildes, clutching her youngest child, also raced for the edge of the woods.

MARTIN REGISTER

Cypress trees line the edge of five-mile-long Billy's Lake. Today, this reservoir has no shoreline, a situation which has existed since the completion of the Suwannee River sill. Most locals today believe a chieftain known at that time as Billy Bowlegs led the raids on white settlements during the "Seminole War." An island – known as "Billy's Island" – and this lake apparently were named however for a friendly Seminole named Billy who farmed on Billy's Island as late as the 1820s. He, ironically, was murdered by whites, an act which outraged the sparse white population in and around the Okefenokee at that time.

Most of their efforts were in vain. Maxey Wildes was killed near his doorsteps, along with three of his children. Mrs. Wildes, still clutching her child, was cut down as she apparently stopped to look back in horror at the carnage. Two of Wildes' sister's children were also among those murdered in the rampage.

Finally sated in their murderous endeavors, the Indians retreated after killing eight at the homestead. It is assumed – but not known for certain – that they also took the provisions from the smokehouse, then torched the Wildes house.

The fears of generations of white settlers in southeast Georgia had at last come to pass for the Wildes. The Okefenokee frontier, generally lawless and yet orderly for the most part, would never again be the same.

With Panic Ensuing

Four of the Wildes' sons, indeed scattering in different directions while fleeing for their lives, managed to survive, reaching neighboring houses across the edges of the Okfenokee to tell of the horrors of the attack. Within hours, shock turned to outright panic.

Many of the homesteaders had known and come into contact with elements of the nomadic Creeks of that day. Some, in spite of scattered clashes between the natives and settlers, had developed a tolerant and reasonably respectful – if uneasy – attitude toward the natives.

Indeed, the murder a decade earlier of Indian Billy, a Creek living and tending his garden peacefully on Billy's Island deep in the swamp, had provoked outrage among many settlers who called for the punishment of Billy's white killers.

By 1838, however, with a continuing war between U.S. Army troops and Seminoles raging to the south in Florida, times had changed. Indeed, the Georgia-Florida frontier had been a dangerous place for settlers for generations, and even before the coming of white settlers, the area had marked the contentious boundary for many Indian tribes for centuries, perhaps even for millennia, according to Dr. C.T. Trowell, retired assistant professor of history at South Georgia College in Douglas, Georgia, and author of the 1992 treatise "Exploring The Okefenokee: Letters And Diaries From The Indian Wars, 1836-42."

Long before the largely Celtic settlers arrived at the edge of the Okefenokee, once-powerful Native American Indian groups had been decimated by disease and other maladies following initial contacts with European explorers who also enslaved them when necessary. The impoverished and ragged remnants of these once-proud Indian cultures were left to be further impacted by additional waves of settlers.

The great Timucuan culture encountered by Ponce de Leon, whose dominance stretched from what today is central Florida to southern Georgia, reigned for over 2,000 years, but they had become extinct before any but the very first white settlers in Georgia reached the new land.

Into this void drifted disaffected Creeks, Yuchis, Hitchitees, and vestiges of other tribes. It was they who had abandoned the Creeks and become what came to be known as the Seminoles.

Ultimately, with battles raging across Florida, some members of the tribe began slipping through the adjoining Pinhook and Okefenokee swamps to raid the new white settlements and homesteads in southern Georgia. Such was the case involving the Wildes family.

Despite their ability to live off the land, the Seminoles were suffering under desperate conditions at this time – sometimes starving. A series of harsh winters and theft of their cattle by bands of white rustlers had decimated their food supply.

Complicating matters was the fact that over recent years, the Seminoles had become accustomed – even dependent upon – the Europeans for whiskey, iron tools and cloth, among other domestic goods. Archaeologists today have discovered few Indian-made artifacts in south Georgia which date later than 1650.

A Legend Eclipsing All Others

Though many accounts of this early history in our nation record only the atrocities of the Native Americans, there were depredations on both sides. In the aftermath of the Wildes Massacre, however, horror and survival were foremost in the minds of the other surviving white settlers. Taking what they could with them, they staggered – stunned by the horrendous murders – toward the safety of the forts ringing the Okefenokee.

Two of the Wildes boys ultimately were taken in by a family in nearby Waresboro; the two others were sent north of the Altamaha to grow up there. It seems almost frivolous to describe such circumstances today, but one needs only to imagine the pain and suffering youngsters endured after seeing parents and other family members killed and dismembered, forcing the surviving family members to be permanently separated and relocated to benevolent though strange families for the duration of their adolescence.

The shock waves of the Wildes Massacre reverberated from the halls of the state capital at Milledgeville to the chambers in the national capitol at Washington City, right to the desk of the president of the United States.

The Wildes Massacre was not the worst of the Seminole-settler incidents, nor was it the first. However, it did mark a watershed moment in southeast Georgia history, and indelibly seared into the south Georgia psyche a story which quickly became a legend.

The legend might not have grown to nearly its ultimate dimensions had not four of the Wildes children survived to tell the grisly story. What they told, and what settlers arriving at the scene recorded, eclipsed an 1836 U.S. military action against a group of Creeks believed to have raided the south Georgia settlement of Roanoke where a white settler was murdered near the mouth of Suwanoochee Creek in Ware (present-day Clinch) County.

Though the horrors in south Georgia at this time were laid almost solely at the feet of the Seminoles and their Creek brethren, much confusion and lawlessness was responsible for at least some of the depredations. Indeed, John Wildes, 12 years of age at the time of the massacre, told federal officers just after the attack that one of the warriors involved in the attack on his family fell over him as he cowered in a palmetto thicket as his family was being murdered. To his astonishment, Wildes said the warrior was white.

A Lt. Darling reported that the boy told him the white attacker "asked him why he did not run." According to the report, Wildes responded that he told the white attacker that he would indeed flee if the man would let him go – which he did.

Growing Confusion

The Wildes murders galvanized settlers' fears, led to calls for action from local volunteers and pleas for Georgia militia and federal troops. It also set in motion scores of communications between the Okefenokee frontier, the state capital at Milledgeville, and the federal government in Washington, all the while fanned by exaggerated or non-existent claims of further Seminole atrocities.

It soon became plain however, that the Wildes massacre was neither exaggeration nor wild rumor. It shocked settlers and initiated four long years of military action.

Lt. Darling's letter concerning the murders, published in the *Niles National Register* of August, 1838 and reprinted in the *Jacksonville Journal*, told of a horrific scene:

"...a man came full speed into the camp with the cry of Indians. I asked where. He said about five miles off, that he had just removed a family who heard the report of guns and screams of people. We were in our saddles in a few minutes, and under full speed to the spot where the alarm originated; and O, God! Of all the scenes I ever saw, or ever wish to see, presented itself to view.

"On reaching the ground, a man, his wife, and four children of his own, and two of his own sister's had fallen by the Indians. Three children of the six were alive when we reached the spot, one about three years old had been shot through the abdomen and lay asleep on the dead mother, another about two rods from the mother.

"But Oh, horrid to tell, I found a fine young lady of 18, shot in two places and dirked in another, with about 20 hogs around her, and she yet alive and had her senses perfectly. This was the most trying time I had ever seen. I gave her cold water, which she wished much.

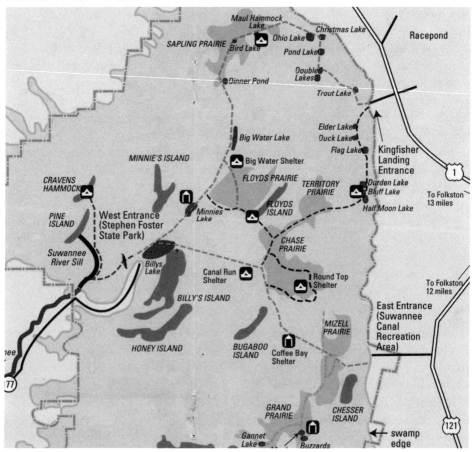

"I remained with her as long as I could, till obliged to go in search of the Indians. We left a guard to protect them, and administer to them all that they could, but all expired in less than twenty minutes after we left..."

Despite a considerable search, the Indian murderers of the Wildes family were never found, a story that would be repeated time and again in the ensuing four years, as troops conducted largely fruitless searches in the wake of further attacks.

Various reports put the number of Seminoles involved in the Wildes Massacre as low as five and as high as 50. Subsequent estimates on the total number of Seminoles in the Okefenokee ranged from zero to more than 500. For two years, rumor, insufficient and sometimes contradictory information, and a growing resentment of the federal officers by militia members combined to accomplish little.

Accepting the Unthinkable

In the period following the Wildes Massacre, "Alarms" came and went. Settlers, particularly in the area of the Saint Mary's River to the southeast, were attacked and murdered, and some Creeks, attempting to flee into Florida, were shot on sight.

Certain officials in Lowndes County to the west seemed bent upon spreading exaggerated claims of Indian attacks, and confusion reigned in addition to panic.

In his work on the subject, Prof. Trowell quotes letters from Major Greenleaf Dearborn to his wife, Augusta, late in 1836, 20 months before the Wildes Massacre. Many of these are quite enlightening regarding the circumstances at that time.

In one, Dearborn wrote of marching from the Okefenokee rim into Lowndes County, where "I suppose we are not wanted...for I can not find a person who has ever heard of Indian depredations there, & I think in Florida all must soon be settled..."

In another letter, dated October 29, 1836, he wrote to his wife of leading "an inactive life, except when marching, there are no Indians now, I believe all are gone, except there may be a few straggling ones..."

From southwest Georgia came accounts of slaughter of Creek men and women by militia members, and Col. Thomas Hilliard wrote with seeming remorse to Gov. William Schley of an attack by militia on an Indian encampment north of Waresboro in which six Indians were killed and four were taken prisoner, including two women.

The issue of dealing with Indian women and children – Creek or Seminole – who were taken as prisoners, soon became a major problem. Prof. Trowell's research revealed that several white vigilante groups "dumped" wounded survivors after "Indian hunts."

If the Okefenokee frontier had been short on law before, it now found itself caught between vigilante groups of settlers, armed militia, federal troops, peaceful Creeks passing through, and hostile Seminoles attacking from an Okefenokee so treacherous in most places that pursuit by white settlers was impossible.

In point of fact, the "Indian problem" was out of control, and so were armed and dangerous white settlers. At the same time, rumors of further Indian attacks could not be substantiated.

Dishonorable Tactics

The war dragged on in Florida, under the command of the controversial General Thomas S. Jesup. "Although his military efforts were no more effective than his predecessors, Jesup was successful in carrying out his orders," Pro. Trowell wrote. "He captured the Indians and moved them west.

"Jesup's tactics were simple. He invited the Seminoles in for a friendly talk under a flag of truce and captured the unarmed Indians."

Among those captured were the revered Osceola and the charismatic young Coacoochee. Osceola's ensuing death in prison has become immortalized in legend, but Coacoochee – who may go down in history as the more dynamic – actually escaped, recruited warriors, and inspired other leaders of small Seminole bands to renew terrorist attacks on outlying settlements and isolated army patrols.

Jesup's "dishonorable tactics" proved unpopular with the press, with white citizens, and even with legislators, who deemed it removed from the fair play of wartime protocol, though in fact the Florida action, as well as the resulting spillover into south Georgia, was far from the protocol of war as perceived by Europeans.

Although Jesup was unpopular in many quarters, he removed many of the Indians from the valuable cattle grazing lands of central Florida. Still, his efforts were frustrated on still another front when Florida leaders developed a fear that the area might ironically be settled by Northern anti-slavery forces.

Therefore, as the guerrilla war continued, "Many whites used the pretext that the Negroes living with the Seminoles were dangerous escaped slaves to whip up fear and hatred of the Indians," Trowell recorded.

Charles R. Floyd

"Exasperated by the confusion following the [Wildes] massacre, Brigadier Gen. Charles R. Floyd took action," Trowell wrote.

Floyd, the son of a wealthy Camden County plantation family who had gained notoriety for his effective actions in removing the Cherokees from north Georgia, made a triumphant return home via Milledgeville, where he was celebrated by the governor, and Savannah, where he was greeted by an escort by Chatham Hussars.

Floyd kept a diary, and it is by far the most complete record of military action – and inaction – in southeast Georgia during the "Indian troubles."

"Floyd was a very complex personality," writes Trowell. "He was a romantic in the early 19th century definition of the term. He lived in a world of heroes and villains, absolute good and evil, glory and dishonor. To Floyd, history was made by individuals, not institutions. His dream from childhood was to be honored as a great warrior."

As a boy in 1813, Floyd had served alongside his father, Gen. John Floyd, in the wars against the Creeks. He was accepted and dismissed from the U.S. Military Academy at West Point for disobedience, a circumstance he described as being "on a point of honor."

At the age of 20, he received a commission as a lieutenant in the U.S. Marines, where his tenure was marked by a series of feuds, vendettas and duels with other officers, although Trowell writes such actions were typical of the times.

He was granted leave in 1821 to tour Europe, after which he returned to manage the family plantation, Bellevue, near Saint Marys, according to Trowell. A few years later, before his 30th birthday, his father gave to him an adjacent property known as Fairfield Plantation.

He organized a company to fight the Seminoles in Florida in 1835, but void of a command, soon returned to his plantation. He then found adventure in the removal of the Cherokees, and returned home to the aftermath of the Wildes Massacre.

Into The Okefenokee

Floyd may have been a leader, but his activities in pursuit of the attacking Seminoles led him not to war, but to what amounted to the first far-ranging exploration of the Okefenokee by a white man. His diary, recorded in "The Complete Journal of Charles Rinaldo Floyd" and housed in the Georgia Historical Society in Savannah, recalls the trivialities of drunken militiamen, rainy mornings, receipts of provisions – but not one encounter with the Seminoles.

Floyd reported encounters with other "scoundrels" and "knaves" as he trudged the southern boundary of the Okefenokee, and at last arrived at Fort Gilmer (near present-day Fargo) on the western side of the swamp.

From there, on November 11, 1838, he and his forces marched up the bank of the Suwannee River, eventually reaching the end of The Pocket, and then marched "about four miles... half the distance through muddy and dismal swamps...," through territory to... "an island called by the Indians Chepucky (Billy's Island).

"On this island is an old field and the remnants of an Indian town called Chepucky te Fa Fa, which means Chepucky's town," Floyd wrote. "On the western edge of the island is a small lake (Billy's Lake), which I expect to be connected to the Suwannee River near its source. Built a fort on the island and called it "Fort Walker" in compliment to a gallant officer..."

From there, Floyd and his men headed northeast to one of Floyd's intended destinations – the island celebrated by the noted naturalist Charles Bartram sixty years previous as a paradise populated by beautiful Indian maidens, although Bartram certainly only heard of it and never came close to actually seeing it.

Since Bartram's time, the island had been thought by many to be a myth. Floyd felt, if it indeed existed, it was quite probably the seat of Seminole encampment. The maidens may have been mythical, but the island turned out to be quite real, and the fact that Floyd and his men actually marched through the quagmire to an island still barely accessible 165 years later is nothing short of amazing.

Island Myth Revealed

The adventurous Floyd realized the significance of the trip. He described the torturous journey in his writings:

"Our course was N.E. with very little variation for eight and a half hours through one of the most horrible swamps on the face of the earth. Below us was mud and water...sometimes nearly waist-deep and roots and logs and above and around were briars, vines and bushes, forming altogether obstacles that no language can accurately describe. . . we emerged from the swamp and entered the island which we sought, never before beheld by the eyes of the white man. It was, as I expected, the headquarters of the enemy."

Floyd's company had discovered an Indian camp and town "with comfortable houses," but the Seminoles had deserted the island months earlier.

Floyd's officers named the remote island in his honor, an act which in his diary he correctly predicted would from that point on bear his name.

The men burned the Indian village, camped "in a beautiful hammock of live oak and laurel trees," and on the following day explored the island, which he overestimated to be 20 miles in length.

Upon striking out for the eastern edge of the swamp on the following day, Floyd realized the gravity of the situation.

"...at times we were bewildered," he wrote. "...Several times I sent men up trees to look for land, for we felt as if we were in the ocean, and at last, near sunset, we were rejoiced at seeing the green tops of pine trees over the gloomy cypress about five miles distant."

Long after dark, the party emerged from the swamp as "the most miserable creatures that ever walked on two legs," he wrote. "...wet, hungry, and nearly dead from fatigue...several men were bogged so deep that it required two men to pull them out, and many on landing were without pantaloons and shoes, these articles being torn off by briars, roots and quagmires.

"I marched at the head of the troops, carrying my haversack of provisions as a common soldier and suffered greatly, but it is a satisfaction to me."

The Final Victors

In the end, the Indian wars in southeast Georgia didn't close with military victory, great or otherwise. The situation merely petered out, dying a slow death marked by weary disinterest in the face of rapidly changing times on many fronts.

What had exploded with the Wildes Massacre ended with a whimper. Seminole raids from the Okefenokee slowly tapered off.

In Florida, the war went on for another decade as the Seminoles retreated ever farther southward, finally taking up residence in another great swamp – The Everglades – as the federal army at last recalled its exhausted troops in 1854.

Gen. Charles Floyd, his honor insulted when he was passed over for a much-coveted military command, retreated to his plantation, where his health gradually deteriorated and his bitterness over the perceived military slight grew stronger with each passing year, even as death approached.

By the 1840s, the scattered Okefenokee families – toughened further by their common experience, had begun to coalesce into the closely-knit, deeply independent cul-

MARTIN REGISTER

ture which would evolve into the celebrated "Cracker" culture, tied by blood, lifestyle and a determined grasp on the essence of the Celtic heart.

The gradual retreat of the Seminoles, the trek across the swamp by Floyd and his men and the settlement of the Okefenokee islands and its perimeter by Okefenokee folk and their descendants, all played a part in the evolution of the swamp families.

In the end, they were the final victors of a complicated period defined, rightly or not, by the Wildes Massacre.

Luther Thrift, a local historian in Waycross, Georgia, holds the only remnant of any historic identification of the Wildes Massacre site in the Okefenokee Swamp. The sign is actually somewhat ineffective, since the actual site of the massacre may have been located slightly further south. Today, the exact location has been erased since the forest undergrowth has reclaimed the site.

A CENTENNIAL REMEMBRANCE OF THE 1906 ATLANTA RACE RIOTS

The Road to Riot

During the age of Reconstruction, the Ku Klux Klan, and Jim Crow laws, tension in Atlanta between the races mounted and boiled to the brink of eruption. In 1906, a barrage of incendiary reporting in local newspapers inflamed Atlanta's passions, triggering a sequence of confrontations that culminated in violence and death. On a humid September evening, the Gateway to the South rioted, unleashing a mob's fury on a city ill-prepared for social upheaval.

JOSHUA OWENS

L ong-time Atlanta Constitution editor Henry Grady and his protégés well understood that in turn-of-the-century Georgia the key to power was newspaper ownership. Publishers and editors effectively held a monopoly on community discourse. They acted as mirrors and, whenever possible, guides of public opinion; consequently, clever political candidates aligned themselves with influential newspapers.

The two Democrat hopefuls vying for a spot on Georgia's 1906 gubernatorial ballot were Clark Howell and Hoke Smith, editors of the *Atlanta Constitution* and *Atlanta Journal*, respectively. Their publications operated without pretense of political objectivity. Competition before primaries was especially fierce: Georgia was a one-party state and victory in the Democrat primary was tantamount to election.

As the two candidates campaigned for votes, they engaged in a highly publicized dance around the maypole of black disfranchisement, a policy that many white southerners of the day favored. This doctrine has now faded into obscurity, but at that point in history many prominent politicians in the South were brazenly racist.

Throughout Georgia, Hoke Smith, the more radical of the two candidates, crusaded to virtually eliminate black voting rights. The slightly more moderate Clark Howell insisted that Smith's goal was pointless: the political pull blacks wielded was negligible, Howell argued, and the ill will generated by disfranchisement would outweigh the benefits.

In addition to blatant political bias, Atlanta's white newspapers frequently published lurid accounts of black male against white female assaults. For most white southerners of that era, these reports aroused a deep-seated desire to protect white women from "the ravages of the black brute." The ultimate social shame of the era was miscegenation (that is, interbreeding of the races), and many white males abandoned civility in order to prevent it.

In the stifling Atlanta heat in the summer of 1906, politically motivated and exaggerated newspaper reporting combined with white society's ingrained antipathy toward black "assaults" creating a tinderbox that required only a spark to ignite.

The Peril of Politics, the Power of Press

A few months after the riot took place, Northern journalist Ray Stannard Baker investigated the Atlanta newspaper reports of black crime and found that in most instances the assaults were exaggerated. Baker noted, "Of twelve such charges against Negroes in the six months preceding the riot two were cases of rape, three were aggravated attempts at rape, three may have been attempts, three were pure cases of fright on the part of the white woman, and in one the white woman, first asserting that a Negro had assaulted her, finally confessed attempted suicide." Baker pointed out that

News of the rioting reached Europe where the French newspaper *Le Petit Parisien* printed this sketch of the events.

COURTESY ATLANTA HISTORY CENTER

Hoke Smith, editor of the *Atlanta Journal*, and Clark Howell, editor of the *Atlanta Constitution*, vied for the Democrat nomination for governor in the elections of 1906. Both published incendiary – and highly exaggerated – accounts of black atrocities to whip up support among voters. Smith won the 1906 election and achieved black disenfranchisement through literacy and property requirements.

three similar cases involving white assailants received comparatively little attention from the press.

On the eve of the riots, Atlanta's journalists were anything but analytical. Toward the end of August 1906, the *Atlanta Evening News* issued a "Call for 1,000 Good and True Men" to administer justice to black offenders. Rival newspapers censured the News and authorities denounced vigilantism; nevertheless, many ordinary citizens heeded the request for retaliation.

The Independent – a black-owned daily newspaper edited by Booker T. Washington disciple Benjamin Davis – and J. Max Barber's militant monthly magazine *Voice of the Negro* impugned the defamations of Atlanta's white newspapers but were ultimately powerless against the rising tide of the city's anger. Whites were infuriated and indignant. Blacks were fearful and anxious. Atlanta approached the boiling point.

(Author's note – diary entries are creations of the author based upon historical events)

From the diary of Levi Holly, a 36-year-old white Atlantan:
Tuesday, September 18, 1906
I've had enough! Something must be done about the obstinate Negro. A few weeks ago Sheriff Nelms said that we must rid our fair city of all black brutes who endanger the purity of our women, even if it means killing every one of them within a thousand miles. I'm beginning to realize how right he is.

Day after day the newspapers tell of vicious Negro assaults upon defenseless women. What would I do if it was my wife who was degraded and forced to live the rest of her life with her head hung in shame because of some lustful beast?

Bishop Henry Turner advised the members of his congregation to purchase firearms to protect themselves during the rioting.

After their feeble pursuit of political power was squelched in the '90s, I thought the blacks would be silent and compliant. Instead, it seems they are attempting despicable miscegenation, corrupting what is dearest to our hearts: our precious women. I'll be a dead man before I allow it to happen even once more!

Why can't all Negroes be like the Kenseys? They are upstanding and reliable. Cassandra Kensey has washed our laundry for nearly a decade, and her husband, Benjamin, delivers it like clockwork each Friday. He always shows the utmost respect and has never uttered even the slightest wayward word. But most of them aren't at all like the Kenseys.

I heard Hoke Smith of the Journal speak at the Peachtree Auditorium when the candidates for governor debated in June. Smith may've sympathized with colored folks years ago, but he has since straightened his ways. He now staunchly calls for full Negro disfranchisement, and with Tom Watson behind him, I can be sure Smith is trustworthy.

Hoke cautioned that unless we take action and quickly there will be political Negro domination. Smith said blacks would constitute a voting majority in 79 of our counties if just one in ten white Democrats defected and voted for another party. Giving them control over the fate of our nation is like placing a loaded pistol in the hands of a toddler.

The Kenseys wouldn't be so foolish as to seek social equality. They know their place in society.

From the diary of Sylvia Pennson, an eleven-year-old black Atlantan:

Wednesday, September 19, 1906

I'm scared.

Mama says there's nothing happening we can't handle, that the Good Lord will help us through whatever crosses our path like he led his people across the Jordan. I know Mama means well, but I suspect she doesn't fully believe what she's saying; she just aims to comfort me.

But I cannot ignore the looks my father draws from white folks on the street when we leave Brownsville. They have a mixture of emotions in their eyes: some display hate, some scorn, and others disgust…but all have a measure of fear. I hear their grumblings after we pass; they make sure we do. They don't care that Father is the most respectable colored physician in all of Atlanta. To them, he's little more than a beast.

Why do they hate and fear us so? What are they afraid of? We pose no threat. Daddy said pretty soon his suffrage would be taken away and he'd have no way to combat the raving politicians. Daddy's friend, Mr. Bowen, looked especially grim when he called on us last

Atlanta's mayor called in the Georgia Militia to restore order.

Tuesday. He and Daddy spoke in hushed whispers in the parlor while Mama and I prepared dinner and tried not to listen. Daddy looked ten years older when Mr. Bowen left.

I noticed later that Mr. Bowen left a copy of the Independent. Daddy calls it watered down and cloyingly complaisant. I don't know precisely what that means, but I can tell from his face that it's bad. Mama says it promotes Booker T. Washington's ideas about race uplift. She believes that if we work hard and don't step on the white men's toes then they will grow to respect us. She thinks Booker is a hero.

I read in Mr. Bowen's paper that "Tom Watson and Hoke Smith in their present insanity and greed for office are just about as fit to be trusted with the ballot as the average Negro." If a crazy man is in line to become governor then what hope do we have?

Unnerving Reports

More reports of assaults against white women were published in Atlanta's papers on September 20, 1906. The news spread like wildfire through the city.

One news account detailed how Mrs. Knowles Kimmel was approached on her porch by a black man clothed in shabby military regalia. He requested a drink of water, which she politely declined to provide. He then "threw me to the ground and assaulted me," lamented Mrs. Kimmel to the Journal. Search parties combed the area for the assailant, and the Journal affirmed that "if caught, the Negro will be lynched, as citizens of that section are greatly excited."

The second account related that 18-year-old Orrie Bryan's home was visited by an inebriated Luther Frazier, who entered late in the evening through a window. Bryan at first thought it was her father, and recoiled at the intimidating black figure staggering toward her. She dove into a closet and locked it. By this time her mother had dashed outside and called for help; neighbors arrived immediately and restrained Frazier.

The next morning, the intruder was tried by the city recorder, Judge Broyles. Orrie Bryan's father, a Methodist Episcopal preacher, was present at the proceeding. During

the hearing he interrupted and earnestly petitioned the court: "I have no weapon, neither pistol nor knife. I have only these hands and fingers that God gave me, but if you will let me use them I can settle this case in a few minutes."

Broyles refused and allowed Frazier an opportunity to speak. The defendant admitted, "I don't remember a thing that happened last night. If the white folks say I was in that house, I reckon it must be so. I got drunk with another Negro and the last thing I remember was when I was in a barroom on Decatur [Street]." Without delay, he was whisked through the hostile crowd and conveyed to the county jail.

From the diary of Levi Holly:

Saturday morning, September 22, 1906

The idling Negroes flock to Decatur Street to sate their evil desires, frequenting dives, finding escorts, purchasing drugs. I read in the Journal that "the wild, vile passions of the vagrant can have no stronger vent than through the open dram shop. From the wedlock of the Negro vagrant and the liquor den come the unspeakable crime." It is no surprise that bestial, decadent Negroes desecrate our women after indulging their vices. Like the Journal said today, we must "Drive out the Negro dives!"

Poor Miss Annie Poole was accosted by Frank Carmichael, a colored male, less than two months ago. The perpetrator got just what he deserved. Carmichael has become an example to all other scum like him that in the South requital is swift, sure, summary. We will not allow punishment to be delayed by legal technicalities and drawn-out court proceedings.

My foreman, Allen Wright, was present with over four dozen others at Carmichael's lynching. The police made no arrests, probably because some of them helped. Any man who was there will tell you straightforward that he willingly participated: there is no shame in justice. It is truly the dawn of a new age in the New South.

Day of Death

The passage of two days [change "two days" to "several days" if you omit the blue

127

shaded text above for space reasons] did little to quell unrest among white citizens. At 2 p.m. on September 22, 1906, the front page of the *Evening News'* first edition included four headlines reproving black improprieties: "Insulting Negro Badly Beaten at Terminal Station," "Bold Negro Kisses White Girl's Hand," "Hundred Lashes and '23' For Squeezing Lady's Arm," and "Negro Insulter Heavily Fined."

Just two hours later, the Journal's first extra – the day's regular edition with an added front page containing breaking news – hit the streets as its peddlers cried, "Negro attempts to assault Mrs. Mary Chafin near Sugar Creek Bridge!" The *Evening News* asserted that the perpetrator was the same who had victimized a Mrs. Kimmel two days before.

Shortly thereafter, an *Evening News* extra blared "Second Assault" in headlines covering the top half of the page. Several hours and four News extras later (most of the other newspapers also issued one or two extras apiece) Atlanta was a seething cauldron: the press had reported four separate assaults and the city was thrown "into a veritable state of panic. The news in the extras was taken as truthful; for the city was not in a mood then for cool investigation."

From the diary of Sylvia Pennson:
Saturday afternoon, September 22, 1906
My neighborhood is gripped with fear. Children aren't allowed out past six o'clock and women only leave their homes if they must. We're losing our business, too. Mother has sewn for white clients for years, but most of them have decided to buy from seamstresses of their own color. Mrs. Abbey told Mama she "wished to support a better type from now on." Daddy is certain this is due to what's been in the newspapers recently, but I haven't read them. "Some people will believe whatever they read even if it's as false as a zebra with polka dots," he told me, "but we mustn't hold the ignorance of the ignorant against them."

I heard Mama talking once about the boy down the street, Sam. He was walking from the fruit market and accidentally brushed a white woman on the street. Mama said Sam was lucky the woman didn't scare easy or he would've been arrested for assault. As it was,

he stood frozen for a moment gaping at her in terror. Once he regained his mind he sprinted full speed to the nearest alleyway. He said it was the scariest moment of his life.

Last Sunday at church Bishop Turner told us to buy guns. He's been saying it for months. That's quite an odd thing for a preacher to say. He thinks we ought to be ready if there's a fight coming.

Daddy listened. After the sermon he and Mr. Bowen went directly to the pawn shop. That night before bed I overheard Mama asking why he had done it. Daddy assured her we wouldn't need it. "A firearm is simply a safeguard," he said.

The Mob Assembles

By 9 p.m. on September 22, there were roughly 2,000 persons gathered in the vicinity of Decatur Street and its numerous "dives," or disreputable clubs. Agitated Atlantans passed around copies of newspaper extras. The black "assaults" were the topic of everyone's conversation. From "every side one heard the same words, 'What are we going to do about it?' and the emphatic statement, 'Something must be done.'"

On the corner of Decatur and Pryor Streets, an unidentified man mounted a makeshift rostrum and upbraided the audience for withholding immediate retribution from black reprobates. The impassioned demagogue flourished the Evening News extra with the imposing words "Third Assault" while he harangued the crowd.

Many listeners were bystanders simply enjoying a social event: "At first it was almost good natured. There was not an angry face in the crowd. Even the Negroes who ran the gauntlet seemed to mind but little the blows which hammered them and bent their efforts at reaching a side street, where they might escape." Before the man had vacated the podium, however, the crowd was thirsty for violence.

The mayor of Atlanta, James Woodward, was present. He ascended the same dry-goods box and fervently pleaded:

"For God's sake, men, go to your homes quietly and leave this matter in the hands of the law. I promise you that every Negro will receive justice, and the guilty shall not escape. I beseech you not to cause this blot on the fair name of our most beautiful city. What you may do in a few minutes of recklessness will take Atlanta many years to recover from. I implore you to leave this matter in the hands of the law, and save the bloodshed that is sure to follow if you allow yourselves to be governed by these reports, which are certainly exaggerated."

Woodward's appeal was disregarded. At 10 p.m. bars were closed and 3,000 tipsy customers poured onto the streets, where they diffused amongst the swelling crowd. The mayor utilized his authority in hopes the multitude would disperse. He summoned Mayor-elect Joyner, who also served as the city's fire chief, and ordered the lingerers drenched by fire hoses.

The rowdies simply regrouped outside the reach of the water. Another man jumped onto a dry-goods box and proclaimed, "It's an outrage for men to let a little water scare them. I will lead the crowd right up Decatur Street." By 10:15 the burgeoning mob was some 10,000 strong.

From the diary of Sylvia Pennson
Monday morning, September 24, 1906
Atlanta has gone crazy.

Mama woke me in the night on Saturday and told me that there was a riot; a mob had come to our house and we needed to stay together. I got out of bed and stumbled half-asleep to the living room, where Daddy had set a barricade up in front of our door. He was pacing with his shotgun and glancing out the window every few seconds. He told me everything would be fine: the mob had passed through but they only yelled and jeered at us; they didn't attack.

The rest of that night passed uneventfully. The next day Mama, Daddy, and I went to Gammon Seminary because we heard the blacks were gathering there for protection. The streets were completely empty. When we arrived, I saw women and children huddled together. The men were keeping watch like soldiers, solemn and armed. We passed the time by praying.

Then late last night Walter White and his father, the postal worker from Darktown who can pass for a white man, showed up at Gammon. They had been visited by the mob too. As Daddy and Mr. White spoke, I asked Walter what had happened to them. He only said the mob was going to attack his house and he nearly had to shoot a man but they left before he had to. That was all he would say.

I asked if the mob had hurt anybody. Walter looked like his mind was in another place when he responded, "Yes. How many I don't know. There is at least one dead, probably many more. I saw a poor crippled bootblack hobbling pitifully for his life from them. He didn't stand a chance. He was beaten to death."

I didn't ask Walter any more questions. Mama told me that we are crossing the Jordan right now and we'll be on the other side soon, and not to worry if I can't see the other side because we'll get there anyhow. I heard her tell Daddy that perhaps purchasing a firearm wasn't such a bad idea.

The Death Toll

After the riots erupted on Saturday, September 22, 1906, Mayor Woodward called in the state militia. Despite martial occupation, scattered violence continued for days and was not fully subdued until Tuesday, September 25.

Official reports tally twelve deaths due to the riot: ten black and two white. Others estimate the toll was as high as three hundred, notes Mark Bauerlein, author of *Negrophobia: A Race Riot in Atlanta, 1906*. Bauerlein gives a more conservative estimate of thirty to forty killed. Quite possibly many victims of the mob were never found or identified.

From the diary of Levi Holly

Monday evening, September 24, 1906

What evils have we wrought? I sought only justice, yet I'm afraid in our ardor we have become murderers. A mob and a jury both comprise men, but a jury is calm and rational. A mob is blinded with its zealous hatred.

The killing began Saturday night. It was not the black offenders who were targeted, it was harmless bicycle couriers, streetcar passengers, and whomever happened to be both colored and in the way.

One man was murdered as he prayed for mercy. Another, young bootblack Will Marion, was shot in cold blood just after he finished shining a man's shoes. Two barbers were beaten, mutilated, and shot in their own place of business. After their lives were extinguished, their killers paraded them around Henry Grady's memorial statue and piled them nearby in the most macabre and grotesque fashion as an altar for the bloodthirsty. How can we claim to be civilized?

The violence continued late into that night, but Sunday was quiet. Today, just hours ago, a contingent of county police endeavored to disarm Brownsville even though there had been no hint of a violent response from that section. The officers were joined by armed citizens. The blacks were simply protecting themselves, and in the darkness, the approaching group must have looked like a mob. I don't know who fired first, but I know that Officer Heard is dead along with four more blacks. John Bowen, president of Gammon Theological Seminary, was struck without provocation with a rifle-butt. I know him personally and he is a good man; that abuse was uncalled for.

Whites are gathered all over town in exactly the same manner as they were, expecting reprisal from blacks, and it would be preposterous to disarm them without due cause. How then can we atone for the deaths of innocent blacks like 70-year-old Civil War veteran Wilder, or hardworking brick mason McGruder, or intelligent and capable Dr. Pennson? These men were no criminals and had nothing to do with the riot. They did not deserve their fates.

Sixty black men were apprehended for Heard's death. So far as I know, no whites have been arrested for the atrocities they have committed. This is not justice. God forgive us!

A Changed City

After the riots, black citizens left Atlanta in droves, but those who remained would inhabit a forever altered capital of the New South. The races became increasingly segregated, resulting in nearly all-black enclaves like Auburn Avenue. Another long term result of the riot – according to Saudia Muwwakkil, co-curator of the Martin Luther King Jr. National Historic Site's upcoming Atlanta race riots exhibition Red Was the Midnight – was the further separation within the African-American community between black elites and the working class.

This fractured society survived for half a century, until the same quarters which had once exploded in racial violence became the spearhead of a nationwide civil rights movement in the 1960s. Ironically, Atlanta was one of just a few major Southern cities that did not violently oppose the dissolution of Jim Crow and segregation.

The author and Georgia Backroads *sincerely thank Mark Bauerlein and Saudia Muwwakkil for their gracious assistance in preparation of this article.*

At the time he authored this article, Joshua Owens was a 19-year-old assistant editor for Georgia Backroads *magazine. At the time of this printing in 2008, Joshua is a senior at West Georgia University.*

Sources
Baker, Ray Stannard. "Following the Color Line."

Bauerlein, Mark. "Negrophobia: A Race Riot in Atlanta, 1906."

Mixon, Gregory. "The Atlanta Riot: Race, Class, and Violence in a New South City."

Period publications – newspapers, magazines, etc.

An extensive bibliography is located at http://www.1906atlantaraceriot.org/html/body_resources.html.

Mixon, Gregory. "The Atlanta Riot: Race, Class, and Violence in a New South City." pp. 20

Which, along with the two candidates' newspapers, included the *Atlanta Evening News* and *Atlanta Georgian*

Baker, Ray Stannard. "Following the Color Line." pp 5.

Mixon, Gregory. "The Atlanta Riot." pp. 108

Tom Watson, who led the failed Populist movement of the late 19th century and later became a U.S. senator, enjoyed tremendous support from agrarian and working class sectors.

June 9, 1906 issue of the *Atlanta Independent*

Bauerlein, Mark. "Negrophobia: A Race Riot in Atlanta, 1906." pp 121-22

September 8, 1906 issue of the *Atlanta Journal*.

Baker, Ray Stannard. "Following the Color Line." pp. 9-10

Bauerlein, Mark. "Negrophobia." pp. 34. This instruction was originally printed in the *Voice of the Negro*. The author assumes Bishop Turner would have shared this sentiment with his congregation as well.

Harper's Weekly. Vol. 50, Issue 1457.

From the Atlanta Georgian, quoted in "Negrophobia." pp. 146

Bauerlein, Mark. "Negrophobia." pp. 147

Historic Watkinsville
Once A Wicked & Lusty Town

It was deemed to be so wicked, that it was rejected as a site for the new university scheduled to be developed in the area. Today, however, the little town of Watkinsville has come a long way since its earliest days some 200 years ago.

KATHLEEN WALLS

In the early 1800s, Watkinsville—a stagecoach stop a short distance from Athens, Georgia—was considered so rowdy that it was declared "off limits" to students at Athens' newly founded University of Georgia. The center of this decadent community was the Eagle Tavern – a regular stop on the route between Milledgeville and Athens.

The Eagle gained notoriety as a place one could obtain a meal, alcoholic beverages, a room for the night, and a lady of the evening if one so desired. Watkinsville is named for Colonel Robert Watkins, a prominent attorney and war hero from Augusta.

The earliest known building in Watkinsville may have been a small blockhouse. The first documented evidence refers to "a fort." In the late 1700s, Watkinsville was the far-

Eagle Tavern

thest frontier outpost for settlers pushing westward from the original thirteen colonies.

The earliest occupation of Watkinsville was recorded in 1789 in the small fort which once existed at the site. Sometime between 1794 and 1801, the Eagle Tavern was built.

Through the years, owners of the tavern added to the original structure to accommodate the growing community. In addition to being a stagecoach stop, Watkinsville was also the county seat of Clark County.

In 1821 Richard Richardson purchased the Eagle and began a series of renovations, ultimately adding six rooms to take care of the town's court proceedings and the growing clientele from the stagecoach business. Richardson's daughter, Martha, married a man named Edward Billups. When they were killed by Indians, their daughter, Belle, took over the business.

Popular legend maintains that Watkinsville was rejected as a site for the University of Georgia because of the "Wicked Tavern" located there. The Eagle, however, played a part in the life of the early students, becoming an oft-used site for a little drinking and illegal fun.

By the 1840s, the Eagle Tavern had achieved a measure of respectability – if only moderately. Harold W. Mann mentioned the tavern in his 1965 biography of 19th century Methodist preacher Rev. Atticus G. Haygood of Watkinsville.

"Most of the liquor was consumed in three established saloons, one of them at Watkinsville in the Eagle Hotel," Mann wrote, "where Athens lawyers stayed during the court sessions. Liquor drinking by respectable gentlemen in the 1840s is not to be confused with the riotous backwoods life of Georgia, especially two and three decades earlier."

Interestingly, despite its notorious nature – and it connection with the court proceedings of the county – the Eagle escaped destruction when troops under the command of General William T. Sherman marched through the area in 1864. In 1959, the old tavern – on its last legs by that time – was deeded to the Georgia Historical Commission and later to Oconee County.

Following renovations, the tavern today houses the offices of the Oconee County Welcome Center, and Watkinsville has gained a regional reputation as a haven for artists. The scenic little town is also attracting an increasing number of tourists.

Today, the old tavern houses many artifacts relevant to life in the 19th century. Halford Lowder, a local resident, loaned one of the newest displays – a large loom and spinning wheel once used by women of the era to spin cotton into thread and weave cloth.

The downtown area around the Eagle Tavern building was designated as a Historical District in 1979, and houses many shops offering art objects, crafts and antiques today. The entire length of Main Street is faced by old homes and businesses, each with a different story to tell.

Another unique structure in Watkinsville is Elder Mill Bridge. This aged conveyance was built in 1880, and is one of the few covered bridges remaining in the state. Once covered by scores of covered bridges, all but a handful have disappeared from the landscape today.

No visit to the bridge would be complete without a word about its self-appointed guardian, Al Cumings, who built his home next to the aged structure when it was in serious disrepair. Al successfully lobbied then-Governor Jimmy Carter for funds to stabilize and preserve the bridge. He continued with his fund-raising efforts for the bridge until the necessary funds were granted and the structure was repaired.

At 80+ years of age, Al still hasn't slowed down. He continues to guard the bridge like it is his own personal responsibility. He has also turned his efforts to another form of conservation – the breeding of rare Asian birds. His Black Swans and exotic pheasants are stunningly beautiful, and have become an awe-inspiring addition to the landscape.

The Haygood House which also figured in the early history of Watkinsville was built in 1827, and was the birthplace (1839) of Bishop Atticus G. Haygood, and his sister (1845), Laura Askew Haygood. The home served as the parsonage of the Methodist Church until 1972.

Atticus Haygood was president of Emory College and later Bishop of the diocese. He died in 1899.

Laura Haygood was principal of an early school for girls in Atlanta. She was also one of the first female missionaries to China. Another Haygood brother and sister are buried on the Haygood House property in Watkinsville. The headstones marking their final resting places still remain in the front yard today.

In 1999, Kathy and Jerry Chappelle bought the Haygood House and began a

Elder Mill Bridge

restoration which lasted two and a half years. They recently opened the historic home as The Chappelle Gallery, a retail business which features American crafts from artists with a national reputation.

The Chappells are no stranger to the art world of Watkinsville. In 1970 they converted an old farm and created the now renowned Happy Valley Pottery and Art Colony. They named the enterprise after a Walt Disney Studios production of Mickey & The Beanstalk, and like the mythical bean plant, the business grew rapidly.

Jerry Chappelle however, recalls it wasn't all sunshine in the early years. He says he and Kathy moved to the farm and began turning chicken houses into studios, but "from the day we moved in, everybody laughed at us because they didn't know what a potter was. At our first little summer festival we had thirty five people, but in 1999, the festival drew between 2,500 to 3,000 people, and it's still growing."

Jerry says the festival offers an artistic home base for other disciplines as well as pottery. Visitors can watch Jeff Bishoff throw a clay pot on his wheel and Judy Williams create a mosaic in stained glass. Loretta Eby shares the magic of glass-blowing with onlookers as she creates one of her renowned "Witch Bottles." She works her magic on a piece of molten glass as she shapes and colors it, and deftly removes it from the long pipe-like blower she handles so skillfully. She and her husband, Jeff Jackson – who works with metal and stained glass – collaborate on many projects.

The Witch Bottle legend began in medieval European glass-blowing studios. Often the craftsmen would be called to war and have to leave their studios. The last object created would be a colorful ornament with a hole left in the center. The evil spirits reportedly would be attracted by the bright colors and find their way inside. When the artist returned, he would throw the bottle into his newly fired furnace, thus destroying the malignant spirit.

Visitors to Watkinsville can find examples of the Jacksons' work, as well as that of other local artists at Ashford Manor, another historic home reincarnated into a thriving bed and breakfast inn. Ashford Manor was built in 1893 by Alexander Woodson "A.W." Ashford and his wife, Elizabeth (Loula) Ashford, who raised their brood of nine children in the structure.

Over the years, Ashford Manor has been witness to both good and bad times. A. W. Ashford died of a heart attack in the home after what came to be known as "Black Friday" – the Stock Market crash of 1929. Ashford's son committed suicide in the family bank when he was unable to cope with financial pressures.

The Victorian style of Ashford Manor lends itself well to the whimsical decorating styles of its current owners, Jim and Dave Shearon and Mario Castro. The trio had become tired of fighting Northern winters and decided to find a house that would lend itself to their idea of a bed and breakfast inn.

Today, Ashford Manor is home to several annual charity events. Grace's Memorial Birthday Party is a fundraiser for local animal charities held in June in memory of Jim's canine companion who died several years ago. Another is the annual Fall Wine Fest held in October to benefit the arts.

Bishop Haygood preached many a sermon in the Ashford Methodist Church located next door to Ashford Manor. This religious sanctuary from yesteryear enjoys a rich history of its own. During the U.S. Civil War, one of Sherman's officers quartered his troops' horses in the basement of the church.

Today, the church has been expanded to meet the needs of a modern congregation, but one can still observe the original exposed wooden beams overhead, as well as many of the hand-made bricks in the walls.

In the late 1700s, huge parcels of land on what then was the western frontier were granted to Revolutionary war heroes as a reward for service. One such grant was made to William Daniell.

Built around 1790, the William Daniell House is believed to be the oldest house still in existence in Oconee County. This structure, located in Founders Grove Subdivision near Watkinsville, is considered a magnificent example of Plantation Plain architecture. The house was once the center of Daniell's 500+ acre plantation in Oconee County.

William Daniell died in 1840 at the age of 97. He lived a full and no doubt lusty life, fathering 24 children. His first wife, Rachel Howe, died in childbirth bearing their eleventh child. William then married 17-year-old Mary Melton. Many of the Daniell descendants continue to live in Oconee County today.

Of course, there are other things to see and do in Watkinsville besides the exploration and admiration of the many historic structures. For fine dining mixed with art, the area's newest restaurant, Le Maison Bleu, offers exhibits by talented artists as well as food with an artistic touch.

Nearby Harris Shoals Park boasts a great nature trail that winds along a secluded creek and crosses a small lake. A picnic area and lots of wooded acreage offer a great place to enjoy nature at its best.

History buff, art connoisseur, or just plain tourist, you'll almost have to agree that though Watkinsville was once known as wild and wicked, it has earned the title today of "Wonderful Watkinsville." Plan to spend a day there on your next trip to Athens.

Robert Elliot Burns

Georgia's Notorious "Chain Gang" Fugitive

In 1922, Robert Elliot Burns was convicted of an armed robbery that netted him less than $2 and a prison sentence of 10 years. Amazingly, he escaped twice, wrote a book while on the run, saw his exaggerated story told on the big screen by Hollywood filmmakers and, finally, was granted a pardon. Some say he was a prison reformer. Others maintain he was nothing more than a con artist and a common criminal.

Jackie Kennedy

A convicted armed robber's two escapes from roadside work details — and the book he wrote chronicling his life in Georgia's notorious "chain gang"–played an important role in reforming the South's Depression-era prison system. Robert Elliot Burns' book, *I Am A Fugitive From A Georgia Chain Gang*, coupled with the 1932 movie based on the book, ultimately influenced lawmakers to investigate allegations of abuse in prison work camps, and positive changes were made.

But while some hailed Burns as the catalyst to reform, others saw him as a mild-mannered con man prone to exaggeration. Both views contain elements of truth, while either picture of Burns without the other tells only half the story of this complex character and his intriguing adventure.

The Beginning

A Brooklyn, New York, native born in 1891, Robert Elliot Burns gave up a job paying $50 a week in 1917 (a substantial salary in those days) and volunteered for service when the United States declared war on Germany during World War I. He returned two years later, "shell-shocked…a badly broken soldier, mentally and physically," according to his brother.

And, Burns was bitter. His pre-war girlfriend had married someone else, and his well-paying job was gone. The new position he was offered paid only $17.60 a week.

Robert Elliott Burns labored on a chain gang building a road in Troup County, circa 1929.

Depressed and dejected, Burns adopted the lifestyle of a hobo, hopping trains and traveling around the country working odd jobs. By February of 1922, he was in Atlanta where, he recalled, "a heavy, dismal sleet" had been falling for two days.

His circumstances soon became even more dismal.

The Crime

At first, Burns was only mildly interested when two strangers offered to pay him for helping them on an undisclosed project. Perhaps his interest was piqued after he hitched a ride on a train later that day and was discovered and forced off by the conductor. Flat broke and busted, Burns no doubt found the strangers' offer more enticing.

The next morning, he met his new acquaintances on an Atlanta street. It was not until then, Burns later wrote in his book, that he realized the "project" was the robbery of a grocery store. After committing the crime, the three men hurried off with a measly $5.80.

Later, after being caught, Burns insisted to police that he was an unwilling participant in the heist, and had been forced, at gunpoint, to assist his two accomplices. When they were arrested a scant 20 minutes after the bungled robbery, Burns presented himself as a victim – at least as much of one as the grocery clerk whose pants pockets he'd searched for cash during the hold-up.

At his trial, Burns pleaded guilty and begged the court's mercy, explaining how he was forced to take part in the robbery. Viewing him not as a victim but as an armed robber, the court sentenced him to six to 10 years hard labor – a stiff penalty for a robbery that profited him only $1.93.

In explaining the harshness of the penalty, prison officials pointed out that it wasn't for mere robbery, but for "armed" robbery, a much more serious offense in which an innocent victim might have been killed.

The Time – Take One

Burns began his sentence at work camps in Fulton County (Bellwood and Sandy Springs) and Campbell County. At Sandy Springs, he pounded rock at a quarry from sunup to sundown, pausing only for dinner and a brief rest. The days were long, hot and relentless.

The nights were even worse. The warden and guards, according to Burns, routinely walked the bunkhouse, often choosing five or six men who, in their opinion, had not put in an adequate day's work. Those convicts, according to Burns, were taken into the mess hall, stripped and beaten with "the leather." Ten licks were doled out to each man as the others listened to their wails of agony.

After two weeks of enduring what had come to be called "chain gang" life (which he described as "a vicious, medieval custom…so archaic and barbarous as to be a national disgrace"), Burns began to think he would never complete his sentence.

There was an old saying on the chain gang: "You either work out, pay out, die out or run out." A convict who "worked out" completed his sentence and was released on schedule. One who "paid out" purchased a pardon or parole, the price of which was $2,000, cash Burns couldn't come by. To "die out" meant you remained in prison until you died. To "run out," however, meant you successfully escaped.

Burns decided the latter would be his route to freedom. Two weeks later, he was transferred to Campbell County. For the next few weeks, he spent every waking moment trying to conceive a method of removing the chains that bound him.

One day, as he was racking his brain, Burns noticed one particular black man on

A chain gang north of Atlanta poses for a photograph, circa 1925.

The interior of the Troup County Prison about the time of Burns's incarceration from 1929 to 1930.

the gang whose many years in chains had made him an expert with a sledgehammer. That man's expertise would pay off for him, Burns reckoned.

Freedom – Take One

Determined to "hang it on the limb," Burns solicited assistance from the master sledge hammer swinger who, with three strong whacks on each ankle shackle, changed the shape from circular to elliptical, a maneuver that allowed Burns to remove his feet from the devices and regain the ability to run for freedom.

A few days later, on June 21, 1922, he was back on the roadbed and taking what the guards believed would be the usual two-minute break to relieve one's self. After finding a secluded spot, Burns tugged the shackles from his feet and made a run for it.

After realizing the convict was not going to return, lawmen and tracking dogs began a quick pursuit. Burns, however, had been lucky. He had somehow been able to coax a ride from the driver of a passing automobile. This eliminated his scent from the trail and allowed him to quickly remove himself from the search area.

After riding into Atlanta, Burns' luck continued to hold. He bumped into an acquaintance from Sandy Springs who was a sympathetic former chain gang member himself. He allowed Burns to stay in his hotel room for the night. The next day, the escapee dodged law officers as he left Atlanta by train and ultimately made his way all the way to Chicago.

After arriving in the "Windy City," Burns found work in the city's stockyards, earning $3.20 a day. Though that was not much money to some people, it was a huge improvement for Burns, who thought that things could only get better.

Life and Love in the Windy City

In 1923, approximately a year after his escape, Burns – using an alias – was renting a room at a boarding house. He eventually struck up a relationship with his landlady's daughter, Emilia del Piño Pacheo, and the young lady fell in love with him.

With an entrepreneurial flair, Burns had an idea for a new magazine he wanted to publish, but he didn't have enough money to launch it. Emilia, who had frugally saved an untold sum of money, loaned him the necessary funds to start his magazine.

Things went well for awhile, and Burns even married Emilia in 1926, though he later claimed it wasn't for love, but because she had threatened to betray him if he didn't. She had learned of his secret past by steaming open a letter from his father. When she gave him the choice of marrying or being exposed, Burns met her at the altar.

Their stressful union rocked on for three years until Burns met another woman at a dance hall in February of 1929. He fell in love with Lillian Salo, decided to move into an apartment with her, and asked Emilia for a divorce. The next day, his jilted wife wasted no time in seeking quick revenge. She mailed a letter to Georgia prison officials revealing the precise location of the escaped convict.

Robert Burns was imprisoned in the Troup County Stockade (photographed in the 1950s) in 1930 after his second escape from the Georgia penal system.

Bargaining

The state of Georgia immediately requested that Burns be returned to serve the remainder of his prison sentence. Chicago authorities, however, were anything but cooperative. A group called the Burns Citizen Committee wrote letters and signed petitions calling for his pardon. They lauded Burns as a model citizen in his community.

Burns' jilted wife, however, made a different claim, charging that her husband was "wicked and unworthy," a "grifter" who had extorted and embezzled funds, bragged of killing four railroad strikers and operated a raunchy carnival striptease show. It was he, his wife claimed, who had begged her to marry in order to gain access to her money.

Whether a saint or a scalawag, Burns nonetheless had been convicted of armed robbery and had not completed his jail term. That's the way the state of Georgia saw it, plain and simple. And after Gov. Eugene Talmadge issued extradition papers, Illinois Gov. Louis F. Emmerson reluctantly signed them.

Burns fought the extradition, and proceedings on a writ of habeas corpus were initiated. As a result, a judge with the Georgia Prison Commission offered Burns a deal: waive extradition, abandon the habeas corpus, pay the state of Georgia $350 (the cost for his recapture), and return south to serve 45-90 days of easy time. Do this, and you'll be a free man, he was assured.

Burns, hoping to legally become a free man again, took the Prison Commission up on its offer. He accompanied the authorities back to Georgia, fully believing he'd serve no more than 90 days and return to Chicago a free man. He should have gotten it in writing.

The Time – Take Two

Burns landed back in the state he loathed in July of 1929 and soon learned to his abject disappointment that his stay could actually be extended up to 12 months. "You are now in Georgia and things will have to be handled from the Georgia viewpoint," he was advised, and was shortly returned to the Campbell County chain gang from which he'd escaped seven years earlier.

While in Campbell County, he later admitted he was "treated intelligently, fairly and from the viewpoint that I was not a desperate criminal." However, he was later transferred to the Troup County Stockade, reportedly for his inability to pay $500 for his pardon. There, Warden Harold Hardy ran the toughest and strictest chain gang camp in the state. The *LaGrange Graphic-Shuttle* reported that because no prisoner had escaped from the new jail, the prison commission often sent "particularly important or clever prisoners from other counties here."

Burns, considered both important and clever, called it "the worst chain gang camp of them all...a place feared by every one of Georgia's 5,000-odd felons."

At Troup County, Burns wrote that he worked 15 hours from dawn to dusk and shared his days with criminals considered to be the "tough eggs...the most desperate of Georgia's felons." Warden Hardy doled out discipline with a firm and cruel hand according to Burns, who said punishment included being stretched in the stocks and

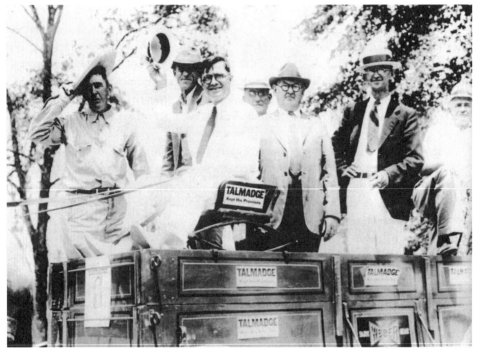

Governor Eugene Talmadge, photographed in Troup County, signed the extradition papers to the state of Illinois for Robert Burns in 1929.

spending time in the sweatbox, a three-feet-square by six-feet-high box where the worst offenders spent up to three days in the sweltering confine for misconduct.

An escape from the Troup County prison was an eventuality not even contemplated by many of the convicts simply because they felt it was so unlikely, but Burns began plotting immediately. "I felt I would rather be dead than in such a place," he wrote.

Freedom – Take Two

After two unsuccessful tries to secure his parole, and repeated attempts by his brother, Vincent, and his mother to persuade the Georgia Prison Commission to keep their promise, Burns nonetheless remained incarcerated. What had been described as 45 to 90 days of deskwork had become 14 months of "endless heart-breaking toil."

If the system wouldn't free him, Burns decided he would once again take matters into his own hands. On Sept. 4, 1930, he made his second escape with aid from a local farmer he paid to drive him to Atlanta. On the day of his escape, Burns wrote, he "sprang at full speed," dashing from his spot in the work line to the waiting getaway car, running with his heart beating rapidly, even as guards lifted their shotguns to firing positions.

Burns, however, exaggerated the actual circumstances of this escape considerably. (He had numerous other exaggerations in his book as well.) According to Warden

Hardy, Burns was actually given considerable freedoms at Troup County. He was a trustee and pulled light work, bringing water to the work crews. It was a chore that separated him from the guards – sometimes up to an hour at a time. He had been gone for more than an hour before anyone realized he had escaped once again.

Hiding in the rumble seat of his anonymous friend's coupe, Burns made his way to Atlanta, and on to Newark, New Jersey, where his brother wrote as he dictated the book that would make him a household name nationally.

A Book, A Movie, and More Notoriety

True Detective magazine bought Burns' story and began publishing it in January of 1931. A year later, Vanguard Press published it in book form as *I Am A Fugitive From A Georgia Chain Gang*. While the writing skips about and is heavy on exaggerated prose, the book received good reviews, and was commended in the North for "baring Georgia's incredible penal system."

In November of 1932, Warner Brothers released the movie version of Burns' book, dropping "Georgia" from the title. Produced by Darryl F. Zanuck, it was heralded as a "Broadway sensation."

Still "hanging it on the limb," Burns remained a fugitive, even as his public acclaim swelled. Unable to resist publicity and the opportunity to cash in on his notoriety, he began giving interviews, promoting himself, his book and the movie. The flaunting of his fame enraged Georgia officials who beefed up their efforts to locate him and, in December 1932, he was finally arrested in Trenton, New Jersey.

Gov. Harry Moore of New Jersey was served with extradition papers and soon after, as was the case three years earlier in Chicago, letters and telegrams from Burns supporters in New York began pouring in, urging the governor to refuse extradition. At the December 21 hearing, Arthur Garfield Hays of the American Civil Liberties Union declared Burns was not a fugitive from justice, "but a fugitive from injustice."

Moore subsequently denied the extradition and Burns was released, a safe man as long as he remained in New Jersey.

The Book and Movie vs. Reality

Meanwhile, back in Troup County, Georgia, the movie version of Burns' experience began playing in area theaters the same week Gov. Moore refused to extradite the convict. Not only was the former chain gang resident free; his life had been sensationalized in the movies. It was a king-sized slap in the face for Georgia. Never mind that the state's name had been dropped from the movie title; everyone knew the true location of Burns' incarceration. And as the nation got an eyeful of Georgia's questionable penal system, the folks in Georgia – and especially in Troup County – gave an earful back.

"Governor Harry Moore...did more than to pass unjust judgment on our state," read an editorial from the *LaGrange* (Troup County) *Daily News*. "He gave official sanction to the increasing number of pictures which have come out of Hollywood glorifying law breaking and pointing the finger of scorn at police and prison officials the country over...Making heroes and martyrs of hold-up men is certainly one of the explanations of the astounding increase in crime in this country."

Warden Hardy called Burns' book "a good story...sadly lacking in veracity." The warden was amused that the convict made his escape from Troup County sound so glamorous. "Burns touched up the story and made himself appear a hero. There wasn't anything daring about his escape."

The movie exaggerated the escape even more. In his portrayal of Burns, actor Paul Muni escaped by stealing a truck and leading prison officials on a high-speed chase. The chase, and the movie, ended with the escapee blowing up a bridge with dynamite, leaving his defeated pursuers stranded on the opposite side.

Warden Harold Hardy

Warden Hardy charged that Burns "drew upon vivid imagination" when describing conditions at the stockade. "We do have a stock at the camp, but we never have had a sweatbox." And while prisoners in the movie were depicted sleeping chained to their beds, such was not reality.

In 1932, a *LaGrange Daily News* reporter allowed Warden Hardy to put him in the stocks that Burns had called "an instrument of torture." The reporter described it as "fairly comfortable."

Troup County policeman R.B. Carter told reporters in 1937 that Burns had easy work driving a dirt cart while at the county stockade. He often expected favors and, according to the article, actually told Carter that "all of his famed book was fiction and that he had not received any such treatment at the hands of any official or any gang while in Georgia."

Burns himself admitted publicly – but only after the movie was released – that he in fact had exaggerated the brutality of the chain gangs.

A Pardon At Last

Upon receiving reprieve from extradition in 1932, Burns said: "I am through with publicity."

And, for the most part, he did remain out of the headlines from that point on. Although he never again enjoyed the success he had managed while in Chicago, he did fare well as a tax consultant in Union, New Jersey. And while he was never reunited with his beloved Lillian Salo, he did remarry and had several children.

In 1933, Warden Hardy and two other state prison officials filed suit against Warner Brothers Motion Pictures, seeking damages for false portrayals in the film. The suits reportedly were settled out of court.

In 1937, Burns' request for a pardon again was turned down. That same year, a federal study discovered 125 county-operated chain gangs in Georgia and urged that they be abandoned "in the interest of decency and humanity."

Though public awareness and the need for prison reform was on the upswing, not much changed until 1942 when reform candidate Ellis Arnall was elected governor. The following year, he banned the use of chains on prisoners, and strengthened the ban on whipping.

Finally, in 1945, upon a request from Gov. Arnall, the Georgia prison and parole board granted clemency to Burns. Upon hearing of their decision, Burns, who by then was 54, reportedly had to struggle to keep from crying. Whether this was an additional attempt at drama from the convict is unknown today.

Looking Back

As a result of his experiences, Burns had made it his goal to destroy the chain gang system. While reform already was in a slow-cooker mode, publicity sparked by his book and movie definitely turned up the heat. By the time he died in 1955, chain gangs in Georgia had ceased to exist.

While Burns was prone to exaggeration and even later admitted that certain parts of his story were fiction, his actions did shine a national spotlight on what had been a shadowy prison system. This illumination, it can be certain, helped bring about some necessary changes.

Whatever his true character, Burns, although short in stature, was definitely tall in tenacity; and although most jailbirds are forgotten the moment they fly, the story of Robert Elliot Burns and the Georgia chain gangs will live on for many years to come.

Sources

I Am a Fugitive from a Georgia Chain Gang by Robert E. Burns, 1932; *LaGrange Daily News; LaGrange Graphic-Shuttle; Atlanta Journal;* "How Hollywood Reformed the Georgia Prison System" by Kaye Lanning Minchew, *Georgia Journal,* Spring 1992; and "A Fugitive's Epic" by T.H. Watkins, *Constitution,* Fall 1993.)

Ogeechee River Ordeal

An adventurous canoe trip with college chums in the 1980s led to a repeat trip down the same river approximately 15 years later with my sons and father-in-law. As in my original excursion, the tough Ogeechee let me know in no uncertain terms just who was boss.

DANIEL M. ROPER

Funny how an idea gets in your head and grows like kudzu on a sharecropper's shack. Twenty years ago, I heard two college professors reminisce about a 1950s trip down the Oconee and Altamaha rivers. Their words penetrated deeper than any classroom lecture, for even today I vividly remember the details – how they built their canoe, portaged the expanse of Lake Sinclair, awoke one morning on an Altamaha River sand bar to find a wild bull outside their tent, and finished two weeks later at Two Way Fish Camp near Darien. Fascinated with the thought of this adventure, I resolved to do pursue something similar – minus the wild bull – before I graduated.

Introduction to the River

That is how I ended up lost in a South Georgia swamp one spring afternoon several years later, beset by long-legged spiders, eyeing the setting sun, wishing I had spent my last college spring break in Daytona Beach rather than paddling the Ogeechee River's dark water. Instead of an idyllic week floating, fishing, and hunting along this pristine river (as I had imagined), the experience was more in line with *Deliverance* and *Swamp Water*, classic novels about Georgia canoeing trips gone bad.

The author (left) and David Dekle at breakfast beside the Ogeechee River, March 1986.

(L-R) David Dekle, Dan Roper, and Dan Forster at the end of their 125-mile Ogeechee River trip in March 1986.

Just an hour before, my two companions and I had blissfully guided our canoes down what appeared to be the river's main channel, only to have the waterway melt into a jungle of cypress, tupelo, willow and maple trees. We had been through this routine before, each time forging ahead, eventually bushwhacking our way back to the main river, but it was disconcerting each time it happened.

So once again, we pushed on through dense foliage, brushing off annoying spiders and sending countless maple seeds down the backs of our shirts, expecting at any moment to find the main channel. This time, however, the expanse of cypress swamp stretched ahead as far as we could see.

It was somewhat unnerving to say the least.

Finally, we halted for a council of war and discussed our options. I favored turning back to find the point where we had left the river, but my friends preferred to proceed on ahead. Totally flouting common sense and universal wilderness wisdom, we elected to split up and see who could find their way out first.

Lost On the River

Vowing to remain within shouting distance of each other, David and Daniel went ahead, while I reversed course and paddled up a narrow channel, flanked by tangled thickets of willow and alder.

A short time later, I saw another channel to my left that looked promising. Noting the proximity of the sun to the horizon, I decided to give it a try, hoping that it would prove to be a shortcut. I figured that we had – at most – an hour until dark. With mounting concern, I yelled a loud "whoop!" toward my friends and heard a disconcertingly distant reply.

Dipping my paddle into the dark water, I propelled myself down the new channel.

151

Once again, the course narrowed and I began breaking through undergrowth until, a few minutes later, the waterway disappeared into yet another impenetrable brush barrier. I glided to a stop in a box canyon, surrounded on three sides by twenty-foot high walls of interwoven willow branches. This was spider heaven. . . .

"Whoop!" I called to Daniel and David. This time there was no answer.

"Whoop!" Louder, and with a touch of desperation, but still no response.

With the lengthening shadows signaling that dusk was approaching, I realized I was stranded and alone in this maze. I pictured myself tying the canoe to a tree limb, lying down in the bottom, passing a restless night listening for alligators, mashing spiders, and hoping that a snake did not crawl in beside me.

Presence Of Mind

Reminding myself not to panic, I picked up my paddle and backed out of the box canyon. I reentered the cypress swamp, turned northwest, and proceeded upstream in the opposite direction from my friends, paddling toward the place where we had left the Ogeechee an hour earlier.

It wasn't long before dusk and the gloomy swamp surrounding me took on a menacing aspect. I tried another "Whoop!" Once again, there was no reply. Placing my paddle in my lap, I allowed the canoe to drift to a stop. I suddenly had to admit to myself that I did not know which way to go next.

I carefully stood up in the canoe, balancing precariously, and peered ahead through the thick undergrowth. I could sense, more than see, an open area to my left. I paddled in that direction for a minute or two, stood again, and....there it was! The broad, unobstructed channel of the Ogeechee River flowed just ahead. A few determined strokes propelled my canoe through the remaining tangles and I jubilantly emerged onto the river's sparkling expanse.

Spring time on the Ogeechee, March 1986.

Now I needed to locate my friends, but nothing but silence greeted my next hearty "Whoop!" The sun had slipped behind the treetops and shadows stretched all the way across the river. Weighing my options, I decided to continue down the river – though it angled away from the point where we had parted earlier in the day – in hopes of finding them somewhere downstream.

I paddled fifty yards and

hollered once again. No answer. A little further, same result. Yet again and, this time, far to my left, I was just able to hear a distant reply.

Joyous Reunion

Needless to say, I felt immense relief at the sound of my friends voices, and shouted, "Are you in the river?" Echoes transformed my shouted query into incomprehensible garble. To minimize the effect of the echoes, I tried shouting one word at a time, allowing each echo to fade away before bellowing the next word:

"ARE…..YOU…..IN…..THE….RIVER?"

Then came the reply, "NO!....ARE….YOU?"

Using this method of communication, we decided that they would come to me, periodic "whoops" serving as a homing beacon. For the next ten minutes, there was no sign of them. Then I heard splashing, muffled conversation and muttered oaths. Suddenly, in the gloom, I saw my friends struggling through thick vegetation. They stood immersed to their waists in swamp water, like Humphrey Bogart and Katharine Hepburn in *The African Queen*, pulling their canoe around trees and lifting it over obstructions.

Dragging the boat across a small sand bar and the last alder thicket, my bedraggled companions finally joined me on the river. Joyful greetings ensued and we shared our misadventures with relieved laughter. Then, with a worried glance to the west, we pushed off, paddling downstream to search for a suitable campsite before dusk turned to total darkness.

Fortunately, the remainder of the trip passed without any major mishaps. We found a campsite and spent the third of our five nights by the river. It turned out to be a wonderful journey. Over six days and 126 miles, we stopped at rustic riverside towns like Midville and Scarboro; prepared oatmeal breakfasts and Dinty Moore beef stew dinners over campfires; bathed beneath a geyser of cold artesian water; and slept snugly in sleeping bags each night while great horned owls hooted loudly in the shadowy forest.

At the completion of our trip, we vowed steadfastly to return, but that vow remained unfulfilled with the passage of the years and our advancing responsibilities in life.

A Return to the River

Seventeen years later, I told my children about that trip and they talked me into doing something similar. I contacted my old friends to gauge their interest, but they were unable to make the trip this time, so after careful planning, I agreed to take my 9- and 6-year-old sons, John and Jackson, and my father-in-law on a three-night trip in October of 2003.

We scheduled the trip in autumn hoping for a lower water level, a more obvious river channel, a diminished likelihood of rain, and fewer annoying bugs. Both of my boys are veteran paddlers, but I reminded them about the threat of poisonous snakes, wasp and hornet nests, and sudden deadfalls sometimes encountered when rounding bends in the river. Overall, I considered the risks relatively small and I was reassured when Allan Wadsworth, an experienced paddler who is a member of the Georgia

(L-R) Jackson and John Roper, and Jack Legg, deal with a deadfall in the Ogeechee.

retrospect, it was probably only two or three. The going was really slow.

With sunset approaching, we selected a rather dreary little sandbar on the left bank for our camp. We tried fishing (no luck), set up tents, cooked dinner, swatted mosquitoes, admired a rising full moon, and listened to great horned and barred owls hoot and great blue herons "craaaaank!" in the distance. Twice that night, I enjoyed one of my favorite camping sounds – the rumble of an approaching freight train on tracks paralleling the river a quarter-mile away.

We awoke at sunrise, ate breakfast, broke camp, and put back on the river before nine, expecting to reach Herndon Bridge before lunch. The first 15 or 20 minutes were serene and beautiful with no obstacles barring the way. This stretch of the Ogeechee is remote, flanked mostly by willow thickets and dense forest. There were some magnificent, gray-barked, moss-festooned cypress trees and wildlife was abundant. Allan, who paddled point, saw many alligators along the way too.

I crossed my fingers and hoped that we had cleared the morass of logjams, but no such luck. By 9:30 a.m. we were back in a stretch with deadfalls at nearly every turn and spent the next three-and-one-half hours fighting our way downstream. The drudgery eventually took its toll, especially on my father-in-law who did not have much experience paddling a canoe in these conditions.

Sometime after 1:00 p.m., we came to a tight bend where the river makes a U-turn with the mouth of the U facing left. At the bend, a large tree had fallen perpendicularly across the river. Limbs and branches obstructed most of the channel and the only way through this huge obstacle was a narrow gap between the tree and the steep,

155

Capsized on the Ogeechee, October 2003. No canoeist takes pleasure in such a sight.

muddy bank. The current sweeping through this little keyhole passage was strong. Adding to the difficulty, a stub of a sawn off branch angled down from the trunk making the passageway even tighter.

Capsized!

By the time I rounded the curve and saw the keyhole, Allan had already maneuvered through it. I turned my boat around so that I could pull myself through backwards. This worked well for me, but I realized it was a mistake nonetheless. When I was about halfway through, my father-in-law and 9-year-old rounded the bend upstream. Following my lead, they too began to turn their canoe, but as they did, they struck an underwater limb, and promptly capsized.

I watched with mounting concern as both paddlers popped quickly to the surface. My father-in-law gained his footing, standing chest-deep on an underwater limb. He tried to keep hold of the canoe despite the strong current. John had his arms securely latched around his grandfather's waist.

I quickly paddled back upstream to help them. I was troubled by the fact that there was no apparent way for my father-in-law to get his canoe ashore due to the steepness of the bank, the depth of the water, and the strength of the current.

Compounding the problem was the fact that their gear had fallen out of their canoe, and some of it began popping to the surface as well. As I tried to help them, I accidentally knocked a fishing pole out of my own canoe.

John soon climbed onto the capsized canoe and then hopped into the bow of mine, beside his younger brother. Both boys then scrambled up the bank using roots and

156

cypress knees for handholds. It was a relief to me when they both were safely ashore.

I retrieved as much of their gear as possible from the water and from beneath the capsized canoe and pulled it into my boat. Then came the task of righting the canoe in deep water.

Tough Resurrection

My father-in-law and I tried unsuccessfully to pick the canoe up and turn it over. Neither of us could get secure grips under the conditions in which we were working. I decided to try a new tack.

I paddled a short distance upstream and tried to pull my canoe out of the water, but heavy, wet gear filled the boat and the bank was steep. I began tossing things out and had to grab hold of the canoe several times when it started sliding down towards the river. I finally got it unloaded and securely ashore.

My father-in-law was still doing his best to hold onto his canoe in the rushing current. By now, he had been in the water for ten or fifteen minutes, and I could tell he was growing weary. Allan rejoined us and, for several minutes, we worked to get the canoe out of the water or turned right side up. No luck whatsoever. There simply was no place to stand and no way to get a good grip or leverage. The effort was quickly sapping our strength.

Suddenly, the limb my father-in-law had been holding onto with one hand broke. He had to let go of the canoe – which floated a few feet downstream into a tangle of limbs – and swim ashore, totally exhausted.

I eventually decided that the only way to extricate the boat was to get it downstream through the keyhole into quieter water. So I pulled off my shirt and scrambled down the bank into the murky yet surprisingly refreshing water. I worked the canoe free from the tangle of limbs, but it hung up on another submerged limb in the keyhole. The canoe was almost completely under water by this point, its bow sinking deeper by the moment. I was losing the battle and began having doubts about recovering it at all under these circumstances.

At this point, I decided the odds of losing the canoe were about 50-50. The current threatened to wedge it tightly beneath the logjam, but then I found firm footing on a stout limb submerged beneath the keyhole. After working the canoe back and forth, trying to raise it over the obstruction, I finally got it free and then pushed and pulled it through the passage into the unobstructed water downstream.

I set my sights on a sandbar near the left bank, but feared that I would be unable to maneuver the heavy, cumbersome craft over that way quickly enough. Shallow water extended beyond the sandbar to midstream, however, and just a few seconds later, I found secure footing. Relieved, I pulled the canoe onto the sandbar and flipped it over.

Assessing the Damage

The crisis had passed. I got into the canoe, pushed off into the river, and guided it downstream using my hands as paddles. I made for the opposite bank where Allan

This placid stretch of the Ogeechee River isn't indicative of the river's often tempestuous nature.

had earlier parked his Mohawk canoe on the muddy shore.

We next retrieved our gear, carried it to the canoes, fixed lunch, and began to assess the damage inflicted by our misadventure. We had lost three fishing poles and a few other miscellaneous items. Much of our food was wet as was nearly all our clothing and my father-in-law's sleeping bag. On the other hand, we were grateful that no one had been hurt.

About then, two fishermen in a johnboat puttered upstream. They informed us that the channel downstream to Herndon was mostly clear but that we were still 5 miles from the bridge we had expected to reach before lunch. I took their estimate with a grain of salt since boaters using motors are notorious for overestimating distances, but even so, I did not relish the idea of facing additional hazards and two more hours on the river.

After hours of battling deadfalls and then capsizing, with no way to dry out the wet sleeping bag and our clothing, realizing that we were far behind schedule and unlikely to reach our rendezvous point 30-miles downstream, our morale was low. We therefore elected to call it quits and pull out when we reached the bridge, ending our trip two days ahead of schedule.

Ultimately, the final "five-mile" stretch of river turned out to be less than two miles with only a couple of obstructions that we cleared without difficulty. We pulled up to the boat ramp at Herndon at 3:00 p.m. and, luckily, found a homeowner willing to

The 2003 version of the "Ogeechee River Ordeal" ended here.

drive us back to our vehicles at Colemans Lake. An hour later, after changing into dry clothes and loading our canoes, we parted ways with Allan and headed home.

I was disappointed that we had to cut our trip short, but felt certain it was the right thing to do under the circumstances. My father-in-law certainly did not express any reservations. The next evening, while watching the University of Georgia Bulldogs whip the Tennessee Volunteers, he announced with a smile, "I believe it was worth getting thrown in the river to come back and watch this."

I took a healthy bite from a slice of key lime pie and mumbled a happy agreement. Meanwhile, in southeast Georgia, the dark Ogeechee rushed headlong toward the Atlantic, uncaring and unrelenting, just as it has since the dawn of time.

The Luckiest Man On Earth?

A small-town boy from Georgia advanced through the ranks of the journalism world, endured a horrible experience at the hands of a criminal, and went on to become one of the captains of American society today.

MARY ANN ANDERSON

Just down the road from Gainesville, Georgia – about twelve miles or so – is the tiny town of Hoschton in Jackson County. This little burg is really nothing more than a crossroads communi-ty of about a thousand people, but one of its residents is per-haps the luckiest man in the world.

Reg Murphy came from humble beginnings – a small town boy who was the son of a country store owner and a first grade teacher. He rose above the ranks of his contemporaries to accomplish an array of amazing achievements – many of which others can only dream.

He has been president of the National Geographic Society, and editor and publisher of three of the most widely-read, Pulitzer Prize-winning newspa-pers in America, including the *Atlanta Journal-Constitution*. He counts golfing great Arnold Palmer and former President

George Bush (41) among his closest friends. He has been president of the U.S. Golf Association and regularly golfs in Scotland. He has traveled the world many times over, and married a woman whom he still calls the "best thing" that ever happened to him, and that only scratches the surface of his accomplishments.

"Lady Luck" may be Murphy's greatest asset. Many Georgians remember his days as editor of the *Atlanta Journal-Constitution*, but he is perhaps best remembered for a singular, mind-numbing incident 30 years ago that clouds his past darkly.

In 1974, when he was editor of the then singularly-named *Atlanta Constitution* (present-day *Atlanta Journal-Constitution*), he was kidnapped by an assailant, stuffed into the trunk of a car, and held for ransom under the worst of conditions for a staggering forty-nine hours. His abductor – William Williams – demanded (and received) $700,000 from the *Constitution*, and after the ransom was paid, Murphy's ordeal came to a close.

The Beginning

John Reginald "Reg" Murphy is the son of the late John Murphy, a shipping clerk who also ran a small country store, and the late Mae Ward Murphy, a first grade teacher. Both parents grew up mostly in Jackson and Hall Counties in north Georgia. The family wasn't wealthy by any stretch of the imagination. "We weren't starving," Murphy says of growing up in Hoschton, "but we certainly didn't have any money either."

Somewhere along the way, John Reginald became simply Reg, a moniker that seems to perfectly fit his laid-back lifestyle. Even though Reg has enjoyed a sterling career in journalism, he originally set out to go to medical school. After he was graduated from Gainesville High School, he enrolled at Mercer University in Macon to begin his studies.

While he was at Mercer, his life began moving in a different direction after he sought employment to help pay his expenses in school. He was hired as a reporter for the *Macon Telegraph*, the city's daily newspaper. Following his indoctrination into this profession and the world of business, his notions of medical school were put on the back burner.

Murphy found he had a knack for the writing profession. He did not complete his studies at Mercer, choosing instead to move to Massachusetts after winning a fellowship to Harvard University.

After he left Harvard (he didn't earn a degree there either, and still does not hold one, which is quite noteworthy considering his accomplishments in life), he worked as a business consultant for a company based in Philadelphia. "While it was an interesting world," he says of that time, "it really was not what I wanted to do."

Still searching for his niche in life, Murphy left the company and began working as a freelance writer. Then one day, his life changed – forever.

"I was freelancing when I got a telephone call from some people I had worked for at the *Constitution*," he recalls. "They asked me if I would like to come [to work for] the newspaper."

To make a long story short, the answer was "yes." As first a political reporter and then later as editor of the *Constitution*, Murphy became well-known in Atlanta, especially for his editorials, of which there eventually were hundreds and hundreds. When he sat down to figure it all up years later, he said the number of words he had written was "mind-boggling."

"That was eight hundred words a day, seven days a week, for seven years," he smiles in remembrance.

With his photo and editorials gracing the pages of the *Constitution* daily, Murphy generated a lot of public recognition for himself. Unfortunately, this attention also caught the eye of a radical individual with an axe to grind and criminal notions in mind.

Kidnapped!

On a winter day in February of 1974, Murphy was at his home when a stranger named William Williams appeared at his door. From the beginning, Murphy says he suspected something was amiss.

"It was clear that he was very nervous," says Murphy. "My little girl was upstairs, and I knew the only thing to do was to get out of the house, so I went out with him."

Under the pretense that he had 300,000 gallons of heating oil that he wanted to donate to charity, Williams, who was 25 years of age, instead pulled a gun on Murphy and told him that he was going to "straighten out the lying leftist press of America." That's when the nightmare began.

Williams immediately swathed tape over Murphy's eyes and forced him at gunpoint to get into the trunk of his car. Frightened of the unknown but realizing that he had no choice in the matter except to protect himself and his family, Murphy complied with everything Williams demanded, even to having his hands tied behind his back, which left him completely helpless. From that point forward, the nightmare steadily worsened. For the next forty-nine hours, it would prove to be the most horrible experience of Murphy's life.

After securing the startled editor in the trunk of his car, Williams began to drive around Atlanta, stopping occasionally to phone in ransom demands to the *Constitution*. Claiming that he represented a right-wing militia group, Williams demanded $700,000 from the newspaper in return for Murphy's release. While that may not sound like a lot of money today, in the early 1970s, it was a considerable sum, especially for a ransom.

A Terrible Ordeal

While the police, the FBI, and the newspaper scrambled to action for the next two days searching for Williams's car and gathering the cash needed for the ransom, Murphy, for the most part, was forced to remain helpless in the trunk of the car, all the while blindfolded and with his hands still securely tied behind his back. Not only did he fear for his life and the lives of his family, but he also was extremely uncomfortable in the darkness of the cramped trunk. One cannot completely imagine the horror of an experience of this nature without actually enduring it personally. For most individuals – even hardened soldiers or lawmen – it would be terrifying.

"We wandered around, drove around for most of the time," Murphy remembers. "A couple of times, I was allowed to get out of the car, but I was still blindfolded."

When I asked him about the worst part of the kidnapping, there was no hesitation as he described two of the most harrowing moments of the entire ordeal. "I was lying in the trunk of the car, listening to the radio," Murphy explained. "Williams had been listening to the news on the radio, which was all about the kidnapping. A newscaster interviewed my father and asked, 'How is your son going to handle all of this stress?' My father answered, 'Well, he's only afraid of one thing. He's afraid of snakes.' I could just imagine that Williams was going to drop some in the trunk of the car while my hands and feet were tied."

As bad as that could be for him, Murphy said his darkest hour – his most disheartening moment – actually came later. He remembers it clearly too: "Another time I was listening to the broadcast, and someone was taking one of the officers at the newspaper through my office. And I'll never forget this. They were talking about me in the past tense. They were saying 'he was,' and 'he did.'"

The thing that Murphy didn't know as he listened to himself being spoken of in the past tense was that several times the FBI had been close on Williams's trail because they knew where he was going to pick up the ransom money. "But when darkness came, they lost him," Murphy recalls. "They couldn't keep up with him."

While Williams seemingly lacked any compassion at all, at one point, he took Murphy to a hotel. When I asked him why he didn't take that chance to escape, Murphy explained simply, "I was just too tired. I just fell across the bed and went immediately to sleep. There were other people outside of the door or somewhere close by, but I was so exhausted that I didn't know what time it was or anything. I was still blindfolded."

After more than two days of Murphy's sinister captivity, Jim Minter, the *Constitution*'s managing editor, took two suitcases crammed with cash and delivered them to a remote spot off Georgia 400 Highway north of Atlanta. By delivering the money, the *Constitution* had held up its end of the bargain, and now it was time for Williams to honor his. The anguished Murphy knew the ordeal was finally coming to an end – one way or another.

Free At Last!

With the money in hand, Williams set out to release Murphy early in the evening. "He stopped the car and told me to get out," Murphy remembered. "I assumed then he was going to leave me dead in a ditch. I could see through the blindfold, and given the fact that I could identify him, I assumed I was going to die. Instead, the car drove away, and I found myself in the parking lot of a motel on the outskirts of town. As soon as I went in the door, the motel clerk knew who I was...because there was so much publicity..."

The clerk benevolently opened a room for Murphy, and then called the authorities. The nightmare, for the time being, was finally over.

Acting on good information and detective work, the authorities closed in on Williams. Within just six hours, he and his wife, Betty, were captured at their home just outside of Atlanta and the ransom money was recovered.

At the highly publicized trial some time later, Williams attempted to plead mental instability because of his drug use and the abuse he had received as a child. The jury, however, didn't buy it, and Williams was convicted of kidnapping and extortion, for which he received a sentence of forty years in prison. His wife was convicted of concealing the crime, and she was placed under three years' probation.

Most people would have thought the trauma was over at that point. However, the verdict, amazingly, didn't stand in Georgia.

"After the first trial in which he was convicted, the court overturned the verdict because of what it termed 'prejudicial pretrial publicity,'" Murphy explained. "He was tried again in Florida, where he was again convicted and got the same sentence."

Williams eventually served nine years in the federal prison system before he was paroled on the condition that he stay out of the state of Georgia. When that condition expired, Williams, who had become a born-again Christian and who had since remarried, returned to Atlanta, where he still resides today.

Reflecting Back

Now, more than thirty years later, Murphy says he still remembers many of the details of those two days quite vividly, including his thoughts during those chilling hours in the trunk.

"I actually played every golf course in my mind that I had ever been on to keep my sanity," he related. "I imagined hitting every shot and making every putt just to keep my mind occupied and doing something."

When I asked him if he still thinks or dreams about the kidnapping, his answer was matter-of-fact: "No, I don't dream about it, but I think about it all the time, because people ask me about it all the time. And I don't flinch when people ask about it – and they do, probably at least once a week, even now – but then, it had gotten to the point where I couldn't walk down the street without people asking me about it."

In the early 1970s, there was a rash of bizarre kidnappings, including the sensationalized incidents involving heiress Patty Hearst and Barbara Jane Mackle, but Murphy decided early on not to let his experience either define him or deny him his freedom. Clearly part of the reason he has come to terms with the kidnapping with such civility and fortitude is because he decided at the moment he ripped off his blindfold, that he would talk about it with anyone who asked. He says he realized that if he repressed his memories, it wouldn't be good for his heart or his soul.

There was still one question that I knew I had to ask. During the trial, Murphy, who describes himself as "very much so" religious – then and now – depicted Williams as "mean as hell." Noting the conviction with which he had described his religious beliefs, I asked him, "Have you forgiven Williams?"

"No," Murphy answered with a finality that indicated forgiveness might be long in coming – if ever. "That was a cruel thing to do to a human being. You just don't treat people like that."

"Even as a Christian, you haven't forgiven him?" I pressed.

"It has nothing to do with religion," he answered straightforwardly. "It has everything to do with the civil rights and the human rights of an individual."

I wanted to know, too, if he thought that Williams's crime against him was the catalyst for his becoming so well known in his career.

"Not really," he answered, once more with simple candor. "I look at it exactly in the opposite way. I overcame it. I didn't become a recluse; I didn't become all preachy. I pursued a career in spite of it rather than because of it. The answer is that I don't think it did me any good. I'm sure there were people who recognized my name because of the notoriety, but notoriety won't make you do a good job. Notoriety won't make you a good manager. Notoriety won't give you a continuing series of successes. A kidnapping won't do that for you; in fact, it won't do anything for you. The only thing it does do for you is that it tells you how you will react under extreme pressure and whether or not you will stay calm."

Sparkling Career

It was at this point that Reg Murphy offered another insight to his remarkable life. He laughed that he "couldn't keep a job" following the abduction experience. He said he left the *Constitution* not very long after the kidnapping, moving west to take over as publisher and editor of the *San Francisco Examiner*. He was recruited for the job, and he left Atlanta with little hesitation, content to leave the kidnapping behind him. But after he was in California for approximately six years, he said he "felt a need to get to some other place."

He ultimately moved back to the East Coast, to Baltimore, where he became publisher of the *Baltimore Sun* – again because he was recruited and not because he sought that particular job. At that time, four families owned the newspaper.

"They graciously let me buy into their stock," he related. Not only did his stint at the *Sun* allow him to become wealthy, but it also gave him the opportunity to revitalize the newspaper and help change its culture by introducing new editors and writers.

The *Sun* would bring him even better things, too, because it was there that he met his wife, Diana. She was well into her own career in advertising and circulation at the newspaper, and they found they had a great deal in common. The two married in 1991.

And without any sort of bragging whatsoever – only as a matter of fact – Murphy will tell you that on his wedding day to Diana, he just happened to play golf with George Bush – who just happened to be president of the United States at the time.

Reg Murphy's newspaper career at the *Constitution*, the *Examiner*, and the *Sun* helped pave the way to greater things too – even greater than playing golf with the president on his wedding day. He would eventually be recruited for one of the best and most sought-after jobs in journalism: the presidency of the National Geographic Society.

National Geographic Calls

Murphy says he wasn't really looking for a job at the time, but when he was offered a position with *National Geographic*, with the knowledge that he would more than likely become its president, he couldn't turn it down. Murphy says he has tremendous respect for *National Geographic* and the impact it has had on education. He relished an opportunity to be at the helm of what is undoubtedly one of the most glamorous jobs in print journalism, but he also maintains it was "the hardest" job he's ever had too.

"When I first took the job, it [the magazine] was so badly overstaffed that I had to cut from 2,300 employees down to about 1,200 in a year," he said. "That was as painful a job as I have ever done, but to survive, it was necessary." He explained he discovered that some individuals literally were employed as assistants to assistants to assistants. Something had to be done, and he eventually pared the employee roster down to a workable number.

During his five-year tenure at *National Geographic*, he was also recruited as president of the United States Golf Association. He loved both jobs with their glitz and travel, but there were also disadvantages. "For two years there, I didn't have a single day off, not one. But I had a great time!" he smiled.

At *National Geographic*, Murphy nurtured many changes in the famous publication, including the forging ahead with twenty foreign language editions of the magazine and the cable channel.

And if you're curious about the sort of writer who makes the cut into *National Geographic*, he'll tell you. "Not many people [get into *National Geographic*]. That's a tough market to crack. It takes somebody who is worldly, who has been around a while, and who understands how to put together a personal adventure. All of it is first person adventure...and it's the ability to see what other people might not see and the ability to translate scenes and emotions into words. But what it takes, also, is wonderful photography. A photographer will go out and work three or four months on a story, and he or she will shoot anywhere from eight hundred to a thousand rolls of film. That's twenty to thirty thousand pictures, and only about twenty-five of those will be published. An enormous amount of work goes into a quality story and photography."

While there was never any question as to *National Geographic*'s role in journalism, there was one particular event during Murphy's time as president of the Society that propelled the magazine even more dramatically into the public spotlight: the publication of Robert James Waller's *The Bridges of Madison County* and then the subsequent movie of the same name that starred Clint Eastwood as a *National Geographic* photographer who has an affair with an Iowa farmwife played by Meryl Streep.

Murphy laughs when he recalls the spectacular fuss that both the movie and book made. "It bore very little relationship to what we did everyday," he says with amusement. "But that was notoriety that was planted in a lot of people's minds to what they thought we did."

While sales of the magazine didn't spike because of the movie, the attention to it did. "The magazine was doing okay then, but the movie was more of a catalyst to propel the magazine into new realms," he stated. "So while it was not an epic event, it did help."

Diana and Reg Murphy at their Sea Island home in 2004.

Welcome Retirement

When Reg Murphy retired from *National Geographic* in 1998, he and Diana went through a very long and detailed search for a new place to call "home." He had been fortunate that he had been able to continue living in Baltimore while he worked at *National Geographic* in nearby Washington, D.C., but following his retirement, the couple was ready for a change.

Although they looked, as he says, "all up and down the East Coast and California," and despite the fact that they could have lived almost anywhere they chose, Murphy's roots ultimately called him back home to Georgia. He and Diana found their dream home on Sea Island, a place where they still live today. His verdant backyard lies on a canal, and on any given day he has plenty of herons and egrets for company, as well as the occasional otter. "I've just never found any place that I thought was as nice as this," he states.

Though he has left employment at the National Geographic Society, the word "retirement" isn't really in Murphy's vocabulary. He still stays busy all the time, and he swears that he will one day write his own autobiography. He says he plans to title it, not surprisingly, *The Luckiest Man I Ever Met.*

He has already penned other books, including *The Southern Strategy* with Hal Gulliver (Scribner, 1971) and *Uncommon Sense: The Achievement of Griffin Bell* (Longstreet Press, 2001). He has been involved with writing "lots of other books," and is now working on the Carl Drury story.

While he is still writing, traveling, and enjoying fine wine and food, he is also a trustee of Mercer University and on the boards of several international companies, including the National Geographic Society. He also attends a weekly Bible study class – when he's home. Most of the year, he is gone at least two or three nights a week. He still plays golf too. Some of his current golfing partners include his wife Diana; former U.S. Senator Sam Nunn; CBS broadcaster and Meet the Press moderator and Sea Island neighbor Bob Schieffer; and of course, Arnold Palmer and George Bush.

From a former marriage, Murphy has two daughters, Karen and Susan. Karen lives in Alpharetta, Georgia; she is the mother of two boys, Jonathan and David. Susan is, like her dad, a writer. She lives in Midtown Atlanta. No matter what else he does or where he goes, Murphy always makes time for his family.

Before our interview ended, I asked Murphy what he considered his most crowning achievement in his career. "That was the active recruitment of me for one job while I held another," he says without hesitation. "I have never applied for a job in my life. That was an indication that people saw the results of what I was doing, and they wanted to hire me to do it for them. And it's important to me that I turned down more jobs than I accepted, because that's a fairly significant thing. You just don't start out expecting to have that much good fortune unless you were born under totally different circumstances than I was. Everything has to fall into place. You have to be extraordinarily lucky."

Lucky indeed – the luckiest man on earth.

The Allgood Family Tragedies

They came to the northwest corner of the state to take advantage of the abundant water-power and establish a major mill at a time when cotton was becoming king in the South. Their efforts were successful, but along the way, they suffered death and despair at the hands of others.

Deborah Malone

In 1880, at the age of 26, DeForest Allgood took over the reins of Trion Factory in northwest Georgia's Chattooga County after his father, Andrew Perry Allgood passed away. The elder Allgood had brought progress and prosperity to the area, and his son who succeeded him proved to be his equal. A scant eight years later, however, DeForest's life would be cut short when he was killed in a terrible accident which still perplexes historians even today.

Interestingly, DeForest's killer was a man he had known all his life – indeed, he was a relative. The families of the two men had enjoyed cordial relations for many years, and both were considered among the most prominent in the region. What precipitated this terrible violence?

To obtain a full understanding of the events which transpired to cause this tragedy, one must go back to the earliest days of the town of Trion, Georgia, back to a time when the first white residents arrived in the region. One of these families – the Allgoods – would experience remarkable successes, as well as pain and suffering.

(L-R) Andrew Perry Allgood, DeForest Allgood, and A.S. Hamilton.

Trion Manufacturing Company employees gather in front of the factory's store in 1877.

Beginnings

In 1832, most of northwest Georgia (including the area comprising present-day Trion) was surveyed and divided into 160-acre land lots for which ownership was granted via a land lottery. Soon thereafter, settlers began arriving in the area, dispossessing the native Cherokees who were soon to depart in the infamous "Trail of Tears."

In the late 1830s, Spencer Marsh from Chatham County, North Carolina, opened a business in the tiny but growing northwest Georgia community of LaFayette. A short time later, Andrew Perry Allgood followed, opening a store of his own in the town.

Instead of becoming rivals as one might have imagined, the two men became fast friends. Marsh and Allgood, in fact, got along so well that they decided to go into business together.

Other evidences of this bond may be found in the fact that on June 22, 1842, Andrew Perry Allgood and Mary Marsh (Spencer Marsh's daughter) were united in matrimony. Andrew was 26 and Mary was a youthful 15 – a not unusual age for marriage in those times.

After examining several places, the two men settled on a spot known at the time as "Island Town," later to be renamed "Trion." They made several purchases in the area with the last being 160 acres procured from a Mr. William Penn.

Penn, no doubt, was known as a tough businessman, because according to one account of the transaction, he demanded to be paid in gold coins (other accounts list silver). As a result, Allgood and Marsh were reported to have produced $6,000 in gold, pouring what then was a fortune on Penn's table in order to allow the crusty curmudgeon to count the shiny coins.

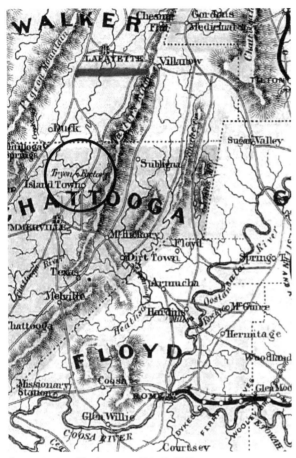

"Tryon Factory" is shown on this Civil War-era map.

Though the above transaction in general is accurate, some of the details – handed down through time – may have been exaggerated or misstated. According to *Chattooga County: The Story of a County and Its People*, "Penn may very well have demanded gold for his land, but deed records zshow that he was paid $1,100 for the land, not $6,000."

According to records in the Chattooga County Courthouse, a third investor – Col. W.K. Briers – joined the men. The company they created had a capital investment of $25,000. These men obviously knew how to generate capital, because sums of this nature in the wilds of north Georgia were practically nonexistent in the 1840s.

The First Mill

On October 12, 1845, the men opened their new factory and embarked upon what would become a productive career. In its first days, the business employed 40 hands – enough to run the first 600 spindles.

By 1862, the mill had prospered, and a town – "Trion" – (in deference to the triumvirate of men who began the community's first business) was incorporated by the State Legislature. The original town limits extended for one mile in every direction with the mill as the center of the community.

Trion Factory enjoyed the distinction of being the first cotton mill in northwest Georgia. Its nearest competitor was located more than 100 miles away in Roswell, Georgia. Still in existence today, the Trion mill has operated continuously since 1847, with little interruption. For only a short period in 1858, it was shut down due to a typhoid epidemic; again for approximately 12 months near the end of the U.S. Civil War; and finally for several months due to a fire in 1875.

Somewhat miraculously, the mill even survived the onslaught of General William

T. Sherman's infamous "March To The Sea" across Georgia. According to Scott Thomas, historian and development manager of what today is called "Mt. Vernon Mills," the endeavor actually avoided destruction as a result of a "Yankee" connection.

"Allgood, from what I have read and heard, was what was known as a Union man," Thomas explained. "He wasn't that supportive of the war. They did have contracts with the Confederacy to supply them with goods, but it has been said that if there was a [Unionist] in the area that was in trouble, Allgood would help him out.

"When Sherman came through, he actually stayed the night in Allgood's house," Thomas continued. "Allgood reportedly agreed to stop operations until the war was over. This might have been the contributing factor that saved the mill and kept it from being burned down."

This explanation may or may not be the total story. One might wonder if a relationship or relationships above and beyond a simple agreement to cease operations until the end of the war existed between Allgood and the Union authorities. There were far too many other mills (Roswell Mill being a good example) that provided ample proof of ownership by individuals non-supportive of the Confederacy, which nevertheless were burned to the ground.

According to *Chattooga County: The Story Of A County And Its People*, there was in fact an official Georgia state investigation into this matter on June 11, 1869, five years after the war. According to Allgood's formal statement to state officials, "When General Sherman passed our place in October 1864, he stayed all night with me & next morning gave me protection papers. Gen. O.O. Howard sent a large guard to

By the early 1900s, Trion Manufacturing had become a substantial enterprise.

the factory to protect all the property there and showed no disposition to destroy any of our property except provisions. I took extra pains to let the Union men of the county know my status or position and rendered them all the aid I could when they were in trouble & [I] was known as a Union man. We stopped running on May 10th, 1864 & run no more – until peace."

This explanation must have satisfied the state investigators – whatever their purpose – but it also became the catalyst for retribution attacks against Allgood by Confederate loyalists in the area. There had been much suffering at the hands of the Union Army in the 1860s, and the memory of these deprivations was burned deeply into the minds and souls of the Southern families who survived it.

Ironically, even though there were many with Southern sentiments who felt betrayed by Allgood, his decision to shut down the mill during the war not only benefited him, but, indirectly, the area residents as well. The fact that he was able to save his factory and fortune (since he did not invest in Confederate bonds or currency) meant the difference between commerce and financial ruin for many people and businesses in Chattooga County in the years immediately following the war.

Fire At The Factory!

Despite the fact that Allgood saved his factory from Sherman's torch, it ultimately fell victim to a fire nonetheless on April 10, 1875. The conflagration had obviously been set by arsonists. A news account in the Rome *Commercial* newspaper chronicled the incident:

"The well known and valuable property Trion Factory situated on the Chattooga River twenty-five miles from Rome and five miles from Summerville, was completely destroyed with all its machinery last Saturday night," the *Commercial* detailed. "The factory was the joint property of Judge Allgood, living at Trion, and Mr. Spencer Marsh of Lafayette.

"The fire was undoubtedly the work of an incendiary," the *Commercial* intoned. "It was first discovered about half past eight o'clock. So soon as discovered, someone was sent up the channel to raise the gate so that a supply of water could be had. So soon as that person returned to the burning factory, some...scoundrel let the gate down, thus cutting off the water. Again someone was sent to raise the gate, and again was the gate was let down. For the third time was the water gate lowered. After this third repetition of villainy, a guard was stationed at the gate, but now it was too late, and the fire fiend had wrapped its withering arms about the building and it melted away as frost before the hot rays of the sun."

Clearly, Andrew Perry Allgood, as a result of his announced Unionist stance, had created a number of enemies in northwest Georgia. Area Confederate loyalists were not about to allow him to "have his cake and eat it too."

The mill was a total loss, but this did not deter Allgood. It was said that as soon as he knew the fire would destroy the mill, he sent men to the woods to scout out trees that would qualify for use in the rebuilding of the mill.

Barely six months later, a new and more grandiose mill – Trion Manufacturing Company – had been erected and was in operation. It boasted 258 looms, and two stories with the lower made of brick.

Andrew Perry Attacked

Allgood's problems, however, did not end with his factory. On February 24, 1874, just a little over a month before the factory fire, an attempt was made on the judge's life by an individual named John Fant. Little is known concerning this incident today, other than the fact that it occurred at the mill in Trion, and there evidently were five individuals who witnessed the attack, or some portion of it. Fant subsequently was arrested, indicted by a Chattooga County Grand Jury, and charged with assault with intent to commit murder.

Although nothing in the court records indicates the reason for Fant's attempt on Allgood's life, the motive once again could possibly have been Allgood's Unionist sentiments. This was a very incendiary issue at the time, and damage to the property of and assaults on untold numbers of individuals – both Unionists and Confederates – routinely occurred.

In 1875, Spencer Marsh passed away, and management of Trion Manufacturing Company fell solely to Andrew Perry Allgood. Not long thereafter, however, Allgood's health began to decline as well. No doubt the stress of rebuilding the mill and the dangers of his community had taken a toll on the feisty businessman.

In 1880, the elder Allgood turned over management of the mill to his only son, DeForest – affectionately known as "Deedy." Two years later, Andrew Perry Allgood passed quietly away.

At the young age of 26, DeForest Allgood inherited a sizeable task – the management of the affairs of a large and growing mill. Despite his age, however, he was not a stranger to the workings of the enterprise. Having been mentored by his father since the age of 14, he actually was well-qualified for the job.

DeForest represented a new generation at the mill, and began to inject new life into the business. He began by improving the physical condition of the mill. He then turned his attention toward making improvements in the mill village and encouraged community leaders to make improvements as well.

During his eight years at the helm of the mill, DeForest replaced the business's water power with gas-generated power. Another major accomplishment that would further advance the mill into the 20th century was the arrival of the railroad in 1888.

Death For DeForest

Just as he was gaining momentum with improvements and new developments at the mill, tragedy struck young DeForest. It was a catastrophe that remains shrouded in mystery even today.

According to official records, DeForest met death at the hands of a person who not only was his brother-in-law, but a medical doctor as well. Dr. J.B.S. Holmes of Rome, Georgia, was married to Addie M. Allgood, DeForest's sister.

The Allgood House, built by DeForest Allgood in the 1890s, was demolished in the 1970s.

Like DeForest, Dr. Holmes was well-liked by most people in his community. He was a skilled and dedicated physician as well as able businessman. The 1888 Rome City Directory described Dr. Holmes as follows:

"Strong in physique, in mental powers, in mental forces and in finances; such is the man whose name stands sponsor for this sketch. In his robustness, Dr. Holmes is refreshing to look upon. In his cheerfulness of disposition, he is the embodiment, the beau ideal of a life crowned with success and at peace with all mankind.

"Dr. Holmes is still a young man, but he has achieved such success as comes to but few. As a director in the Rome Land Company, and the Rome Street Railway Company, he takes an active interest in developing the growth and propriety of his city, and every enterprise of worth finds in him an ardent and liberal friend."

What events transpired between these two men to cause Dr. Holmes to feel the need to take the life of DeForest, his wife's brother? Mr. DeForest Hamilton of present-day Rome, is the grandson of Alford Shorter Hamilton, the husband of Margaret Marsh Allgood, DeForest Allgood's sister. Mr. Hamilton was kind enough to share some of the family history with this writer.

Rome's Armstrong Hotel was an impressive piece of architecture when completed in 1888. It was outside this building that DeForest Allgood was shot and killed by his brother-in-law, Dr. J.B.S. Holmes, in 1890.

Shooting Details

Interestingly, Mr. Hamilton's father, DeForest Allgood Hamilton, Sr., wrote a history of his family which has survived to the present day. Judging from what the elder Hamilton wrote, the precipitating factors in the shooting which took the life of DeForest Allgood were nothing more than simple pride and insulting behavior on the part of the combatants. If the facts bear out the explanation provided by Mr. Hamilton, the incident was a ridiculous, rash, and tragic accident.

"It happened this way," Mr. Hamilton wrote. "The two men had many arguments over the merits of their horses and bird dogs so I've been told. On this date, Dr. Holmes drove up to the front of the Armstrong Hotel, located on Second Avenue (Rome) and had his shotgun in his buggy. DeForest Allgood came out of the hotel and reached for his hip pocket in which he had both a gun and a handkerchief. Dr. Holmes, thinking he was reaching for his gun, raised his shotgun and killed him. Dr. Holmes was tried by a jury and acquitted."

According to other testimony of the incident, it was believed that Allgood had a cold and was simply reaching for his handkerchief. Had Dr. Holmes actually believed that Allgood was reaching for his gun? It is unknown today what might have caused him to so fear for his life that he felt the need to take so rash an action as shooting Allgood. One has to wonder if other motives were afoot to instigate such a tragic event.

Digging through the courthouse records, this writer discovered Criminal Docket Book #5 in the Floyd County Superior Courthouse. On page 205 of this record, dated March, 1890, the verdict of "Not Guilty" in the murder case of The State Vs. J.B.S. Holmes is listed.

Further attempts to locate a transcript from the trial proved fruitless. This writer did, however, find an interesting note that was written by someone who had attended the trial. It was discovered among the papers in the John L. Harris files in the Rome/Floyd County Library. An excerpt from the note reads as follows:

"I suppose it was just curiosity – no ill feeling that brought me in to listen while Dr. Holmes was delivering his address to the jury – keeping his hand on his forehead most of the time.

"He (Dr. Holmes) explained that he and Mr. Allgood had had a quarrel, about some property I think, and that he had left town and gone hunting to avoid him. Coming back he had stopped at the Armstrong Hotel, for a quick drink, I imagine, at the hotel bar – a usual ornament at hotels then, his own fine home being only two blocks off on Second Avenue."

It is unknown today if the above statement was written by John L. Harris, or if it is some bit of information he collected during his tenure as the court clerk of the Rome/Floyd County Superior Court. Along with this statement was a cryptic notation "minutes of Floyd Superior Court #24, page 256."

Was DeForest's death really simply the result of rash action? Was there some dark foreboding secret which caused Dr. Holmes to lash out? Perhaps we will never know all the details today.

Aftermath

Whatever the circumstances, DeForest Allgood was laid to rest in LaFayette in the family plot. A short time later, however, the body was removed and secretly interred in a plot in Griffin, Georgia, where it remains today. The *Chattooga News* made the following bit of information public on August 9, 1893:

"On the evening of January 20th D.F. Allgood boarded Dan Ramsey's train at Trion bound for Rome. He was in his usual cheerful and happy mood, and if there was a shadow to mar his future, or a foreboding of his impending death, his fellow passengers could not detect it by his conduct.

"That night he was killed, and on Wednesday following, the body was placed on Dan Ramsey's train to be carried to Trion where thousands were waiting to see him dead, who had loved him dearly while living.

"Again, last Monday, Conductor Ramsey had the body on board his car for removal to Griffin. Past the homes of those who had known him from boyhood up; past the busy, humming mills that had been his pride; past the beautiful home that promised more of earthly happiness than falls to the lot of most people; past all these and away among strangers save one, as it goes now for a final resting place."

Following DeForest's death, the operations of the mill were turned over to his brother-in-law, Alfred Shorter Hamilton. He was married to Margaret Marsh Allgood on April 10th, 1888. Under his guidance from 1890 to 1910, many improvements were made to the mill, but it was a tenure that was not without its problems.

In 1911, Trion Mill surprisingly faced bankruptcy, and was sold to Mr. Benjamin D. Riegel of New York. Although this would be the end of the Allgood dynasty in the mill, the enterprise has continued to thrive and has become one of the leading denim manufacturing factories in the nation today.

According to Scott Thomas of Mt. Vernon Mills, "The mill has 1,100,000 square feet of manufacturing space, consumes 2,500,000 pounds of cotton each week (3,500 acres-worth) and produces 2,700,000 square yards of denim each week (over 850 miles)."

Though the Allgood family endured their fair share of triumphs and tragedies, the mill Andrew Perry Allgood founded in 1845, still provides many employment opportunities and much commercial enterprise for his beloved community of Trion, Georgia. Both Andrew and DeForest would be proud.

The Last Promise In Braswell

They met during the trauma of World War I in a tiny community in northwest Georgia. She waited for him in vain, but kept him in her heart forever.

Carol Thompson

"I guess I've lived a long life for many reasons. I've always trusted in God. I drink a glass of water every morning, and well...I've never been married," my 98-year-old great aunt once said to me, with a hint of laughter in her voice. I knew, of course, that her solitary life was not by choice...then again, in actuality, it was.

I don't guess I'll ever forget this conversation with Aunt Irene. A native of Braswell, Georgia, she lived in the old Camp homeplace for most of her life. Born in 1897, Irene Camp saw many changes over part of two different centuries, and she passed on some valuable lessons to us children.

At the time, heritage wasn't that important to me, and I guess the opportunities I missed in talking with her about life in general will haunt me forever, for she was not just a living breathing part of history, but part of my personal history as well.

Looking back over the years, it could be

Irene Camp

said this woman, born in the mountains of northwest Georgia during a very difficult time in history, paid a supreme sacrifice of sorts. The oldest of six children, she accepted a lot of responsibility – as did most during that age. She cooked, scrubbed, made soap, milked the cow, and took care of the younger children, and never once complained.

The Early Years

Her home was in the foothills of Braswell Mountain on historic Brushy Mountain Road in Paulding County, Georgia. She lived all of her 98 years on the same family lot. Her family did have to rebuild and renovate a couple of times because of tragic fires, but always on the same lot.

Families had settled on the fertile farmlands in the Braswell area after the creation of the Southern Railroad through the vicinity in 1882. Upon completion of a depot, the town of Braswell was established in 1895. It was named after a prominent citizen –

The Camp family at the homeplace in Braswell. L-R (rear) Bealie Camp, Thomas G. Camp, Sarah, Irene, and Maude; (front) Bersha, T.G., and Bernice.

Henry Braswell – who owned a sizeable sawmill there and also worked for the railroad.

In earlier years, Aunt Irene had spent time working in Battey Hospital in nearby Rome. This facility was used almost exclusively for the treatment of tuberculosis at one time.

Aunt Irene attended Berry School (present-day Berry College), but it was nowhere near as elite and prestigious a school as it is today. Ironically, during her days there, Berry was a school for the poor and indigent.

Aunt Irene also spent time at Wahsega Camp in Dahlonega, Georgia. Interestingly, some 70 years later, this same camp would host me, her great niece.

Most of my aunt's adult years were spent as the teacher at Braswell School. It was this role in life for which she was best known and loved.

One of the most interesting and romantic times in her life occurred around the year 1914. Our country was in the midst of World War I, and chaos was being played out overseas. Although that conflict seemed a world away, safeguards were soon initiated to protect valuable resources right here in her hometown in the Braswell Mountains.

At that time, Irene was in her early teens. Life in the hills consisted mainly of working, "churching," and enjoying what little entertainment could be found within walking distance of one's home. A social life depended on who in the community was

Friends of the Camp family pose on the Southern Railway tracks just below Braswell Depot.

within your age limits and walking area.

The little community of Braswell had a very small population, and there weren't many – if any – opportunities for romance for Aunt Irene. Unbeknownst to her however, a change of pace was on the way.

Soldiers In Our Midst

Although the world was in turmoil and had been for a couple of years, little had changed in Braswell until sometime around the summer of 1914. At that time, American soldiers were sent to guard the tunnels in the area which were suspected to be a red hot target of any enemies wanting to damage the lifelines of the military.

Southern Railways was used to transport much needed food, military equipment and supplies to the front line, and a main line passed right through the Braswell Mountains. An injury to this direct line could prove very injurious to the U.S. military.

In 1904, the Seaboard Railroad was also graded through the area, and, just as Southern Railway, the builders had to tunnel through the rough terrain of Braswell Mountain to establish their line. The Seaboard tunnel is named Brushy Mountain Tunnel, but the Southern tunnel, to my knowledge, has no formal name. It has always just been called the Braswell Tunnel.

Interestingly, it was known that the President of the United States sometimes traveled to various destinations using the Southern Railways line. As a result, the little town of Braswell was suddenly deluged with new faces and a dramatically-changed lifestyle as military men came to town. It went from a community of less than 100 people to a town with at least 100 new temporary residents.

According to details supplied by my grandmother who is Aunt Irene's sister, (for Irene was a very shy and modest lady), she (Irene) often traversed the customary routes of the soldiers in those days. The assigned troops would march several times daily from one tunnel to the other (there were several). Their horses and wagons were housed at my great-grandfather's place.

Mr. and Mrs. Joel Walker at Braswell Depot, circa 1914.

The soldiers usually stopped at the well at the Camp's home place to get a sip of the cool, sweet water. Irene initially avoided the soldiers, because they and their strange uniforms, guns, and equipment scared her younger siblings. However, in the course of several weeks, she suddenly changed her habits and began instead to regularly patronize the soldiers' routes. It seems one young man among the troopers had caught her fancy.

One day, it just so happened that she was drawing water at the well at the exact same moment that the troops marched by, and also by coincidence, she noticed that very same soldier that she had fancied was smiling at her. After a couple of bumbled attempts to speak to one another amidst a fear that the commanding officer would punish the young man for fraternizing with a young lady, the soldier finally succeeded in greeting Irene and introducing himself.

He explained his name was Newal Short. Weeks went by with the same routine. Irene and Newal would just happen to "desperately need" a drink of water and would hurry to their meeting place. Hours of conversation and preliminaries of courtship would be packed into stolen minutes at the well. Love is a funny thing... For many people, once they have it, they never lose it. Such was the case with Aunt Irene.

Although the world was at war, Irene and Newal lived only for their brief encounters each day. As the couple's love progressed, they were unaware that the war was inextricably drawing them apart day by day.

The two entrances to the Braswell tunnel, photographed in 2004. The north side remains fully open, but sediment has filled the lower half on the south side.

As the days passed, the couple continued to enjoy their stolen moments. They knew that it might not be long before the war would need Newal some place else, but when it was over, he could always return.

Off To War

Finally, several months into their newfound relationship, Newal received the crushing news that he and his fellow comrades would be sent overseas. The Germans were advancing more than the U.S. had hoped and additional troops were needed.

Military decisions are usually swift and decisive, and this troop relocation was no exception. The men were packing and on the move before most knew why or where.

Knowing only that he and his comrades were leaving to go overseas to fight on the front lines, Newal desperately wanted see Irene one last time. He ran to the well and waited for her despite the unusual time of day.

When Irene saw him waiting earlier than usual, her heart dropped. She had a gut-wrenching hunch that something wasn't quite right. This time, their conversation was more brief than usual. Newal was desperate, and undoubtedly feared he might never see his beloved again. He promised, however, to come back if she promised to marry him upon his return. It was a request to which Irene gladly agreed. The promise was sealed with the only kiss ever exchanged by the two. With his hat in his hand and a tear in her eye, the couple bid each other a sad farewell.

Not long after that, life returned to normal in the little town of Braswell, despite the turmoil of fighting occurring a world away in Europe. At first, Irene received letters from Newal, most of which reconfirmed his commitment to her. Irene read them and held them close to her heart, longing for the day this promise would come true.

Love Unrequited

One day, however, the letters ceased, and Irene eventually realized – much to her sadness – that her love would remain unrequited forever. She spoke little of the soldier at the well thereafter, and most people never even knew he had existed until Irene was way up in her years. She, nevertheless, grieved terribly for him, and that was obvious to many people.

Over the years, most of us eventually learned the story of her lost love, but knew that discussing "romantic issues" with an elderly spinster was not proper etiquette. We knew that this had been the love of her life and she would never know exactly what had happened to him.

Some of us wondered if her love had merely lost interest while he was overseas, but she quelled that suggestion one day by saying, "Newal was a good person. He would have told me if he changed his mind so as I wouldn't worry. He made a promise, and promises are made to keep."

I guess Aunt Irene kept her promise as well. She lived ninety-eight years in the hills of Braswell where she grew up. She never married, and I suspect there wasn't a day when she didn't miss her one true love. She's gone now, and I suspect there will never be a day when I don't miss her either, but the lesson of her strength of character will live with me to my dying days.

Epilogue

Although the above story has been told many times in my family, the details of Aunt Irene's lost love remain unverified. I have searched military records numerous times for Newal Short's name, using many different variations of spellings, all to no avail. I have written to the U.S. government for some form of service verification but have received nothing.

Mr. Short's hometown is a mystery of equal proportions today. Some of my family members "think" it was New York. I did find a "N. Short" that was "Killed in Action" in 1916 but he was from the United Kingdom. I guess this individual might possibly have been him, but here again, I have little information to confirm that possibility.

It is also unknown by this writer if the railroad tunnels through Braswell were actually strategic sites during World War I. Some old-timers in the area still tell of the days when the soldiers "guarded the tunnels," but I have been unable to find any confirmation of this in historic archives.

Regardless of the circumstances, I hope my Aunt Irene discovered immediately after her own passing that her heart had been right. Personally, I would like to know where he was buried and the details of his war service, but in retrospect, I guess it really doesn't matter. He was Aunt Irene's love and they are both gone forever. I have simply put pen to paper to document this wonderful yet traumatic account of love and war which took place so many years ago in a small town in the hinterlands of northwest Georgia.

The Murders Of Lawmen
Virgil Griner and Harbard Smith

Nathan S. Hipps

Documented from court records and newspaper reports, the following dramatized account of the cold-blooded murders of these two law enforcement officers still haunts Ben Hill County in south Georgia.

Three slices of sweet potato pie were missing when Etta Smith checked the refrigerator. She had expected it. Her father, Harbard, had a habit of taking food down to the jail on weekends for his prisoners. His generosity with her cooking always irritated Etta. She didn't want her culinary efforts going into the stomach of some common criminal, but there was nothing she could do or say about it. Harbard, the long-time jailer of Ben Hill County, did pretty much as he pleased, and this often included a stern but compassionate care of his prisoners in the county jail.

He'd become even more stubborn in old age, if that was possible. He worked whether he felt good or not, and on most days, in his own mind, he felt fine. In a year's time, he would celebrate his fiftieth anniversary on the job, a feat unparalleled in Ben Hill County's history. He planned to retire at the end of 1952 and finally begin taking it easy for a while. He was seventy-seven years old, and his reflexes just weren't as sharp as they had been in his youth.

Etta nagged Harbard constantly about retirement. She couldn't understand for the life of her why he wanted to keep working. "You're an old man; too old to be running off after some chicken thief!" she complained.

Harbard's reply invariably irritated her even more. "Maybe I am old, but I can assure you that the chicken is glad I'm still doing my job," he would say.

His flippant attitude riled Etta to distraction. She often warned him that he was playing with fire, and that one day he would be badly burned. She didn't know it at the time, but her words would prove to be terribly prophetic shortly.

Jailer & Jailbirds

Harbard waited outside the jail cell while his three prisoners greedily wolfed down the sweet potato pie he had brought them. They were harmless folk for the most part. One was drying out after an all-night drinking binge. The other two were cooling off after a public brawl over a woman of questionable repute.

Despite the relatively harmless nature of the men, Harbard nevertheless cautiously kept himself out of arm's reach of the prisoners. He nervously jingled a pocketful of change. The clinking noise reverberated through the cells, a sound reminiscent of

The Murders Of Lawmen Virgil Griner and Harbard Smith

LEFT: John Harbard Smith was the jailer at Ben Hill County Jail, and died instantly from a gunshot wound to the chest. RIGHT: James Virgil Griner (55) was the sheriff of Ben Hill County for 15 years, and was highly respected in the community of Fitzgerald. He was fatally wounded by Allen Spires during an investigation in 1951.

myriad coins tap dancing down a flight of stairs.

"If you boys feel the need to visit here again next weekend, I can promise each of you a slice of the tastiest pecan pie you'll ever put in your mouth," Harbard smiled. "My daughter-in-law is making it to celebrate my forty-ninth year on the job."

"Forty nine years?" one of the men slyly asked, incredulous. "You that old Mr. Smith?"

Harbard chuckled. "That and then some. I've been locking people up in this jail way before you boys were born. I even locked up your daddy, Ernest. And for doing the same thing you did – fightin' over a woman."

"I wouldn't have to be fightin' at all if some back-stabbin' polecat had kept his paws to himself." Ernest then spat at his rival, Cal, in the adjoining cell.

"Knock it off Ernest," Harbard quickly commanded, as he collected the prisoners' empty plates. "You want me to add another day to your sentence?"

"If it meant not having to look at his ugly mug I wouldn't mind it!" Ernest shot back, glaring at the object of his hate.

"Fine by me," Cal responded. "It'd just give me an extra day with your woman!"

Ernest slammed his open hand against the cell bars, seething once again with rage. "I'm gonna kill you Cal!" he screamed.

By this time, Harbard had heard enough. "Shut up!" he suddenly yelled. "Both of you! If I so much as hear a peep out of either one of you somebody's gonna be sleepin' under the jail tonight!"

When Harbard Smith was serious, he could still bore holes through a person with a single glance. He meant business, and both of the boys knew it. They turned their backs on each other and stood in stony silence.

A Moonshine Suspect

When Harbard returned downstairs to the office, Sheriff Virgil Griner was sitting with his feet propped up on his desk. "I thought you'd be gone for the rest of the day," the jailer said, surprised to see his superior.

"Me, too," the sheriff replied with a smirk on his face. "I got side-tracked. Saw that Ford station wagon out on the highway again. I doubled back and followed him for awhile. Think I spooked him though, cause he headed straight for home. Didn't turn off the highway or go into town. Went home like any good ol' boy would do who was totin' a load of 'shine in his car with the sheriff on his tail."

"You think he's our man?" Harbard asked, his interest piqued.

"I know he is. What else would he be doing on the Ashton Highway as much as he is? And don't tell me it's just coincidence that there's a still right off the highway next to the county line and he just happened to be ridin' by it."

"How come you didn't stop him?" Harbard asked as he placed the dirty dishes into a bag.

"I didn't actually see him come up off the old county road onto the highway. For all I know, he could've been out for an innocent Saturday afternoon drive," Virgil replied, glancing over his shoulder at Harbard. "And if you believe that, I got a parcel of land down at Ocmulgee Swamp you might be interested in."

"What do you want to do about him?"

"Why don't we take a little trip down the Ashton Highway in the morning," the sheriff smiled contemplatively. "Park the car in that clearing just east of the county road and see if Mr. Spires pays us a visit."

Harbard could see the wheels turning inside the sheriff's head, formulating a plan to catch the suspect red-handed. He circled the next day's date – August 26, 1951 – on his calendar, reminding himself to let his prisoners go before he and Virgil went looking for Allen Spires.

A Fateful Day

The following morning, Etta got up early – just in time to see Harbard leaving the house. It was Sunday, and she expected him to transport her to church as he did every Sunday. He wouldn't say why he was leaving the house so early, or even when he'd be back.

"Well how am I supposed to get to church?" Etta pouted.

"Get a ride with Junior and Lou. It won't kill you to vary your routine, Etta," Harbard replied, as he closed the car door and drove off.

Etta watched from the doorway, muttering to herself how unappreciated she was.

Meanwhile, back at the jail, Harbard released his three prisoners and sent them on their way before Virgil showed up. Ernest was still cranky and started to go after Cal,

Fitzgerald Herald

OFFICIAL ORGAN OF BEN HILL COUNTY

FITZGERALD, GEORGIA, TUESDAY, AUGUST 28, 1951   NUMBER 69

Slayer Is Still At Large

Officers Disperse As Trail Of Slayer Cools

Ben Hill county jailer, John H. Smith is dead, and Sheriff J. Virgil Griner is in Piedmont Hospital in Atlanta, with four bullet wounds in his shoulders following a shooting affair in which Allen Spires is alleged to have done the shooting.

According to Frank Ellis, deputy sheriff, Sheriff Griner and his jailer, John H. Smith, were taking their usual Sunday morning ride out Ashton road and were listening to a special song service that was being played over the local radio, as was their usual habit, when they passed a maroon station wagon being driven by Allen Spires.

Spires is said by Ellis to have a court record involving illicit whiskey dealing.

The sheriff overtook the station wagon and ordered Spires to drive to the side of the road and stop. Instead, according to Mr. Ellis, Spires increased his speed, with the sheriff out running him and forcing him to

but Harbard quickly cuffed the boy on the side of the head and threatened to re-jail him, putting an end – at least for the moment – to the aggressive youth's behavior.

Harbard then turned his attention to preparations for the morning patrol with Virgil. The sheriff arrived shortly, and the two then drove out to the clearing east of the county road as planned. The car was virtually invisible to anyone passing from north to south toward the Ashton Highway. A stand of pines and thick undergrowth concealed their presence.

The two lawmen waited in silence, neither daring to speak for fear of tipping their hand. Harbard's senses were on full alert. If anything was stirring in the woods around them, he'd know it.

Harbard checked his watch. It was eight-thirty. They might have to wait all day for Spires if he was to pass by at all.

Suddenly, however, a car engine could be heard in the distance slowly being cranked. It sputtered a few times, and then someone eased it into gear. Sheriff Griner rose expectantly in his seat, his fingers at ready on the ignition. An automobile appeared in the distance and made its way down the dusty county road. As the car crept past, Harbard – watching between two large pines – got a good look at the driver. It was Allen Spires.

The suspected bootlegger pulled his old station wagon onto the highway and headed east toward town. Sheriff Griner let him travel about a mile down the road before emerging from the clearing.

Spires was easy to follow. With a cargo of moonshine in the rear of his car, he was taking it slow and easy, careful not to exceed the speed limit. When the two lawmen pulled up alongside him and motioned for him to pull over, Spires cursed and then floored the accelerator. He obviously had no intention of giving up that easy.

"He's running!" Griner yelled, gunning the police car in reply. "Hang on!"

After a brief high-speed chase, the sheriff was able to force Spires off the road where he came to an abrupt stop. The two lawmen, having tamed many bootleggers in this manner over the years, assumed most of the hard work was over.

Cold Blooded Murder

"Turn off the engine!" Sheriff Griner ordered the suspect behind the wheel of the station wagon as he walked toward the car.

Spires, however, sat motionless in the car, assessing his options.

"Turn it off I said!" Griner loudly repeated.

Spires deliberated more, then decided to take a rash action. A .38-caliber pistol was concealed on the seat next to him. He quickly but unobtrusively grabbed the pistol and waited for just the right moment.

"Step out of the car" the sheriff added, accustomed to being obeyed at this juncture. Neither the sheriff nor Harbard were armed. Few people ever defied them, and moonshine suspects usually were routine arrests.

Spires, however, opened the door of his station wagon, and with no warning whatsoever, leveled his .38 at Griner who was the nearest to him.

"Don't shoot!" the sheriff loudly plead as Spires nonetheless quickly pulled the trigger five times. Four of the bullets tore into the sheriff's chest. He moaned and fell to the ground.

The whole thing happened so fast that Harbard also was caught off-guard. In all of their experiences, neither of the two lawmen had ever seen a moonshiner respond in this manner – as a cold-blooded killer.

Spires never hesitated. Just as quickly, he shot Harbard with his last round. The bullet struck the jailer in the chest, piercing and practically destroying his heart.

Mortally wounded, Harbard collapsed, too. The asphalt quickly turned dark crimson with the blood of the two men.

Spires then calmly got back into his car and drove away.

A Witness

Meanwhile, a short distance down the highway, Mr. Eddie Myers had heard the two cars collide as the lawmen forced Spires to the side of the road. Myers thought an accident had occurred, and ran in the direction of the cars to lend assistance if necessary.

As Spires left the two lawmen prostrate in the road, he cruised slowly down the highway – barely above the speed limit – in his black station wagon. Mr. Myers got a quick glimpse of the assailant, then continued on toward the accident site.

As he ran on down the highway, Myers noticed what looked like two men lying in the road. At about this same time, Myers saw another car drive up. Mr. Talmadge

Rutherford, who happened to be driving by, quickly stopped his car and jumped out, shocked at what he saw.

"What happened?" Myers quickly asked as he ran up.

"Looks like they've been shot," Rutherford shouted, as he quickly began loading the two men back into the police cruiser.

"Get me to the hospital. I'm hurt bad," Sheriff Griner reportedly moaned.

The two men gingerly placed the two men back inside the patrol car and Rutherford then sped off. He pushed the car as fast as it would go, spraying loose rocks and dirt in his wake.

An older model station wagon was just ahead. Rutherford didn't notice the man in the white shirt and straw hat as he roared past. He was too busy shouting encouragement to the critically injured sheriff.

The attack on the two lawmen had been savage and brutal. Though he lived for four more days, the sheriff's wounds ultimately proved fatal. Harbard wasn't even a consideration. He was pronounced "dead on arrival" at the hospital, and in fact had been dead since he hit the ground, his heart shattered by the assassin's bullet.

Felon's Flight

Since the sheriff had been wounded and the jailer slain, the deputy sheriff and other law enforcement officials did not immediately realize the perpetrator was still free. A group of lawmen eventually were organized to search for the murderer. Several hundred citizens even joined the lawmen to search for Spires.

The search effort would include the woods bordering the Ashton Highway. The forest was dense and dark, and on some days, visibility was reduced to three or four feet even at high noon. Trailing someone in the vast Ocmulgee Forest and swamp had been the undoing of many a lawman.

Meanwhile, Allen Spires had proceeded directly to his house from the murder scene. He ran into the house, re-stocked his supply of ammunition, took what little cash he had, then began his flight from the justice.

He headed west on the Irwin County Highway toward the small town of Arp. Once he was beyond the city limits, he picked up speed. He had not grasped the gravity of his murderous actions until just now – as he drove away from his home and family. He felt nauseous, and had to pull over to the side of the road to vomit.

Fueled by a consuming paranoia, Spires drove even faster, proceeding recklessly down the road in a vain attempt to escape the demons tormenting him. He jerked the steering wheel into a left turn, nearly overturning his vehicle and striking another car which was also turning into the road.

Changing course, Spires turned east, toward town, then veered north on Arbor Church Road. It was almost high noon, and he figured the search for him was intensifying by now. He drove several miles north to an oak ridge across from the old Player Cemetery, near Reubens Lake. He pulled up beneath the oak tree thicket, got out, and began gathering brush to conceal the car. Clutching his revolver in his left hand, he set off on a course deep into the woods.

Spires traveled south and then east, half running then walking a two-mile distance until he came across an old house on the Tharpe Fitzgerald farm. He watched it from the security of the forest while catching his breath. He hadn't eaten since sunrise, and the delicious smell of frying chicken wafted across the yard to him.

Sliding the revolver inside the back of his pants, Spires approached the house. A middle-aged black woman answered his knock at the door. She wore a bandana over her hair and a grease-stained apron across her waist. She eyed Spires suspiciously, wondering what a white man was doing this deep in the woods.

"What do you want?" she asked with caution.

Spires explained that he had been fishing down at the lake and had been separated from his friends, and that he needed to get back to town but didn't know the way. Following this explanation, he asked the woman for some of the chicken she was cooking, explaining how hungry he was.

After giving Spires directions to town and a piece of chicken, the woman watched as the strange man set back out across the woods. Shortly thereafter, she was listening to the radio when she heard a report about the shooting and a description of Spires. She then quickly sent someone to contact the sheriff.

Giving Up

After leaving the black woman's home, Spires wandered through the dense forest for days, trying desperately to leave the terrible memories of his actions behind him. He crossed Bowen's Mill Road near Bowen's Mill and then made his way into the swamps where he hoped to lose his pursuers.

Five days had passed since the murders, and the combination of hunger and sleep deprivation had ruined him. Try as he might, Allen Spires could not sleep at all, despite an overwhelming exhaustion. The mosquitoes were relentless, and the creatures of the forest constantly alerted him to their presence. He was delirious and beyond exhaustion as morning dawned once again.

When the sun rose full in the sky, Spires continued downriver. He stopped at a house along the way and rested on its front porch. The occupants – an elderly couple – watched the stranger from the front window. He looked to them as if he were sleeping – his head leaning forward and touching his chest.

"Are you all right sir?" the man inquired.

Spires breathed deeply, as if he was snoring. Despite its hardness, the porch felt good. He could lay back and sleep here forever. "Could you please do me a favor?" he asked.

"If I am able I will," the elderly man replied.

"Do you happen to have a pencil and a scrap of paper?"

"Yes."

"Could you bring them to me please?"

The old man complied with Spires' wishes, laying the paper and pencil on the floor next to him. Spires scribbled something on the paper and then folded it several times before handing it to the man.

"Would you mind taking this into town and giving it to your sheriff? I need help," he sighed. I'll wait right here."

As requested, the elderly man delivered the note, and as promised, Spires waited on the front porch – until the sheriff arrived, handcuffed him, and took him off to jail where he slept for the remainder of the day and through the evening. He was then taken to Cordele where he awaited extradition to Ben Hill County.

As simply as that, one of the most heinous murderers in recent history in Georgia was captured and brought to justice.

The Trial

On the day of the trial of Allen Spires, the onlookers settled into an uneasy silence as the court was brought to order. Spires' defense team had him testify on his own behalf. When asked by his attorneys why he had shot the two lawmen, he had responded that he thought he had the right to defend himself. "I didn't know what was going to happen," Spires said.

His defense team knew it had an uphill grind to win a case of this nature. They did not deny that Spires had shot Harbard Smith and Virgil Griner. What they challenged was the point of provocation. While damning, they felt Sheriff Griner's testimony was not beyond reproach. They presented a theory that Spires had acted in self defense, claiming he did not know what the two men were after when they bumped into his car and caused him to pull over.

When it came time for him to cross-examine Spires, Prosecutor Harvey Jay had the assailant exactly where he wanted him. He had waited for over seven months for this moment.

"Mr. Spires, you stated that you did not know what would happen next. Is that correct?" Jay inquired. With his back to Spires, the prosecutor approached the jurors, his hands nonchalantly dangling from his pockets.

"Yes. That is correct," Spires responded.

"Mr. Spires, had you ever seen the sheriff's car prior to August 26, 1951?" the prosecutor baited the accused.

"I'm sure I had," Spires answered.

"Is there something that distinguishes that car from any privately owned vehicle?"

"What do you mean?"

"Anything you might have noticed that would identify it as an official vehicle?"

Spires hesitated. "It has an emblem on the side if that's what you mean," he offered.

"That's exactly what I mean, Mr. Spires. So you were aware when these two men chased you, bumped your car, and pulled you over that they were in an official car."

Again Spires hesitated, glancing at his attorneys. "I did not see it while they were chasing me, no."

"That may be," Jay replied, "but when they pulled you over, and your car was facing them, could you not see that emblem?" Prosecutor Jay now faced the jury, looking deeply into their eyes.

"I might have seen it but things happened so fast. I did not know what they wanted," Spires replied again.

"Mr. Spires, prior to August 26, 1951, had you ever seen Harbard Smith or Virgil Griner before?"

"Yes."

"And did you know them to be the deputy sheriff and sheriff of Ben Hill County?"

"Yes," Spires squirmed.

"So Mr. Spires, if you knew them to be law enforcement officials, why were you so concerned about what would happen next? Don't they have the right, the duty, to stop citizens whom they suspect of criminal activities? Is that not their job as deputy sheriff and sheriff?"

"I did not know what they wanted with me," Spires cowered.

"Is that any reason to gun down two law enforcement officials?"

"Objection!" Defense Attorney Watson exclaimed.

"I withdraw the question your honor," Prosecutor Jay acquiesced. "Mr. Spires, did you give the sheriff and his jailer ample time to tell you what they wanted before you shot them?"

Spires panicked, closing his eyes, praying that everyone would just go away and leave him in peace. More than anything else, he wished that the events of August 26, 1951 had never occurred.

"Well Mr. Spires?" Harvey Jay pressed.

"I don't recall," Spires answered, defeated.

"Did they threaten you Mr. Spires?"

"I don't recall."

"I see. The sheriff and his deputy pull you over, you shoot them, but you don't recall if they explained why they pulled you over or if they threatened you. Is that correct?"

Spires barely breathed. "Yes. That is correct."

"I have no further questions your Honor."

The jury in the case of the State vs. Allen Spires deliberated an hour before sending word that a verdict had been reached.

When the jury filed back into the courtroom, Judge Horne read their verdict. "We the jury hereby find the defendant, Allen Spires, guilty of murder in the first degree," he intoned.

Though he escaped a death sentence, Allen Spires drew a lengthy prison term.

Meanwhile, back in Fitzgerald, Georgia, life goes on, but many of the citizens there still remember a horrible day in August of 1951, when the unbelievable happened in their sleepy little community in Ben Hill County.

(Though all basic facts in the above article are, to the best of the author's knowledge, true and accurate, some portions have been extrapolated and added for dramatic effect.)

The Strange Death
of Capt. Abner Zachry

Hugh T. Harrington

The murder of this former prominent farmer from Morgan and Putnam counties is shrouded in mystery today. Due to the passage of time and the absence of leads, it quite likely will never be solved, but it remains a captivating incident in the history of the area.

Thousands of vehicles speed past the tiny family cemetery each year, and hardly a person ever takes notice of the historic site. In appearance, it is just another of the countless family plots which frequently are found along what once were quiet country lanes. This cemetery, however, is unusual in that it contains the last remains of Captain Abner R. Zachry, whose gravestone proclaims – in large letters – that he was "cruelly assassinated in Morgan County, December 17, 1896.[1]

So just who was Abner Zachry? Why was he assassinated, and by whom? The first question is easy to answer. The second, however, is much more difficult, if not impossible.

The story begins with Zachry's birth in rural Putnam County on June 6, 1841. Two years later, his father, a successful farmer, died. His mother remarried and so Abner grew up living with his mother and step-father. In an ironic twist of fate, Abner's own children would all later grow up with a step-parent of their own.

Young Abner attended the schools in his community. In 1860, at the age of 19, he was recorded as attending class and interestingly, that he had assets worth $20,000. In that day, that was a lot of money, and it had come from his portion of his inheritance from his late father's estate.

In June of 1861, Abner enlisted in the Confederate army as a corporal in Company G. 12th Georgia Infantry. From December, 1861 to July, 1864, he was promoted three times, the last of which was to the rank of captain.

During his service, Abner was wounded three times, the most severe of which occurred at Ft. Stevens, outside Washington City, where he received a severe wound to the chest. He was captured by Union forces at this point in 1864, and taken to various hospitals and prisons including Old Capitol Prison in Washington. In October of that year, he was sent to Ft. Delaware where he remained until he was released on June 17, 1865.

While he was in prison, Abner was described as having a sallow complexion, light colored hair, blue eyes and being six feet four and one-half inches in height.[2]

Upon his return to Putnam County, Abner Zachry wasted no time getting on with his life. On January 25, 1866, he married 19-year-old Eugenia Lyle and returned to farming. Abner apparently was both an intelligent and resourceful farmer, because according to records, he prospered in his profession. As his wealth grew, so also did his family.

In January of 1885, however, tragedy struck the family when his wife died a few days after giving birth to a tiny girl named Eugenia. This loss left Abner with seven children ranging in age from his 16-year-old daughter, Lilla, to newly born Eugenia.

Immediately upon the death of her mother, Lilla assumed full responsibility for the care and well-being of her siblings. She was assisted by her sister, Hattie, who was 15.

Not only was there the newborn to care for, but also Abner, Jr., a two-year old. The older children included nine-year-old Guy, seven-year-old Bertie, and five-year-old Percy. Lilla apparently took her new role very seriously and conscientiously. She diligently cared for the children and effectively ran the household.[3]

After 13 months, Abner, now 44, remarried. His bride was 36-year-old Martha Singleton, known as Mattie. Mattie had been the children's school teacher. She immediately displaced Lilla, taking over all responsibility for the children and the household, a fact which was known to have been greatly resented by Lilla.

Five years later, in 1891, Lilla's sister and confidant, Hattie, left home when she married. Hattie's new home was only a few miles distant from the Zachry farm.

Today, the actual relationship between their stepmother, Mattie, and the children is unknown. It is known, however, that there was an uneasy truce during this span of time, and much resentment quite possibly existed.

Meanwhile, Abner Zachry continued to prosper in the farming profession, becoming one of the wealthiest men in the county. He continued to prosper, and life went on for the Zachry family.

However, on December 17, 1896, tragedy again struck the

Abner Zachry's grave alongside busy U.S. Highway 441 in Morgan County, Georgia.

HUGH HARRINGTON

family. At 7:00 p.m. that cold evening, Abner Zachry and Mattie were sitting by their fireside as was their custom in the evenings. Lilla, then 28, was in the adjacent room playing cards with 16-year-old Percy, 13-year-old Abner, Jr., 11-year-old Eugenia and their eight-year-old half-brother, Robert. The two older children – Guy, then 21, and his sister Bertie, 18 – were in a buggy on their way to a party in nearby Godfrey.

According to a report of the incident, a youngster from a neighboring farm – Frank Durden – came for a visit at the Zachry home. Upon entering the room, he expressed surprise and related how he thought he had just seen Percy – who was sitting in the room – outside the house.

The next instant, two loud gunshots in quick succession were heard in the next room. The children all rushed into the room and through the acrid black gunpowder smoke, they, to their abject horror, saw their father lying on the floor in a pool of blood. Much of his head had been shattered and blown away by the blasts.

The shots had been fired through the window of the home. Young Percy quickly dashed outside to see if he could find the murderer of his beloved father. No perpetrator, however, could be seen or found.

Back inside, Mattie struggled to get her husband onto a bed. Farm hands were sent to inform Hattie and to find Bertie and Guy. Hattie's husband was not at home, and was reported to be possum-hunting. Bertie and Guy were located on the road in their buggy.

Investigating authorities had little to go on. Rain that night had obliterated any traces of the killer.

Abner Zachry's fatal wound had been caused by two deadly shots from an old-fashioned muzzle-loading shotgun firing No. 6 and No. 7 shot. Along with the shot, brown paper wadding was found in the wound and in the room.

Interestingly, Mattie had been sitting next to Abner and had moved just prior to the moment the shots were fired through the window. It is curious today, that despite the fact the shots were fired from directly outside the windows, none of the family members reported seeing anyone outside.

In the days that followed, area newspapers trumpeted the tragic story with headlines of "That Foul Deed, The Assassination Of Capt. Zachry," and "His Head Shot Off." The papers told the same story.

Abner Zachry apparently was popular in his community and had no known enemies. The crime was a complete mystery. No real leads for the killer could be found anywhere.

One unfortunate – a black man named Judge Perryman – was arrested temporarily solely because he was seen carrying a muzzle-loading shotgun and used brown paper as wadding. No case against Perryman, however, was ever made, since he was on good terms with Zachry and could not be tied further to the incident. He subsequently was released.[4]

On Saturday, December 19 – just a few days before Christmas – the body of

The Strange Death of Capt. Abner Zachry

Captain Abner Zachry was laid to rest in the small cemetery on what today is busy U.S. Highway 441. His many friends, former comrades at arms and family attended.

Conspicuously absent from the funeral, however, was Abner's wife, Mattie. She had taken her eight-year-old son Robert, and a wagon-load of possessions to her family home in Eatonton. She abandoned Abner's children by his first marriage, leaving a note behind which stated that she had never been treated right by them, and could not live with them after the death of her husband. Mattie soon moved to distant Waycross, Georgia, where she would live for the rest of her life.[5]

Following the death of her father, Lilla again took over the role of "mother" for the younger children. The older boys continued to manage the farm. They all eventually married – all except Lilla. She eventually moved in with her sister Hattie, and mothered yet another generation of children. She lived until December 13, 1931, almost 35 years to the day of her father's violent death.

No killer was ever tried for the murder of Abner Zachry. No real evidence or motive ever surfaced. Some, perhaps unkindly, suggested that the gunshots had been meant for Mattie Zachry, and that her sudden movement just prior to the gunshots, had saved her life.

Despite the fact that Mattie was unpopular with her adopted children – as is often the case with stepchildren – it would seem unlikely they (one or more of the children) would have conspired to have her killed.

Today, the unsolved murder of Abner Zachry is long forgotten – a dusty record in the archives of Morgan County history. Abner's last child – young Robert who was taken to Eatonton after the shooting by Mattie – died in 1955. The few people who take the time to stop at the little cemetery and read the epitaph of Abner Zachry will always wonder who he was and how he came to be "cruelly assassinated" on a cold winter day in December of 1896.

Endnotes

1. Zachry, Clare H., *The Zachry Family Tree, Southern Branch*, privately printed, n.p., n.d., circa 1985, p. 83.
2. Ward, Dorothy Haizlip, *The Zachry Family*, privately printed, Ft. Lauderdale, 1991, p. 61.
3. Eatonton Messenger, December 26, 1896, *Atlanta Constitution*, December 19, 1896.
4. Ward, Dorothy Haizlip, *The Zachry Family*, privately printed, Ft. Lauderdale, 1991, p. 61.

Murder on Main Street

In the 1890s, two separate cold-blooded shootings in Baldwin County, Georgia, demonstrate the import attached to the public defense of a lady's honor prior to the 20th century.

Hugh T. Harrington

Much has been said and written over the centuries about deeds done for the sake of a lady's honor. On the edges of these memories are vague recollections of formal duels and damsels in distress being rescued by knights in shining armor. These "chivalrous" defenses continued to occur right up into the 20th century, causing innumerable tragic injuries and deaths among ordinary people; often even among friends.

In 1892 and 1893 in Baldwin County, Georgia, two such incidents occurred in which the perceived or real threat to a lady's honor resulted in death. Through an examination of these cases and the legal outcomes, an interesting glimpse inside the minds of the participants and the juries is available.

The first incident took place on the quiet Sunday afternoon of May 29, 1892, in the churchyard at Lingould's Chapel about four miles south of Milledgeville.[1] The calm that spring day was interrupted by the staccato sound of 7 rapid gunshots which left two men grievously wounded.[2]

A young man, Charles

Richardson, had recently been rejected as a suitor by Cora Barnes, the sister of Richardson's friend, William D. Barnes. The previous week Cora had married another man.

Visually demonstrating his objection to the wedding and despair at his rejection as a suitor, Richardson wore black crepe – a notable sign of mourning in that day – in his hatband. He also uttered remarks that Cora's brother took as offensive.[3]

Deadly Confrontation

Angered by the remarks Richardson had made, Bill Barnes later went looking for him after the nuptials had been completed. He found him attending Sunday School in Lingould Chapel.

Barnes called Richardson out and the two walked into the churchyard arguing in undertones. Suddenly one of them shouted, "Then we will settle it here!" and at that exclamation, both men reportedly pulled revolvers and began firing. One witness said that Barnes hit Richardson with a stick as Richardson's revolver became entangled in his handkerchief while he was drawing it, thus enabling Barnes to get his own revolver into action.[4]

It is not known today who actually fired first. However, Barnes was hit twice; once in the shoulder and once in the side with the ball lodging next to his spine causing paralysis. Richardson was hit in the right side with the ball lodging in the muscles of his back.[5]

At first, it appeared that both men would die from the exchange of gunfire. However, after a few weeks Richardson's wounds were healing satisfactorily. Barnes, however, never regained consciousness, lingering for almost two months before dying on July 21. He was buried in Memory Hill Cemetery.[6]

Immediately after Barnes' death, Richardson was arrested for his murder. He was released in a few days, however, after posting $2,000.00 bail.[7]

Despite the serious nature of the matter, Charles Richardson was never brought to trial for the murder of Bill Barnes. The Baldwin County Grand Jury, meeting in September of that year, returned a "No Bill," thus ending the case.

At the time, area newspapers had referred to the incident as a "duel," perhaps indirectly assigning some sentiment for legitimate acquittal, but in reality, the shooting was not a duel at all in the formal definition of the term.[8] This was simply a fight between two men, former friends, over the perceived insult by one to the other's sister.

Gooden Shooting

The following May, a similar act of violence took place in the small hamlet of Stevens' Pottery[9] in the southern part of Baldwin County. There, a young man named Daniel Gooden had for some time been making unkind remarks about the wife of another young man, David Upshaw.

Finally, on the afternoon of May 16, 1893, Upshaw could ignore the remarks no longer. He picked up his double barrel shotgun and went to Stevens' Pottery in search of Daniel Gooden.

HUGH T. HARRINGTON

The Stevens' Pottery building still stands in Baldwin County. Daniel Gooden was shot and killed in front of this building in 1893.

Upon his arrival, Upshaw learned that Gooden was inside the Pottery building, and he waited on the porch for him to come out. As Gooden walked into the street, Upshaw came up behind him and when approximately 8 steps away fired his shotgun at Gooden's back.

Seriously wounded, Gooden turned after he was hit and Upshaw resolutely fired the second barrel directly into the horrified man's face, and then quietly walked away.[10]

Daniel Gooden did not die instantly. He was carried to his house where he expired, no doubt painfully, during the night.

Witnesses To Murder

A Coroner's Jury held, "over his body," an inquest the day after the shooting at the home of Daniel Gooden. Several witnesses provided testimony.

The first witness to the incident was young Johnny Gooden, the grief-stricken nine-year-old son of the dead man. He had gone to town with his father to pick up the mail. He clearly saw his father shot in the back and then again in the face by Upshaw as he went from the Pottery office to the shop.[11]

Another witness, Jack Scott, saw Gooden going from the Pottery office to the shop when David Upshaw shot him in the back with a "double barrel breech-loading shotgun." According to Scott's testimony, Gooden turned and "threw his hand to the place where he was shot and says, 'Oh, don't kill me,'" to which Upshaw replied, "God damn you" as he shot Gooden in the face. Upshaw then reportedly reloaded the shotgun and walked away.[12]

Sometime after the shooting, a Dr. Gilmore was called in to render assistance. He reached the dying man about 11:00 pm. He testified that Gooden's left eye was shot out and several shot had struck his face. The wound in the back, which the doctor did not think would have been fatal, was from his buttocks to his shoulders. The shotgun had been loaded with "small shot."[13]

McCullar Testimony

Lewis McCullar who also testified, was able to shed some light on events that had preceded the shooting. He explained that in "early spring," David Upshaw and another man had come to ask his advice, saying that Gooden "had been using some bad language and telling scandalous tales about Upshaw's wife."

McCullar said he referred Upshaw to a lawyer who informed the distraught man that he could indeed sue Gooden, but that he "didn't think it would amount to much, and advised [Upshaw] not to spend any money on it." McCullar then described how Upshaw had told him he could not live and have a man talking about his wife in that way.

Upshaw, according to McCullar, had also even considered moving away to reside elsewhere. McCullar said he suggested to Upshaw that he simply go speak to Gooden and ask him if he would "not make any more remarks about him or his wife." Upshaw, to his credit, indeed did speak to Gooden and Gooden reportedly agreed not to talk about Upshaw or Upshaw's wife in the future.

Unfortunately, on the Sunday preceding the shooting, McCullar said he saw Upshaw who told him that Gooden was still talking about his wife. Upshaw did not say what he was going to do, but did relate that he "couldn't put up with it."[14]

In his testimony, Joe McCullar continued by explaining that he was then asked by Upshaw to go into town with him the morning of the shooting. On the way, Upshaw reportedly never spoke of Gooden. When the two men reached Stevens' Pottery, Gooden walked past Upshaw who said, "Dan, I suppose you have been talking about my wife again." Gooden replied to Upshaw's statement, but McCullar said Gooden's words were too low and indistinct for him to understand what he said.

"I thought Mr. Upshaw was going to shoot Gooden, and I walked off to keep from seeing it," McCullar said. "I went in the house as soon as Upshaw and Gooden commenced talking."[15]

Brown Testimony

W.E. Brown testified that a few days prior to the shooting, Daniel Gooden had told him that he saw Mrs. Upshaw "and a man go into the bushes together, but would not tell the man's name." Brown said he informed Upshaw what Gooden had said, and Upshaw flew into "a heat of passion and said, 'God D___ him! He had promised not to mention me or my wife's name any more.'"[16]

After listening to this testimony, the Coroner's Jury found that Daniel Gooden "came to his death by gunshot wound inflicted by David Upshaw and. ...decide the same to be voluntary manslaughter."

The following morning David Upshaw turned himself in to the authorities in Milledgeville. He posted his bail and was released. His trial was scheduled for July.[17]

The trial consumed two full days with evidence and opposing arguments. "Great interest was manifested in this remarkable case," one newspaper intoned.

A large crowd packed the courthouse anxious to hear the attorneys' arguments. The newspaper article continued by describing how the arguments were "opened by the Solicitor General in his usual strong and forcible manner, followed by J.D. Howard, M.W. Hall and Joseph E. Pottle in able speeches for the defense [with] Robert Whitfield closing for the prosecution in a speech of wonderful power."

HUGH T. HARRINGTON

The Baldwin County Courthouse in which a Grand Jury returned a "No Bill" for Charles Richardson and a standing jury acquitted David Upshaw, also still stands in Baldwin County.

Preconceived Verdict

It is not known today what evidence was produced for the defense. There clearly was ample evidence for the prosecution. The jury got the case on a Thursday evening and deliberated until Saturday morning but could not reach a verdict. The judge called in the jury and recharged them and sent them back to the jury room, but they still failed to agree and Saturday afternoon the judge declared a mistrial.[18]

At the next term of court the case was tried once again. Again the trial took two days. At this trial the defense introduced no witnesses other than David Upshaw. He testified simply that Gooden had persistently slandered his wife, and he had killed him. The jury was out for only two hours before returning with a verdict of "Not Guilty."[19]

It seems somewhat inconceivable today that a man could even hope to get away with a killing where he intentionally sought out his victim and shot him in the back. A defense based solely upon the shooter feeling the need to stop a man from making unkind – although perhaps true – comments about his wife is, at best, "grasping at straws."

Nevertheless, in 1890s Milledgeville, the honor of a lady – even a lady who may not actually have been honorable – carried a great deal of importance, not just with the men who defended their honor with a gun, but also with the juries who passed judgment upon their actions.

Endnotes

1. Now called Oak Grove Methodist Church, original church building has been replaced. From center of Milledgeville follow Business 441 south for 4 miles. At bypass, 441 turns left. Follow 243 south .6 miles; turn left onto Colony Farm Road. After .8 miles turn right on Lingold Street. Continue .1 miles to churchyard.

2. *Union Recorder*, May 31, 1892.

3, 4, 5 ibid

6. *Union Recorder*, July 26, 1892, Harrington, Susan J. and Hugh T., and Gardner, Floride Moore, "Historic Memory Hill Cemetery, Milledgeville, Georgia, 1804-1997," Milledgeville, 1998, p. 367. Grave is unmarked, located on west side, lot #38.

7. *Union Recorder*, August 2, 1892.

8. *Union Recorder*, September 6, 1892.

9. Stevens' Pottery is 9.5 miles south of Milledgeville. From center of Milledgeville follow Business 441 south for 4 miles. At bypass 441 turns left; follow 143 south 5.1 miles to J.F. Hall Road. Turn right. Follow J.F. Hall Road .4 miles to the railroad tracks. Pottery building is across the tracks on the left.

10. *Union Recorder*, May 23, 1893.

11, 12, 13, 14, 15, 16, 17 ibid

18. *Union Recorder*, August 15, 1893.

19. *Union Recorder*, January 23, 1894.

The Georgia Nuclear Aircraft Laboratory

Red Sky in Morning

At the height of the Cold War in the 1950s and '60s, a secret military laboratory concealed in a remote section of the north Georgia mountains carried out pioneering atomic experiments and research.

Dwayne Keith Petty

What if the ruins of a former nuclear facility, once operated in isolation and semi-secrecy, existed in your own back yard? For the residents of Pickens, Forsyth, Cherokee, and Dawson Counties, that "what if" is a reality. Welcome to the Dawson Wildlife Management Area, a 10,000-acre forest currently owned by Hartsfield-Jackson International Airport and overseen by the Georgia Department of Natural Resources. A pristine wilderness serving campers, hikers, equestrians, and hunters, this stretch of land was also once the home of the Georgia Nuclear Aircraft Laboratory, an atomic research facility operated by Lockheed Martin Corporation, the United States Air Force, and the Atomic Energy Commission.

The reactor at the Georgia Nuclear Aircraft Laboratory in the "raised" position. When not in use it was lowered into the concrete-enclosed pit or pool below.

This aerial photograph of the reactor site shows the reactor building and the railroad tracks.

The primary goal of the Georgia Nuclear Aircraft Laboratory (GNAL), which commenced operations in the late 1950s and was decommissioned in 1971, was to create a nuclear propulsion system for military aircraft. The facility, spread out over several square miles of mountainous terrain, included a hot cell building, a nuclear reactor site, and a cooling site for irradiated materials. These three locations were connected by an onsite narrow-gauge railway with rail cars that transported materials to and from the three facility stations.

For the purposes of this article, I interviewed an anonymous source who worked for Lockheed Nuclear Products Division from 1957 until 1960 in nuclear shielding, and later for NASA and Huntsville's nuclear rocket program. My source recalls that the Dawsonville site was selected for several reasons. First, the plant, known as Air Force Plant # 67, was, my source states, "an easy commute for the technical and nuclear wizards of Marietta's Air Force Plant # 6." The location also afforded low population density and was in what was labeled a "well-shielded area," meaning it was sparsely populated.

The 10-million watt reactor was positioned in a hollow. It was stored in a concrete "pool" or pit when not in use and raised from the pit when it was to be operated. When the reactor was operating and conducting tests or irradiation procedures, employees took shelter in underground quarters. Once the reactor had been raised and turned on, or "flashed," as it is known in the industry, employees waited for the procedure to end and the reactor to be returned to its pool before emerging from their quarters.

The GNAL reactor at Dawson Forest was what is termed an air-shielded reactor. This means it operated in the open and was unshielded (except by air) when removed from its storage pool. Therefore, each time it was in operation it irradiated the surrounding landscape and forest. After only a few uses, all the foliage surrounding the reactor area died from the effects of radiation.

Lockheed continued research on nuclear-powered aircraft for several years. At the height of the Cold War, the U. S. government and military, apprehensive about Soviet advances in the same area, made this project a top priority. In theory, nuclear-powered aircraft did not need to land and refuel and could therefore remain aloft for weeks at a time. In the minds of military strategists, this capability would have been invaluable. Imagine bombers able to lurk near an enemy's border for days on end, able to strike at a moment's notice. Their vision, however, was never realized.

Lockwood

Specialists in the field of nuclear study soon recognized that vari-

1. The entrance to the laboratory: The railroad tracks terminate at the hot cell building, which had concrete and steel walls four feet thick. Inside, "cell blocks" (or rooms) housed materials that had been exposed to radiation. Physicists studied these materials by peering through glass and oil-panel windows. These specially constructed
continued next page

windows had glass panes on either side of the wall and a mineral oil filling the space in between. The mineral oil absorbed harmful radiation and also allowed a clearer view inside each cell than would a four-foot thick pane of glass. Physicists used mechanical arms to manipulate the materials in the cell blocks. Overgrown Entrance – The entrance to the underground facility is overgrown with brush today. State officials regularly bulldoze dirt against each opening to prevent unauthorized entry. 2. Hot Cell Building: Barbed wire bars access to the hot cell building where residual radiation still poses a risk.

3. Bridge Abutment: Concrete bridge abutments are relics of the GNAL railroad.

ous materials took on new properties when irradiated, and this led to the creation of the Lockheed Nuclear Products division. During this phase of the facility's operation, products were loaded onto rail cars and transported to the reactor site. Once exposed to the reactor's radiation, the products where transported by rail to the cooling site and retrieved by plant workmen.

One such product was wood. Transformed in strength and durability by the irradiation process, ordinary pine, infused with a type of resin or polymer, was loaded onto the facility rail cars and delivered to the reactor site. My source recalls that Lockheed Martin Corporation then marketed the irradiated wood under the name "Lockwood." Some of this wood was used for flooring at the Atomic Energy Commission facility in Germantown, Maryland.

Unnatural Experiments

Beginning in 1958, the Lockheed/ Dawsonville reactor site was also the location of extensive radiation studies and animal experiments. Conducted by the University of Georgia, Emory University, and the U.S. Atomic Energy Commission, these studies subjected wildlife, both indigenous and introduced to the area, as well as the surrounding landscape, to massive doses of radiation.

In his research report The Effect of Neutron-Gamma Radiation on Free-living Small Mammals at the Lockheed Reactor Site, Jay H. Schnell chronicles an experiment with various types of rats that took place in August 1960 at the Dawsonville facility. In this testing, researchers under the direction of Emory University's Dr. Robert B. Platt released various populations of rats into the fields and forests surrounding the reactor site. These rats, having been tagged, were later recaptured in baited traps after the area had been exposed to intense radiation in order to document effects and mortality rates.

Lethal radiation doses for rats range from 500 to 650 rads (a rad is a unit of measurement for radiation). This same dosage is also lethal to human beings. During the experiments described by Schnell, the reactor emitted as much as 7,394 rads into the experimental area. The reactor operated for three weeks at varying radiation levels except on weekends and during personnel shift changes. The effects on the rat populations included increased mortality rates (often 100%), immobility, disorientation, and graying or whitening of pelts.

In a separate report from this same period, Some Effects of Neutron Gamma Radiation on Late Summer Bird Populations, Schnell documents the results of the irradiation process and experiments on birds including Carolina wrens, bobwhites, common yellowthroats, white-eyed and red-eyed vireos, and indigo buntings. From July 26, 1960, until August 20, 1960, the percentage of these birds in the irradiated areas dropped dramatically. Schnell estimates that some birds received as much as 27,700 rads of radiation.

The University of Georgia's Eugene P. Odum stated in 1965, "Experience with the unshielded reactor at Dawsonville, Georgia, provides a good example [of the effects of radiation]. After one of the high energy runs the entire population of marked cotton rats living in the adjacent field was exterminated...Small birds entering the radiation field were also undoubtedly killed...'"

Fallout

Another study measured the effects of a simulated nuclear war on the forest around the reactor site. In Code Red Alert: Confronting Nuclear Power in Georgia, the authors noted, "Further, studies were done using nuclear reaction energy levels 'giving radiation doses up to supralethal' to simulate nuclear war without 'the heat and blasts associated with bomb tests.' The forest was irradiated in two acute exposures in June 1959 and August 1960, and it was recommended that the area be called a 'radiation subclimax' as the 'radiation disturbed community is not in the normal successional pattern.' A forest develops in an established pattern. In this case, the pattern was altered due to the high levels of radiation."

Of the two acute exposures, the most detrimental effects from the reactor emanated into the forest environment during the middle two weeks of June 1959. At the time, scientific study dictated a release of neutron and gamma rays for the express purpose of documenting both immediate damage to pine and deciduous trees and to study the long-term effects on tree growth, tree resiliency, and leaves.

This study was one of two initiated by the Environmental Sciences Branch of the Division of Biology and Medicine of the U.S. Atomic Energy Commission. The other took place at Brookhaven National Laboratories on Long Island, New York. In both instances, the threat of nuclear war with the Soviet Union necessitated a comprehensive understanding of the ultimate effects of nuclear war and our nation's ability to recover.

In a study conducted through Emory University, Robert A. Pedigo stated, "One of the most urgent reasons for vastly increasing our inventory of radiation sensitivities is that of intelligently planning for the problems which would arise in nuclear warfare. In this case the essential elements of our renewable natural resources could have received drastic, in many cases lethal, doses [of radiation] and the efficiency with which society can recover will be due in large measure to the reconstitution of our renewable natural resources."

One of our most important natural resources was our verdant woodlands, so the Dawson Forest was an ideal location for the tests. With the reactor operating at full power, the gamma-neutron field extended to distances 3,000 feet or more from the

reactor, depending on terrain – an area covering some 300 acres. Trees closest to the reactor absorbed as much as 100,000 rads during the operation, with absorption rates declining as distance from the reactor increased. In short, the physicists at GNAL successfully reconstructed the impact of a ground-zero detonation of a nuclear weapon using the reactor instead of a bomb.

The effect on the forest of this simulated catastrophe was disastrous. Leaves on trees closest to the reactor, especially pines, immediately began to turn brown and die. Archival photographs of the area show stands of loblolly pines almost identical in appearance to stands of pines infested with Southern pine beetles today; and even deciduous trees, though not killed, suffered dramatic effects due to the radiation.

During the two years that followed the June 1959 irradiation of Dawson Forest, hardwood trees shed their leaves an average of six weeks early each autumn and began producing buds six weeks later each winter and spring. Even then, bud and leaf production was dramatically reduced. In addition, growth of all trees within the test field suffered considerably, and the gamma-neutron field area, extending about one mile in radius from the reactor, remained a recovering wasteland and a location for irradiation and animal experiments for the next several years.

A final tally of the irradiation processes from December 1958 until December 1960 shows approximately 100,000 rads of radiation absorbed within a 1,000-foot radius of the reactor, with taper levels of rads extending up to 4,000 feet from the reactor. Of this radiation, most would have been contained inside the test field; but neutron radiation, which is the type associated with fallout from nuclear weapons, could theoretically have been lifted into the atmosphere and carried various distances according to prevailing winds. This, however, is not a matter of documentation but rather conjecture.

Radiation Relics in the Forest

Today, decades after the Cold War, Red scares, blacklisting, air-raid drills, and H-bomb shelters, the remains of the Georgia Nuclear Aircraft Laboratory are quite evident within the Dawson Wildlife Management Area. Numerous foundations of leveled buildings peer through weeds; the clearly visible bed of the rail line leads across the Etowah River and deeper into the forest to the still-contaminated cooling area which is enclosed by a fence; abutments of two demolished bridges, once a part of the railway, adorn the banks of the river; and the hot cell building stands intact near the entrance to the management area.

According to Georgia Forestry Commission employee Nathan McClure, who managed Dawson and Paulding Forests from 1991 until 2004, the hot cell building wasn't razed because of the immense difficulty and expense involved in demolishing its 48-inch thick steel and concrete walls. Still, all openings to the building have been sealed with concrete blocks overlaid with steel plates. Additionally, two fences, the outer topped with barbed wire, surround the building, which was identified several decades ago as a radiation hot spot due to remaining traces of Cobalt 60 and Europium 152. McClure states, "Our charge was to keep folks away from this building for a variety of safety concerns – mostly the hazards associated with getting injured while climbing in, around, and through the building."

In addition to these surface relics, the remains of the underground facility at the reactor area also exist. This was the structure that shielded physicists and workers during irradiation tests. It consists of three underground levels and a tunnel that led to a parking area. Due to water table, these underground compartments had to be continuously pumped during the '50s and '60s and are now completely flooded. Each entrance has been sealed by bulldozed mounds of earth.

These measures do not always work, McClure notes. "We continuously had to seal up the three openings to the tunnel and underground area because folks occasionally dig them out."

Residual Risk?

As for the radiation dangers within the Dawson Forest today, little, if any, threat

exists according to the Georgia Forestry Commission and the Environmental Protection Division. Within the hot cell and cooling areas, some hot spots of Cobalt 60 and Europium 152 remain, but having already spent their half-lives plus an additional decade-and-a-half, their radiation levels probably pose no more peril than do background radiation (radiation that occurs naturally in the environment).

Still, as a precaution, the areas remain restricted to the public today. Additionally, the Environmental Protection Division placed radiation monitors in questionable areas throughout the forest, and assessments are conducted every three months to ensure continued public safety. The Etowah River is likewise tested regularly.

These safety measures don't always quell the rumors, however. Though it is difficult to persuade those with accurate information to talk about GNAL, its impact upon local legend is indelible. Stories of accidents, sickness, and animal mutations persist. Hunters report bucks with extra sets of antlers or an absence of antlers and deer with atrophied legs and albino pelts. At one point, the tale of a Cyclops-like deer circulated.

Such stories remain by and large unsubstantiated, though it is known that genetic mutations can be hereditary. Of his thirteen years at Dawson Forest, Nathan McClure jokes, "I've never seen any five-legged deer or other strange creatures on the site."

Other residents of Cherokee, Dawson, Pickens, and Forsyth Counties remember the days of the red sky in 1959, which many at first thought to be a sign of the end of the world but later attributed to GNAL operations. During this period, the sky in this vicinity reportedly became a deep crimson color and some families gathered inside to pray, fearing the Apocalypse.

Was this phenomenon related to operations at the Georgia Nuclear Aircraft Laboratory? No one knows for sure. Although June 1959 was the period of most acute irradiation of the forest, those who remember the red sky do not remember exact dates so it is not possible to correlate with the days when the reactor was in operation. It does not seem likely, though, because the type of radiation emitted by the reactor was not visible to the naked eye (although there is some debate about that even today).

Many people living in the vicinity of the Dawson Forest still question the impact of the GNAL site on the environment. In regard to these concerns, I contacted a University of Georgia physicist and asked if the public should be concerned. His response was a resounding, "No!" According to him, even at the time of the nuclear experiments, radiation damage only extended as far as the visible damage to the forest. It seems that the reactor, though capable of producing destruction to immediate surroundings, did not emit the type of radiation that would travel beyond the visible limit of impact.

This conclusion was reinforced recently at a February meeting of the Marble Valley Historical Society in Jasper, Georgia. Six former GNAL employees were present and spoke at length about the limited effects, in terms of range, of the radiation in use at the Lockheed facility. Likewise, during the facility's operation, Lockheed took extraordinary safety measures, especially for those employed there. These steps included use of dosimeters badges, regular checkups by physicians, and limits on exposure to radiation.

The former employees present at this meeting expressed gratitude to Lockheed for choosing Dawsonville as the site of operations, primarily because the plant gave a much-needed economic boost to many families. One gentleman fondly remembered earning $120.00 per week in the 1950s, an impressive sum at the time. His wife, a secretary at the plant, received $100.00 for working one Sunday; and together, the couple described the blessing of being able to pay for a sick child's needs through Lockheed's liberal health insurance benefits. In the end, those present agreed that the facility had been a godsend.

Since the Georgia Nuclear Aircraft Laboratory was carefully guarded and shrouded in secrecy, many mysteries remain regarding its operation and the effects of its experiments. Without question, it will remain a topic of conversation, rumor, and legend for those who live in these mountains area, even though any danger may have long since passed.

Was Michael Shaw Hanged for a Crime He Did Not Commit?

On April 30, 1877, a young wife who had previously been abused by her husband was found dead, brutally murdered in her own home. The evidence, all circumstantial, pointed to her husband, but not necessarily convincingly.

In 1878, 26-year-old Michael Shaw was hanged in Milledgeville, Georgia, for the brutal 1877 murder of his 24-year-old wife, Ardeoro. Did the evidence support Shaw's conviction? While we do not have the benefit of the trial testimony today, we do have contemporary newspaper accounts which provide good descriptions of the murder investigation and the events which transpired afterwards, including the hanging. A review of these newspaper articles may leave some doubt as to the guilt of this man in this horrendous crime.

The initial article on this sensational incident appeared on May 1, 1877, the day after the crime. It described how Mrs. Shaw, living in the country eleven miles west of Milledgeville, "was murdered yesterday morning by two black fiends in human shape."

According to further details in the newspaper article, Mike Shaw had left home in the morning to cut firewood. He reportedly heard a gunshot at his house and returned to "find his wife lying at the door with her brains beaten in with a 'lightwood knot' – her skull broken in several places." The article went on to explain that Mrs. Shaw's arm and hand – which she apparently had used to ward off the terrible blows – were also broken terribly in several places. As if the trauma of this bludgeoning was not enough, Mrs. Shaw had also been shot in the head, presumably with Mr. Shaw's pistol which was missing and never found.[1]

Compounding the horror of this incident was the fact that the couple's blood-splattered baby daughter, four years of age, was discovered sitting by Mrs. Shaw's body. According to the child's tearful revelations, "two black men" had killed her mother.

Investigating The Crime

The neighbors were soon on the trail of the two mysterious black men. They found blood smears on a fence which suggested the direction in which the perpetrators had fled. However, when bloodhounds were brought in to track the murderers, they were unsuccessful in locating the scent. Milledgeville's law enforcement officers later picked up two "suspicious-looking negroes" and put them in jail as they were "unable to give a satisfactory account of themselves."[2]

Within a few days the focus of the investigation had begun to change with dramatic results. The first newspaper article describing this investigation appeared in

HUGH T. HARRINGTON

Milledgeville's Union Recorder. It had been written based upon a report from a brother of Mike Shaw. According to the article, the four-year-old child had recanted (changed) her story, stating instead that it was her father, Mike Shaw, who had actually killed her mother.

Shaw's mother-in-law, Sarah Moore, had strongly believed her daughter had been murdered by Shaw all along, and was pressing for prosecution. Rumors "of the most damaging kind" began to circulate in the area. Some residents recalled that Shaw, as a member of the Ku Klux Klan, had been arrested previously for the murder of a black man in 1875, but since no one could positively identify him as the perpetrator, he was acquitted after being given a stern lecture by the judge.

The gravestone of Sarah Moore, mother of the murdered Ardeoro Shaw. Moore steadfastly maintained that Ardeoro's husband, Michael Shaw, was her killer, and pressed unerringly for his conviction.

According to a report in the May 5, 1877 issue of the *Atlanta Constitution*, following these developments, Mike Shaw was arrested and charged with the murder of his wife. The two black men who had been arrested earlier were released from custody.[3]

Dubious Testimony

At Mike Shaw's preliminary hearing, several individuals were called upon for testimony. Dr. I.L. Harris had performed the post-mortem examination of Mrs. Shaw. He stated that the left side of her head was badly bruised and gashed and that there was a hole in top of the skull from a bullet. He also said that there were scratches on the face of Mike Shaw. Mr. Shaw's defense counsel objected to the testimony of the scratches, but was overruled. According to the May 8, 1877 issue of the Union Recorder, this testimony was entered into the court record under protest.[4]

Sarah Moore, the mother of the dead woman testified that she had heard a person scream twice on the day of the murder. Later, looking out from her house she said she saw Mr. Shaw and his little daughter coming toward her house with blood on the little girl's cheeks and clothing. Mrs. Moore further stated that Mr. Shaw said his wife had been killed by someone and that the child said it was a negro. Mrs. Moore also said she knew there had been "a bad state of feeling between Shaw and his wife."

A hired man, described as "a half-witted sort of a man" who lived with the Shaws – David Butler – stated that on the day of the crime he had gone out to plow, and that Mike Shaw had gone out to cut logs. Butler said he had heard a gun fired and that Shaw had yelled to him asking where the firing had come from. Butler said he had replied that it was from the direction of Shaw's house.

In further testimony, Mrs. Moore stated that she had heard screaming and then a gunshot, then had heard Mike Shaw call to David Butler. She said it had been "about a minute" from the time of the screaming to the time Shaw had called to Butler. She also said that just the week before the killing, Mrs. Shaw had told her that she was on better terms with her husband now than she had been for 12 months.

As a result of this testimony and other evidence in the preliminary hearing, Mike Shaw was bound over to be tried for murder. According to the May 8, 1877 issue of the Union Recorder, he was sent to the jail in nearby Richmond for safe-keeping while awaiting his trail which had been scheduled for August in Baldwin County Superior Court.[5]

Court Of Public Opinion

Despite what could be described as condemning testimony, the case against Shaw was in fact based solely upon circumstantial evidence, and the Baldwin County District Attorney wanted more hard evidence before the trial. Shaw's pistol had never been located, and there was no evidence directly tying Shaw to the crime himself.

The D.A. sent to Atlanta for Captain E.C. Murphy who had earned a reputation as an excellent detective. Murphy spent several days in and around the area where the killing had occurred.

During this period prior to the trial, whisperings had begun around Milledgeville that Shaw had been cruel to his wife and that he was a "terror to the neighborhood, especially the colored population, who regarded him as a member of the Klan. It was thought that some of the witnesses were afraid to testify against him." Shaw was suspected in the killing of several blacks.

According to the October 7, 1877 issue of the *Atlanta Constitution*, an anonymous note was received by a Colonel McCombs stating that the skeleton of a black man could be found in his well. According to records, a search of the well did indeed turn up the purported skeleton. The author of this note was never discovered.

The article in the October 7 issue of the *Constitution* went on to explain that it was also rumored that Shaw was the leader of a local band of "desperate men" known as "The Georgia Tigers." No evidence, however, surfaced to connect him with any of these activities but the rumors persisted nonetheless.[6]

Adding to the confusion of the investigation, "half-witted" David Butler ultimately changed his story. At his own request he was locked in the county jail for protective purposes after disclosing new information to Detective Murphy which now implicated Shaw in the crime. He was released when arrangements were made for him to relocate to a different area in Baldwin County.

According to Butler's new testimony, he saw Shaw beat his wife with a piece of wood then drag her into the house. He said he then heard gunshots from inside the house, adding that Shaw had emerged from the house and upon seeing him (Butler), had put a pistol to his head and told him he would kill him if he ever told what he had seen. This testimony, however, became less credible when it was learned that David Butler had signed an affidavit that he had received money to testify against Shaw. He later maintained that the affidavit had been an error.[7]

Despite all this confusing evidence and testimony, the case against Michael Shaw ground along, and the court of public opinion had convicted him long before his actual trial. Detective Murphy eventually returned to Atlanta leaving the impression that the case against Shaw now was even solid.

A Trial & Conviction

The trial of Michael Shaw consumed two days, which was a long trial by the standards of that day. The jury nevertheless eventually returned with a verdict of "Guilty." According to a somewhat dramatic article in the August 28, 1877 issue of the Union Recorder in Milledgeville, the judge pronounced sentence that Shaw was "to be taken to Fulton County jail in Atlanta for safe-keeping, and on the 12th day of October next be returned to Baldwin County, and between the hours of 10:00 AM and 2:00 PM be hanged by the neck until he is dead, dead, dead."

During this same time-period, Shaw was also indicted for having murdered a black man by the name of James Bostwick whose bones had been discovered in McComb's old well near his residence.[8] It is unknown today how it was determined that the bones were actually those of Mr. Bostwick. The evidence used to implicate Shaw in this crime is equally lacking today.

Interestingly, on the night of October 2nd, 1877, Michael Shaw and another convicted murderer, Gus Johnson, cut through iron bars and then amazingly tunneled out of the Fulton County Jail. It is believed they were the first inmates to successfully make such an escape from this prison. They were "at large" for several days before being apprehended near Powder Springs, northwest of Atlanta.

The Atlanta Constitution, in an article in its October 7, 1877 issue, detailed how Shaw had been arrested in the past for beating his wife. Mrs. Moore, the murdered woman's mother, stated that her daughter had often told her that Shaw had threatened her life and that she was in constant fear and dread of him. Physically, Shaw was described as a man with almost super-human strength, and also possessed of a "peculiarly brilliant and baleful eye – what is commonly called the 'snake eye.'"[9] In the midst of all this incriminating circumstantial evidence, Shaw might even have been

HUGH T. HARRINGTON

The spot at which the gallows upon which Michael Shaw was hanged once stood. This site is on the Oconee River one-half mile from Milledgeville.

Satan himself according to his accusers' obviously free-wheeling imaginations.

Shaw's Last Hours

Shaw's hanging was delayed as his attorneys took the case to the Supreme Court in January of 1878. The case was delayed yet again and it was not until June that the Supreme Court decided against hearing his case. Shaw was returned again to Baldwin County where he was escorted to the courthouse by the "Baldwin Blues," the local militia unit.

Upon pronouncing sentence, the judge asked Shaw if he had anything to say. He reportedly replied, "Nothing more than I said before, that I have not had a fair trial." The death sentence was scheduled to be carried out on July 12th. Curiously, despite all the publicity and sensationalism connected with this crime and trial, it was the order of the court that the execution of Shaw be conducted in private.

Throughout the ordeal of his arrest and conviction, Shaw reportedly was exceptionally composed, displaying a courage that the reporters strangely found "admirable." "Alas! that a man possessing these manly powers – this great physical courage – should not have the moral force to restrain his evil passions," one reporter penned.

During his last days, Shaw was visited in jail by his friends, attorneys, and his mother and even his young daughter. In clarifying his statement that he "had not had a fair trial," he said that David Butler had sworn falsely against him. He steadfastly maintained that he was innocent and had no confession whatsoever to make.

Late in the same afternoon, despite his courageous demeanor throughout his ordeal, Shaw reportedly attempted suicide by taking strychnine which he had brought with him from Atlanta concealed in the binding of his Bible. When he began convulsing, doctors were immediately summoned to his assistance. As he was yet conscious, he was informed by the doctors that strychnine would result in a very painful and horrible death. Upon learning this, Shaw reportedly took a prescribed antidote and recovered. He was then returned to Atlanta to await the day of his execution.

Desperate Rescue Attempts

Shaw's brother circulated a petition asking that his brother's sentence be commuted to life imprisonment. He received many signatures. Some said that they "would not hang a dog on Butler's testimony." The petition was then sent to the Governor by Shaw's defense attorney, Judge DuBignon. The Governor, however, refused to commute the sentence. The June 18, 1878 issue of the *Union Recorder* commented that "a large majority of our citizens never had any doubt of his guilt.[10]

On July 1st, one of the prosecuting attorneys, D.B. Sanford, received a warning:

"I have been unhappily placed in a position to know there will be an effort to relieve the guard of Shaw on the railroad by parties that you least suspect. I would sign my name but it would place me in antagonism of my dark friends. Signed: A. Friend"

In response to this communication the Baldwin County Sheriff and three deputies went to Atlanta to pick up Shaw and did not disclose by which train they would be returning. No attempt was ever made to "relieve" them of Shaw. The Baldwin Blues guarded the jail during the night, and Shaw was chained to the floor and two guards remained inside the cell with him.[11]

During his last hours, Shaw was visited by three Catholic priests who prayed with him. He talked with his guards but did not sleep. He refused requests by the press for interviews. Despite the announcement that the execution would be private, a huge crowd of 3,000 to 5,000 people filled Milledgeville for a chance to glimpse Shaw as he was taken to the gallows.

The Hanging

The gallows had been erected near the Oconee River bridge (south of the location of the present-day river bridge) with an 18-foot fence around it. At noon the Sheriff took Shaw from the jail and placed him in a carriage for the half-mile ride to the river. He was escorted by the Baldwin Blues and fifty cavalrymen. Shaw rode in silence with his eyes on his open prayer-book.

According to an account of his last moments, at the river, Shaw spoke to the crowd while standing in the carriage saying, "I have nothing in the world against any man. The county officers have all been very kind to me, and I do not want my people to think hard of them. I have committed many great sins, but have prayed to God and do hope that he has forgiven me." He next recited the service which his spiritual advisors had arranged for him, and then entered the gallows enclosure.

According to articles in the July 16, 1878 *Union Recorder* and the July 13, 1878 *New York Times*, Shaw ascended the scaffold with a firm step and seemed to be absorbed. He prayed for 15 minutes while standing on the trap with his hands and feet bound, his head was covered with a black hood, his neck placed in the noose. He asked the Sheriff if he could have a few more minutes as he was "not ready yet" and the sheriff granted his request.

Shortly thereafter, Shaw notified the Sheriff of his readiness, saying, "Good-bye. Tell your wife good-bye for me." He resumed his prayer and while the words, "O God have mercy…" were on his lips the trap opened, he dropped suddenly through it, and his soul flew into eternity. Shaw's body reportedly trembled and jerked for several minutes and then a crucifix which he had been holding fell to the ground. After 37 minutes the doctors pronounced him dead. Upon a final examination, the doctors found that Shaw's neck had not been broken by the fall, and that he unfortunately had died slowly from strangulation.[12]

The Burials

In the Union Recorder article, it was pointed out that while on the gallows Shaw never stated that he was innocent. However, it should also be pointed out that he never admitted any guilt, either.[13]

The day before his attempted suicide Shaw wrote a letter to his mother. In it he asked his mother to "take care of my baby and meet me in Heaven, for I feel that I am better off than the ones that has sworn my life away. Now I hope that those who has done all they can against me are satisfied. I don't want my friends to stop work until they find out the right party. It will be found out some day, when it is too late for me. I know my treatment and my wife's wishes, for I worked as hard for my wife as any man that ever lived, and I am as clear of my charge as a baby, and God that is in Heaven knows."

Later, in the same letter, Shaw stated "Bury me by my wife and baby if it is agreeable with all parties; if not agreeable with all parties suit yourself."[14]

Today, the burial location of Michael Shaw is unknown. Unless his body was cremated, his last remains lie in an unmarked pauper's grave for eternity. Immediately following the hanging, his body was shipped to Stevens Pottery in the southern part of Baldwin County. It is unknown what transpired thereafter.

Ardeoro Shaw is buried in West-Neil Cemetery, a small family cemetery now grown up in brush, trees and vines off County Line Road in Baldwin County. Her grave had been marked in earlier years, but is no longer discernible today. Her mother, Sarah Moore, who spoke out so strongly against Michael Shaw, has a small simple headstone on her grave. It reads, "Sarah Moore, born April 15, 1828. died June 2, 1900, She Hath Done What She Could."[15]

Final Thoughts

Was Michael Shaw in fact guilty of the murder of his wife? Today, one might not be so certain. It would be easy to question the weight placed upon the changeable testimony of the "half witted" David Butler and wonder if he was actually pressured by Shaw to make his first statement or by Detective Murphy to make his revised statement.

However, there is also the question of Shaw's violent past and the rumors surrounding him which undoubtedly were taken into consideration by the jury. Also, the story told by the four-year-old child is open to speculation today as well. History – particularly recent cases – have demonstrated how easily a child can be influenced to both speak and personally believe terrible untruths.

While there were no other solid suspects at which to point a suspicious finger, there was little solid evidence relating to Michael Shaw as well, so the questions will always remain: Was Michael Shaw guilty of murder? Or, was an innocent man hanged for a crime he did not commit?

Endnotes

1. *Union Recorder*, May 1, 1877.
2. *Union Recorder*, May 2, 1877.
3. *Atlanta Constitution*, May 5, 1877 and Union Recorder, July 16, 1878.
    4. *Union Recorder*, May 8, 1877.
5. *Union Recorder*, May 8, 1877.
6. *Union Recorder*, May 22, 1877 and Atlanta Constitution, October 7, 1877.
7. ibid.
8. *Union Recorder*, July 16, 1878.
9. *Atlanta Constitution*, October 7, 1877.
10. *Union Recorder*, June 18, 1878 and Union Recorder, July 16, 1878.
11. *Union Recorder*, July 16, 1878.
12. *Union Recorder*, July 16, 1878 and New York Times, July 13, 1878.
13. *Union Recorder*, July 16, 1878.
14. ibid
15. *Union Recorder*, July 16, 1878 and Dawson, Elizabeth L. and Louise M. Horne and Anne M. King, *One Hundred Three Lost or Found Cemeteries of Baldwin County, Georgia 1814-1999* (Milledgeville, GA, Mary Vinson Memorial Library, 1999) p. 190.

The Night, the Alligator, & Me

JOYCE KRAMER

L iving with the alligator is a part of life in the country on Lake Seminole in the extreme southwestern corner of Georgia. Most of the time, animal and human get along just fine, respecting each others' turf. However, occasionally, the alligator gets frustrated with the ever-growing invasion of its domain, and strikes back. This is when the Alligator Control crew with the local office of the Georgia Department of Natural Resources (DNR) comes to the rescue.

When alerted to a troublesome "gator," the DNR crew will capture the offending critter and take it to a new location, usually a swamp well away from human contact. In my job as a news reporter, I was once asked to come along on one of these hunts. It turned out to be quite an adventure too.

Now just as with most women, I have no desire to be out on the black water of an

This sizeable alligator obviously had lost much of its fear of humans, and was called in to the Georgia Department of Natural Resources as a nuisance case. He had become so bold that he was attacking the watercraft of boaters as they were being launched.

DALE KRAMER

immense river at night, looking for – of all things – alligators. My husband, Dale, however, loved the idea of this adventure and eagerly volunteered to take my place. This action took place in a back-water swamp off the Chattahoochee River, and Dale later described this adventure to me as follows in great detail.

A Big One Ensnared

"Hey!" Two DNR officials with the Alligator Control Unit in a 13-foot boat thrashed their arms wildly through the air in the inky blackness of the night, calling to the shape of the smaller, twelve-foot DNR boat containing two additional DNR personnel assisting in the hunt. They were barely visible against the wild foliage of the immense Chattahoochee.

"We got us a big one here!," they called, their trap surging from the violent escape attempts of the enraged animal. "Over ten feet!"

Sitting in the boat with the DNR men, Dale was somewhat unnerved. "This is my first hunt. Can't we start with an eighteen 'incher?'" Dale knew alligators are unpredictable, and are more than powerful enough to sever arms and legs, and the larger ones are definitely capable of killing humans, as they have demonstrated over the years.

One of the DNR crewmen directed the light from his helmet to the black water around the small boat in which they were seated. What he saw made him immediately uncomfortable. All around the men, the red eyes of other alligators indicated the beasts had gathered in an unusual number, their eyes shining like Christmas lights, twinkling with false merriment.

As Dale sat in the front of the larger, thirteen-foot boat and watched the men, his apprehension caused him to unconsciously flex and un-flex his hands. He could only find it ironic that barely one-half hour ago, he had been at home, comfortably and safely reclined in his big, overstuffed easy chair, feet propped up, watching National Geographic's, "When Good Animals Go Bad!"

As the men in the 13-foot craft maneuvered through the many tree stumps and water grasses to the side of the smaller boat, they brushed up against the side of the ensnared 'gator. "Watch out!" one of the men cautioned as the large 'gator snapped viciously at the side of the boat, his teeth leaving sizeable indentations in the sturdy metal.

"Boy! Is he mad!"

Securing The Beast

It was a troublesome 'gator just such as this which had recently been reported as attacking watercraft being launched at a nearby ramp. The men knew they had to relocate this trouble-maker to a safer environment. Otherwise, he would just have to be euthanized.

Dale was visibly shaken as he helped steady the boat against the thrashing tail of the three hundred and fifty pound reptile. The 'gator suddenly dived and the boiling

DALE KRAMER

Gators aren't always easy to spot. Nature has made their hides impenetrable and practically invisible against the dark waters of their natural environment. They have been waiting thousands of years to meet us. We just have to make sure it's not a "dinner date."

water between the boats became calm once again.

At that point, the night air was almost too thick to breathe, the humidity hanging like a veil across the great body of water. The only sound was of playful frogs on the distant shoreline, seemingly laughing at the follies of the men in the boats.

Collectively holding their breath, the men cautiously looked all around.

"Where do you think he is?" Dale whispered as harsh admonitions for silence followed his words.

"He's probably under the boat," came the answer as a light from a helmet scanned the water.

Bump! Bump! Oh yes, the 'gator was there alright, hitting the bottom of the boat. Suddenly, the water erupted, sending a shower of droplets which would have put Old Faithful to shame. The animal writhed wildly. Twisting and thrashing, powerful jaws snapping in a staccato pace, and tail threatening to crush everything in its path.

Using the technology of their trade – and just brute force – the men eventually wrestled the strong beast into position. For some unknown reason, once a 'gator's mouth is permanently shut, the animal becomes somewhat sedate, and one of the men quickly announced, "We have to tape that mouth!"

A hunter in the smaller boat quickly picked up a paddle which had been laying dormant inside the craft. A huge hunk was missing from the fat end. As if reading Dale's mind, the man explained simply, "From the last gator."

Using a technique honed from many hunts on the rivers and swamps of Georgia, the DNR man then lowered the paddle down toward the thrashing animal who immediately snapped at it, closing it's three hundred pounds-per-square-inch of jaw pressure around the wood.

"Tape it! Tape it!" he yelled as the other two men reached over and fiercely held the dangerous mouth closed.

"Hey, I need you to grab around him by his hind legs," one of the men told Dale. "We need to keep that tail still!" the hunter gasped, already out of breath.

Dale quickly did as he was told. His life flashed before his eyes. It had been a good one. Short, but good.

Despite his momentary lapse, Dale knew he had to keep his end up. These guys were depending on him. He reached over the side and grabbed the hind legs. No fear!

One of the men quickly taped and taped for what seemed like an eternity. Finally, the mouth and legs were all taped down and confined securely. The big dangerous animal wasn't going anywhere now.

'Gator On Board

"Let's bring him in the boat." the DNR man said with a heave.

Dale looked at the two men in the other boat. No room there! Were they really going to bring this leviathan into the boat with him?

"Pardon me," he said somewhat apprehensively, "Is there going to be 'three' in this boat?"

"Yep. Just remember, this ain't the Love Boat and he's not the recreation director!" the DNR man responded with a grin on his face.

The men steadied the boat, then rolled the big reptile on board.

Dale watched in awe as the 'gator's eyes roamed over his new surroundings. It was hard to believe this ten-foot three-inch, three hundred fifty pound animal was now draped from bow to stern, up over one seat, down onto the floor, up over another seat and on over the side of the boat.

As one of the men attempted to start the boat motor for the trip back to the truck, the engine suddenly sputtered, coughed and died. Puzzled, he tried to restart it. "I just filled the gas tank before we left," he said, somewhat exasperated, "so I know it's not that."

Once again, Dale's eyes trailed over the huge body of his "ship mate," an animal whose jaws could crush your thigh like a watermelon.

Suddenly, there it was. The men saw the huge 'gator's body had been draped on top of the gas line, cutting off the flow of fuel! Dale's partner grabbed the alligator's front and he grabbed the 'gator's hind legs. They then rolled him over, off the gas line, and the engine immediately coughed to life. Once on their way, the men were quickly back at the boat launch ramp and the truck.

The next task was to wench the sullen alligator up into the bed of the pick-up truck. As the beast laid still, Dale reached down and grabbed onto its foot, feeling

JOYCE KRAMER

Donalsonville, Georgia, resident Dale Kramer pilots his craft down a slough off the Chattahoochee. "An alligator we call 'Grumpy' once chased us here," he smiles.

the power located even there. He had to reflect back over this adventurous evening with awe.

The cool professionalism and confident demeanor of the DNR men was inspiring. Their actions tonight may help rid the area of one troublesome animal, but Dale knew that the alligator is a species which has been around since prehistoric times. They will always be around and there will always be alligator problems – no doubt right up until the end of time.

Looking back over the excitement of the evening, Dale mused that he probably would like to go out and experience this action again! Well, maybe.

THE 7TH CAVALRY RIDES INTO HISTORY

Georgians at the Battle of the Little Bighorn

MICHAEL WILLIAMS

They were a part of one of the most famous military engagements of all time. They did not know it at the time, but one of these Georgians was destined to emerge from the fateful battle unscathed, and the other to suffer a horrible death and then eternity in a grave on a lonely hill in present-day Montana.

June 24, 1876, was a particularly hot, muggy day in Montana Territory. The riverboat Far West slowly chugged its way up the Little Bighorn River. A black plume of smoke could be seen for miles as the craft made its way to the point of rendezvous south of the sacred Black Hills. It had been sent to rendezvous with Lt. Col. George Armstrong Custer to re-supply his vaunted Seventh Cavalry. Within this group of soldiers were two native Georgians and one later citizen of the state, all of whom were destined to soon become ignoble footnotes in history.

The captain of the Far West slowly piloted the boat close to the shoreline where he was to await the arrival of Custer and the Seventh. Within moments of mooring, the seaman saw a cloud of dust rising above the horizon. Approximately 650 cavalrymen soon became visible, galloping toward the Far West, the thunderous pounding of their horses' hooves growing louder by the minute. Full-force, the Seventh Cavalry was an impressive fighting force, and certainly one to be feared as an organized unit.

Unfulfilled Career?

Upon reaching the riverboat at its moorings, Custer dismounted, as did his men. The famed leader had distinguished himself in the U.S. Civil War, rising through a succession of battlefield or brevet promotions to the rank of brigadier general at the unprecedented age of 22. He had continuously demonstrated unbridled courage in numerous battles as a Union army commander, but his men also had repeatedly suffered extremely heavy casualties.

While serving in the West, however, his career has been described as stellar by some and unimpressive by others. In late 1867, he was court-martialed and suspended for a year for being absent from duty without leave. In 1866 he had been appointed lieutenant colonel (his permanent rank) of the Seventh Cavalry, but almost lost this command when in 1876, he was temporarily relieved of duty by President Ulysses S. Grant for further misdeeds.

In nearly 11 years in and around Fort Abraham Lincoln in Dakota Territory, Custer

Lt. Colonel George A. Custer has remained one of the best-known figures in American history long after his death at the hands of Lakota and Cheyenne warriors at the Battle of the Little Bighorn on June 25, 1876.

had truly won but one battle – Washita Creek–against the Indians. Depending upon the reference source today, this battle was either an honest victory over fierce opposition – or a massacre basically of women, children and elderly natives while most of the warriors were out hunting. Regardless of the circumstances, Custer's contempt for the Native Americans was obvious in his battle strategies and general relations. It was a trait that would one day return to haunt him.

During its re-supply trip to Custer's men, the Far West had brought the soldiers food, clothing, blankets – and most importantly – four months worth of back pay, reportedly paid in gold and silver coins. In 1876, the U.S. Army was notorious for falling behind on payrolls to the troops, so paydays were always morale-building days.

In this instance, however, the morale of the Seventh Cavalry apparently was so low that Custer ordered no payment was to be distributed to the men until they were five days out of Fort Abraham Lincoln on their next mission. This was done in order to prevent desertions. No rational man would desert so far from the safety of the fort or his comrades. Most of the troopers had witnessed first-hand the ferocity of the Indians and the mutilations they imparted upon their victims, and certainly none of the soldiers wanted ever to endure such torture themselves.

Georgians Among Them

In this particular mission, the Seventh Cavalry had been sent to put down an Indian uprising which had resulted from the encroachment of prospectors on the Black Hills where a gold rush had been touched off following the discovery of the precious yellow metal. The Black Hills were sacred to the Indians who resented the violation of their homeland by the white settlers. In response, thousands of Sioux, Unkpapa, Blackfeet, Arapaho and Cheyenne had united and converged upon the hills to inflict a "stiff" price – literally – upon their invaders.

Sitting Bull was a prominent leader among the Lakota Sioux who defeated Lt. Colonel George Custer at the Battle of the Little Bighorn.

The Seventh Cavalry under Custer consisted of approximately 650 (some reports indicate 655) men. Four Custer family members also accompanied the 37-year-old commander. They were: Tom Custer, age 38, George's older brother; Boston Custer, age 19, George's younger brother; brother-in-law James Calhoun, and a nephew named Audie Reed. By the end of the mission, they all would be dead.

Two native Georgians also accompanied Custer on this ill-fated mission. James Manning of Houston County, Georgia, had enlisted in the Seventh three years earlier. He was a blacksmith by trade whose skills were always in demand. He was described as 5 feet 8 inches in height with hazel eyes and black hair. He was 33 years of age.[1]

William Rye, another trooper in the Seventh, hailed from Pike County, Georgia, where he was born in 1849. He enlisted with the Seventh in 1875. He was described as 5 feet 8 inches in height, with gray eyes and brown hair.[2]

Along with Custer, there were two other officers strategically involved at the Little Bighorn campaign – Major Marcus Reno and Captain Frederick Benteen – both of whom would go down in history as major players in the engagement.

Captain Benteen hailed from Virginia. He had served during the Civil War under General James Wilson and had been present during the infamous Battle of Columbus, Georgia in 1865 (Readers please see "The Tragic Battle Of Columbus," *Georgia Backroads*, Winter, 2004, pp 46-50). Following his military career, Benteen would move to Atlanta where he would spend his final years. He was described as tall, with curly blond hair and a pudgy face. He hated Custer and the feeling was mutual, and this relationship may possibly have played a decisive role in the disastrous outcome of the Battle at Little Bighorn.

Early Mistakes

In addition to the aforementioned supplies unloaded from the Far West, two large Gatling guns initially were taken ashore for use by the Seventh Cavalry. Custer, however, reportedly studied the guns intently then made the first of several catastrophic decisions which ultimately doomed his command. "Those are too big, too heavy," he reportedly stated. "Besides, we won't need them anyway," he added confidently, demonstrating his trademark disdain for the Indians.

Ironically, the two Gatling guns just might have saved Custer's command in the engagement at Little Bighorn, and at the very least would have given his men better odds against the Indians who outnumbered the Seventh Cavalry overwhelmingly. The Gatling consisted of six gun barrels mounted in a revolving frame which could spew out murderous continuous fire at enemy combatants. A later version with ten barrels was able to fire an even more deadly 320 rounds per minute. Custer, however, was supremely confident in his leadership and his troops' abilities on the battlefield, and in fairness, the sizeable guns no doubt would have been burdensome to haul over the rough terrain in the Black Hills.

The Seventh remained camped on the Little Bighorn River throughout the night.

There reportedly was a festive mood as the men ate, socialized and relaxed before the campaign began.

At dawn, the Far West weighed anchor and steamed back downriver. Custer dispatched three Indian scouts – Curly, Bloody Knife, and Half-Yellow Face – with orders to find the Indian camp and report back to him as soon as the camp was discovered. Meanwhile, he and his command broke camp, mounted up and headed toward the Black Hills themselves.

The cavalrymen rode in formation at a slow gallop into the Little Bighorn Valley searching for any signs of hostiles. Their presence no doubt was soon made known to the Indians as the shrill notes of *Gary Owen* – Custer's favorite song – were played by the regimental piccoloist.

Around 9:00 a.m., the three scouts returned, galloping quickly up to Custer to deliver their report. He halted his command as the scouts approached. Half-Yellow Face appeared alarmed.

"There are many lodges," the scout reportedly explained. "More than I have ever seen before. The village is very, very big."

Custer turned to his brother, Tom, to discuss their course of action. Before he could begin, however, Half-Yellow Face reportedly interrupted him with the ominous warning, "They know we are here. They have seen us. You must attack, now!"

After conferring with Tom, Custer decided he needed instead to reconnoiter the situation before acting. He wanted to ride up to a prominence known today as Sharpshooter Ridge. From there he would be able to see for several miles and get a better understanding of the Indian positions.

Deadly Division

Before he departed, Custer called Capt. Benteen and Major Reno forward. He instructed Benteen to take three companies (Companies D, H & K) and head southwest. Reno was instructed to take three companies as well (A, G & M) and cross the river. William Rye from Georgia was in one of these companies.

Custer himself would take five companies (C, E, F, I and L) and head north. James Manning from Georgia was among these troops. In the Seventh Cavalry, a company usually consisted of 40 to 50 men.

The last company of just over 40 men under the command of Capt. McDougall remained in the rear to escort the pack or supply train.

Custer led his men toward Sharpshooter Ridge. From his experience, he had become aware that most Indian villages consisted of perhaps 300 to 400 natives. Some later estimates placed the Indians' numbers in this village somewhere between 4,000 to 10,000 natives, but many knowledgeable historians today estimate the hostiles' actual strength on that day was somewhere in the neighborhood of 2,000 warriors, which is still almost a 10-to-one advantage over the 210 men directly under Custer's command that day in the decisive battle.

Around noon, Major Reno reached the Little Bighorn River not far from the

LEFT: Capt. Frederick Benteen was one of the survivors of the fateful battle at the Little Bighorn. He retired from the U.S. Army in 1888 and moved to Atlanta, Georgia, purchasing a home overlooking Grant Park in the city. He died there ten years later in 1898. RIGHT: Major Marcus Reno failed to come to Custer's relief even after being summoned by the famed commander. As a result of his actions, he was charged with cowardice and barely escaped being court martialed.

Indian village. He crossed at the shallowest spot.

"...We got the skirmish line formed and here the Indians made their first charge," said Sergeant John Ryan who survived the engagement and was later interviewed. "There were probably 500 of them coming from the direction of their village. They were well mounted and well armed."

Sergeant Ryan explained how Reno's command was quickly overwhelmed. "They could not cut through us, [but] they strung out in single file, lying on the opposite side of their ponies from us...They overlapped our skirmish line on the left and were closing in on the rear to complete the circle."

Reno, armed with a pistol, also returned fire at the attackers. He knew the Indians had the advantage since they were firing and moving downhill toward him and his men who were huddled in a low-lying grassy area next to the river. He also knew he had to counter that advantage.

Reno's Response

Stunned by the events unfolding before him, Reno realized that matters were worse than he had thought. There were more Indians than he could count. Some were riding horses, but many were on foot, stalking his troops slowly through the tall grass. All were armed with rifles, pistols, knives or bows and arrows. The air was filled with war whoops, gun fire and the thunder of horses' hooves. The Indians came by the scores, rushing Reno's position continuously, inflicting casualties at a steady rate.

Reno's men soon began falling as the Indians' guns found their marks. The tall grass provided excellent cover as the Indians crept up on the troopers before ambushing them. Reno's heart pounded as more and more warriors began pouring out onto the hillside to engage his vastly outnumbered force. He quickly turned to a private and shouted "Go find Benteen! We're going to be overrun!"

George Herendon also managed to survive the battle and was later interviewed regarding the incident.

"Reno [had] advanced about a mile from the [river] ford to a line of timber on the right and dismounted his men to fight on foot," Herendon explained. "...After skirmishing for a few minutes, Reno

Two Moons was chief of the Cheyenne who conquered the Seventh Cavalry at the Little Bighorn.

fell back to his horses in the timber. The Indians moved to his left and rear, evidently with the intention of cutting him off from the ford...The command headed for the ford, pressed closely by Indians in large numbers...The Sioux, mounted on their swift ponies dashed up by the side of the soldiers and fired at them, killing both men and horses. Little resistance was offered, and it was a complete rout to the ford."

Suffering heavy losses, Reno and the remainder of his men fell back to a hill on a bluff. "I saw the Indians coming up the valley from Custer's right," Herendon continued. "Reno was moving his command down the ridge toward Custer, but the Indians crossed the river below Reno and swarmed up the bluff on all sides. After skirmishing with them Reno went back to his old position which was on one of the highest fronts along the bluffs [above the river].

"As soon as it was dark, Reno took the packs and saddles off the mules and horses and made breastworks of them," Herendon added. "He also [ordered us to drag] the dead horses and mules on the line and sheltered the men behind them. . . . The fight lasted until it was too dark to see to shoot.

"At the peep of day, the Indians opened a heavy fire and a desperate fight ensued, lasting until 10:00 o'clock," Herendon stated. The Indians charged our positions three or four times, coming up close enough to hit our men with stones which they threw by hand."

Reno soon was joined by Capt. Benteen's men and the fighting continued in earnest. Benteen, realizing that their ammunition would run out, gave orders that only his best shooters were to return fire until Custer could reinforce them.

Courting Disaster

Meanwhile, farther down the valley, Custer was about to have his hands full as well. Shortly before 3:00 p.m., with approximately one-sixth of the strength of the Seventh Cavalry with him, Custer began to make his way toward Sharpshooter Ridge. To reach the prominence, he would have to ride through a small valley surrounded by bluffs, trees, rocks and bushes. He halted his command for a brief moment to assess the situation.

At this point, Half Yellow Face gave a final warning to the vain-glorious leader. "They know we are here. We should turn back."

Custer, growing weary of the scout's ominous warnings, gave the order to proceed. The cavalry began to ride at a steady gallop down into the valley. Suddenly, all Hell broke loose. Intense gunfire rang out from every peak, bluff, tree and shrub surrounding the valley, as the Indians, like angry hornets, set upon Custer and his men.

Mitch Bouyer, a half-blood scout, reportedly turned to Curly and said, "You are a young man. Save yourself!" At that, Curly turned his horse toward the entrance of the valley and raced frantically toward freedom. Bullets whizzed by his head, but he held on tightly to his horse and made good his escape. Many sources maintain that Curly was the lone survivor from Custer's men, but other reports indicate that Custer had sent three other scouts back out of harm's way just prior to the conflict.

One fearful soldier, realizing that disaster was imminent, reportedly observed Curly's daring escape and decided to flee as well. He rode frantically and laid low in the saddle, but was not as fortunate as the scout. Several bullets ripped into his flesh, causing him to twist and sag in the saddle before collapsing onto the ground. His horse fell only seconds later, cut down as well by the intense gunfire.

Eliminating The Horses

Meanwhile, Custer, who had experienced many engagements such as this over the years, was not yet worried – despite the fact that by this time, he was already taking considerable fire from the Indians. Wolf Tooth, a Cheyenne, had been scouting with 40 to 50 warriors when he noticed Custer and his men. The Indians immediately set upon the soldiers, peppering them with fire.

Custer sent Algernon Smith and E Troop to find a spot for the men to cross the river. After quickly reconnoitering the area and discovering a ford, Smith and E Troop returned to Custer. Then, still disdainful of the Indians' strength, Custer divided his men even more, taking Companies E and F and setting out northwest along a ridge-line toward a broad plain and the river. He left Companies I, C and L to fight Wolf Tooth's men.

As Custer and the troops from E and F approached the river, they began taking still more fire from a group of warriors who were guarding the women and children at the Indians' camp. Custer ordered F Company to dismount and set up a skirmish line, and then made yet another strategic mistake. Instead of having every fourth trooper hold four horses each (as was required in 1876 cavalry tactics), Custer ordered a still smaller group of troopers to hold eight horses each in order to increase his man-power (and thus firepower) on the skirmish line.

This tactic ultimately proved disastrous. Waving blankets and firing their weapons at the soldiers' horses, the Indians, who had virtually surrounded the troopers, began stampeding the frightened animals, isolating more and more of the men of Companies E and F. Finally, with most of F Troop on foot, Custer realized the entire operation and his immediate command were in grave peril. He was completely surrounded and about to be overrun, and many of his men now were without mounts.

Desperate Message

With more and more bullets buzzing around his head, Custer quickly scrawled a note addressed to Benteen ordering him to come quickly and bring lots of packs. He gave the note to a young private and instructed him vehemently to find Benteen.

Though Custer had no way to know it at the time, Benteen had encountered far too many hostiles himself to come to the aid of his commander. Even had he been able, Benteen, was a more prudent (if possibly cowardly) leader than was Custer, and would not have ridden into the face of almost certain death.

Nonetheless, the private, with his grave orders from Custer in hand, mounted his horse and made a mad dash toward the entrance of the valley. Miraculously, despite a hail of gunfire raining around him, he made good his escape, just as had Curly before him.

From a nearby peak, Curly reportedly stood and watched helplessly as the vaunted Seventh Cavalry fell under what he undoubtedly knew was a deadly siege. For a while, the troopers – with their longer-ranged firepower – were able to hold many of the Indians at bay. The big .45-70 caliber Springfields were able to reach much farther more accurately than the Indians' rifles and bows and arrows. However, the Indians had at least 200 of the repeating Winchesters in their possession during the conflict, and once they began overtaking the soldiers, the repeaters naturally proved superior to the single-shot Springfields.

As a result, the soldiers under Custer increasingly were overwhelmed as the Indians stalked them in the tall grass which provided excellent concealment for ambushing

Photographed in 1879, three years after the disastrous engagement, this grisly scene of bleached bones, strewn equipment and other paraphernalia littered the ridgeline and gullies on Last Stand Hill as Capt. George Sanderson and his 11th Infantry began cleaning up the site. Notice the many horse bones from the poor mounts sacrificed to provide cover for the terrified troopers.

the troops. Many of the Indians were making suicide rushes too, totally ignoring the gunfire from the troopers. Making matters worse, virtually all of the Indians who had been attacking Reno and his men soon turned their attention to Custer.

Last Stand Hill

Custer looked around him desperately, searching for a more defensible position. The shouts and gunfire and whinnying horses no doubt were deafening by this time. The ridgeline down which he had earlier galloped was high ground and certainly more defensible than the low-lying river-plain where he currently was taking heavy casualties. Today, this brief rise is known as "Last Stand Hill."

Company F began retreating back toward this ridgeline where much of the remainder of Custer's men had gathered. At first, the men tried to force their horses to lie down so they could be used as cover from the intense gunfire. Many of the horses, however, bucked and resisted, frightened by the noise and heightened panic around them, as well as by the painful bullets from the Indians which were piercing their hides. Finally, realizing they had no choice, the troopers began shooting their mounts to establish desperately-needed breastworks on the hillside.

Despite the losses, Custer rallied his men. Lying behind their horses, the men con-

"Last Stand Hill:" To honor the soldiers – including Georgia's James Manning – who died here, small marble markers were placed at the site where each soldier fell. The bodies of these soldiers were all later re-buried in an adjacent cemetery, with the exception of Custer, whose body was re-buried at West Point Military Academy.

tinued to return fire, though it was becoming increasingly obvious that their efforts were futile. In the end, the Indians simply overwhelmed them numerically. Since the men were horseless, the end was inevitable.

More and more soldiers fell as they were cut down by the Indians. Custer no doubt looked around one last time, hoping he might spot Benteen riding to his rescue. Benteen, however, was nowhere to be found, nor would he be.

Suddenly, a deadly round hit Custer, ripping into his left temple, dropping him in his tracks. A second round – possibly a trophy shot – was later fired by one of the victorious hostiles into Custer's left breast, but by that time, the spirit of the Seventh Cavalry commander had already departed. His time on earth had ended.

Today, some historians and battlefield analysts speculate as to whether Custer's two wounds both came from enemy combatants. Some maintain the wound in Custer's left temple may have been self-inflicted, since blood had flowed from it but not from his chest wound, meaning the chest wound was made sometime later, after his heart had stopped pumping blood.

Custer – better than most of his men – knew of the horrors inflicted by the Indians upon captured soldiers. He knew how terrible were the tortures, and certainly did not intend to have to endure that suffering himself under any circumstances. Did he actually commit suicide? Perhaps. Perhaps not. It undoubtedly will never be known.

Whatever the circumstances, Custer's men by this point were leaderless. Panic no doubt set in for the few that were left alive. The ground on Last Stand Hill became spotted and stained with the blood of scores of cavalrymen.

Utter Annihilation

At this moment, the Sioux, Cheyenne, and their united brethren decided to rush forward to finish the attack on Custer's men. Perhaps 2,000 warriors snuffed out the lives of the remaining troopers in a bloodbath. If the earlier portions of the engagement at Little Bighorn had been nightmarish to Custer's men, this final annihilation must have been abjectly horrifying to the handful who remained alive long enough to witness it. The heat was intense and the air filled with the smell of death and the war whoops of thousands of warriors as they shot, stabbed, slashed, crushed and mutilated the bodies of all the soldiers.

One last desperate group of 15 to 20 soldiers from Company E managed to survive for a brief moment. They were surrounded and out of ammunition and made a last-ditch attempt to escape through a nearby ravine, carrying their empty weapons which they used as clubs. They, however, were quickly cut down.

In the end, the bodies of 210 dead cavalrymen were left scattered about the ridgeline. Included in the dead were five members of the Custer family and Georgia's own James Manning.

At this point, death was actually a merciful relief for the soldiers, for the natives were not yet finished with their victims. The Indian women, children and elderly now converged upon the battlefield themselves for the ritualistic mutilations, cutting and hacking at the bodies of the fallen soldiers at will. According to Indian tradition, if a man was missing an arm, a leg, a head or other body part or organ, he would spend all eternity without that part, searching for it indefinitely. All of the fallen soldiers were mutilated horribly.

Custer himself was not spared this final indignity. His body was discovered two days later on June 27 by Lt. Edward Godfrey. He had not been scalped, but his left thigh had been slashed to the bone (the Indians believed it would impede his mounting a horse in the afterlife), a finger had been severed, and an arrow shaft had been shoved into his private parts.

The warriors set about collecting the rifles, knives and any other personal possessions of the soldiers that might be of use. They also looted the pockets of the bodies for valuables.

The gold and silver coins which had recently been paid to the men as back pay were gathered together and placed in two saddlebags. This cache – worth in excess of $30,000.00 in 1876 – would be worth millions today. No reports have ever surfaced of the discovery of this treasure which may yet be buried at an unknown site in the vicinity of the battle. Treasure hunters still search for this valuable cache even today.

No Rescue From Reno

Meanwhile, around 3:00 p.m. on the fateful day, a lone rider rode frantically toward Benteen and Reno's position. By now, the gunfire surrounding them had subsided as their assailants had turned their attention to Custer. The rider handed the note to Benteen. It was the frantic hand-written order from Custer. It stated he was under attack and to bring packs quickly.

Intense gunfire could now be heard coming from the north as the Indians were wiping out Custer and his troops. Reno knew he needed the ammunition and other supplies in the packs being held in the rear, but they were too far away to be called up immediately. Benteen and Reno conferred, and Reno ultimately decided to hold where they were.

In retrospect, some battlefield analysts have called the actions of these two men cowardly. Others have maintained they were wise. No one, however, can argue the fact that their decision to hold their positions at that point quite likely saved the lives of many men in the Seventh Cavalry who otherwise would have perished.

Despite these observations, the men of both Benteen and Reno respected the courage of their commanders, and did not hesitate to testify to this later after the battle. "Captain Benteen saw a large mass of Indians gathered on his front to charge," added trooper George Herendon, a seasoned frontiersman who survived the battle. "Benteen led the charge and was upon the Indians before they knew what they were about and killed a great many... All the time he was going about through the bullets, encouraging the soldiers to stand up to their work and not let the Indians whip them... He never sheltered his own person once during the battle, and I do not see how he escaped being killed."

Nevertheless, Reno's controversial decision not to proceed to Custer's relief later resulted in his being charged with cowardice. He barely escaped a court-martial. Benteen testified on Reno's behalf and said "If we had gone to relieve Custer, we all would have been killed."

Soon, the gunfire surrounding the two commanders and their men intensified as the Indians who had defeated Custer were now rejoining the assault on the remainder of the Seventh, seeking to annihilate them as well. The two commanders were uncertain what course of action to take. They had the advantage of higher ground but they were still heavily outnumbered and cut off from water and supplies. "The bullets fell like a perfect shower of hail," Lt. Francis Gibson later remembered.

Waiting For Rescue

Despite taking 73 more casualties (13 killed; 60 wounded), the surviving troopers from the Seventh successfully held off the Sioux and Cheyenne for almost two days. The men knew that General Alford Terry was scheduled to bring in another regiment within those two days, and they were determined to endure the onslaught until relief

Though the soldiers were laid to rest in graves in an adjacent cemetery, the spots at which they fell as they died were marked for posterity.

could arrive.

For the next 48 hours, the gunfire was not as intense, but remained steady nonetheless. The heat and sparse cover left Benteen's and Reno's troops parched, drained and weary, and desperate for water. A few brave cavalrymen made the ultra-hazardous trek down to the creek under cover of darkness, braving almost certain death, to retrieve precious water for the men.

By this point, however, the men would not have been so uneasy had they known the status of their attackers. The Sioux, Cheyenne and their brothers in arms knew they had successfully conquered a great foe, but that in doing so, there would be a price to pay when reinforcements for the soldiers arrived. The Indians, therefore, were breaking camp, making preparations to flee the fresh cavalrymen they knew would undoubtedly be arriving shortly.

On the 27th of June, Benteen caught a heart-warming glimpse of an American flag in the distance. General Terry had finally arrived. Benteen's bugler began desperately blowing reveille to alert Terry to their position. Terry ordered his men to follow the sound of the bugle.

Upon his arrival, Terry was stunned to hear that the men had been under siege for two days and Custer's whereabouts was unknown. He ordered Reno and Benteen to have their men mount up. They joined Terry as all rode north to search for Custer.

About 30 minutes later, the soldiers, to their horror, found the bloated mutilated bodies of Custer and his men – all now at the mercy of the scorching sun and the buzzards. Terry ordered the men to quickly bury the bodies as best they could, using pans or anything that would serve as a digging implement. As soon as the last body was buried, he organized his men and they left the Little Bighorn Valley.

Killing Ground Revisited

Terry's command returned a month later to give proper burials to the fallen soldiers. Custer's body was removed and taken back east where it was later interred at West Point Military Academy. The Indian tribes who had allied for their great victory soon scattered to the four winds. Many later were captured and sent to reservations.

The battlefield at Little Bighorn was designated a national historic site 10 years after the infamous engagement. A monument lists the names of all the 210 men killed with Custer, as well as the 53 who were killed in Reno's command. Another monument was erected where each of the soldiers fell. The markers read simply, "U.S. Soldier Seventh Cavalry Fell Here June 25, 1876."

The body of James Manning from Houston County, Georgia, was laid to rest at the Little Bighorn cemetery. Georgia native William Rye was one of the luckier ones. He was a part of Reno's command and survived the battle. In September, 1877, he apparently decided he had been in the military long enough, and deserted the army. Today, his circumstances beyond that date are known but to God.

Interestingly, in 1888, Captain Frederick Benteen – one of the most sensationalized survivors at the Battle of Little Bighorn – officially retired from military life and moved to Atlanta, Georgia. He and his wife bought a home at 39 Pavilion Street overlooking Grant Park. He spent his time peacefully as a farmer while his wife, Kate, socialized and enjoyed Atlanta culture, frequently attending the opera.

Benteen ultimately became acquainted with a number of later icons in Atlanta (and American) history, including author Joel Chandler Harris (of Uncle Remus and Br'er Rabbit fame), the Candler brothers (founders of Coca-Cola), Mayor Charles Collier and Georgia Governor William Atchinson.

Benteen was far luckier than many of his former compatriots at arms, dying peacefully in his warm, safe home on June 22, 1898. He was buried three days later in Atlanta's Westview Cemetery – on the 22nd anniversary of the Battle of Little Bighorn. Four years later, his body was disinterred and reburied in Arlington National Cemetery in Washington, D.C. All his trials were now over.

Endnotes

1. *Men With Custer, Biographies Of The Seventh Cavalry*, p 205.
2. Ibid, p 291.

Carpetbaggers & Crime
and the Georgia Piney Woods

JANE WALKER

Southerners familiar with the history of the U.S. Civil War are well-acquainted with the term "carpet-bagger," particularly if they are descended from families directly afflicted by this pestilence. In 1868, just such a torment descended upon residents in a quiet middle Georgia region.

Throughout the ages, land wars have been the fodder not only of great litera-ture and famous legal battles, but also of the shattered lives of those with the misfortune to be involved in them. During the latter part of the nineteenth century, the people of what came to be known as the Three Rivers Area of middle

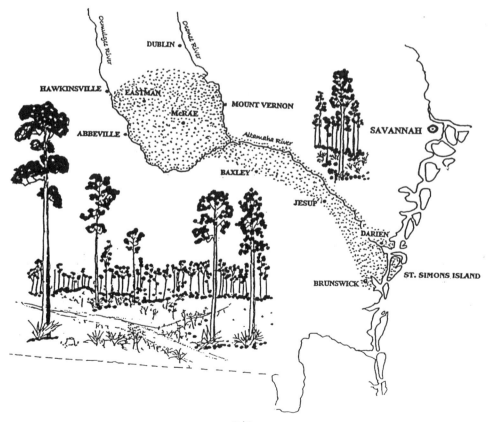

Georgia were involved in just such a "war," which, amazingly, continued for forty years after the War Between the States.

When I chanced to move to the Three Rivers Area in Georgia's Telfair County in 1960, I knew nothing of its beguiling history. I knew nothing about the pine trees that once stretched over a hundred feet into the sky; trees that had grown untouched for hundreds of years. I knew nothing about the rafting of these giant trees to the coast during the latter portion of the 1800s either. Indeed, I also did not know that it was these same trees which had lured Northern "carpet-baggers"– with larceny in their hearts – to this area during this period. It was an action which ultimately became so incendiary that it resulted in murder and mayhem and untold grief for local landowners in the area for many years.

I had recently married, and almost immediately, my new husband began to acquaint me with the area's past, especially the turmoil of the late 1800s. As an attorney, he was fascinated by the legal ramifications of the land seizures, a fascination that continued until his death in 1994. It was only after he passed away that I realized that I, too, had become captivated by this true but relatively unknown bit of Georgia's history.

To find the Three Rivers Area on a Georgia map, one must look for the Ocmulgee,

the Oconee, and the Altamaha. The first two rivers converge at a place called "The Forks" to form the larger Altamaha River. Lying along and between the Ocmulgee and the Oconee are the counties of Telfair, Dodge, Montgomery, Laurens, and Pulaski, more than five hundred square miles of land which became known during the latter part of the 19th century as "the Dodge lands."

In 1868, only a few years after the end of the U.S. Civil War, William E. Dodge of New York, along with other Northerners such as William Pitt Eastman and William Chauncey, came to this region with questionable deeds to this vast area of more than 300,000 acres of some of the finest longleaf yellow pine timber in the world. Welcomed as harbingers of peace and prosperity and as businessmen who had come to help the beleaguered and devastated South, these Northerners at first ingratiated themselves with the local people. This initial warm reception, however, was short-lived, as their true intentions became obvious.

The Dodge Family

William E. Dodge erected at his own expense a magnificent courthouse and gave it to the people of the county which bears his name. Known for his strict religious beliefs, Dodge was a Prohibitionist. He did not believe in the consumption of alcohol in any form. He claimed he was a devout Christian and he, along with William Pitt Eastman, became steadfastly involved with the churches and Sunday Schools in Eastman. Dodge also opposed any form of labor on the Sabbath. These and other qualities made a good impression, initially, upon the local Georgia residents.

The Prohibitionist New Yorker had seven sons, three of whom were active in the land confiscations and timber industry in the Three Rivers Area. These three were George E. Dodge, Norman

This group of hardy raftsmen was photographed circa early 1900s in south Georgia, and are very characteristic of the crews harvesting timber during the Dodge era.

W. Dodge, and A.G.P. Dodge, also known as "Alphabet Dodge," because of his use of so many initials in his name. (A.G.P. was the father of Anson Dodge who rebuilt Christ Church on St. Simons Island after the Civil War depredations there. He served as its rector for fourteen years until his death in 1898).

The Dodge title to the lands in question is so extensive, complex, and ambiguous, that it is difficult to attempt to explain it even today, particularly in the context of this article. The local people rightfully assumed that they – not the Dodges – owned their land. After all, they had lived on the land for generations and had aged deeds to prove their ownership. Herein, however, began their descent into the maelstrom of land confiscations and lawsuits by the Dodges which resulted in a forty-year land war that took the lives of many people on both sides of this volatile issue.

Bending The Law

In the late 1860s (and even today), Georgia law decreed that an individual could claim ownership of land after twenty years' possession without a deed or after only seven years' possession with color of title. This is the law known as "adverse possession" and it is still Georgia law today.

This is a story in the truest sense of how "carpet-baggers" from the North came to the South to use the federal legal system to take advantage of poor, devastated landowners following the U.S. Civil War. Articles in several newspapers of that time lamented the fact that this land war was being waged by "one-legged Confederates and old widows" against a powerful land monopoly from the North.

A painting of William Pitt Eastman.

As their stranglehold on the land tightened, the Dodges hired armed woods riders who intimidated and threatened the local people into giving up their land to the Dodges. Some, fearful for their lives, ceded their land without a fight, while others fought to the bitter end.

In 1870, two statutes were enacted by Congress entitled simply Revised Statute 5508 and Revised Statute 5509. Though originally intended for use in dealing with issues involving the freed slaves in the South, these statutes authorized federal courts to deal with incidences of "conspiracy" and to

BILLY WARE WALKER, JR.

The Executive House from the former Dodge empire in south Georgia still stands on Highway 341 a mile below Chauncey in southern Dodge County.

determine the punishment for conspiracy. As a result, these statutes were used successfully by the Dodges' attorneys to move cases – which constitutionally should have been tried in the state courts – into the federal courts, where the judges and juries were much friendlier to the northern Dodges' interests.

This happened repeatedly with the land ejection suits brought by the Dodges against the local landowners. These Georgians, some of whom were pathetically poor, were forced to travel long distances to the federal courts in Macon and Savannah, sometimes a hundred miles or more in the days when horses and mules were still the standard method of transportation. This proved to be just one of many hardships the local landowners faced in trying to hold on to their lands. These statutes were repealed in 1910, but for forty years prior to that time, the people of the Three Rivers Area were at the mercy of the Dodge family and the federal courts, and they paid a dear price.

The Dodges ultimately faced three crises during the early 1890s that heralded an end to their dynasty in Georgia. Despite this fact, legal battles involving the Three Rivers Area properties raged on until 1923, when the final land ejection suit was finally removed from the court dockets.

Forsyth Slaying

The first of these crises occurred in 1890, when John C. Forsyth, chief agent of Norman W. Dodge, was shot and killed, presumably by irate "squatters," at his home in Normandale in southern Dodge County. "Squatters," of course, was a slanderous misnomer the Dodges used to label the local residents who were simply fighting to hold on to their lands.

John C. Forsyth managed the Dodges' tremendous sawmill at Normandale (a community called Suomi, today). Normandale was named for Norman W. Dodge, one of the seven sons of William E. Dodge who died in 1883.

Five men were tried in the federal court in Macon and found guilty of the murder of Forsyth. They were sent to the remote Ohio Penitentiary to serve their sentences. Four were from Telfair County and one was from Dodge County.

By invoking the federal conspiracy statute, the Dodge lawyers successfully moved the murder case from the constitutionally mandated state court system into the fed-

This logging scene from south Georgia appeared on a postcard from the early 1900s. The oxen pull what appears to be a "butt cut" of virgin longleaf pine or cyprus. Notice the immense size of the trunk upon which the driver sits.

eral court system which ultimately sent the Wright brothers, attorney Luther Hall and others to prison.

Lawyer Luther

Several of the individuals who were convicted of the crime were prominent men from highly regarded families who maintained their innocence for the rest of their lives. One was Luther Hall, a brilliant attorney who lived in Eastman and who had represented the local people against the powerful legal battery of the Dodges on many occasions. The elimination of Hall was tremendously beneficial to the larcenous efforts of the Dodge family. Others imprisoned for the crime were the two Lancaster brothers, Wright and John. Wright Lancaster, amazingly, was the young sheriff of Telfair County at the time of his conviction.

According to newspaper articles of that day, Luther Hall – who no doubt was no angel – had often denounced Norman W. Dodge, his agent, Forsyth, and the federal court, once urging the local landowners who were battling with the Dodges to meet his agents with shotguns and to "cram their carcasses down gopher holes."

An awesome presence because of his huge physique, a scarred cheek, and a green shield over his sightless eye, Hall became an impassioned orator in a successful bid for the Georgia State Legislature when he dramatically shouted, "Who shall rule, Dodge or the people?" and further intoning, "You people have your guns. The nights are dark. You can do your own work."

Other Crises

The second crisis of the early 1890s was the burning of the huge sawmill at

Normandale in 1892. According to several articles of that day, the sawmill was the largest in the South at that time. After the sawmill burned, it was never rebuilt, for the Dodges had already depleted the timber in the area, and thus had no reason to rebuild.

Of course, they still had their large sawmill at Willcox Lake on the Ocmulgee River which was their river headquarters. The Dodges also had tremendous sawmills at St. Simons and later at Darien. Their sawmills on St. Simons were located where the present-day complex Epworth By The Sea – a Methodist conference center – is located today. In fact, the fireboxes of their mills can still be seen on the grounds of Epworth. An historical marker, explaining the significance of the site, stands nearby.

The third crisis occurred in 1894, when Norman W. Dodge filed a land ejection suit against Lucius Williams of Telfair County and 380 other residents in the Three Rivers Area. This particular lawsuit dragged on until 1923, when it was finally resolved and removed from the court dockets.

Lucius Williams Killing

Local folklore maintains that the Dodges finally met their match in the person of Lucius Williams. He was from a large and prominent family, and he was a former sheriff of Telfair County who rose to the rank of captain in the Confederacy during the War Between the States. When the Dodges' logging crew or "log choppers" came onto Williams' land, he met them with a loaded weapon and fired over their heads to frighten them away, but in doing so inadvertently killed one of the loggers.

Feeling that he would not receive a fair trial in the federal court, which he felt would certainly hear his case, Williams decided to elude the federal authorities. When

A timber tramroad and rail processor at Temperance in Telfair County, Georgia, photographed circa 1900.

COURTESY JULIAN WILLIAMS

This sawmill on Willcox Lake on the Ocmulgee River was the hub of the Dodges' Ocmulgee River timber business.

federal marshals came to arrest him, his family and friends came to his rescue with drawn weapons as handcuffs were being placed on his wrists. After freeing him, they then whisked him away to safety. The startled marshals were forced to free their prisoner and return to Macon empty-handed. Williams hid out in the Ocmulgee River swamp where family and friends brought him food and provisions for months.

Eventually, Norman W. Dodge sent Williams word that he was willing to "negotiate" with him about the land, if he would only come out of the swamp. Williams, who was tired of running and suffering from exposure to the elements, decided to return to his home and see what type deal he might be able to arrange with Dodge for his land and timber. It turned out to be a poor decision.

Norman W. Dodge never approached Williams about negotiating a fair deal for his land. Instead, one day while Lucius Williams was asleep on the front porch of his home, federal marshals from Macon pulled up in their buggy. The newspaper accounts of this incident varied in reporting who fired the first shot. Some said Williams fired first; others swore the marshals fired first. Regardless of the circumstances, Williams was killed by the first few shots, and even after he was obviously dead, the marshals continued firing rounds into the house in which women and children huddled until all told eighty-one bullets had been fired into the dwelling. Miraculously, no one else was injured.

Immense Devastation

The Dodges continued their merciless devastation of the longleaf yellow pine timber in the Three Rivers Area of the state until the turn of the century. Where once a "forest primeval" had existed, nothing remained but a land of stumps and treetops as far as the eye could see. Not only was this devastation an eyesore on the landscape, it also proved to be a substantial impediment to farmers in their attempts to eke out a living on the scarred land.

In the midst of their immense timber empire, the Dodges built railroads and tram-roads all over the counties in which the timber was being harvested. The two major ones in Telfair County were the Ocmulgee and Chauncey or Normandale Railroad, which stretched from the sawmill town of Normandale to Willcox Lake on the Ocmulgee River, and the Horse Creek Railroad, which ran northward from the boom on the Ocmulgee River into the pinelands of Telfair County. Some of the tram-roads were movable once the timber had been exhausted in an area.

Oxen and mules were used to transport the hewn timber to creeks (for rafting) or to rail cars. Oxen were used in swampy areas because of their cloven hooves provided them with better footing, while mules were used in dry areas.

The felled trees were sent either by rail to the Macon and Brunswick Railroad which ran by the sawmill town of Normandale, or they were dragged to nearby streams to be floated down to the booms on the Ocmulgee River. (A boom was a holding area where logs were collected to be bound into rafts.)

Today, it is difficult to imagine the majesty of the immense stands of towering pines which once existed in the Three Rivers Area prior to the arrival of the Dodges in 1868. A 1932 Dodge County newspaper article recounts the harvesting of one excep-tionally tremendous longleaf yellow pine in the county. The tree was fifteen to sixteen feet in circumference and yielded some 5,000 board feet of lumber when processed. According to its growth rings, it was 175 years old.

Some of the trees that the Dodges cut in the Three Rivers Area were several hun-dred years old, so they quite likely were even larger than the one described in the article. Other newspaper articles of that day recorded that some of these trees were so large that they required forty-eight oxen to move one tree. Some were so tremen-dous that one tree reportedly could provide enough lumber for the building of an entire house.

Independent Rafters

In an effort to take advantage of the timber on their property and beat the Dodges at their own game, some local landowners continued rafting their logs themselves to Darien during this era. The rafting of timber to the coast during the 1800s was a way of life for many of these landowners, intent upon cashing in on their timber before it was taken by the Dodges. An article written in 1883 from Clayville (on the Ocmulgee River) in Telfair County described how more than a hundred rafts passed by the Dodges' Boom on the river. Of these, "thirty-six were sent by the Dodge Company."

Raft hands were a hardy lot. They had to be resilient just to survive. Neophyte rafts-men often paid with their lives if they were unfamiliar with the vagaries and caprices of the rivers. Oftentimes, after reaching Darien with a raft, the raft hands were also at the mercy of unscrupulous timber inspectors who would refuse to give their timber the proper grade it deserved, knowing that the raftsmen couldn't float their rafts back up the rivers.

If a hard rain, or "freshet," swelled the rivers and caused the water to rush and swirl, knowledgeable raft hands knew to wait until the rushing water had subsided before continuing to drift down the rivers. Those who did attempt to ride their rafts through this swift water often would be found days later, floating face-down in the water.

Maggie and Lucius Williams

Wild & Wooly Darien

A rafting trip from Willcox Lake to Darien was a distance of around two hundred miles. Depending on the weather, the length of the trip could vary from five days to a week or longer. The raftsmen slept and cooked on the raft, though sometimes they would pull over to the bank and spend the night on the riverbank.

Prior to the advent of the railroad in 1870, raft hands often walked back home after floating their rafts to the mills. This walk sometimes was a distance of several hundred miles, sometimes in freezing weather.

Darien was a world-renowned port during the latter part of the 1800s. Ships from around the globe came to load the fine longleaf yellow pine timber for markets elsewhere.

Raft hands were known to be a tough lot, particularly if cornered or mistreated. After spending days and sometimes weeks on the rivers, they were a dirty, stinking lot with very little patience.

After they had sold their rafts at Darien, the raftsmen would attach their cooking utensils, tools, and other gear to their belts. Walking the streets of Darien, they would present such a clanking, dirty appearance that passersby reportedly would veer away from them as they passed.

Interestingly, Darien had a number of saloons and brothels at that time which vied for the money of the newly-paid raft hands. Sometimes, these hard-working men would drink to excess and later discover that they had spent all of their hard-earned money on the bars and women. The ones who suffered that misfortune truly did have a long, cold walk back home.

Dodge Legacy

Over a hundred years have now passed since the heydays of the Dodge presence in the Three Rivers Area of Georgia, though they were actually in the area for fifty-five years, from 1868 until 1923. The Dodges were not only very wealthy, educated, and

BILLY WARE WALKER, JR.

The Lucius L. Williams home still stands (as of this writing) in the Cobbtown community in Telfair County. This home was the site of the Lucius Williams killing in 1895. Eighty-one rounds were fired into this home by federal marshals.

cultured, but also on the cutting edge of the reconstruction of a shattered nation – despite the disreputable nature of their deeds in the Three Rivers Area. Their achievements are legendary – especially those of William E. Dodge – in the construction of canals, sawmills, and railroads in the United States and Canada.

Despite their successes, the name Dodge in the Three Rivers Area of Georgia will always be connected with the misery and strife of the forty-year land war. Only the exemplary life of Anson Dodge, grandson of William E. Dodge and the protagonist in Eugenia Price's *Beloved Invader*, has lessened to a degree the animosity felt by local residents toward these "invaders" from the North.

In a dramatic recreation of the Dodge Era in Georgia, Dr. Delma Presley, a retired English professor and museum director at Georgia Southern University, has penned the script for an outdoor drama – The Lightwood Knot. This theatrical production was presented in performances in 1997 and 1998 to capacity crowds at the Little Ocmulgee State Park in Wheeler County, near McRae. The Lightwood Knot is one of four recognized outdoor dramas in the State of Georgia. Plans currently are being made to involve area colleges in an anticipated revival of the drama.

Jane Walker's historical novel, *Widow of Sighing Pines*, set during the Dodge era, was honored with the President's Award for Best Adult Fiction for 2003 by the Florida Publishing Association. She also has co-authored a non-fiction volume of history entitled *The Dodge Land Troubles, 1868-1923* with Chris Trowell, associate professor emeritus at South Georgia College in Douglas, Georgia.

The Murder of Eleanor Bustin, and the Legend of Justice Lamar's Suicide

Hugh T. Harrington and Eileen Babb McAdams

On July 4, 1834, Judge L.Q.C. Lamar put a handgun to his head and pulled the trigger, ending his life instantly. Seven and a half months earlier, he had sentenced a man to death who quite possibly was innocent of the murder for which he was charged. A legend eventually grew which maintained Lamar had killed himself as a result of depression over sentencing an innocent man to death. In actuality, nothing could be further from the truth.

One of the more well-known individuals who has lived to date in Baldwin County was Lucius Quintus Cincinnatus Lamar. His brother, Mirabeau Buonaparte Lamar (1798-1859), became the second president of the Republic of Texas. L.Q.C.'s place in the history of Baldwin County, however, is somewhat ignoble.

L.Q.C. Lamar was a distinguished lawyer who became judge of the Superior Court of the Ocmulgee Circuit which included Baldwin County. His life, and his potential for great achievements, was cut short by his suicide July 4, 1834 at the age of 36.

A major part of the legend of L.Q.C. Lamar revolves around the presumption that he became depressed after learning he had sentenced an innocent man to the gallows and in his despair killed himself. It makes a good story; but it is not true.

In November of 1832, Baldwin County was shocked by the discovery of the body of 13 year old Eleanor Bustin. The young girl had been choked to death with a hank of cotton yarn tied around her neck.[1]

Eleanor had lived at the home of her sister, Nancy, and her husband John A. Johnson, a minister. Their home was a farm in the northern part of Baldwin County near the Oconee River. Today, this area is covered by Lake Sinclair.

On Tuesday, November 13, 1832 Eleanor did not return home in the evening. The next day, friends and neighbors began a search for her. She was nowhere to be found.

On Thursday the search continued. Small footprints were discovered in the woods several hundred yards from the home of the Johnsons. The tracks of a man were found as well.

Unfortunately, the searchers could not successfully follow any of the tracks. One searcher, William Dunn, met the Reverend Mr. Johnson in the woods. Dunn told Johnson that he was about to search a particular section of woods and was told by Mr. Johnson that that area had already been thoroughly searched.

Later in the day that particular section of woods which the minister had said had been searched was searched again, and the body of the girl subsequently was discovered. The man who found her, Benjamin Askew, said that he saw the body and called

HUGH HARRINGTON

Judge L.Q.C. Lamar's impressive headstone stands at his grave in historic Memory Hill Cemetery in Milledgeville.

out to bring other searchers to the scene.

The searchers who gathered near the girl's corpse did not immediately touch the body, but inspected it carefully. Askew said Eleanor looked as if she were on her knees. Her hands were lightly touching the ground. She was inclined forward with her knees just touching the ground. Her head was a little more than a foot above the ground.

A hank of cotton yarn was tied to a hackberry bush and to the little girl's neck in a running noose. The noose was loose enough around Eleanor's neck for the witness to slip his fingers between her neck and the cotton line. The end of the length of yarn was tied to the bush at such a low height that if the girl had been standing she could not have been choked by it.

There were some abrasions on Eleanor's fingers, and the ground was somewhat disturbed under her hands. It strangely did not appear that she had struggled with her feet as the ground under them was not marked in any way.

The men also discovered a bruise on Eleanor's arm and one on her shoulder. Due to the stiffness of the body (rigor mortis), they agreed that she must have been dead since Tuesday when she first was missing. They also saw bruises and abrasions indicative of a whipping on her body.

The body was taken to the Johnson home where an inquest was held. There, witnesses testified that Mr. Johnson said a "great deal" about the girl. After her body was laid out he accused her of putting cobalt and jimson weed in his milk to poison him. Johnson spoke harshly about Eleanor and said that every time he whipped her he thought of her trying to poison him. He said that "she was a lying, roguish girl, and would steal little frivolous things."

At the trial, testimony revealed that after the inquest, Mr. Johnson stated that "if anybody thought he killed her, he was ready to abide the law." This was said before anyone had accused him of the murder, raising suspicion even more.

A neighbor, Mrs. Mary Moore, testified that in August she had seen marks of a

255

whipping on Eleanor's body. On the Sunday evening before Eleanor's death, Mrs. Moore was walking with Eleanor to the Moore home when Eleanor showed her more whipping marks. The marks appeared to be very large, as if they could not have been made with a switch, and the flesh was very badly bruised, with blood oozing out. There were a great many marks from the waist to the ankles.

Mrs. Moore further testified that on Monday evening the day before Eleanor disappeared, she (Mrs. Moore) had gone to the Johnson home and spoken with Mr. Johnson about the beatings he was giving to Eleanor. He freely admitted beating her and promised not to do it again.

At the time of this conversation between Mrs. Moore and Mr. Johnson, Eleanor was at the Moore home. Johnson and Mrs. Moore walked back to the Moore home together. Johnson was angry and called to Eleanor to come out and go home with him. Mrs. Moore, fearful that he would beat Eleanor again, sent her own daughter with them to spend the night at the Johnson home. The Moore's daughter returned home on Tuesday morning. Tuesday afternoon Eleanor was murdered.

Mrs. Moore also testified that she recognized the hank of cotton yarn tied around the girl's neck as being identical in color and design pattern to cotton that she had seen in the home of the Johnsons.

The Baldwin County Grand Jury indicted Johnson for the murder of Eleanor Bustin with the damning words, "...not having the fear of God before his eyes, but being moved and seduced by the instigation of the Devil,..."

At his trial, in August of 1833, Johnson pled not guilty. He did not take the stand in his own defense. The legend surrounding the case maintains that his own wife testified against him, but in point of fact, she did not testify at all.

The jury, when presented with the testimony of the witnesses to Johnson's attitude toward the dead girl and his behavior after the discovery of her body, ultimately found him guilty of murder. The law allowed Judge L.Q.C. Lamar only one course of action in this case. He sentenced Johnson to hang on November 15, 1833 and "delivered a very feeling and eloquent address."

The *Georgia Journal* mentioned that "the case in...prominent features is striking similar to that of Avery; but the evidence against [Johnson] is not as strong, we are told, as against [Avery]."[2]

The "Avery" case to which the *Journal* refers was a remarkably similar crime that may have had a bearing on the Johnson trial. In December of 1832, the body of a girl by the name of Sarah M. Cornell was found hanging from the pole of a haystack in Tiverton, Rhode Island. Initially, it was thought the girl had committed suicide. Soon, however, new evidence came to light that she had been pregnant and that a Methodist minister named Ephraim K. Avery of Bristol, Rhode Island was the father of her child.

The Avery case had received national attention. The trial, in May of 1833, lasted for about a month. The prosecution presented a large mass of circumstantial evidence

Since the Bustin murder occurred in Baldwin County, the trial took place in Milledgeville, which was the state capitol of Georgia at that time. The Legislature took an interest in the case since only circumstantial evidence had been produced to link the suspect to the crime. The old Georgia state Legislature is pictured here in Milledgeville.

but could not submit any direct evidence that Reverend Avery was guilty.

The defense, funded by wealthy Methodist church members, presented a large body of materials trashing the character of Sarah Cornell and making a case for suicide. Avery ultimately was acquitted. There was a nationwide popular outcry against him and he fled the region fearing for his life.

Since the Bustin murder occurred in Baldwin County, the trial took place in Milledgeville which was then the capital of Georgia. At the time, the state Legislature was in session. The Legislature took an interest in the case as only circumstantial evidence had been produced to link Johnson with the murder.

At the time, many people actually thought that Johnson was innocent or that there was enough doubt about his guilt that he at least should not be executed. A bill was introduced in the Legislature to pardon Johnson. Governor Wilson Lumpkin gave Johnson a respite for a week, delaying the scheduled execution until Friday, November 22, so the Legislature could debate the merits of the bill.

The *Georgia Journal* described the scene in the State House thusly: "A substitute [bill] was offered to commute his punishment, with his own consent, to imprisonment for life. This was objected to by some as unconstitutional. The printed evidence was examined and its principal points commented on in able and animated debate, in which it was viewed in various aspects. The case was well argued on both sides.

Every motive of sympathy, of mercy, of compassion, was eloquently appealed to; the condemning features of the evidence were addressed fairly and fully, and every claim of the long sighted humanity, of severe example and the claims of public justice, were powerfully urged. After an ineffectual motion to adjourn, it was moved to lay the bill and substitute on the table for the residue of the session, which prevailed."[3]

The motion to "lay the bill and substitute on the table" was the same as a rejection. The *Georgia Journal* added the editorial comment that, "this second edition of the Rev. E.K. Avery is to be hung in Milledgeville on Friday the 22nd instant."

Johnson was hanged in public view. It was estimated that there were three to four thousand spectators for the event.[4] This is a huge number considering that the white population of Baldwin County at that time numbered only 2,750 individuals.

Today, few contemporary accounts of the hanging remain in existence. The Federal Union commented that "a painful uncertainty still hangs over this case. Johnson was convicted on circumstantial evidence alone; he has never confessed himself guilty; and he approached the awful moment, with remarkable composure, and firmness, and seemed to be devoutly engaged, in the exercise of religious feelings, in preparing to meet his God. This case furnishes a strong argument in favor of a proposal now before the Legislature, so to alter the law, as to substitute perpetual imprisonment, for death, wherever the conviction is founded on circumstantial evidence alone."[5]

According to the Southern Recorder, seven and a half months after the execution of Johnson, Judge L.Q.C. Lamar "put a period to his life, on the afternoon of the 4th inst. [July 4, 1834] by a pistol shot, through the brain." The Inquest determined that Lamar died "in a state of distraction."

The Southern Recorder also states that "this condition of mind has been brought about by the wretched ill health under which Judge Lamar has labored for a number of months past, and of that peculiar disease, which always brings as its attendants the greatest degree of gloom and despondency." The newspaper continues, "...he has certainly, at intervals, for some time past, labored under mental hallucination. The peculiar kind of hallucination under which Judge Lamar labored at the time of his death, was an overwhelming fear of impending mania, which doubtless, led immediately to the fatal deed..."[6]

The Federal Union had much the same impression as to Lamar's mental health. "It is no doubt the effect of aberration of mind. He is the victim of dyspepsia, that gloomy scourge of the student. Laboring for some months past under this depressing disease, a deep despondency had settled over him; he feared that the faculties of his mind were impaired; the awful apprehension of insanity, was a sword piercing his brain; it became the terrible disease of his soul. In an agony of despair, believing himself insane, he committed the fatal act."[7]

The *Georgia Journal* adds some description by saying that Lamar had attended the festivities of the 4th of July and that "his deportment through the day had been much as usual of late, generally grave and even sad, he was sometimes slightly cheerful, but often so much abstracted that it was noticed and remarked at the time." The newspaper continued, "...arriving home a little before sunset, he wrote a short note of farewell to his family, walked into the garden, placed a loaded pistol to his head and in a second was a corpse."[8]

It is significant that no account at the time of Lamar's death in 1834 makes mention of the Johnson murder trial. That was an embellishment to the suicide story that would come in later years.

Nine years later, on June 20, 1843, the Federal Union reprinted an anonymous letter, dated Monroe County, May 31st, 1843, originally published in the *Georgia Messenger*. The letter reads, "By inserting the following information in your paper, you will do an act of justice to the family of the late unfortunate Mr. Johnston [sic], who was executed at Milledgeville, for the supposed murder of his wife's sister, during the sitting of the Legislature in 1833, but who was perfectly innocent of the crime for which he suffered an ignominious death, there being no positive testimony brought against him. I trust the next Legislature will make some donation for the support of the family of this unfortunate man."

The information provided by the anonymous letter writer states, "Some time since, a gentleman traveling from Alabama, put up at the Union Hall in Forsyth, and in a conversation had with the proprietor of the house, stated that a Negro fellow had been taken up for having committed violence upon the body of a white female, and that during his examination, he confessed that he had committed a similar act upon the body of a white female near Milledgeville, and that after he had gratified his brutal desire, he hung her with a bunch of cotton thread. He stated that it was not his first intention to murder her – but to accomplish his object he was obliged to choke her finding (as he stated) she was so near gone, he continued to hang her, in which situation the body was discovered. The Negro also stated that Mr. Johnston [sic], was executed for the supposed murder, and that he was an innocent man: that he himself had committed the murder, and that there was no person concerned with him. These facts having come to my knowledge, I felt it a duty I owe to the family of this unfortunate gentleman, to give them to the public." The message was signed simply with the word "Justice."

This anonymous letter was the origin of the legend of the gallows confession of the "real killer" of Eleanor Bustin. As it is a third-hand account, with no details, it is impossible to make any attempt to verify the statements. As nine years had passed since the suicide of Judge Lamar it is impossible that he was influenced by it. Even if the story had come to his attention, one would certainly doubt that he would take much notice of such a nebulous source.

In 1858, *The Bench and Bar of Georgia: Memoirs and Sketches* was compiled by Stephen F. Miller. Here, the former law partner of Judge Lamar, Joel Crawford, gives a biography and personal reminiscences of Lamar. Crawford writes that "the true and only cause" of the suicide was "insanity, resulting from accidental derangement of cerebral organism. The disease of which the judge died may therefore be assumed as a natural one, and as explicable on pathological principles, as apoplexy or any other malady of the brain."[9]

The retired actor, Solomon Smith, published his *Theatrical Management in the West and South for Thirty Years* in 1868. Smith was a witness to the trial and hanging of John Johnson. His recollection 35 years later is a bit cloudy. He says that Johnson's guilt "appeared undoubted, although the evidence was all circumstantial." He also said that Johnson said, on the gallows, "I die innocent." Smith then says that "fourteen years afterward a negro was hung in Mississippi who on the gallows confessed that he committed the crime..." He makes no mention, however, of a connection between the murder trial and Lamar's death.[10]

In September of 1886, yet another man was hanged in Milledgeville. Reporting on that event, the *Savannah Morning News* mentioned the Johnson trial and printed the legend, as fact, that Lamar committed suicide upon learning of the gallows confession of the actual murderer of Eleanor Bustin.[11]

That article elicited a response from a reader, Hamilton W. Sharpe, which appeared in the October 2, 1886 edition of the Savannah Morning News. Sharpe had been a member of the state Legislature at the time of the trial 53 years earlier. Sharpe wrote that Robert Toombs "made a telling speech against the accused" which convinced many people of Johnson's guilt. Sharpe did not mention Judge Lamar but he did say that "it is well known that a burly Negro, who was hung for murder in Alabama some years after, confessed to the murder of the girl, exonerating Johnson, leaving his character without a blotch or stain."

Ten years later, *The New York Times* picked up the story in an article about the circumstantial evidence laws in Georgia. In this account, John Johnson's name is erroneously printed as "Frank Johnson." The additional inaccuracy of stating that his wife testified against him also appears. The Times also added that "many years after this execution a Negro was convicted of murdering his master in Mississippi, and upon the gallows he confessed..." to having killed Eleanor Bustin as well.[12]

In 1911, *The Savannah Morning News* reprinted an article from the *Washington Post* about the Lamar family. That article says that Judge Lamar "committed suicide because, it is said, he had to preside at a trial of a man accused of murder who was found "Guilty" by a jury, and sentenced to death by him. It was afterwards established that the accused man was innocent and Judge Lamar brooded over his having sentenced the man to death."[13] An interesting and important twist to this rendition of the story is that the article was quoting one Lucius Q. C. Lamar, a lawyer newly admitted to practice before the U.S. Supreme Court. So, now the Lamar family was even repeating the legend.

The Union-Recorder reprinted a long article from the *Macon Telegraph* which was originally written by Judge E.E. Brown in 1884. In this article Judge Brown recounts the Johnson-Bustin murder and its connection with Judge Lamar. Unfortunately, Brown included a wide variety of embellishments. He referred to Johnson as "a perfect terror to evil-doers. . ." that made him "known throughout the entire country." Brown wrote that "nearly all the Methodists throughout the State were impressed with his innocence and began efforts to have him pardoned."

Brown said that Johnson's wife "whose testimony was largely instrumental in his being convicted, was on the gallows with him, and stuck to him to the last. Like a woman, she wanted her husband to forgive her before he suffered the extreme penalty."

According to Brown "several years later a Negro was hanged in Mississippi for murder and while on the gallows confessed that he killed the little girl whose murder was charged to Johnson."[14] The only part of the legend that Brown did not repeat was that Lamar killed himself due to the confession of the mysterious man on the gallows.

Other well-respected biographies continued to cite Crawford's description of Lamar's mental health, not stating that Lamar committed suicide over Johnson. These biographies included Wirt Armistead Cate's 1935 biography of Judge Lamar's son, Lucius Q.C. Lamar, *Secession and Reunion*[15] and James B. Murphy's *LQC Lamar, Pragmatic Patriot.*[16]

In 1978, *Milledgeville, Georgia's Antebellum Capital* by James Bonner was published. Regrettably, even this much-respected history gave new life to the old legend. Bonner stated that "the minister's wife was the principal witness against him..." and that "Lamar developed his own doubts about the guilt of the condemned man, and later, after the minister was hanged, a man in Mississippi confessed to the deed from the gallows. In a fit of melancholia, Lamar came into his house, quietly kissed his wife and children, then walked into the garden and shot himself."[17] Bonner cited as his source for this information the 1884 article by Judge Brown that was reprinted by the *Union-Recorder* in 1919.

The case as seen from a distance of almost 175 years is still intriguing. The weight the jury placed on the circumstantial evidence in the case against Johnson will always be debated. Also to be considered is the influence the E.K. Avery case may have had on the minds of the jury.

The truth is that Judge Lamar actually played an almost insignificant part in the drama. However, legends never seem to die but instead tend to grow with time.

In Milledgeville, L.Q.C. Lamar's grave will always be pointed out to visitors as belonging to the judge who became despondent after learning of a gallows confession, quietly kissed his wife and children good-bye, walked out into his garden, and killed himself. By this tragic act, he guaranteed that his name will live on, in legend, forever.

Endnotes

1. All references to testimony are from a pamphlet titled "Evidence In The Case Of The State vs. John Johnson, on an Indictment in Baldwin Superior Court for Murder" which was printed in 1833 to be distributed to members of the Georgia state Legislature as they considered a bill to pardon John Johnson.
2. *Georgia Journal*, September 4, 1833.
3. *Georgia Journal*, November 16, 1833.

4. *Georgia Journal,* November 28, 1833.

5. *Federal Union*, November 27, 1822.

6. *Southern Recorder*, July 9, 1834.

7. *Federal Union*, July 9, 1834.

8. *Georgia Journal,* July 9, 1834.

9. Miller, Stephen F., *The Bench and Bar of Georgia: Memoirs and Sketches*, 1858, Philadelphia, J.B. Lippincott & Co., p. 137.

10. Smith, Solomon, *Theatrical Management in the West and South for Thirty Years*, 1868, New York, Harper & Brothers, p. 100.

11. *Savannah Morning News*, September 25, 1886.j

12. *The New York Times*, February 15, 1897.

13. *Savannah Morning News*, January 16, 1919.

14. *Union Recorder*, September 16, 1919.

15. Cate, Wirt Armistead, Lucius Q.C. Lamar, *Secession and Reunion*, 1935, Chapel Hill, University of North Carolina Press, p. 19.

16. Murphy, James B., LQC Lamar, *Pragmatic Patriot*, 1973, Baton Rouge, Louisiana State University Press, p. 6,7.

17. Bonner, James C., Milledgeville, *Georgia's Antebellum Capital*, 1978, Athens, University of Georgia Press, p. 39.

Searching for the
Ghost Airmen of Harris Neck

MARY ANN ANDERSON

Today Harris Neck Island is a place of exquisite beauty and solitude, a National Wildlife Refuge where the sounds of nature, even the deafening calls of the teeming bird life, augment the tranquility. During World War II, however, it was alive with the roar of dozens of high-performance engines as pilots maneuvered fighter planes just above ground level. So what happened to these "top guns" and their "secret" air base at Harris Neck?

The storm came quickly, as spring showers often do, its silver- and charcoal-striated clouds racing across the sky with the wind. Here and there, lightning flashed, signaling that rain would soon fall. Even with the storm fast approaching, I scrambled up the steep incline of the dam at Woody Pond in Harris Neck National Wildlife Refuge. Mixed in with the rumbling thunder from the storm, I heard the steady clamor of what had to be a million birds chattering all at once. That's what it sounded like, anyway. The thing was, I couldn't see them yet.

The airfield's P-39 and P-40 fighter planes were housed in this hangar (photographed in 1963).

A few more steps and I reached the top of the dam. Then I stopped abruptly in my tracks, completely awestruck, my mouth wide open. I remember whispering something under my breath like "Gosh" or "Holy moly" or "My word" or something equally as Southern and silly.

There were indeed birds, maybe not the millions I had envisioned just moments earlier, but countless thousands. Most seemed to be calling, creating a cacophonous symphony of avian song that seemed as loud as anything I had ever heard. The pungent scent of guano – bird droppings, probably measured in tons – percolated with the humidity of the upcoming storm, making the moment a bit surreal.

Everywhere I looked there were birds: in the trees, on the shore, among the cattails, in the wax myrtle, in the water, over

The runup at the end of the old runway.

the water, on top of the water. Here a bird, there a bird, everywhere a bird-bird.

Herons, egrets, and ibises blended together in clouds of white and grey and pale blue. I saw anhingas and ducks of every type and even endangered wood storks. Just then, a whirl of red, white, and black caught my attention from the forested side of the dam. I glanced up at the trees where a pair of pileated woodpeckers flapped their wings and cackled their wild, unearthly call like something you might hear in an asylum or the deepest jungles of Africa.

On the Edge

I had never seen a bird rookery before and I was utterly mesmerized at the scene; so mesmerized, in fact, that I had no idea that my position near the pond's edge was a precarious one.

"Careful," my friend whispered. "Be very careful. There are 'gators in there."

I momentarily took my eyes off the birds to scan the thick, green algae along the pond's perimeter. Sure enough, an alligator regarded me warily, its eyes as bright as embers but also cold and heartless. It was about six feet long by my estimate, but the dense aquatic vegetation prevented a clear view. With a soft "bloop," it disappeared beneath the surface and only the silent rippling of water suggested it had been there.

Within minutes, fat drops of rain began to fall and a storm was upon us. With a final glance back at Woody Pond, teeming with birds so that when I squinted it resembled a pasture blanketed in snow, we returned to the comfort of the car.

Forgotten Past

That was my first visit to Harris Neck National Wildlife Refuge some three years ago. I was completely captivated by its incredible profusion of birds and wildlife, but I also realized that my knowledge about it was limited, to say the least. So I returned several times to study and enjoy its ethereal beauty. I also read dozens of articles about its ecosystem, wildlife, and beguiling history. In the process, I learned that while Harris Neck is both a remarkable and a compelling place, surprisingly little has actually been written about it over the years.

Today, the murmuring and screeching of hundreds of birds fill the skies over Harris Neck, but sixty-five years ago the high-pitched whine of the engines of P-39 and P-40 fighter planes was the order of the day. At that time, Harris Neck Army Airfield occupied this little strip of land on Georgia's coast. Since then, the old network of roads, runways and buildings has reverted to an expanse of fields and meadows overgrown with cactus and pine. Now the birds - especially the endangered wood stork with its five-foot wingspan giving it the appearance of some prehistoric creature - circle above the runways, taking off or touching down very much like the fighter planes that flew here so long ago.

Harris Neck Island lies near the north end of a long, narrow isthmus between Sapelo Sound and St. Catherines Island. The refuge encompasses 2,824 acres with a variety of habitat including open fields, mixed forest, saltwater marsh, and freshwater impoundments. The rest of the island is a mélange of million-dollar mansions and mobile homes with little in-between except a few churches and plenty of armadillos.

The Plantation Period

Harris Neck's modern history dates back to the 18th century. Until then it was mostly the domain of the Guale Indians. Then land grants to English and Scottish settlers in the 1750s opened the area to well-to-do planters. From that point until after the Civil War, Harris Neck supported a plantation society. The relatively high ground and good soil were perfect for growing crops like rice, indigo, and Sea Island cotton. Timber and livestock also contributed to the economy.

Originally known as Dickenson's Neck, Harris Neck takes its name from the 750-acre William Thomas Harris Plantation. Perhaps the best known of the area's antebellum residences was, however, Jonathan Thomas's Peru Plantation. In 1923, Jonathan's descendant, Edward J. Thomas, wrote about his memories of Peru Plantation in *Memoirs of a Southerner*, 1840-1923:

265

"I was born in Savannah, Georgia, March 25, 1840, but a few years after we moved to the old homestead in McIntosh County, some forty miles from this city. My first recollection was of this plantation. It was called "Peru" on account of its fertility – the legend of Pizarro's gold find being not yet forgotten – situated on South Newport River, a bold and wide salt water stream emptying into Black-Beard Sound. My grandfather lived at one end of this plantation of three thousand acres, and my father lived at the other. I remember my grandfather very distinctly; he wore no whiskers, and, not shaving daily, would catch me in his arms and rub his face against mine, scratching me with his beard, much to our mutual delight. This impressed me with the belief that old men had beards and young men had whiskers, for father wore whiskers except the moustache, which, to wear in those days, was considered "horsey." Grandfather, Jonathan Thomas, died a few years later, leaving his many plantations – Peru, Belvidere, Baker, and Stark, comprising some fifteen thousand acres and about one hundred and twenty-five slaves. His remains are buried by a large oak in our private burying ground on the banks of South Newport River, and there he rests while the restless waters ebb and flow nearby. His portrait now hangs over my fireplace, and kindly smiles down on his great, great, great grandchildren."

Tobacco and Tuxedos

Following the Civil War, the plantation society of Jonathan Thomas's era quickly faded away. Former slaves acquired small plots of land and survived by raising a few cows and chickens and planting gardens. This growing African-American community eventually became known as Lacy (or Lacey) although that name later fell into disuse.

The late 1880s and early 1890s brought an influx of well-to-do Yankee entrepreneurs to Georgia's scenic coast. These included prominent families like the Carnegies and Rockefellers who acquired vast acreages on Cumberland and Jekyll Islands. At Harris Neck, Pierre Lorillard (1833-1901), a wealthy tobacco magnate (who, incidentally, is also credited with inventing the tuxedo) built a fabulous winter retreat complete with fountains and swimming pools.

Despite Pierre's presence, Harris Neck never became a popular winter retreat on the order of the Sea Islands. With the exception of Lorillard and a few others, Harris Neck remained the dominion of former slaves and their descendants.

Airfields and Airmen

The African-American community flourished for decades, but the 1930s brought change when the U.S. Department of Commerce came a callin'. This agency established Harris Neck Intermediate Field, an emergency landing strip for commercial aircraft on the Jacksonville, Florida to Richmond, Virginia routes. This facility was illuminated for the benefit of aircraft experiencing trouble at night, but otherwise did not offer any amenities.

The Intermediate Field had little impact on Harris Neck's quiet ways, but World War II wrought greater changes and challenges for the black community. After the Japanese attack on Pearl Harbor in 1941, the War Department began aggressively

The old Army Air Corps runway at Harris Neck is in a state of disrepair but it is one of the few surviving relics of the World War II airfield.

building military bases. In July 1942, the government condemned 1,200 acres on Harris Neck for an Army Air Corps base. Most of this land belonged to poor black farmers whose families had lived there for generations. They stood no chance against a government focused on wartime needs. Soon the landowners were forced off their property and out of the only way of life most had ever known.

While the black community suffered, Harris Neck Army Airfield thrived. It was an ideal location for submarine reconnaissance by pilots in P-39 Airacobra and P-40 Kittyhawk fighters. These keen-eyed pilots flew patrols along the coast looking for German U-boats (no idle threat since several Allied merchants ships were torpedoed within sight of gawking civilians on nearby St. Simons and Jekyll Islands).

The little airfield eventually grew to include eleven prefabricated buildings including hangars, supply depot, maintenance and machine shops, warehouses, NCO (non-commissioned officer) club, and officer's club. At its peak in the autumn of 1944, the airfield housed 130 officers and 400 enlisted men who utilized thirty-two P-40s and five BT-13 aircraft for fighter-bomber training and gunnery practice. All of this activity amidst the hush-hush secrecy of wartime eventually led to rumors among the local populace that Harris Neck was a "secret" base used to train "hot" pilots.

Already fading into mists of antiquity

Surprisingly, next to nothing of Harris Neck Army Airfield exists today, adding a touch of mystery to all those rumors about top secret wartime activity. In the 1970s,

1st Lt. Marvin H. "Sam" Snead (no relation to the golfing great) was stationed at Harris Neck for a time.

Savannah attorney Charles Rippin wrote "The Harris Neck Army Air Field 1941—1944", an article for a local magazine. Rippin went to Washington, D.C. to search the U.S. National Archives for photographs of Harris Neck, but failed to unearth a single photograph of the base.

He likewise failed to locate any of the pilots or other personnel once stationed there. He summarized his frustrations by noting, "Given the fallibility of human memory, the encroachments of time and decay, the transience of all things generally, and perhaps most importantly, the remoteness of the place, it is not surprising that few people along the Georgia coast recall the army airfield at Harris Neck."

Rippen did not strike out entirely. He obtained records from Maxwell Air force Base that shed light on Harris Neck's day-to-day activities. These records reveal, for example, that July 1944 was a "very hot and routine month" that included "a review of all military personnel. Distinguished Flying Crosses were presented to veterans of the China Theater and the Southwest Pacific Theater. Four Bronze Oak Leaf Clusters to the Air Medal were awarded to First Lieutenant Francis H. Hoye, an instructor pilot. Hoye had flown a P-39 with the 18th Fighter Group at Guadalcanal."

Rippen also learned that several soldiers were killed in accidents at Harris Neck. The first happened in August 1944 when flight officer James E. Beard perished on a training flight when his P-40 crashed into the sea. The second fatality occurred just two months later when a staff sergeant died from injuries sustained in an automobile accident.

Autumn Hurricane

The airfield faced yet another peril that autumn. A storm brewing in the Gulf of Mexico grew into a late season hurricane that screamed its way across Florida, killing more than a dozen people as it bore down on Georgia. On October 18, two days before the storm hit Georgia's coast, Harris Neck's aircraft and personnel were sent inland to Waycross out of harm's way.

When the men returned to the base they found debris and downed trees blocking the base roads and that the South Newport River boat landing was heavily damaged by high tides and heavy winds. The cleanup began, but the hurricane nevertheless hastened the airfield's demise. With the Allies moving toward victory in Europe, the Army began consolidating bases. Nearly everything at Harris Neck, including supplies, equipment, files, and publications were shipped to the army air base at Warner Robins. By December 31, less than three years after Harris Neck Army Airfield opened, everyone and everything was gone.

After the war, Harris Neck had a chequered history at best. McIntosh County acquired the base to develop a municipal airport, but the airfield and the neighboring Lorillard estate were looted and vandalized. The federal government later reclaimed the property from the county and on May 25, 1962, Harris Neck became a National Wildlife Refuge.

The refuge today

Today, Harris Neck NWR is administered by the Savannah Coastal Refuges Complex that also manages six other NWRs (Pinckney Island, South Carolina; Savannah; Wolf; Wassaw; Tybee; and Blackbeard islands). On May 13, 2005, a new field office and visitors' center opened with a ceremony attended by dignitaries, media, and federal, state, and local officials who enjoyed a Low Country boil, iced tea, and a special commemorative cake.

Visitors to Harris Neck National Wildlife Refuge may enjoy the winding drive through a natural melody of creeks, marsh, and ponds with distinctive names like Woody, Bluebill, Goose, Teal and Greenhead. The route takes drivers by Wigeon Pond, Barbour River Landing, the South Newport River, and Gould's Cemetery where the remains of early coastal settlers and Harris Neck's black residents lie. Few of these visitors recognize the crumbling roads and runways and realize that this was the site of a World War II fighter base.

Harris Neck Island is on the Atlantic Flyaway and Georgia's Colonial Coast Birding Trail and is a marvelous place to view Coastal Georgia wildlife and shorebirds. During the spring and summer, countless wood storks, egrets, and herons nest in the swamps. Winter brings a variety of ducks, especially mallards, gadwall, and teal. In spring, the brilliantly-hued plumage of the painted bunting creates an unmistakable and unforgettable sight against Harris Neck's verdant forests.

Harris Neck is once again a peaceful place of astonishing natural beauty and serenity. As you stand near the marsh watching the sunset spin golden strands of light, you would never guess that squadrons of fighter planes revving their engines once disrupted nature's rhythmic hum. The Kittyhawks and Airacobras are but dim memories now and wood storks and alligators once again reign supreme.

Today, Harris Neck's golden marshes are a serene, wild place.

Helpful Information:

There is no admission fee to Harris Neck NWR. The refuge is open to the public daily from dawn until dusk. Additional information is available by calling the Visitor Center (912-832-4608), the Savannah Coastal Refuge (912-652-4415), or the U.S. Fish & Wildlife Service (800-344-WILD). You may also visit the website at http://harrisneck.fws.gov.

Getting there: From Savannah, travel south on I-95 to Exit 67 (South Newport). Proceed south on U.S. 17 approximately one mile. Turn left (east) on Harris Neck Road and continue seven miles to the main entrance.

Murder Moonshine
and the Ku Klux Klan

R. ALLEN WILBURN

At the height of prohibition and the bootlegging era, a North Georgia minister endeavored to purge alcohol and its evils from his community. In doing so, he unwittingly set in motion a sequence of events that culminated in his wife's untimely death and incited a show of support from an unlikely source.

Early one November evening in 1924, gunfire erupted in normally quiet Draketown, a small farming community in Northwest Georgia. The volleys left a well-known resident – the wife of a local preacher – mortally wounded. The shooting sent shock waves rippling through Georgia and drew nationwide attention to the once-serene location.

The events that ultimately led to bloodshed began weeks earlier. During the Prohibition years, Reverend Robert Stewart, a devout Methodist minister, unleashed powerful sermons against the manufacture, sale, and use of spirituous liquors. He was a man who practiced what he preached, so he also participated in search and destroy missions for local moonshine stills.

Word of Stewart's exploits and declamations from the pulpit filtered into the com-

Like many other preachers in rural areas, Rev. Stewart "rode the circuit" (he served a number of churches in the Draketown area). District Line United Methodist Church in Haralson County was one of his charges at the time of his wife's murder.

munity reaching remote, secluded valleys in Haralson and Paulding counties where many of these stills were tucked away. As locals tell it today, the bootleggers made at least two visits to Stewart, plainly stating that moonshine was their only source of income. "If the sheriff catches us, that's his job," they explained. "It is not a preacher's work. You can preach against us, but leave still destruction to the law."

Unheeded Warnings

Since these warnings did not influence Stewart, his continued exertions posed a genuine threat to the outlaws' prosperity, so they resolved to teach the "Raiding Parson" a lesson.

On the fateful autumn evening, Stewart and his wife Alice were at home. Whether their two daughters, Lorine, 7, and Tannie, 17, were also present is not known today. After dark, two groups of armed men arrived at the Methodist parsonage in separate cars. The exact chronology of events that followed is muddled at best.

The November 20, 1924 issue of the *Haralson County Tribune* reported that Alice Stewart later declared from her deathbed that the night-riders had arrived at about 9:30 p.m., asking for Stewart. The clergyman answered the door dressed in his bed clothes. He immediately sensed that something was amiss. When he hesitated the bootleggers grabbed him and wrestled him towards a waiting vehicle.

Another witness, Earnest H. Goldin, recollected that the moonshiners had difficulty forcing the parson – "a short, stout man"– into their vehicle. During this commotion, one of the malefactors shouted at him, "Damn you – you have made your last raid!"

One can only imagine Mrs. Stewart's state of mind as this horror unfolded. Thoroughly alarmed by her husband's plight, she fetched a gun – according to one report a pistol, while another source states it was a shotgun – and ran out into the front yard to make her stand.

Shots Fired

The firearm wielding woman in an evening gown demanded that the ruffians release her husband; when they refused to do so, she fired two warning shots into the air in rapid succession. One or more of the kidnappers panicked and returned fire. Mrs. Stewart was hit and fell to the ground.

Amidst this mayhem, Stewart made his move. He struggled from the clutches of his captors and ran to his injured wife. He grabbed her weapon and fired twice at the outlaws as they scurried back to their cars and made their escape from the bloody scene.

Fumbling about in the darkness, Stewart gave what aid he could to his gravely injured wife. Alice had been shot twice. One bullet penetrated her elbow while the second entered near her spine and turned upward, shattering several vertebrae.

Dr. B. F. Eaves, a local physician summoned to the scene, arrived quickly and transported the critically hurt woman to Wesley Memorial Hospital in Atlanta. There wasn't much they could do for her. She lingered two days and managed during that time to give a statement about the night's assault. According to her husband, she even identified some of the perpetrators.

Mrs. Stewart's wounds proved too severe and on November 15, 1924 she perished. Her remains were taken to her hometown, Helen, Georgia, for burial in the Chattahoochee Methodist Church cemetery.

Alice Stewart's slaying shocked Draketown and prompted outrage throughout Georgia. From the state capital, Governor Clifford Walker issued a proclamation decrying the brutal murder and offered a $200 reward for information leading to the arrest and conviction of those responsible.

The Ku Klux Klan Steps In

The residents of Draketown likewise offered their condolences and comforted the mourning minister. Sympathy also came from a rather unlikely source – the Ku Klux Klan.

On the Sunday following Mrs. Stewart's death, a twenty-car caravan arrived at the parsonage. The lead vehicle sported a large American flag imparting a parade-like atmosphere. The vehicles carried dozens of Klansmen in full Klan regalia from the nearby communities of Tallapoosa, Waco and Bremen. The Klansmen presented Stewart with $50, a heartfelt resolution condemning the murder, and a pledge of support for local law enforcement in their efforts to apprehend the killers.

Haralson County Sheriff George B. Richards and his deputies worked the case exhaustively. They inspected the crime scene, took statements, and within 48 hours made ten arrests. Those

This marble shaft was dedicated on June 6, 1925 at the site of the Alice Stewart shooting. It honors her memory and served as a pointed reminder to her killer or killers of the evils associated with bootleg liquor. The monument is located on Eaves Drive in Draketown.

District Line UMC today.

charged with Alice Stewart's murder were Jeff Henderson, his sons Herbert and Otis (both minors), Sted Hesteriee, Georgie Hucheson, Tom Bishop, Calvin Bishop, Jr., Tom Gober, Jr., John Carter, and Emmett Hollis.

The accused vehemently denied involvement in the crime and Judge F. A. Irwin apparently found that some of their alibis had merit. At the preliminary hearing in Haralson Superior Court, Judge Irwin dismissed the charges against Hesteriee, Hucheson, Carter, Hollis and Tom Bishop. Those held for trial were the three Hendersons, Gober and Calvin Bishop.

The sensational nature of the killing generated plenty of interest and set the stage for a spell-binding trial. Stewart was one of the prosecution's key witnesses. In response to pointed questions by Solicitor General E. S. Griffith, the parson testified that the defendants were part of the mob that had attacked him the night his wife was shot. He also offered hearsay testimony that his wife – while on her deathbed – identified several of the alleged criminals.

The drama heightened when Mrs. W. L. Hogue took the stand. Not content to merely answer questions, Mrs. Hogue, a well-known Draketown resident, read passages from the Bible, offered a prayer, and exhorted the court and law enforcement officers to obtain justice for the victim and her family. Mrs. Hogue then proceeded to testify that she had witnessed the shooting at the Stewart residence.

The defense presented alibis claiming that the accused were elsewhere at the time of the shooting. To the surprise of many and the delight of the defendants, the jury concluded that there was insufficient evidence on which to base a guilty verdict. The jury returned an acquittal on the charges against O.J. Henderson. The other trials were postponed. Eventually, the prosecutor decided to dismiss the charges and none of the other defendants stood trial.

Justice Delayed

While it seems that Alice Stewart's murderers never paid for their crime, the good citizens of Draketown did what they could to ensure that the slaying and the victim would not be forgotten. They were also determined to remind the perpetrators that one day they faced punishment of a more lasting nature. As a result, a memorial was commissioned for placement at the scene of the crime. A citizen's committee sought contributions and, once again, the Klan came forward in a show of support, participating in the purchase, installation, and dedication of the monument.

At noon on Sunday, June 6, 1925, nearly 5,000 people gathered in Draketown for the dedication service. Several local ministers and dignitaries spoke. Then little Lorine Stewart uncovered the fifteen-foot-high white marble monument featuring two benches and a porcelain photograph of Mrs. Stewart (years later the photograph was destroyed by BB-gun toting vandals).

The inscription on the monument reads:

"Alice Wildie Adams, wife of Rev. Robert Stewart, born May 10, 1888, assassinated November 13, 1924, by rum runners at this place, and died at Wesley Memorial hospital November 15, 1924. She was a kind and affectionate wife, a fond mother and a friend to all. 'Look not thou upon the wine when it is red, when it giveth colour aright. At the last it biteth like a serpent and stingeth like an adder. My fruit is better than gold, yea than fine gold, and my revenue than choice silver.'"

Shortly after this service, Rev. Stewart was transferred by the Methodist Church to the Greene Circuit south of Athens, Georgia. Undoubtedly, this action was taken to remove him from the immediate vicinity of the terrible crime that robbed him of his wife and childrens' mother. His career in the ministry, which began in Dahlonega in 1915, continued until his death on November 6, 1949. His remains are interred beside his wife's in the mountain cemetery near Helen.

Given the years that have passed since that terrible November evening, it is most likely that those with blood on their hands have since entered into their eternal reward. Today, just a few old-timers remain who remember the Raiding Parson and the death of Alice Stewart. On occasion, however, visitors happen upon the weathered marble monument in Draketown, pause to read the inscription, and wonder what led "rum runners" to assassinate a preacher's wife.

The Show Must Go On

Just a few days before Thanksgiving in 1915, a train carrying Con T. Kennedy's renowned carnival approached Columbus, Georgia. It was a merry, magical occasion, but a simple mistake by a railroad worker resulted in a horrifying crash that remains one of Georgia's worst-ever railroad accidents.

Joshua Owens and Michael Williams

I t was November 22, 1915, and showman Con T. Kennedy's carnival was heading to Columbus, Georgia. His gaily-decorated convoy train rumbled up the gentle grade. The trip had been uneventful thus far. The train departed Macon at 7:40 a.m., passed Upatoi Station before noon, and at about 1 p.m. reached Reynolds, where the conductor received clearance to continue through Muscogee Station.

It was late autumn, and the show season would soon end. After Columbus, Kennedy's carnival had engagements in Albany, Georgia, followed by the season finale in Jacksonville, Florida.

The entertainers had just completed a remarkably successful showing in Atlanta, and Kennedy had reason to be pleased. It had been an off year for most of his rival shows, but Con T. Kennedy Shows had enjoyed a series of profitable exhibitions.

Robert Kennedy, his brother and advertising manager, had been in Columbus nearly a week publicizing the upcoming event. Con Kennedy didn't expect Atlanta-sized crowds in Columbus, but he knew that Robert's enticing announcements of daring acrobatic feats, intriguing shows, and exotic animals would draw a multitude of Columbus-area residents to his carnival.

The train continued bouncing and bobbing along. Lulled by the car's rhythmic rocking, Con Kennedy may have relaxed just a bit, overcome by a pleasant drowsiness, and settled in for a midday nap.

The Dispatcher

In 1915, railroads operated by timetables, hand signals, and commands transmitted by telephone. In order to ensure safety, it was imperative to draft and transmit orders clearly and accurately. Railroad companies had developed elaborate protocols to achieve this objective, but human error could not be completely eliminated. On November 22, Train Dispatcher Mercer made a simple mistake when he sent Order 28 to operators at the stations in Columbus and Reynolds. The order specified that "No. 2, engine 1610 [an eastbound Central of Georgia train], will wait at Muscogee until 1:35 p.m. for No. 37 and Extra 1716."

Mercer intended to convey that Train 2 should halt at Muscogee until two west-

bound trains passed through the station. His order should have referred to both westbound engines (1716 and 1759), but he accidentally omitted 1759, giving the impression that there was only one.

The operator at Reynolds Station caught the error and pointed out that the order could potentially be misunderstood. He offered to insert the second engine number by hand, and Mercer assented. The operator made the change and transmitted the corrected order to Conductor Conley on westbound Extra 1716, Kennedy's carnival train.

Wilkerson, the operator in Columbus, also noticed the mistake. He contacted Mercer, who replied tersely, "No. 37 has engine No. 1759." This clarification suffered from the same defect as the original order: it referred to just a single westbound engine. Those who received the clarification might assume it simply corrected the number of the engine pulling Train 37 from 1716 to 1759.

Mercer broke a cardinal rule by allowing the operators at Reynolds and Columbus to transmit orders that weren't identical. Had they been, the conductor on westbound Extra 1716 may have realized the peril created by the ambiguity and straightened out the matter; as it was, the crew members on the westbound train had correct information. Since Rule 202 of the Central of Georgia's regulations specified that "each train order must be given in the same words to all persons or trains addressed," Conley understandably assumed that everything was in order and that the eastbound crew knew there were two oncoming trains.

Eastbound Train No. 2

J.W. Reichert was the conductor on the Central of Georgia's eastbound Train 2. His engineman – and right hand man – was Jerry Fickling. The conductor had the ultimate authority on a train, but the engineman handled everyday responsibilities. That

SEPTEMBER 4, 1915 **The Billboard** PRICE 10 CENTS 80 PAGES

Con. T. Kennedy
GENERAL MANAGER
CON. T. KENNEDY SHOWS

being the case, Reichert relied on Fickling's judgment in handling the train as it lumbered east towards Muscogee Station. Reichert trusted Fickling implicitly, for he was a fine, experienced engineman.

Train 2 departed Columbus at 1:12 p.m. Before boarding, Reichert scanned Order 28 at the telegraph office. He understood the order to require his train to wait in Muscogee until 1:35 p.m. While the 2.3-mile stretch from Columbus to Muscogee was a double track line allowing traffic in both directions, the stretch east of Muscogee was just single track. They would have to wait for westbound traffic to clear the line.

Reichert handed his copy of the order to his baggage master. He had a porter take another copy to Fickling, the engineman, disregarding the policy requiring conductors to personally deliver orders of such import.

After the porter delivered the message, he heard Fickling repeat the order to the fireman: "Wait until 1:35 for train 37, engine 1716." The porter thought nothing of it at the time, but later realized that the order implied that there was just one west-bound train.

When westbound Train 37 sped by on the double tracks just a few minutes later, Fickling thought the track ahead was vacant. Despite the order to halt at Muscogee until 1:35, he decided to proceed.

The Overconfident Engineman

Jerry Fickling was a seasoned professional who knew his trade intimately. He had thirty-four years railroading experience. He had begun as a fireman in 1881 and had been an engineman since 1884. He decided that since the oncoming train had passed, there was no need to linger in Muscogee. His home and family awaited in Macon, Train 2's destination.

Fickling sounded the whistle as the eastbound freight neared Muscogee. He was surprised when someone else aboard gave three shrill blasts of the air whistle, the signal to stop. Fickling paused for a moment to consider the meaning of this additional signal. Then, he remembered that Muscogee was a regular passenger stop, so he slowed the engine to a halt.

Fickling's fireman reported that the baggage master had a message. Baggage Master Frierson, a few cars back, was clutching the order in one hand, his face distraught. With his other hand he signaled Fickling, first raising two fingers and then lowering one, to indicate there were two oncoming trains and that just one had passed.

Fickling, who knew how to read a train order, was irritated by the questioning of his judgment, and he peevishly looked away before seeing the baggage master's hand signal.

The Westbound Carnival Train
Extra 1716 carried one of the premier entertainment troupes of the early 20th century. Con T. Kennedy Shows possessed a sparkling reputation in the carnival world. Con Kennedy traveled with his enterprise throughout the United States as it performed for audiences from Wisconsin to Florida.

An advertisement in the Columbus Enquirer-Sun a few days before had touted the carnival's tantalizing attractions: Sibley's International Diving Girls, Siamese Twins, three French midgets, a Ferris wheel, and the Motordrome, "a veritable cage of death…of the most reckless and dare devil motorcycle riders the world has ever known."

Kennedy was unable to sleep on the train. The show was to commence that evening. There would be a street parade the following day at 2 p.m., likely to be the largest parade in Columbus up to that time. The six-day event would be like an extended holiday for the people of Columbus. Few had experienced anything like this and nearly everyone would want to attend.

Westbound Extra 1716 consisted of 16 flatcars, 3 stock cars, and 9 sleeping cars in that order. Most of the cars were constructed of sturdy lumber. There was an impressive array of well-trained animals caged in the rear cars with horses, elephants, and other fabulous creatures. Mezeppa, the "$50,000 fire fighting horse with the human brain," was one of the chief animal attractions.

Passengers aboard included Mr. and Mrs. Fred Kempf and their 2-year-old daughter Hazel. Fred Kempf was considered a genius for his self-designed and self-built Model City, "a live up to the minute city in the noon-day of activity."

Kennedy tried to suppress the nervousness which always fluttered in his stomach before reaching a new city. He glanced at his watch: 1:15 p.m. A little less than an hour and they would be in Columbus.

The Baggage Master
Baggage Master Frierson saw Fickling look away before seeing his frantic gesture. "Why are we leaving Muscogee?" he wondered. "We've not let Extra 1716 pass."

It wasn't yet 1:35, so the engineman was directly disobeying Order 28. Before the train had gone far, Frierson blew the air whistle again, prompting Fickling to stop the train once more. Frierson left his post in the baggage cars to have a word with the engineman. When he reached the locomotive he told Fickling that Extra 1716 hadn't passed yet.

Fickling flatly disagreed and informed Frierson that there was one train and it had already passed. He herded Frierson away and mumbled that he had read the order and understood its meaning. Fickling started the train moving again, without first receiving a proper signal from the conductor to proceed. The self-assured engineman didn't even read over his own copy of the order to see if he had possibly erred.

Frierson, utterly frustrated, rushed to the rear of the train to find the conductor in hopes that Reichert would realize Fickling's slip and stop the train immediately.

Train Porter Lee was also worried. He remembered Reichert saying that the order called for a stop in Muscogee until 1:35 to allow two trains to pass. It wasn't 1:35 and Lee knew the second hadn't passed yet, so when he felt the locomotive lurch ahead again he rose to speak to the conductor. Then a flushed Frierson scrambled by, and Lee heaved a deep sigh of relief and sat back down. Good, he thought, the baggage master will take care of it.

Conductor Reichert

Reichert was surprised. The stop signal had been sounded by the baggage master twice, an unusual occurrence. He was even more surprised when Frierson, panting and red-faced, stamped into the caboose. "Sir, there is another train coming," Frierson huffed. "I don't think the engineman understands the order correctly."

Reichert's reaction was much like Fickling's. He assured Frierson that the engineman knew what he was doing and that he would surely wait if the two trains had not already passed. It was true that the conductor had spent most of the ride in the rear car and had not actually discussed the situation with the engineman, but Reichert knew that Fickling was not one to make such a careless blunder.

The conductor dismissed the dismayed Frierson, who exited quietly, wondering if he was the mistaken one.

The Crash

Fireman Allison had seen many sights in his 16 years of railroading. There was one sight, though, which he had never hoped to see: an engineman leaping from a locomotive for his life.

At 1:26 p.m., Train 2 was three-and-one-half miles east of Muscogee approaching a sharp curve near Bull Creek. Due to the thick foliage of nearby trees and brush, the crew had a limited line of sight. Allison was hard at work maintaining the boiler fire when he heard the engineman sharply inhale. Then Allison witnessed the startling sequence of Fickling engaging the emergency air brakes, pulling the reverse lever, and jumping from the train.

Rapidly rounding the curve was Extra 1716, Con T. Kennedy's transport, hurtling along the tracks at some 30 miles per hour. An instant later, the two trains collided in a cacophony of screeching, tearing, rending metal and shattering timbers.

On the Central of Georgia's Train 2, shocked passengers flew from their seats without warning, but fortunately even the worst injuries sustained were minor. The elderly Ella May Morris of Columbus was severely bruised and Dr. W. Marshall of Cincinnati suffered a broken wrist. None of the railroad employees were killed, though Engineman Fickling received a serious throat laceration and Conductor Reichert a wrenched back.

The Inferno

The situation on Extra 1716 was much grimmer. Cars near the point of impact began derailing. A truck on the flat car behind the engine contained incendiary items which burst into flame. The fire spread quickly among the wooden cars, and was so intense it "melted the iron beams on…the ferris wheel and the merry-go-round."

One man who was present during the wreck and its aftermath was William Floto, the Kennedy Shows' press agent. In the December 4, 1915 issue of The Billboard, a carnival industry newspaper, Floto described the mayhem: "Nine [of Kennedy's] flat cars were piled one on top of another…and almost instantly the entire mass burst into flames…[The] nine cars and their contents were piled…within a radius of one hundred feet. The ferris wheel, which was on the fourth car back, was found twisted around the cab and safety valve of the big locomotive."

A stunned but uninjured Irving Kempf was one of the first to react and attempt to reach the conflagration. He found his brother, Fred, caught beneath a heavy plank. Beside Fred was his wife, Blanche, who was also hopelessly trapped. "Mrs. Kempf, seeing…no chance to escape, hurled [Hazel] through a window, clear of the train.

Then [she] fell back and was burned alive a minute later."

"For God's sake save me," cried Fred Kempf. "Kill me or pull me out!" Irving strived courageously to extricate his brother, receiving severe burns in the process. Sadly, he failed, and Fred Kempf, along with his wife and Model City, succumbed in the inferno.

Con Kennedy rallied any help he could among nearby men and women and orchestrated multiple rescues. The quick-thinking circus manager, Walter Stanley, uncoupled cars at the rear and organized a crew to push them to safety. As a result of his efforts, several cars which held animals, passengers, and various equipment escaped the holocaust.

Before long, the fire became too intense for the rescuers. They stood aside, watching the train go up in flames. Even normally stoic, strong men wept openly because of their helplessness at the carnage, death, and horrifying injuries.

The Funeral

The passengers aboard Extra 1716 suffered terribly. The Columbus hospital was inundated with burn victims and quickly filled to capacity. Newly-orphaned toddler Hazel Kempf, with her tiny head wrapped in gauze and face slathered in ointment, was among the survivors.

Mrs. Gilman, the child's maternal grandmother, arrived shortly to determine the whereabouts of her family. She burst into tears when she asked Hazel where her father was. The child replied, "Poppa is on the train," and continued playing on her hospital bed, oblivious to the truth.

According to the Interstate Commerce Commission's accident investigation report, seven passengers perished. The *Atlanta Constitution* listed eleven casualties: Albert "Whitey" Johnson, William Batchelor, George Chapman, O.H. Hawkins, Frank Gilroy, Walter Hagan, Fred and Blanche Kempf, and three unidentified victims.

On a gloomy Thanksgiving morning, four hearses carried the bodies of some of the deceased to Columbus' Riverside Cemetery. The funeral procession included thousands of people paying their last respects. Historian Ken Thomas, a Columbus native, recently pointed out that the carnival band played "Nearer my God to Thee," the same hymn played on Titanic as it sank three years earlier. At the conclusion of the service, local Masons "read their impressive ritual" in honor of their fallen comrade, Fred Kempf.

Triumph from Tragedy

Con Kennedy incurred substantial financial losses exceeding $100,000 and mourned the deaths of multiple employees. He canceled the Columbus exhibition, "as he did not care to open…while the dead of his company were lying in local morgues." Kennedy debated whether he could even finish the season under such tragic circumstances.

The owners of competing carnivals and circuses rallied to his aid and placed their resources at his disposal. While he couldn't replace his Ferris wheel on such short notice, in just a week he cobbled together several stand-in acts: Ben Naple Illusions replaced the Coney Island Show, the Busy City took the place of Fred Kempf's Model City, and the Human Silo and Sanges' motordrome replaced the Gold & Hager's motordrome. These reportedly made up a show as interesting as any Kennedy had presented the whole season.

Persistent to the point of stubbornness, Kennedy decided to carry on despite the awful accident. A week later, Con T. Kennedy Shows left Columbus aboard nine rail cars (nineteen less than before) for Albany, Georgia. Though the carnival troupe members still reeled from the loss of family and friends, they knew that the show must go on.

Editor's Note

In our search for photographs of the train wreck, *Georgia Backroads* and the authors contacted museums, historical societies, and railroad enthusiasts throughout the United States and England. No photographs were found despite this tantalizing announcement in the November 22, 1915 issue of *The Columbus Enquirer-Sun*: "McCollum's studio photographed seven different scenes of the railroad wreck shortly after it occurred."

Sources

Many of the details in this article are derived from the ICC's Incident Report which is available at the U.S. Dept. of Transportation's online library: http://specialcollection.dotlibrary.dot.gov/

November 20, 1915 issue of the *Columbus Enquirer-Sun*.

"May Hold Trainmen for Manslaughter," November 24, 1915 issue of *The Atlanta Constitution*.

Floto, W.M. "Complete Details of Kennedy Train Wreck," December 4, 1915 issue of *The Billboard*.

"24 Lives Reported Lost in Fire When Carnival Train is Wrecked in Head-on Crash Near Columbus," November 23, 1915 issue of *The Atlanta Constitution*

November 23 , 1915 issue of the *Columbus Enquirer-Sun*.

Other casualty reports ranged from eight to twenty-four people

Floto, W.M. "Con T. Kennedy Shows," December 11, 1915 issue of *The Billboard*.

November 23, 1915 issue of the *Columbus Enquirer-Sun*

"Blame for the Wreck Put on Trainmen," November 25, 1915 issue of *The Atlanta Constitution*

Floto, W.M. "Con T. Kennedy Shows," December 11, 1915 issue of *The Billboard*.

A Walk Through the Valley of the Shadow of Death

Article and Photography Gary Elam

Blam! The startling noise wakes me from a very shallow sleep. Not a gunshot …not this time…but the thunderous clap of a baseball bat striking a heavy wooden door. Not my door…not yet…but there are more strikes, each a little louder and closer than the last, coming my way. "Here we go again," I think. "Somebody's going to interrogation…go on past my door, I'm tired."

I'm standing in a wooden box of a room about three feet square and six feet high. This is one time that I'm glad to be five-feet-ten inches, because I can stand up straight in the box. With nine square feet of floor space, it's more comfortable to sleep (make that doze) standing up than to try to sit. Besides, the floor is cold.

My box is one in two long lines of boxes in a barn-like building of rough cut,

unpainted lumber. The temperature outside the building is 30 degrees below zero. The floor is so cold. We have been allowed to keep our arctic parkas and boots, so as long as I stay off the floor, the cold itself isn't my main concern at the moment.

Suddenly, a baseball bat strikes my door. The door flies open and I am jerked out of my box. Now it's my turn. A large black hood is thrown over my head and my hands are tied behind by back; my box suddenly seems downright cozy.

Interrogation

It's been a long day, followed by an even longer night. The evening has included, among other challenging activities, crawling across the hard, high-desert floor to the concertina wire, then slowly, ever so slowly and meticulously, picking a path through coiled barbed wire (sometimes referred to as "razor wire"), being recaptured, standing naked in a very cold room among several other nude prisoners, and listening to the ravings and threats of a screaming compound commandant while our clothing is carefully, methodically searched.

Now, wearing the black hood, I'm pushed and shoved by two guards into a room where I face an extremely bright in-the-face light, probing questions, insults, and threats…the insidious individual interrogation.

Later, our entire group is reunited in the outdoor compound. We guess that it's almost dawn, and, knowing that the coldest time of night is just before sunrise, we take turns around a small wood stove in the compound's tiny shack, where a chosen few are again trying to figure a way out of this inhospitable deep-freeze.

If we escape, we'll wind up spending several days in the nearby mountains, at times running just ahead of gunshots, sometimes hiding, and always, always thinking about food – there isn't much game to be caught when it's 30 below in the mountains. At least there's plenty of water if you have time to punch a hole through the ice covering a stream.

Preparing for the Unimaginable

Training. It was all training. A three-week "paid vacation" provided by the U.S. Air Force in the high desert north of Reno, Nevada. Back in the Cold War days of the early '60s, everyone on flight status was treated to the Stead Air Force Base "vacation."

The package included POW training, "escape and evasion" tactics, and survival training, all seasoned with a bit of hand-to-hand combat practice. Good training, made very realistic by instructors who "had been there"…about as realistic as it could be without actual torture.

It gave us an idea what captivity could be like. It certainly made us think, and it made us prove to ourselves that we could indeed endure a lot more than we had previously thought. We were forced to consider the question, "What will I do if I should

wind up in a real POW situation?" Each of us soon understood that no one can answer that question until he has been pushed to his breaking point. And one's breaking point can lie on either side of death.

We also fully understood that we could not really be trained to be a POW. Training cannot duplicate the physical torture, the mental torture, and most of all, it can never duplicate the big unknown: Will I survive this and, if I do, how long must I endure it? How long?

Not by Arms Alone

This "what would I do" question was echoed by Fred Boyles, Superintendent of Andersonville National Historic Site near

Americus, Georgia. Andersonville includes the Civil War prison grounds, the National Cemetery, and the Prisoner of War Museum. Broyles believes that it is important for all Andersonville visitors to ask themselves that question and leave with the understanding that no one can answer it fully. Only then can one begin to know what the museum stands for: to promote the recognition of and appreciation for the extreme sacrifices our POWs made to protect the freedom that so many take for granted.

In addition to overseeing Andersonville, Broyles is also active in the Navy Reserve. I asked him, "Is there anything worse than being a POW?" He replied that he didn't know, but pointed out that there are things worse than death.

Charles Andrews, an American in Britain's infamous Dartmoor prison during the War of 1812, put it this way: "Death itself, with hopes of a hereafter, seemed less terrible than this gloomy prison."

Another POW said, "Few people can understand what it means to live daily with fear. The prisoner never knows when his freedom will be restored, if he will be fed tomorrow, or if he will suddenly become the next victim."

We also need to understand that, insofar as humanly possible, the POW continues to fight. The emblem of the American Ex-Prisoners of War (AXPOW) organization states this succinctly: NON SOLUM ARMIS – "Not by Arms Alone." Escape attempts, subversions, espionage, and communication with underground forces have all been part of POW resistance efforts.

But, so many times, the biggest fight is simply survival: "You're in hand-to-hand combat every day, but your hands are tied behind your back, you're blindfolded...it's a constant battle." Another POW said, "The only thing that separates you from an animal is what you've got inside of you."

Fred Broyles stresses that, from the first stages of Museum planning, all involved agreed that it was imperative to let the POWs themselves do most of the story-telling. Who can better impress upon us that we really don't understand how precious freedom is until we've lost it?

With this in mind, hundreds of hours of taped interviews were conducted with former POWs. Many of these men have since died, so their stories are priceless. The interviews are featured in more than six hours of interactive presentations. These recollections along with rare archival film footage and music combine to evoke emotions and inform the viewer of the pathos and valor of the American POW.

Polly Weister, producer of the museum's documentary, "Echoes of Captivity," comments on the involvement and emotion she felt as the editing progressed: "Each sound, word, picture, and timing is painstakingly reviewed and talked about again and again until it simply feels right."

Images of Suffering and Hope

This dedication is evident throughout the Museum. Donna Doberfuhl, who sculpted the heart-rending bronze sculpture in the courtyard as well as three brick relief panels bordering the courtyard, became so emotionally involved with the project that she took days off to separate herself from her work. Man's inhumanity to man got to her.

The lone bronze figure silently screams a combination of sentiments: hardship and extreme suffering on one hand; yet, having survived imprisonment and once again

tasted the water of life, his eyes are raised toward heaven in thanksgiving.

The brick background panels feature 25 figures of varying size, artfully set into perspective. Each of these figures is compelling and thought provoking.

The water meandering between the lone survivor and the brick wall symbolizes the miraculous Providence Spring that suddenly gushed forth in the Andersonville compound during a storm in August, 1864. It provided pure, clean water to Union prisoners of war in place of the filth-laden stream that had been providing both drinking water and latrine facilities.

Camp Sumter

The Prisoner of War Museum is about freedom. It is dedicated to every American POW, from the Revolutionary War through the ongoing war in Iraq. All of these men and women sacrificed their freedom so that we might have ours.

It is appropriate that the Prisoner of War Museum is part of the Andersonville complex, since Andersonville is a Civil War site. It was during the Civil War era that POW camps came of age. Through the early stages of the Civil War, prisoners were exchanged rather than incarcerated: a sergeant for a sergeant, a corporal for a corporal, a captain for a captain. With this practice in place, and with neither side expecting a long war, POW facilities were just short-term holding pens.

As the war progressed, the prisoner exchange system fell apart, due to various complaints from both sides. Exchange discussions ended on October 23, 1862, when U.S. Secretary of War Edwin Stanton directed that there would be no more exchanges. The existing holding pens immediately became overcrowded, and new facilities were hastily built in the North and South. Andersonville, officially called Camp Sumter, was thus born and long-term internment became a fact of warfare

Museum Origins

The creation of the POW Museum spanned some 30 years. It was around the time of the 100th Anniversary of the end of the Civil War that the U.S. Army decided to no longer operate the National Cemetery and prison park. Local citizens began a push to have the site incorporated into the National Park Service and soon won the support of Congressman Jack Brinkley and Senator Richard B. Russell, who gave Lyndon

Johnson credit for the idea to make Andersonville a memorial to all American POWs. In 1970, the property became a National Historic Site.

As the idea of dedication to all of our POWs gathered momentum, Governor Jimmy Carter commissioned the State of Georgia to erect a monument in the Andersonville Cemetery. The result – an appalling depiction of a trio of poor, wretched victims – was designed by William Thompson of Athens, Georgia and is the only monument at Andersonville erected by a Southern state, and the only one dedicated to all POWs.

In the early 1980s, when Chief Ranger Alfredo Sanchez began discussions with AXPOW, the dream of a National POW Museum first took shape. After Congressional funding was approved in 1990, the serious planning began. AXPOW members from WWII, Korea, and Vietnam were actively involved, especially in the overall building design and the courtyard concept.

Museum construction kicked off in the summer of 1996, and the grand opening was April 9, 1998. The ceremony was a suitable show of respect including speeches by Senator John McCain (who was a POW in Vietnam), Congressman Sanford Bishop, Governor Zell Miller, members of AXPOW, National Park Service representatives, and music by a Marine Corps band.

Designed as a Message

The Museum building is a work of art … a bit more subtle, perhaps, than its contents and the courtyard, but nevertheless it ingeniously mirrors prison camp building blocks. The design of this beautiful structure reflects the elements common to most POW enclosures: high windowless walls, towers, and a constricted approach through black steel gates.

The lobby is well lit by sunlight flooding through the overhead atrium formed by the largest of the towers. The Information and Literature Desk is located here as is a well stocked bookstore and gift shop.

From the lobby, a narrow passageway leads to the exhibit rooms, which hold some

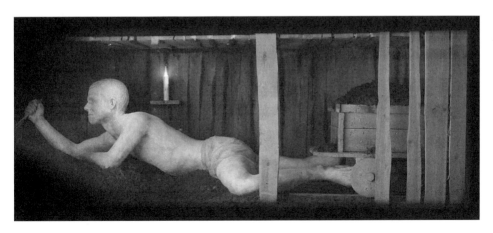

1500 POW-related artifacts, photographs, and videos. The thematic approach to the displays, rather than a chronological approach, was chosen because it better conveys the themes common to all POW experiences.

The initial exhibit answers the question, "What is a POW?" From there, the displays progress through Capture, Journey to the Camp, Living Conditions, News and Communications, Those Who Wait, Privation, Morale and Relationships, and appropriately concludes with Escape and Freedom. These theme rooms flank the central corridor, which contains additional artifacts and photographs as well as quiet resting areas under the two smaller towers.

Lessons

One thing is apparent during a tour of the Museum: the attitudes of captors toward prisoners changed dramatically over the years. During the Civil War, an estimated 194,000 Union soldiers and 214,000 Confederate soldiers became POWs. Approximately 30,000 Union and 26,000 Confederate troops died in captivity, most from disease and malnutrition. Both stemmed from hideous conditions that the captors were unable to correct due to wartime shortages. The deaths weren't due to the intentional mistreatment or torture of the prisoners.

During WWII, forced marches, slave labor with little or no food, solitary confinement, and physical torture were facets of the brutal captivity that occurred all too often in both the European and Pacific Theaters.

During the Korean War, mistreatment of American POWs was kicked up another notch when political "re-education" was perpetrated on the captives. Over 7000 Americans were captured in Korea, 2700 of which died. Adding to this grim figure, 8000 are still listed as missing in action.

During the Vietnam War, many Americans were held as long as seven years, enduring both physical and mental torture on a regular basis. The North Vietnamese claimed that the Americans were "political criminals" rather than POWs, and thus were not entitled to the protection of the Geneva Conventions.

A look at the well-stocked torture rooms of Iraq is ready proof that man is still devising methods increasing the level and efficiency of his inhumanity toward his fellow man. During the 1991 Gulf War, 23 American POWs, including two women, experienced frequent beatings, broken eardrums, and strategically-placed electric shock probes.

We all celebrate Memorial Day and the 4th of July. Some of us also observe Armed Forced Day, Flag Day, and Veterans Day. But few realize that the third Friday in September is National POW / MIA Recognition Day. A visit to the National Prisoner of War Museum is one way to pay tribute to all who have endured enemy captivity. My visit reminded me once again how fortunate I was that my Stead "vacation" was only training for a event that I fortunately never experienced.

Andersonville is 10 miles northeast of Americus on Georgia Hwy. 49. Telephone (229) 924-0343 or visit www.nps.gov/ande for more information.

DISGRACED MINISTER CHARGED WITH MURDER

The Shooting of U.S. Marshal Robert Forsyth and the Legend of Beverly Allen

RAY CHANDLER

At the dawning of our nation's existence, a disgraced and defrocked Methodist minister shot and killed United States Marshal Robert Forsyth in an Augusta boarding house. Forsyth, who had been appointed by President George Washington, was the first marshal killed in U.S. history. Some who believed that the killer was either justified or wrongly accused aided in his escape, thus giving birth to the legend of Beverly Allen.

On January 11, 1794, a defrocked Methodist minister in Augusta raised his pistol and fired through the door of his boarding house room. United States Marshal Robert Forsyth fell dead from a pistol ball through his head. His death earned Forsyth, who was attempting to serve civil papers on the preacher, the unfortunate distinction of being the first federal law enforcement officer killed in the line of duty.

Beverly Allen had once been a flamboyant, powerful preacher who held congregations throughout the Carolinas and Georgia in the palm of his hand. By the time he killed Forsyth, however, he was a notorious rake, stripped of his ministry and surrounded by whispered rumors of a grave sin that had led to his humiliation and the abandonment of his wife.

After the shooting, an aura developed around Allen in Elbert County, where he had made his home in 1792. It was the kind of legend that surrounded Robin Hood, Jesse James, Billy the Kid, and John Dillinger. Not once, but twice Allen escaped from jail with the help of friends motivated by suspicions Allen was a victim of dirty politics.

Allen's second jail rescue came at the hands of a mob that seems to have included some of Elbert County's most respected citizens. Finally, Allen fled to far off Kentucky – so the stories went – but in Elbert County lore his final whereabouts remained shrouded in mystery.

Most stories had him practicing medicine and once again taking up preaching, perhaps in hopes of redemption. If you grew up in Elbert County that is the Beverly Allen you heard about: a romantic rake and a wronged man. Surprisingly, the legend remains as strong as ever.

A close look at what is known of Allen's life reveals that the legend is inaccurate. He was, in fact, a troubled man who had reached the pinnacle of his calling before falling completely out of grace, a victim of his own foibles and, perhaps, church politics.

It seems that Beverly Allen arrived in Elbert County pursued by his own demons and later departed in hopes of escaping them as well as the law. He successfully evaded the authorities, but given what is known of his end suggests that he died a man still haunted by his demons and fears of hellfire.

The Early Church Years

Little is known about Beverly Allen before 1781, the year he was accepted into the Methodist church as an itinerant preacher. Methodist historian Duane V. Maxey did not determine the exact time and place of either his birth or death. His brother, William Allen, with whom Beverly was in the mercantile business at the time he killed Forsyth, was born in Amherst County, Virginia in 1756. Beverly was two years older, so it is possible he was born there. Accounts indicate the brothers also had at least one sister.

MICHAEL KIRTON

Allen possessed considerable charm, which helped him overcome the obstacles and prejudices ministers of the new denomination encountered in the Methodist church's early years. One observer described Allen as a "brilliant young preacher of striking appearance and unusual popularity... He could win his way wherever he went and gain a bearing among all. He managed to carry on an extended correspondence with Mr. [John] Wesley, and for a brief time did an excellent work..."

Francis Asbury, a founding father of American Methodism, was a man who tolerated little or no dissent to his way of governing the church. Beverly Allen, however, was apparently one who reserved the right to disagree with Asbury and it was not long before Asbury sensed this, describing Allen as "a promising young man, but a little of a Dissenter."

There was no question that Allen was an effective minister. He attracted the favorable notice of a Mrs. William Cole at his church in Salisbury, North Carolina in 1783:

"Soon after my return to Salisbury, at the close of the [Revolutionary] war, it was announced that there would be preaching in a schoolhouse by a new kind of people, called Methodists... I went early expecting to see a minister resembling the old parsons; but judge of my surprise, when instead of a stout, good looking, finely dressed gentleman with gown and surplice, in silk stockings and silver buckles, in walked a slender, delicate young man, dressed in homespun cotton jeans. Though plainly attired, I perceived in his countenance unusual solemnity and goodness. The impressions made upon my mind and heart by this sermon — the first I ever heard from a Methodist minister — have never been effaced from my memory. The subject was experimental religion, explained and enforced. To my surprise, the preacher unfolded my experience, and seemed to give in detail all the exercises of my mind, from my first conviction for sin, until I was made happy in the love of God. Not till then did I know that I enjoyed religion; although happy, I did not fully understand why. My experience exactly agreeing with the word preached, I concluded that the preacher, an entire stranger, could not have known so much about me, had not God revealed it to him. At his third visit he formed a small class, of which I was one..."

Allen's success continued at his next post in Wilmington and, at a conference in Baltimore, he was named one of the Methodist church's twelve elders. Then, in 1785, he was sent as a missionary to organize congregations in Georgia. He apparently enjoyed continued success there, especially in Wilkes County, where his brother William had settled after the Revolution.

Disgraced

During this period, there was increasing tension between Asbury and Allen. Historian Maxey speculates that Asbury arranged to have Allen sent to Georgia as a sort of exile for the "dissenter." Years later, Asbury described the deteriorating state of their relationship in his journal: "Poor Beverly Allen ... has been going from bad to worse these seven or eight years, speaking against me to preachers and people and writing to Mr. Wesley and Dr. Coke, and being thereby the source of most of the mischief that has followed."

In 1787, Allen received an appointment as the Methodist church's elder in Charleston, South Carolina, where he continued to excel for awhile. He married into a prominent family (by one account his wife was a wealthy widow who owned a plantation on Edisto Island), but his record darkened here.

Exactly what he did that led to his expulsion from the church isn't recorded in any known account of the Methodist church's history. The details of his supposed sins were apparently carefully kept from public notice. In the 1830s, theological historian Nathan Bangs simply said, "In the notice we have taken of the rise and progress of Methodism in Charleston, South Carolina, we have seen that Mr. Allen brought a great reproach upon the Church in that place by his apostasy. What the particular sin was by which he thus wounded the cause of God, I am not informed."

Beverly Allen was expelled from the church by Asbury in 1792 "for immorality" and a "flagrant crime." He left Charleston in disgrace, followed by allegations that he had abandoned his wife after leaving her destitute.

To the Georgia Upcountry

The disgraced minister next turned up in Elbert County where he went into business with his brother. William Allen was a successful man in his own right, though his life had taken a different tack from Beverly's. William appears typical of the hardworking merchants and landowners who helped settle the upper Savannah River valley, but his actions after Beverly killed Forsyth cast a shadow over his life and that of his descendents for years afterward.

William operated a tavern and mercantile business on the road leading to bustling Petersburg, where he also dealt in the lucrative trade in town lots. Petersburg was a bustling river port thriving on trade in upper Savannah River valley and was, briefly, Georgia's third largest city. William Allen was one of the area's leading citizens and held the rank of captain of the Elbert County militia, a factor of no small importance in Beverly's last jailbreak.

By late 1793, in the face of the uncertainties of trading in land, tobacco, and the coming commodity of cotton, the Allen brothers had overextended themselves with creditors in Augusta and had been named in several lawsuits. It was during a trip to Augusta to try to settle some of these debts that Allen encountered Forsyth.

On Saturday, January 11, 1794, Robert Forsyth and two of his deputies arrived at a boarding house owned by a Mrs. Dixon. According to an account published in the *Augusta Chronicle* one week later, the lawmen approached William and Beverly Allen, who were talking with acquaintances, and asked to speak with them privately. The newspaper account opined that Forsyth wished to spare the Allens the embarrassment of being publicly served with summonses in another lawsuit.

Death in the Line of Duty

There are two different versions of the events that followed. One is that William Allen accepted service while Beverly fled to his second floor room. The other has both brothers fleeing. Since both were arrested later, it seems likely that both fled to their room.

In any case, witnesses attested that when Forsyth approached the door to the room, Beverly warned that if he came any further he would blow Foryth's brains out. Beverly then fired, the pistol ball going through the door and hitting Forsyth in the head, killing him instantly.

The 40-year-old Forsyth had been a U.S. marshal for nearly five years, one of the thirteen original federal marshals (one for each state) appointed in 1789 by President George Washington. Born in Scotland in 1754, Forsyth came to America with his father and lived in New England until moving to Fredericksburg, Virginia around 1774. Two years later, he enlisted in the colonial forces and, in 1779, was commissioned a captain in the light dragoons. Eventually, Forsyth transferred to the commissary department of the Continental Army's Southern Department and ended the war as a major in the First Virginia Legion.

In 1785, Forsyth moved from Fredericksburg to Augusta. He quickly rose in his new community, becoming a county commissioner and trustee of a school as well as working as a tax assessor and a justice of the peace. He was a merchant, a farmer, and a member of the Augusta Masonic lodge. He had a wife and two sons.

Act of Insanity?

At first, both Allens were arrested for Forsyth's murder, but a coroner's inquest charged just Beverly Allen with the crime. He was held in the Richmond County jail, the gallows his almost certain fate. Friends in Elbert County almost immediately rallied to his support, however, and devised a desperate strategy to free him: the insanity plea.

Francis Asbury, writing in his journal, comments about their tactic while seemingly more concerned lest the incident cast a shadow over the church: "The masterpiece of all, is," Asbury wrote, "a petition is prepared declaring him to have shown marks of insanity previous to his killing the major! The poor Methodists also must unjustly be put to the rack on his account, although he has been expelled from among us these two years. I have had my opinion of him these nine years; and gave Dr. Coke my thoughts of him before his ordination. I pity, I pray for him, that, if his life be given up to justice, his soul may yet be saved."

The effort to prove that Beverly Allen was insane showed no signs of working. So six weeks after the shooting, he escaped from the Richmond County jail, reportedly with the aid of a guard. Rewards were immediately offered for Allen's recapture. "The apprehension of this man will be liberally rewarded by the respected inhabitants of Augusta," the announcement in the March 1 edition of the Augusta Chronicle read, "besides the approving voice of every good character in America."

Allen sought refuge from his brother in Elbert County. The fugitive was finally located and recaptured, however, on June 15. This time, his supporters and William's militia comrades rallied to his aid by more direct means.

To Protect Him from Insults

William Barnett, a justice of the peace in Elbert County, later wrote Georgia Governor George Mathews about the events: "On the 15th instant the sheriff of this County with myself an several others went to the house of Mr. William Allen where we had reason to believe that Beverly Allen who had escaped from Richmond County Gaol, was concealed. We accordingly found him very ingeniously secreted in the gar-

The original portion of this house, built by William Allen's sons, stood for many years overlooking the lands along Beaverdam Creek granted to their father in what became Elbert County after the American Revolution. From the early 1800s, it passed through descendants of the Allens until it passed into the hands of Mrs. E.C. Brown. It was sold from the Brown estate in the 1990s and burned in 2000.

ratt of the house of Wm. Allen. We carried him from thence to our gaol. In about two hours after our arrival we were surprised by an armed force to the amount of some thirty odd, headed by Wm. Allen whose intentions he said were to protect Beverly Allen from Insults and from being carried to Augusta, though for some cause best known to themselves, they Retreated without any further molestation."

Barnett called for reinforcements from the militia, undoubtedly unaware of their ties to the Allen family. Two days later, about 40 or 50 armed men with faces blackened arrived at the jail. Badly outnumbered, the officer in charge ordered his men to hold fire.

"The mob advanced and rescued the prisoner," Barnett informed the governor. "We have on slight testimony apprehended four of the party two of which were Militia Captains. It is extraordinary to think of the influence this man has had on the minds of the citizens of this County. I think they are a majority in his favor."

Barnett's involvement in the effort to bring Beverly Allen to justice led to speculation that he had more personal motives. He had been, in fact, a close friend of Robert Forsyth, having been both a tax collector and sheriff in Richmond County before moving to Elbert County in 1790.

To the Frontier

In 1794, Kentucky was still a wild and wooly land that was a natural haven for outlaws. According to legend, Beverly Allen sought refuge there and, based upon the record, this seems likely. He settled in Logan County, Kentucky in an area known as Rogues Harbor, because it was inhabited at the time mainly by "murderers and horse thieves."

There is some reason to believe that Beverly was joined there by his sister. So it would seem that his flight to Kentucky was a fairly open secret among his family and, presumably, his friends. Authorities apparently made no serious effort to pursue the fugitive. The itinerant preacher-turned-fugitive-from-justice finally had a place to settle and by some accounts eventually started a family of his own.

Allen took up medicine and also ran a boarding school in his Logan County home, according to Peter Cartwright, who was one of his students and later a notable Methodist minister himself. Cartwright recorded that the wayward fugitive's last years were wracked with guilt and spiritual torment and, in seeking comfort, he abandoned the Methodist church for the then nascent faith of Universalism, with its less rigid and demanding strictures on salvation. Cartwright, who from his writings was fully aware of Allen's past, makes no mention of him taking up preaching of his new-found faith.

Haunted by Demons

Beverly Allen died near the age of 90, with Cartwright at his bedside, and at the end returned to the Methodist fold even though he held out no hope that returning to the church could save his troubled soul. "It fell to my lot," Cartwright wrote, "after

I had been a preacher several years, to visit the Doctor on his dying bed.

"I talked to, and prayed with him. Just before he died I asked him if he was willing to die and meet his final Judge with his Universalist sentiments. He frankly said he was not. He said he could make the mercy of God cover every case in his mind but his own, but he thought there was no mercy for him; and in this state of mind he left the world, bidding his family and friends an eternal farewell, warning them not to come to that place of torment to which he felt himself eternally doomed."

Cartwright doesn't mention any specific deathbed confessions by Beverly Allen, so we have no clue whether any of his last thoughts were of Robert Forsyth. It seems likely, however, that the memory of January 11, 1794 did visit his troubled mind. It was a tormented end for a tormented man, who would have been further dismayed had he known how he would be remembered in north Georgia.

William Allen suffered no known legal troubles for his role in helping Beverly escape from the Elbert County jail. He settled with his Augusta creditors and continued to thrive as a merchant and plantation owner, always numbered among Elbert County's respected citizens. He had two sons, one named Beverly.

Robert Forsyth was buried in the cemetery of St. Paul's Episcopal Church in Augusta. Both Forsyth County and the city of Forsyth, Georgia were named in his honor and to this day he has an honored place in the annals of the U.S. Marshals Service. In 1981, the Marshals Service created the "Robert Forsyth Act of Valor Award." The award is given to a U.S. Marshals Service employee who demonstrates unusual courage, good judgment, and competence in hostile circumstances, or who has performed an act or service which saved the life of another person while endangering his/her own life.

In 1997, Governor Zell Miller dedicated the Georgia Public Safety Memorial at the Public Safety Training Center in Forsyth. The monument memorializes Georgia law enforcement officers, firefighters, corrections officers, emergency medical technicians and emergency management agency personnel who lost their lives in the line of duty. The first name carved on the memorial is that of Robert Forsyth.

Sources

Lloyd deWitt Bockstruck, Revolutionary War Bounty Land Grants Awarded by State Governments (Baltimore, MD: Genealogical Publishing Company, 1996).

In his memoirs, the Methodist minister Peter Cartwright recounts staying at an inn in Hopkinsville, Christian County, Ky., and identifies the innkeeper's wife as the sister of "Dr. Allen," whom Cartwright knew and had ministered on his deathbed. Quoted in *Beverly Allen: (The Sad and Sobering Story of an Early Methodist Apostate)* by Duane V. Maxey, Digital Edition 11727/99 By Holiness Data Ministry.

Duane V. Maxey, *Beverly Allen: (The Sad and Sobering Story of an Early Methodist Apostate)* Digital Edition 11727/99 By Holiness Data Ministry.

Nathan Bangs, *History of the Methodist Episcopal Church from its Origin in 1776 to the General Conference of 1840*, Vol. I, (New York, 1839).

The Augusta Chronicle, January 18, 1794.

Biography of Robert Forsyth summarized from the website of the U.S. Marshals Service.

Asbury's journal entry quoted by Maxey.

John. H. McIntosh, *The Official History of Elbert County, 1790-1935*, Elberton, Georgia, Stephen Heard Chapter of DAR, pp. 71-72.

Cartwright's recollections of Beverly Allen in Kentucky, written in his memoirs, are quoted by Maxey.

Website of the U.S. Marshals Service:
www.usmarshals.gov/history/forsyth/in_line_of_duty.htm.

Website of Georgia Public Safety Training Center:
www.state.ga.us/gpstc/memorial.html.

Atlanta's Historic Oakland Cemetery

ALEXANDRA KATHRYN MOSCA

A shaded enclave amidst Atlanta's towering skyscrapers, Oakland Cemetery offers visitors a peaceful – and occasionally unsettling – stroll among the remains of thousands of Georgians, both the famous and the forgotten.

I was drawn to Atlanta from New York because of my abiding affection for the city and one of its most famous writers, Margaret Mitchell. Her novel, *Gone with the Wind*, has been a touchstone for my literary interest and I'm a collector of books, documents, and other material about Mitchell. During a recent visit to Atlanta, I made a pilgrimage to Mitchell's final resting place – historic Oakland Cemetery, where as a child she rode her bicycle through the grounds.

Aside from its ties to Mitchell, Oakland Cemetery is a cultural repository for a city that for so long has been the economic and social center of the South. The cemetery is listed on the National Register of Historic Places and encompasses 88 acres. More than 70,000 people are buried there including 6,900 Civil War dead, five Confederate generals, six Georgia governors, and 26 Atlanta mayors. The cemetery is also one of Atlanta's most popular tourist attractions, drawing people who often seek some link to those who once made up Atlanta society.

Oakland's Origins

The death of Mrs. Agnes Wooding, a farmer's wife, resulted in the establishment of Oakland Cemetery. . She was buried on her property and her husband, Alfred, soon found he couldn't bear living so near her grave. So, when the city of Atlanta offered to buy six acres for $450 and turn it into a city cemetery, he sold. The land became Atlanta's first (as well as it's only for the next 34 years) cemetery, as Kevin Kuharic, the cemetery's Recreation and Landscape Manager, explained as we made our first stop on a private tour.

Walking paths bordered by the stately oak trees from which the cemetery gets its name, Kuharic pointed out various plants indigenous to the cemetery including phlox. Its attractive purple flowers suggest "Our souls are united" according to a Victorian era legend. Plantings, Kuharic told me, are taken seriously at Oakland because folklore has it that a scent carried by a wafting breeze is a spirit passing by.

A Gruesome Request

We stopped at the grave of Dr. James Nissen. A physician who died while visiting the city during a medical convention, Dr. Nissen was Oakland's first official "resident." Afraid of being buried alive, he requested, prior to his death, that a colleague, Dr. Noel d'Alvigny, open his casket at the cemetery and sever his jugular vein. A plaque at the site recalls this incident.

Oakland offers many fine examples of Victorian style monuments which are strong on symbolism. At the Neal grave, a woman holds an open book, signifying knowl-

edge known to man, whereas her daughter holds a closed book, which signifies knowledge unknown to man on earth. A Celtic Cross, symbolizing eternal life; redemption and faith, serves as a backdrop.

Other objects on display include urns, signifying sorrow; columns connoting heaven; obelisks representing eternal life; lions symbolizing courage; and lopped tree trunks denoting lives cut short.

Yet, for all the intricately carved stones and mausoleums, many with religious and inspirational inscriptions, I take note of many monuments which are just as poignant in their simplicity. Perhaps that is why the Potter's Field, where 17,000 people were buried in obscurity or anonymity, is particularly poignant. At one time, these graves were marked by wooden crosses. Today, there is a single monument to all who rest in this meadow-like area.

Confederate Dead

The Confederate Section of the cemetery lies in a serene grove of trees which contrasts sharply with the tumult of war. Six acres were set aside during the Civil War as the bodies of Confederate soldiers, and even some Union casualties, would be interred.

A majority of the Civil War dead are known and identified. During the war, wooden markers were placed at their graves. These were replaced later by larger marble headstones issued by the Veteran's Administration.

There are several memorials to the war including The Lion of Atlanta, a 30,000 pound marble statue of a recumbent lion erected to honor 3,000 unknown

Final resting place of Margaret Mitchell, author of *Gone with the Wind*.

Confederate dead who perished during the Battle of Atlanta. The Confederate Obelisk is the tallest structure in the cemetery and at one time the tallest structure in Atlanta, according to cemetery historians. Built of granite mined from a nearby Stone Mountain quarry, the memorial was dedicated on April 26, 1874, Confederate Memorial Day, to commemorate fallen Southern soldiers. A service is held here each year to honor Confederate war dead.

By the start of the Civil War, 860 African-Americans had been buried at Oakland; the oldest believed to be a 125 year old slave from Africa. The first recorded burial of an African American occurred in 1853 after the Atlanta City Council authorized burial of African-Americans in the cemetery, albeit in a section set apart. Until then, Atlanta's African-Americans were buried in church cemeteries or private family lots.

Atlanta's Leaders

The long list of prominent African American's buried in Oakland Cemetery includes former Atlanta Mayor Maynard Jackson, Atlanta's first black mayor, who died in 2003. He is just one of many on the distinguished list of Atlanta mayors buried at Oakland including Atlanta's first mayor, Moses Formwalt, who served from 1848 to 1849. After he left office, Formwalt was murdered by a prisoner while employed as a DeKalb County deputy sheriff.

A monument, dubbed simply The Mayor's Monument, is dedicated to all Atlanta mayors. Names, dating from 1848 to 1976, are inscribed. Another block was added in 2000, to bring the list up to date, leaving room for future mayors.

Another minority group, those of the Jewish faith, also have a special area that is the second oldest Jewish cemetery in Georgia. In this section, monuments are, for the most part, inscribed in English and Hebrew and include interesting religious symbolism. In 1860, a cemetery guide book notes, there were a mere 50 Jews in Atlanta, but their numbers increased as did their impact on the city. They were among the city's leading businessmen, professionals, and manufacturers. Several left indelible marks on Atlanta, establishing icons like Coca-Cola and Rich's Department Store.

After visiting the final resting places of so many who played key roles in Atlanta history, it was finally time to visit the grave that was the most important to me. A small sign pointed the way to Margaret Mitchell's grave, the most visited gravesite in Oakland. I was struck by the relative simplicity of her burial site. In keeping with her modesty, the headstone does not refer to her literary accomplishments. The inscriptions on the marble memorial simply list her name and that of her husband, John Marsh, her parents, and her brother.

Standing at her headstone, I was overwhelmed by the emotion to be visiting the final resting place of the woman who had inspired me as a writer. I walked up to the stone, outstretched my hand, and with my fingers traced the letters etched into the monument. It was a moving experience, made all the more so because Mitchell died on my birthday and was born on the same day as my best friend, who strongly encouraged me to write. I lingered at the grave and, before leaving, placed a bouquet of spring flowers there.

As I exited the cemetery gates, I reflected on the words of Margaret Mitchell: "Do Not Squander Time, for time is the stuff that life is made of." On that day, they never held more meaning.

THE 1814-15 BRITISH INVASION OF GEORGIA

The Final Battle

ARTICLE AND ILLUSTRATIONS MICHAEL KIRTON

The British invasion of St. Mary's, Georgia in 1815 becomes a personal vendetta of the King's commanding officer when a local U.S. Customs agent refuses to cooperate with the invaders. When British troops set out to exact retribution, a carefully laid ambush by American troops results in a bloody battle which, circumstances soon reveal, was completely pointless.

Many Americans have little or no knowledge of the War of 1812, our country's first international conflict. While most recognize the National Anthem, and some have heard of the Battle of New Orleans or are vaguely aware that Washington D.C. was once burned, relatively few associate these with the War of 1812. If asked, a majority might point to the American Revolution or the Civil War. Few indeed would be aware that the final battle of this war took place right here in Georgia.

America's largely unknown and forgotten war was the result of several economic and political factors, the most egregious of which was the British impressment of American seamen. Throughout the Napoleonic Wars, Great Britain needed sailors. To meet this need, the Royal Navy boarded neutral vessels at sea and removed expatriate British crewmen. These "press gangs" were none too discriminating and over the years thousands of American citizens, native-born as well as naturalized, were seized. Impressment galled much of the American populace.

Eventually, President James Madison, under pressure from the political "war hawks" led by Henry Clay, asked Congress to declare war on Great Britain. On June 18, 1812, the House and Senate approved Madison's request.

Sadly, it was a war that need not have been fought. The British repealed the impressment policy on June 22, but news did not reach Washington for a month. By then it was too late; the fighting had already begun.

While the conflict is known as the War of 1812, it waged on for more than two years. Initially the British earned the lion's share of victories, especially in land engagements. For some time, the only bright spot for the United States was its relatively small but scrappy navy. But as the war continued, American ground forces also experienced success. Younger, more energetic generals like Andrew Jackson, Winfield Scott, and Edmund Gaines emerged and achieved victories.

Nevertheless, by 1814 both sides were seeking an end to the war. In August, British and American representatives met in Ghent, Belgium. The negotiations proved long and difficult, but on December 24, 1814, the Treaty of Ghent was agreed to and soon

January 11, 1815, Camden County, GA: Captain Robert Barrie of the Royal Navy, invaded Cumberland Island with 1500 troops and commandeered Dungeness Place for use as British headquarters.

after ratified by Parliament. However, ratification by the United States Congress was also required, and trans-Atlantic travel was slow, so more than six weeks passed before the treaty took effect.

It was during this period that Andrew Jackson crushed the British at the Battle of New Orleans on January 8, 1815. This victory is often portrayed as the last battle of a war that was already over, yet the war did not officially end until February 17, 1815, and the last land engagement was fought a week later along the St. Mary's River.

Invasion

The events leading up to the St. Mary's battle began with the British invasion of Cumberland Island. In December 1814, British Rear Admiral Sir George Cockburn (pronounced "Co'burn") was ordered south from the Chesapeake Bay area to harass coastal South Carolina and Georgia. He was to capture Cumberland Island and the nearby town of St. Mary's, Georgia, thereby severing American inter-coastal traffic and communication.

By early January most of his squadron had assembled at a rendezvous point off Cumberland Island to await the admiral's arrival. Cockburn was unavoidably detained, however, by what he termed "extraordinary bad and adverse weather." As a result, his squadron grew critically short of water and suffered increasing shipboard illness. The senior officer present, Capt. Philip Somerville of HMS *Rota*, decided to alleviate the situation by proceeding with the invasion.

Ill himself, Somerville ordered Capt. Robert Barrie of HMS *Dragon* to assume command of the operation. At daybreak, January 10, Barrie made for St. Andrews Sound and the northern end of Cumberland Island. Accompanying him were detachments of the First, Second, and Third Battalions of Royal Marines as well as two companies of the Second West India Regiment. Additionally, he brought the squadron's barges and the schooners *Canso* and *Whiting*.

By 5 p.m., Barrie's force anchored near the north end of Cumberland Island and a

Two Dungeness mansions have occupied Cumberland Island's south end. The first was completed by Catharine Greene, the widow of Revolutionary War general Nathanael Greene, in 1804. It was occupied by British forces in early 1815. Thomas Carnegie began construction of a new Dungeness on the foundation of the old in 1884. It is the ruins of the Carnegie mansion (pictured here), which burned in 1959, that loom so hauntingly on Cumberland today.

detachment of troops landed unopposed, probably at High Point. This troop proceeded south and camped at an undetermined site, possibly near Parker's Landing. At daybreak the following morning they resumed their march south.

Dungeness

That same morning, January 11, Barrie transported the remainder of his troops south in the squadron's barges. He left the two schooners at the north end of the island to guard the sound's entrance and took the Plum Orchard passage to avoid detection. This party reached Dungeness Plantation later that day. Barrie quickly disembarked his troops and commandeered the manor house.

Dungeness was a massive, four-story tabby-built structure that, at the time, was considered the most magnificent home on the Georgia coast. Revolutionary War hero Gen. Nathaniel Greene began construction of Dungeness in the early 1780s, and, after his untimely death, the work continued under the direction of his widow, Catherine. By January 1815, ownership of the manor had passed to their youngest daughter, Louisa Greene Shaw. Because her husband, James, was ill and indisposed throughout the entire British occupation, she was forced to deal with the uninvited houseguests.

By the evening of January 11, the British had determined that Cumberland Island's food reserves and other materials were insufficient to meet the squadron's needs. Somerville elected to proceed with the capture of Fort Point Peter and St. Mary's on the mainland even though Admiral Cockburn had not arrived. By January 12, the senior officers had formulated their plan of attack for the following day.

Ambush

Early on January 13, 600 troops under the command of Lt. Col. R. Williams crossed the Cumberland River in barges and landed at Kings Bay Plantation. The guide, Lt. John Fitzgerald of the British Army, had once lived in St. Mary's and knew of a trail running from the plantation to the rear of Fort Point Peter.

Although the British landing was unopposed, Capt. Abraham Massias, who commanded the U.S. Army garrison at Point Peter, quickly received news of the British approach and moved to intercept it. Leaving Capt. Elias Stallings and 36 men to hold the fort, Massias led two companies, one rifle and one regular infantry, to a swampy section of the trail later known as Battle Hammock. He positioned a detachment under Lt. Hall on his left, and another, under Lt. Hardee, on his right.

The engagement that ensued, according to Lt. Col. Williams, consisted of "about twenty minutes of rapid firing." The ambush succeeded in slowing, but not stopping the British, and Massias was forced to retreat. John Sawyer, a local citizen, later wrote that, "Captain Massias lost one killed and two or three wounded. I saw two of the British deserters, who state that the British had two killed and several wounded."

Capt. Stallings fared worse. Fourteen of the 36 men of his defense force were wounded and he abandoned Point Peter. The British pillaged the fort, removing can-

January 13, 1815, Camden County, GA: U.S, Army Captain Abraham Messias, and less than 90 soldiers, ambushed a force of 600 British troops advancing along a marsby trail toward the rear of Fort Point Peter. They succeed in slowing, but not stopping the British, and were soon forced to withdraw.

non and supplies before destroying the redoubt, blockhouse and barracks. Lt. Col. Williams, meanwhile, was preparing to advance on St. Marys via the same log causeway used by Stallings and Massias in the American retreat across the North River.

Retreat

At that moment, Col. William Scott, commander of the 3rd Regiment, Georgia Militia, was in St. Mary's organizing its defense. He informed Gen. John Floyd, 1st Division, Georgia Militia: "I have

Archibald Clark built this attractive house in St. Mary's in 1801. Admiral Cockburn occupied the house during the British invasion of Georgia in 1815. Clark, the U.S. customs officer at St. Mary's, was put under arrest for refusing to cooperate with the British. Today, the house is still in the family, serving as a private residence and antique shop open by appointment and when the "open" flag is displayed.

never experienced so much alarm. The inhabitants are flying in all directions. The men, women, and children are all running away."

The citizens urged Scott not to defend St. Mary's, fearing to do so would provoke Admiral Cockburn into burning their town. Their concern was well founded. Like Gen. W. T. Sherman fifty years later, Cockburn was a man known to be careless with matches. He had put much of Washington, D.C. to the torch and left plantations and settlements in ashes up and down the Chesapeake Bay.

Col. Scott decided that he had insufficient troops to mount a defense and reluctantly withdrew his 80 soldiers 20 miles north to the Great Satilla River. The citizens of St. Mary's promptly appointed Major Archibald Clark and Henry Sadler to carry a flag of truce to the enemy and St. Mary's was peacefully surrendered.

To the Victors

Admiral Cockburn arrived on January 14 and found St. Mary's swarming with activity. The British were ransacking the town, carting off anything of value. The waterfront was jammed with items to be loaded aboard local ships that had also been taken by the British. In his report to the Division's Commander in Chief, Admiral Sir Alexander Cochrane, dated January 27, 1815, Cockburn wrote:

"On my arrival at St. Mary's, I found a considerable quantity of American produce had been collected there…and I also learnt that some valuable Shipping had been moved from 20 to 30 miles higher up the St. Mary's River, with the view of placing them beyond our reach. I have consequently determined to hold St. Mary's until the whole of this Merchandize could be Embarked and the River properly examined...The Shipment of the Articles found in St. Mary's was also immediately commenced in Vessels which had been there taken. These Objects (notwithstanding the most indefatigable exertions of all) occupied us until the 23 Instant when every Article which could be removed being Shipped..."

The British withdrew from St. Mary's to Cumberland Island on January 23. It was from his headquarters at Dungeness that Cockburn directed further depredations on the southern coast. He had dispatched HMS *Severn* to blockade Charleston and HMS *Erebus* to blockade Savannah. On January 28, he sent Capt. Robert Ramsey of HMS *Regulus* together with the *Manley* and *Canso* to attack and occupy St. Simons and Jekyll Islands. The troops were under orders to confiscate any merchandise, vessels and livestock found there.

Cockburn also ordered Ramsey to recruit as many slaves "as may be willing to join our standard." The British had instituted a policy of freeing any slaves who, by what-ever means, came under their jurisdiction. Many of these were recruited into the British Army or Royal Navy. The 3rd West India Regiment was comprised, for example, entirely of slaves freed during Cockburn's Chesapeake Bay raids.

Other slaves, both escaped and British-liberated, gathered by the hundreds on Cumberland Island. The British pledged to provide transportation to all individuals, black or white, who desired to leave the United States. A few

Sometime between January 14 & January 23, 1815, Camden County, GA: Admiral Sir George Cockburn had Archibald Clark, the U. S. Customs Collector at St. Marys, arrested for refusing to hand over the more than $100, 000 in revenues he held. Clark's continued refusals and the admiral's greed ultimately lead to the last battle of the war.

white families accepted the offer, but the vast majority were blacks. Most of them were transported to Halifax, Nova Scotia or Bermuda. A rumor persisted for years, however, that some were resold into slavery in the West Indies.

By February 10, 1815, Admiral Cockburn had learned of the signing of the Treaty of Ghent from a European newspaper dated December 27, 1814. But since he had not received official notification, he chose to continue his wartime operations, especially the seizing of prizes.

Loot for the Taking

While nearly everything of value in St. Mary's had been looted, there were other prizes nearby ripe for the plucking. Given its proximity to Spanish East Florida, St. Mary's was a busy and prosperous international port for legal as well as illicit traffic. Its customs house took in large sums annually as Cockburn well knew. This collection amounted to $100,000 in bonds, $12,000 in currency, and $8,000 in bank bills. As admiral of the squadron, Cockburn was entitled to a large part of this prize if it could be taken, and he wanted it.

When Archibald Clark, the customs collector, refused to hand over these funds, he was arrested and imprisoned aboard HMS *Primrose*, then anchored in Cumberland Sound. Cockburn's efforts to force Clark to reveal the location of the booty proved unsuccessful. It was Clark's bullheadedness and Cockburn's avarice that would ultimately lead to the war's last battle.

In reprisal for Clark's stubbornness, Cockburn decided to torch the custom collector's sawmills. The mills were situated near Spanish Creek, a St. Mary's tributary about 35 miles due west of Cumberland Island. By way of the winding St. Mary's River, however, the distance was closer to 50 miles. There was a road from St. Mary's to a point within a few miles of Clark's mills, but Cockburn instead sent his troops by the longer water route.

Attack!

On February 27, Cockburn wrote to Admiral Cochrane to explain that three days earlier he sent Capt. Phillott of the Primrose "with a Division of Armed Boats having a proportion of Light Troops…Embarked in each up the St. Mary's River." The admiral didn't specify the number of barges, troops, and sailors involved in the expedition.

By some unknown means, the Americans learned of Cockburn's plans. On February 28, Lt. Col. William Scott wrote to Georgia Governor Peter Early about the events that transpired:

"I have the pleasure to inform you of a brilliant affair having taken place on the 24th instant, on the St. Mary's River between part of my detachment, 20 men, commanded by captain Wm. Mickler, aided by about 30 of the patriots of Florida, under colonel Dell, and six of the enemy's barges, containing about 250 men, which had attempted to proceed up the river to burn Mr. A. Clark's mills. The enemy were first attacked by the patriots from the Florida shore, near camp Pinckney, when the barges immediately tacked about to retreat but our men being in ambush on this shore gave

On February 24, 1815, a British force of 250 men in six barges sent to burn Archibald Clark's sawmills was ambushed from both sides of the St. Mary's river by a combined force of 50 Americans. The British suffered between 100 and 160 casualties while the Americans had only one man wounded.

them a second reception, and thus the fire was kept up from both sides until they got into a greater extent of river than our riflemen could reach. The reports from Amelia (Island) say that the loss of the enemy was 160 killed and wounded—some say 100— but this I have been credibly informed, they were so cut up as not to be able to work their barges with the complement of oars. We had one man severely wounded through the body and several to receive balls through their cloths, but no further injury. The news of their intentions reached me too late to join the detachment with the remainder of my troops, which is to be lamented, for I am confident not a barge should have returned to Cumberland to carry them the news. While writing this I am informed the enemy are fitting out another expedition to go up the river St. Mary's and if they do I hope they will pay dearly for their undertaking."

The Florida patriots mentioned in Scott's report were a group of Americans, pri-

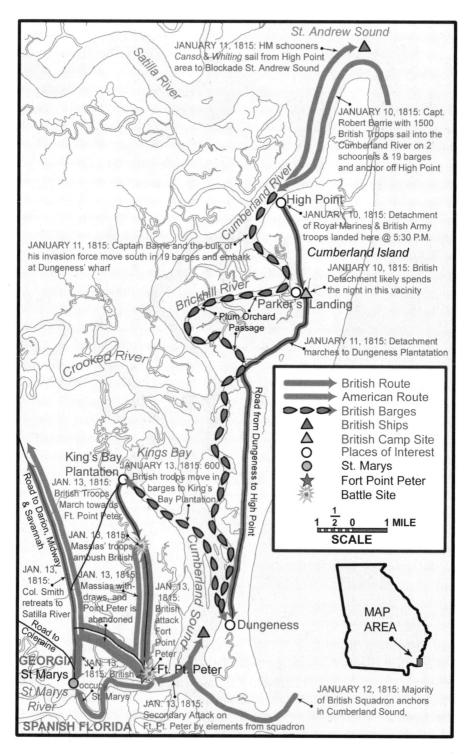

St. Andrew Sound

JANUARY 11, 1815: HM schooners *Canso* & *Whiting* sail from High Point area to Blockade St. Andrew Sound

JANUARY 10, 1815: Capt. Robert Barrie with 1500 British Troops sail into the Cumberland River on 2 schooners & 19 barges and anchor off High Point

Satilla River

Cumberland River

High Point

JANUARY 10, 1815: Detachment of Royal Marines & British Army troops landed here @ 5:30 P.M.

JANUARY 11, 1815: Captain Barrie and the bulk of his invasion force move south in 19 barges and embark at Dungeness' wharf

Cumberland Island

JANUARY 10, 1815: British Detachment likely spends the night in this vacinity

Brickhill River

Parker's Landing

Plum Orchard Passage

JANUARY 11, 1815: Detachment marches to Dungeness Plantatation

Crooked River

Road from Dungeness to High Point

British Route
American Route
British Barges
British Ships
British Camp Site
Places of Interest
St. Marys
Fort Point Peter
Battle Site

King's Bay Plantation

Kings Bay

JANUARY 13, 1815: 600 British troops move in barges to King's Bay Plantation

JAN. 13, 1815: British Troops March towards Ft. Point Peter

Road to Darion, Midway, & Savannah

JAN. 13, 1815: Massias' troops ambush British

JAN. 13, 1815: Col. Smith retreats to Satilla River

JAN. 13, 1815: Massias withdraws, and Point Peter is abandoned

JAN. 13, 1815: British attack Fort Point Peter

Cumberland Sound

½   0   1 MILE
SCALE

MAP AREA

Road to Coleraine

GEORGIA
St Marys

St Marys River

JAN. 13, 1815: British occupy St. Marys

Ft. Pt. Peter

Dungeness

SPANISH FLORIDA

JAN. 13, 1815: Secondary Attack on Ft. Pt. Peter by elements from squadron

JANUARY 12, 1815: Majority of British Squadron anchors in Cumberland Sound, marily Georgians, who had seized control of portions of Spanish East Florida. The U.S. government, fearing that Great Britain was planning a similar move, had taken secret steps to act first. President Madison gave the Florida invasion his unofficial support, but later disavowed any involvement in the incursion.

There is some uncertainty as to who actually commanded the American contingent and the exact size of the British force. There is no question, however, that the British suffered a stinging repulse as American marksmen fired on the invaders from the banks of the river. The amount of British casualties varies considerably with reports ranging from 100 to 180 killed with an equal number wounded.

Dismayed and angered by the whipping, the British immediately began "fitting out another expedition," as Gen. John H. McIntosh noted in a April 2, 1815 letter:

"Cockburn was so enraged when his six boats returned, with two-thirds of their crews killed and wounded, that he made a signal for all boats and marines to come from the vessels, and swore that he would burn St. Mary's and every house between the (rivers) Altamaha and St. Mary's. But the arrival of Maj. Burke with the (official) account of peace prevented him from putting his threat in execution."

Finally, on March 1, 1815, Cockburn, in a letter to Admiral Cochrane, acknowledged having received orders to cease hostilities. He had already dispatched the *Primrose, Brune,* and *Canso* to convoy the Second West India Regiment to the Bahamas.

By March 13, Cockburn had "withdrawn the remainder of His Majesty's Forces from Cumberland Island" and directed "the whole of HM Ships lately acting under my immediate Orders...to Bermuda for further Orders." Five days later, HMS *Albion,* Cockburn's flagship, crossed the St. Mary's bar and put to sea. Her ship's log read: "P.M. Fresh breeze and fine weather; 1:35 weighed sail to the Eastward." The final campaign of the War of 1812 had drawn to a close.

Sources:

Blackshear, David. 1858. *Memoir of General David Blackshear.* Philadelphia, PA.

Bullard, Mary R. 1983. *Black Liberation on Cumberland Island in 1815.* DeLeon Springs, FL.

Northern, William J. (reprinted in Spartanburg SC, 1974). *Men of Mark in Georgia.*

Patrick, Rembert W. 1954. *Florida Fiasco/ Rampant Rebels on the Georgia-Florida Border, 1810-1815.* Athens, GA.

Papers of Sir George Cockburn, 1788-1847. Microfilm. Library of Congress.

Scott to Early. March 14, 1815. *Republican;* and *Savannah Evening Ledger.*

Vocelle, James T. 1914. (reprinted in St. Mary's, GA, 1989) *History of Camden County Georgia.* Jacksonville, FL.

White, George, Rev. 1854. *Historical Collections of Georgia.* New York, NY.

Knight, Lucian L. 1914 *Georgia's Landmarks, Memorials and Legends.* Byrd Printing Co.

Letters from the Nineteenth Century

JEAN A. CURRAN

When the author and her brothers inherit an old family trunk, they find within a treasure trove of letters and other heirlooms that provide a fascinating, intimate look at life of a 19th century Georgia mountain family.

When the last surviving member of my father's family died in 1992, my brothers and I inherited a treasure chest. It was an old cedar trunk which held memorabilia from four generations of our North Georgia family. There were grainy, faded photographs, many of which pictured subjects who were totally unknown to us and likely to remain so. There was a collection of religious poetry composed by our grandmother over a long but sometimes heartbreaking life. There were manuscripts along with their rejection slips, the results of an aunt's efforts at literary publication.

Ancient valentines, love letters, and brown newspaper clippings announcing births, deaths, marriages, and movie news had been stored away along with a recipe for curing meat. The accounting records of our grandfather's "jot-em-down" store in Folsom, Georgia didn't take up much space because they were written on miniature notebooks shaped like Dental brand snuff boxes. Almost all of the correspondence to and from our father's youngest brother who lost his life in Germany in World War II were lovingly preserved there.

Among the treasures was a Bible, brown and stiff with age, with both covers and many pages missing. Carefully tucked within the remaining brittle pages were a number of letters to and from our great-grandfather, Wyatt Adcock, a farmer and veteran of the Civil War who lived near Adairsville in north Bartow County for most of his 63 years.

The letters are a poignant record of a time that was simultaneously simpler and more complex than life in our new century. The time was simpler because the lack of industrial products kept the rhythms of everyday life basic and close to the earth, and the time was more complex for the same reason.

Transportation and communication were so primitive that many basic life functions were difficult or impossible while all the things – the telephones, dishwashers, refrigerators, automobiles, computers, etc. – that make our lives comfortable were non-existent. The written words left by these ancestors link us to a past that mocks us with its serene courage and dignity amid formidable hardships.

Letters from Everyday Life

Before reading this old correspondence, it is helpful to note some of the idiosyncrasies of letter writing in that era. Though the penmanship was usually legible and often surprisingly graceful, usually there was no punctuation, little capitalization, and

A collage of letters from the 1800s recently found in an old family trunk.

no attempt at paragraph structure. The spelling ranged from quaint to downright bizarre, and some words have two or more spellings on the same page.

Reading the letters is not particularly difficult because spelling was often phonetic. Letter headings look strange to those of us grounded in the structure of personal letter writing today, but are consistent throughout the correspondence reflecting either different teaching in an earlier educational system or the dictates of custom.

A letter from Wyatt Adcock's sister, Sarah Adcock Ivey, to Wyatt and his wife, Mary, is indicative of a personal letter to a family member in the late 19th century. I have taken the liberty of lightly editing for punctuation and capitalization and have corrected most of the colorful spelling to make reading easier, but I have kept the grammatical errors and quaint phrasing for the sake of authenticity.

Georgia, Dekalb County, June the 5, 1879
Dear brother and sister. It is with pleasure I take my pen in han to answer you kind letter we reseved a few days a go. We was glad to hear from you all an to hear you was all in common health. These few lines leaves us all in common health. We are very dry at this time and very cold mornings. Crops looks very well. Wheat crops is very good for this section. Well, Polly (this was apparently Mary Adcock's nickname), you wonted to no what was the matter with the old man Poke. He had heart disease an pneumonia fever. He was down a bout four 4 weeks. Mrs. Poke talks of goin back to South Carliner this fall. The place will be sold this fall. She got a letter from hear soninlaw that moved to Texes an her daughter was dead. Polly, I heard from Hanes an Nancy on a Friday a go. They was all well and doin very well. Polly, I aint got a letter from Walton since you was here. I dont no why they dont write. We got a letter from Russel and Frank a few days a go. They was well and doing well. Write soon.

Front and back of a postcard announcing the death of Wyatt Adcocks brother, Barnett.

Corn is sixty cents, wheat one dollar, bacon four or five cent, chickens fifteen to twenty-five cent, eggs twelve to fifteen and butter fifteen to twenty, veagatable is of all prices. Peas are dollar. Polly, they wont be no fruit this year a bout here. The frost kill it. William an Lue is well as common. The babey is fine child. Its name is Jonna. Lener is never well. Lue would like to come to see you all but her children is a most all ways sick. You all must come as often as you can. Well, Wiett, Mr. Ivey says you must come with Mr. Prichett an all of the rest that can come. He says he is going to sell or swap. They is several that wonts this place. We think he would like the place. It is such a publick place an close to Atlanta. He can make a good livin by peddlin on vegatables if he like the trade. Mr. Ivey has one or two places in view if he dont trade with him. Mr. Ivey wonts you to write what time you an him will be here so he will be at home when you com. Tell him we'll look for him this summer. Hanes is going to sell his place and move closer to us. Sebun and Azilla think they would like that section very well so write soon. So I remain you sister until death.

Thomas Ivey Sarah Ivey Wiett Adcock Mary Adcock

Sarah Ivey referring to her husband as Mr. Ivey is a reminder that in the 1800s both husbands and wives used these formal, respectful titles. This manner of address is used throughout Margaret Mitchell's *Gone with the Wind* which covered the same time period as many of the Adcock letters. Sarah misspelled her brother Wyatt's name, and other correspondents referred to him as Wat or Watt.

The subjects covered by most of the letter writers are similar. They usually began by discussing health. The seeming redundancy of the phrase "they was well and doing well" is strange to modern ears, but served to distinguish between physical health and everyday living conditions while "well as common" is a charming but characteristically understated expression denoting average health.

320

Since they were an agrarian people, it comes as no surprise that the price of crops were particularly important to them. Several letters contained a price list similar to Sarah's. For the same reason the weather was of interest and was often described with great detail.

It should be noted that Sarah and Thomas lived in Dekalb County while Wyatt lived in Bartow. Other siblings in Walton County where this branch of the Adcock family first settled in Georgia. Much space in the correspondence was given to relating news of family members.

Usually, Adcocks of that generation were Baptist and religious events were frequently covered in their correspondence. Several letters contained news of "good meatings." A friend in Walton County wrote in 1880: "Wat, you stated In your letter you had a great meeting up with you. I am glad to hear of the Lord's being with you. He has done a great work with us. 10 ten Join in one meeting and several others some at Ebenezer making 15 in all."

In similar fashion, Sarah Ivey reported in 1879, "We have had a heap of good meatings. At sum churches they babtised as high as 34. It is a great thing if they will hold out. Meeting is still going on."

If the people of the 1800s seemed more interested in religion than later generations, it was for good reason. Times were hard, and religious faith gave them hope and comfort during bad times. But religious gatherings served a social function as well. Revival meetings were especially welcome to people who had limited opportunities for social interaction.

It is easy to detect a spirit of weariness in much of the correspondence, and it is tempting to deduce that life for these letter writers was bleak and lacking in humor. But further reading reveals a genuine capacity for merriment. A relative in Walton County described a holiday season in 1886:

The day that Cousin Edmon was here was the coldest day that I ever saw. I bet that Cousin Edmon will never forget that Saturday as long as he lives. I tryed to get them to stay all night but I think that Mr. Scott had a engagement out to go to see his girl that night. If he went to see her that night you may expect for him to come back soon. I tell you that she is a Daisy. Polly, I Wish that you had been here Christmas. You Would been made to fly as a Bird. Everybody seem to enjoy the Beautiful Christmas. It was one to be long Rememberd in this settlement. It was parties and Weddings all the Christmas.

James Henry Barnes wrote with an acerbic pen from Walton County in 1881:

"I hope that some of you all will come this summer. Tell Cousin Jimmie to come and stay A while and see some of the walton girls for they are all as plain as an old shoe and as sour as they all ways was if they ever was sweet. Tell him that Miss Tippie Malcom has married at last and tell Cousin Mit that Bud Hawk is flying A round Cousin Mollie and they are very loving to each other.

On the other hand, the privations these ancestors suffered are difficult for us to imagine. Think of receiving this letter dated July 7, 1881:

Dear Unkle & Cousin Jim

I seat my self to in form you we are all well. But Papa he is very bad off. I don't think they is any chance for him to get well. I have had Two doctors with him. One says it is tiphoid fever & the other says it is brain fever. He is bin Sick Twelve days to day and he don't know any thing nor has not since last Tuesday was a week. So if any of you want to see him any more in this life you had better come right a way.

A postcard dated the next day related the sad news:

Monroe Geo
July 8, 1881
Dear Sir
Your Bro Barnett died this morning at 7 o'clock an will be Buried tomorrow morning at 10 o'clock.
yours t
Joe Greene

Wyatt Adcock was unable to attend his brother's funeral, but in a time when communication and travel required days, weeks, or months rather than hours no one would have expected out of town relatives to attend funerals of family members who lived very far away, even in distant counties of the same state. This limitation that we find hard to imagine was simply a fact of life that was taken for granted by the people of the 19th Century.

From a Civil War Prison

The letters most treasured by the family were written while Great-Grandfather Wyatt Adcock was held at Camp Douglas, a Civil War prison facility near Chicago, Illinois from late 1863 until the end of the war in 1865. The first correspondence is a fragment of a letter from his wife, Mary:

Georgia Cass County March the 6 1863 [sic, should be 1864]
Dear beloved companion,
I seat my self to answer your loving letter that came to han the 6 of this. That made three letters i have got from you. I am sorry that you hant got more of mine. This makes four that I have wrote to you. We are all well at this time and are doing the same what of us is a live. Father and the baby is both dead. Father died the 6 and the baby the 13 of December. You wrote to me . . . . . . be at home by March 1.

The lower half of the page is missing. On the back of the page is written

...if you please send this letter for me. I hope that you will.

RIGHT: Wyatt Adcock (1825-1888) was a Bartow County farmer who served in the Confederate army during the Civil War. Family heirlooms include letters to and from his wife, Mary, while Wyatt was a prisoner of war at Camp Douglas, Illinois from 1863-1865. LEFT: Mary Stokes Adcock (1828-1891) and her husband had fifteen children.

[addressed to:] Wyatt Adcock, Squad 18
Prisoner of War
Camp Douglas, Chicago City
Fourth Cav of [Georgia]
Maj. Gillaspie's Co.
Chickamauga Prisoners

It is interesting to note that Great-Grandmother Mary was still referring to her home county as Cass even though its name had been changed to Bartow County in 1861. It leads one to wonder whether she temporarily forgot the change or simply preferred the original name and stubbornly held onto it.

Wyatt wrote to Mary on February 20, 1864:

Dear wife,
I seat my self to let you no I am well and I hope when these few lines come to han you all may be well and doing well. Mary, I am cared for very well. I get enough to eat and we have dried clothes. I have wrote three letters to you and aint had no answer yet. I hope you get my letters if I cant get yours. I want to hear from you and the children the worst I ever did and our old father and mother. Tell them howdy for me. Let me no something about our Neighbors. Get some of them to write to me so I can get and answer from some of you. I

want to hear from you the worst in the world. Write to me how you are getting along. Write where reuben Woods is. Tell Martha I have got her a nice ring for her. Tell James I want to be at home with him once more. Mary, if I could hear from you and the children once more. You must kiss all the children for me. Your husband

Wyatt Adcock

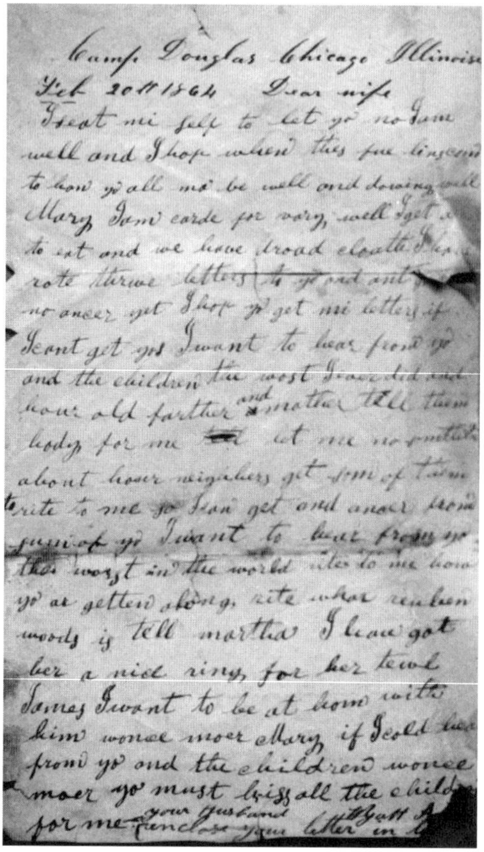

In his Camp Douglas history *To Die in Chicago*, George Levy explained that prisoners were permitted to have money and to make purchases from the post sutler who paid periodic visits to the prison. This likely explains how Wyatt was able to procure a ring for one of his daughters.

On April 20, 1865 (just twelve days after Gen. Robert E. Lee's surrender at Appomattox) he wrote:

COURTESY BRAD MEARS

A letter from Wyatt to Mary while he was at Camp Douglas.

Dear Wife, These few lines leaves me well and I hope they may find you enjoying the same blessings from God. Mary, I have no news of importance. I have not received a letter from you since the 8th of Sept. I want to hear from you the worst I ever did as I fear that you are not a getting a long very well. I want you to write to Mother as soon as this you read. You must also write to Mrs. Pullen and tell her that Thomas is well and doing as well as could be expected. So I must now close by saying you must write as soon as this you read.

Wyatt Adcock

Barrack 217

Co. C – 4th Cavalry

Great-Grandmother Mary

The trunk also contained a manuscript written by my aunt relating family stories about Great-Grandmother Mary. Mary Stokes' grandmother was a Cherokee Indian, which might explain Mary's physical stamina and vivid imagination.

When she was just a girl, Mary and a friend decided to play that favorite game of young girls: fortune-telling. They boiled an egg, cut it in half, removed the yolk, and filled each cavity with salt. This done, they ate their creation. That night Mary understandably dreamed of water. It seems she was standing near a public well and Wyatt Adcock, a young man in the community, handed her a drink of water.

The romance did not go smoothly at first, however, for Mary became engaged to marry a prosperous plantation owner. But when the plantation owner went to get a marriage license he learned that Wyatt Adcock already had a license to marry the same young lady.

If Mary was a bit fickle in the beginning, she certainly proved her loyalty to Wyatt later by bearing him 15 children – ten before the Civil War and five afterward. One of those five was Charles Mulvin Adcock, my grandfather. Mary demonstrated her ingenuity during Sherman's march through Georgia. When some people were hiding silver and heirlooms, Mary hid her most valuable possessions, two family mules, in nearby woods and so brought them safely through the crisis.

A Small Slice of Immortality

As I read and reread these messages from long ago, I am struck by the enormity of the treasure I hold in my hand. The letters permit a glimpse into the personalities, the interests, the hopes and fears of people who were, until now, only names or faces in faded portraits.

Through their words I get to know them and recognize family characteristics which have remained strong through later generations. With this new familiarity I can more clearly mark my own place in the history of this family. Their words become a small slice of immortality, and I am profoundly grateful to my grandmother and my aunts who could not bear to part with these precious messages and so slipped them inside an old family Bible for me to find when the time was right.

When I read that my great-grandmother referred to her husband as "my beloved companion," I know that I sprang from strong and healthy roots. If I could speak across the ages, I would say to Wyatt and Mary, "Thanks in part to your strength and endurance your great-granddaughter is well and doing well."

Endnotes

Wyatt Adcock served in Company C, 4th Georgia Cavalry and was captured in September 1863 during the campaign leading to the Battle of Chickamauga.

Cass County was named for Lewis Cass of Michigan. His pro-Union politics did not sit well with Southerners and the county was renamed Bartow in honor of Francis Bartow, a Georgia general killed at the First Battle of Manassas.

Levy, George, 1994. To Die in Chicago: Confederate Prisoners at Camp Douglas, 1862-1865 (Evanston Publishing, Evanston, Ill.), p. 52.

Murder on the Dover Bridge

Michael H. McDougald

Elliot Padrick, who had not seen his young bride for some time, arranged to meet her at the depot in little Clito, Georgia, in June 1922. He anxiously awaited their reunion, but it was jealousy rather than affection that overflowed his heart.

On the afternoon of June 19, 1922, a man identified in newspaper reports as "Mr. Freeman of Dover" approached the rickety wooden planks of the Dover Bridge, near Statesboro, and found his way blocked by a Ford sedan. The Ford's front wheels were barely on the bridge and its rear wheels remained on the dirt road.

Mr. Freeman saw two women in the car, one in the driver's seat and the other slumped over the front seat. He also noticed a pool of blood forming on the bridge planking and observed that the woman behind the wheel had her head thrown back unnaturally and arms at her side. The second woman had apparently tried to climb from the back into the front seat but failed; she had her head on the chest and an arm around the neck of the older woman up front.

Both women were gravely wounded, perhaps dead. In shock and horror, Mr. Freeman tried to steer his vehicle around the Ford to get help, but there wasn't room. He left his car and ran to Dover, a small town in Screven County about a half-mile away.

Troubled Beginning

By all accounts, 17-year-old Willie Mae Dixon was a pretty young lady. She was from Clito, a small town between Dover and Statesboro. Her parents, Byron and Mamie Lou Dixon, were influential in guiding her through the decisions a young woman must make, but all that changed when Elliot Padrick, the son of an itinerant Methodist preacher, entered her life.

Elliot fell in love with – and soon wished to marry – Willie Mae. Elliot's mother and father concurred, and even his father's congregation agreed that the two should wed. After all, Elliot was a student in seminary and might become the preacher one day. It was important that he have just the right wife.

Elliot Padrick was 20 years old when he met Willie Mae, but lacking judgment and self-control. He had willingly followed in his father's footsteps, attending Asbury Theological Seminary in Wilmore, Kentucky. In fact, with just a year of classes under his belt, he had already preached some six times from his father's pulpit in a little country church in Eureka, another Bulloch County hamlet.

During a visit home, he met the charming Willie Mae Dixon. He was smitten by the young woman, but no real courtship developed. Instead, they became warm friends at first, but there was little doubt in Elliot's mind that he would marry Willie Mae, if she would have him. When she rebuffed his advances, Elliot appealed to both sets of

W.E. Padrick

parents – the Dixons and the Padricks – to intervene.

Mamie Lou eventually cajoled Willie Mae into marriage. When the preacher arrived at the Dixon house to perform the ceremony, though, Willie Mae changed her mind. She wasn't a "runaway bride," so to speak, but an "I'm not coming out of my room to marry him" bride. The ceremony was called off and the few wedding guests went home scratching their heads.

Mamie Lou insisted that her daughter go through with the wedding. It is uncertain why she was so insistent upon the union. Elliot later claimed that Mamie Lou had been forced into her own marriage with Byron Dixon and took twisted satisfaction in forcing Willie Mae to marry someone she didn't love. Whatever the reason, Willie Mae reluctantly capitulated and the young couple finally exchanged vows.

A Miniature Hell

The newlyweds struggled financially, but received ample help from their families. They moved to a farm that Byron Dixon rented for them. Mr. Dixon also co-signed

The Ogeechee River bridge near Dover, Georgia looked much like this one near Guyton, circa 1908. When a "Mr. Freeman of Dover" approached the bridge near Dover, on June 19, 1922, he found the gravely wounded Mamie Lou Dixon and Willie Mae Padrick inside a Ford sedan. The vehicle blocked his way, so Mr. Freeman sprinted to nearby Dover to summon help.

The Clito Presbyterian Church Sunday school class poses for a photo in front of the Clito depot, circa 1937 (the church met in the depot). The author, a six-year-old at the time, is the young boy standing between the two girls beneath the window. The house on the left was the Dixon house in the 1930s (and possibly at the time of the murders in 1922).

a promissory note enabling Elliot and Willie Mae to obtain supplies and farm implements. Elliot's mother gave them chickens to raise.

Willie Mae and Elliot's life as a married couple was doomed from the beginning. "Our troubles started on the day that we were married," Elliot would later state in court. "For on that day she declared that she hated me and said that her mother had forced her to marry me…I believe that my marrying was the mistake of my life. My wife, though young as she was, realized this fact. Realizing this, she became dissatisfied with me, and this caused separation. I still loved her and believed God could make her my ideal, but all the persuasion and kindness of a husband seemed to be in vain. We parted several times but would go back together and have the same disputes. In spite of this, I still held on to God."

The rampant rumors were that they lived apart more than together. No one could put a stop to the fighting and Willie Mae's "I'm going home to Mama" tantrums. Even the governing body of the local Methodist conference learned of the Padricks' marital problems and refused to ordain Elliot as a minister.

"My wife stood the farm life with me for about thirty days," Elliot recounted. "I do not care to repeat the blasphemous outbursts, the cursing and taunting remarks that she flung at me during those thirty days. It was a miniature hell…I believe we would have been on the farm until now if her mother had left well enough alone. But there was no money coming and my father-in-law had notes piled upon him that threatened to deprive him of all his prospects. My father-in-law told me to take my belongings, which consisted of my two suitcases containing my personal effects, and some dozen chickens that my mother had given us, and get out of the community. Thus I was married by my parents-in-law and separated from my wife, my health declined, and there arose in my heart a bitter hatred for them."

Rendezvous in Clito

Even though the marriage was rocky, no one could have foreseen the events of Monday, June 19, 1922, when the preacher's son would forge a $100 check, purchase a .32 caliber five-shot revolver, and summon his wife to meet his train at the Clito depot.

Clito was one of those country towns that thrived in the era when cotton was king. Its railroad depot was directly across from the only general store in the area. Painted a cheery yellow and white, the depot was so small and insignificant that its waiting room had only one bench. For fire protection, a barrel of stagnant rainwater stood at each corner.

Despite the floodwaters of the Ogeechee River, Dover appeared to be a prosperous railroad town in this 1925 photograph.

329

The main enterprise in town was the McDougald-Outland Company, which owned 1,185 acres of farmland, a country store, a cotton gin, and was involved in turpentine distillation. The only gasoline for miles around came from the gravity-fed pump in front of the general store. Inside, soda crackers came in barrels and cheese came in huge 'rounds' covered with cheesecloth. A chunk of cheese, some saltines, and a tin of sardines made quite a noontime meal for cotton pickers, railroad gang workers, log loaders, and plowmen.

Loved Her More than Anything

Prior to the day of the murders, Willie Mae and Elliot Padrick had been separated for some time. During the subsequent trial, Elliot complained that Willie Mae "in her perverseness" often declared that she would kill him with a butcher knife. "For this I do not believe she can be held entirely responsible," he intoned. "For before leaving home and going on the farm I was in the kitchen when I overheard my father-in-law say, as he raised an object from the refrigerator – it sounded very much like a knife – 'Here's something, Willie Mae, you can get rid of him with: a butcher knife.'"

During the many times that the couple was apart, Elliot believed, rightly or not, that his wife was seeing at least one man in Statesboro. While there was no hard evidence of her unfaithfulness, jealous husbands are seldom rational. Suspicions of infidelity tormented Elliot. "On receipt of the news that my wife had become untrue to me a feeling arose within my breast…a hideous plot arose in my mind."

Elliot methodically planned the details of his "hideous plot." He wrote Willie Mae

The old dirt road to the Dover Bridge is serene today.

asking her to "steal" her father's Ford and pick him up at the Clito depot. He suggested privacy, of course, since they had not seen each other for so long.

Kiss of Death

Willie Mae agreed to meet her husband, who was arriving on the train from Dover, but didn't comply with his request that she travel by herself. Instead, Mamie Lou chauffeured her daughter to Clito, where the two met the inbound train. Witnesses described the reunion as "most cordial," although it's certain Elliot was dismayed to see his mother-in-law. By then, Mamie Lou and Elliot had a strained relationship: he secretly referred to her as the "tyrant master" and "witch wife."

On that Monday afternoon, though, Elliot climbed into the Ford, kissed his wife three times and warmly shook Mrs. Dixon's hand. Then the trio started toward the Dixon home. They had traveled just a short distance before turning around and returning to Clito's general store to buy gasoline and oil for the car. Elliot explained to the clerk that he had left his suitcase in Dover, so they would need the extra gas to drive the five miles back to the depot and retrieve it. He paid the bill, appearing flush with cash, which witnesses said surprised both Willie Mae and Mamie Lou since Elliot usually didn't carry much money.

Once more, the Ford departed Clito with Mamie Lou at the wheel. The outwardly happy couple sat together in the backseat. As they left town, they passed two barns, a cotton-weighing station, and the yellow-and-white depot with its four rain barrels. Neither woman could have guessed that this would be their last view of Clito.

Crime Scene

It was shortly afterwards that Mr. Freeman happened upon the scene of the shooting and found the two victims in Byron Dixon's Ford sedan. He promptly reported his gruesome discovery, but it was already too late for Mamie Lou and Willie Mae. Inside the blood-soaked auto, Mamie Lou was already dead from gunshot wounds and Willie Mae perished before medical help arrived. By ten o'clock that night, the bodies of both mother and daughter were taken to a Statesboro funeral home, where an inquest revealed that the fatal bullets came from a new Smith & Wesson .32 caliber revolver.

While Elliot Padrick was unsuccessful at both marriage and the ministry, he certainly wasn't hampered when it came to killing. Autopsies showed that he shot Mamie Lou cleanly through her neck, instantly severing her spinal cord. Then, for good measure, he shot her just under her right arm; that bullet tore through her body.

Willie Mae was hit three times: once through her right arm with the projectile piercing her heart; another bullet penetrated her right cheek, breaking her jawbone; the third entered her head an inch below her left ear. It is amazing that she lived long enough to event attempt crawling over the seat toward her mother.

Abnormal Composure

After mortally wounding his wife and mother-in-law, Elliot knew he had to escape.

He hurried the half-mile to Dover. In crossing the bridge, though, he had crossed from Bulloch County, where the crimes were committed, into Screven County. Thanks to Mr. Freeman, the Screven County sheriff was soon alerted and on the look-out for anyone who had recently come from the direction of the bridge.

When Elliot reached Dover, he approached a local citizen and asked the gentleman for a lift to Millen, some 20 miles distant. The man told Elliot that was too far away and that the roads were in bad condition. The quick-thinking murderer requested a ride instead to nearby Sylvania, and his persistence paid off. The man assented and Elliot climbed in, adding quickly that he was sick and wanted a room in a hotel.

Just two miles outside Sylvania, two police officers halted the vehicle. The June 22, 1922 edition of the *Bulloch Times* described the stop:

"The driver carrying Padrick was questioned as to where he was from and the identity of his passenger and his actions while the trip was being made from Dover. Nothing wrong was noted in the demeanor of the passenger as had first been noted by the driver, and Padrick was reported to be perfectly calm and had talked freely on all subjects. Padrick was questioned by the officials and gave his name and took his bible from his pocket as confirmation of his declared inno-cence of the crime and stated that he was a preacher and believed in the word of God. The two officers then withdrew for a conference among themselves and returned to the car formerly [sic] placing Padrick under arrest telling him that it would be necessary for him to go to Dover to investigate the affair. Then a return trip was begun with Padrick in the officer's car, but only about two miles of the distance had been traveled when the prisoner asked them not to go any further, stating that he was the man who had committed the crime, and asked that he be taken away (from the area) for safekeeping.

Law officials returned Padrick to Sylvania and later, on account of the wide relationship of the deceased in Screven county and fear of violence from them, was taken to Augusta that night for safekeeping in a strong jail."

I Do Not Know Why this has Happened

At the time of his arrest, Elliot Padrick was carrying an unloaded, new Smith & Wesson .32 caliber five-shot revolver. All five chambers had recently been fired. Padrick was whisked away to the Richmond County Jail in Augusta, where he made a full confession. Seemingly dumbfounded by the events leading up to the murders, he stated, "Why all this has happened at the beginning of my youthful career, I do not know. I do believe that the same God who forgave David for murder forgives me and will aid me in my trial, and [I will see] the light of heaven and peaceful joy of full privilege and enjoyment."

The next afternoon, June 20, the coroner's inquest was held in Statesboro. Testimony from witnesses pieced together the time-line and the consensus was that Elliot chose the Dover Bridge for the site of the crime so that he could shoot Willie Mae and dispose of her body in the Ogeechee River, where it would flow down-

COURTESY LEETA MCDOUGALD

The author was unable to locate marked graves of Mamie Lou Dixon and Willie Mae Padrick, but believes both victims were most likely buried in the Union Meeting House cemetery near Clito. The Dixons attended this church at the time of the murders.

stream, never to be found. He would then make the Ford his "getaway car." The investigators concluded that Elliot had, sometime before the murders, forged a $100 check, cashed it, and purchased the pistol.

An unfortunate by-product of his scheme was Mamie Lou. Her death was merely happenstance because she was in the car.

On June 21, 1922, Mamie Lou Dixon and Willie Mae Dixon Padrick were buried together at Union Methodist Church near Clito. A large crowd of family, friends, and curious citizens attended.

Life Sentence

During the ensuing trial in the Superior Court of Bulloch County, Elliot audaciously took the stand and opened his testimony with prayer, inviting the jury to pray with him. He rambled on, as any gifted but demented orator might do, preaching to everyone in the courtroom, judge and jury included. Twice during his theatrical testimony – in which he professed that he "loved his wife more than anything in the world and had rather see her dead than have her continue as she had" – his own lawyer told him peremptorily to sit down and be quiet.

The jury did not buy his harangues, and W.E. "Elliot" Padrick was convicted on the charge of murdering Mrs. Byron Dixon – Mamie Lou to those who knew her – and sentenced to life in prison on November 1, 1922. He never stood trial for Willie Mae's murder.

Elliot Padrick remained in the Georgia State Prison in Milledgeville until his death on March 12, 1961. After 39 years of incarceration – more than double the number of years Willie Mae lived – he at last completed the sentence for his murderous rampage on the Dover Bridge.

Sources

The information contained in this article was obtained from witness statements, newspaper reports from *The Bulloch Times*, and the Georgia Office of Vital Statistics.

He was a Soldier Once, My Father Forever

By Maylinda McRae

The 7th Cavalry, the regiment overwhelmed at Little Big Horn a century before, left Georgia in the summer of 1965. This time they were destined for victory in the Battle of Ia Drang Valley, South Vietnam. One soldier left behind his four-year-old daughter, me. I wouldn't see him again, but my respect, devotion, and love would only increase as the years and decades passed.

Although I'm a "civilian," I live and work near Fort Benning, Georgia. Each time I have the opportunity to meet men and women in the military, I shake their hands and tell them how much I appreciate everything they do for my family and our country.

My father, Paris Dale Dusch, was stationed at Fort Benning when I was born at Martin Army Hospital in 1961. Like so many other soldiers, Dad willingly risked his life to serve his country and help protect the freedom and the privileges that we enjoyed then and continue to enjoy today.

Dad was in Charlie Company, 1st Battalion, 7th Cavalry. His unit was part of the first large-scale commitment of American troops in the Vietnam conflict and was in the first pitched battle at Ia Drang Valley,

Paris Dale Dusch

Republic of South Vietnam, in 1965. During the four-day Ia Drang clash more than 230 Americans died. Most, like my father, were U.S. Army infantrymen. But the casualties also included artillerymen and even an Air Force pilot. Most of them came from small towns like Hopeville, Ohio; Holly Springs, North Carolina; and Carrollton, Kentucky.

If you have read Lieutenant General Hal Moore's book "We Were Soldiers Once and Young" – or perhaps have seen the movie starring Mel Gibson – then you know it's about the Ia Drang Valley campaign. The movie, partially filmed at Fort Benning, was very difficult for me to watch because it depicts those same events my father went through during his last days on earth.

He was a Soldier Once, My Father Forever

My dad, a staff sergeant at the time, was only 32 when he was killed in action on November 15, 1965. I was just four years old when he died, and four decades later I watched the movie with my children – the grandchildren he never met.

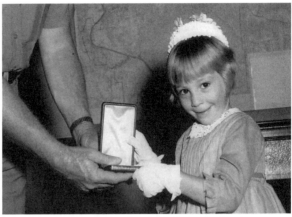

A young Maylinda receives her father's Purple Heart.

At the end of the movie, Mel Gibson, in the role of Hal Moore, who as a lieutenant colonel led the U.S. troops at Ia Drang, stands before the Vietnam Veterans Memorial in Washington, D.C. – we know it now as "the Wall" – and looks upon the names of the brave men who served and died so far from home in Southeast Asia. I sat on the edge of my seat, staring intently at each name as the camera scrolled across the Wall. As much as I tried to focus on the television screen, I wasn't able to because I couldn't stop crying.

Then, as the camera zoomed in on the Wall, I couldn't believe what I was seeing: Dad's name stood out, and for a moment it was almost as if my father and I, his only child, were face to face for the first time since I was a little girl. As the movie ended, my heart overflowed with pride, joy, and even disbelief.

Two of my four children had the unforgettable experience of visiting Washington, D.C. and the Vietnam Veterans Memorial when they were students in middle school. I clearly recall how they expressed their pride and how their hearts were overwhelmed to see and touch the name of the grandfather they never knew but just the same loved with all their hearts.

My hope is that one day I will be able to stand before the Wall and see my father's name and touch the inscription with my own hand – the same hand he held so long ago. I want to embrace the names of his many brothers and sisters who stood with him and likewise made the ultimate sacrifice for us all. That will be enough for me.

A Daughter's Wish

Dear Angel of God: I have one wish both as a child of yesterday and as a woman today,
I'm full of questions and the need for answers about a man so young taken far away.
I've heard so many stories from his family and friends that treasure his memory deeply,
A soldier devoted to his country, my father whose memory I struggle to place.
Six feet tall I know he was from the top of his helmet to the toe of his black-shined boots,
Proud to be the man he was with deep devotion to the family of his Kentucky roots.
A father he was to only one child and I know he loved me with all his heart and soul,
That child was left behind at four and his life is a story that needs to be told.

I don't have many memories of my own and that alone is a battle my heart struggles with,
There are so many unknowns I long to have and stories of him his family needs.
Full of laughter and eyes of brown, his hair was gold and soft as fields of wheat,
The sound of his voice, the smile of his face, a man my heart longs to meet.
I wonder often how many hugs and kisses we shared during our short time,
What songs did he sing, and tickles of laughter that were only his and mine.
Did he bounce me on his knee and brush my hair that was golden like his own,
I know we share deep brown eyes for in his pictures I see them shining at me.
To love someone that you can't remember is a true love from deep within the heart,
Please, Angel of God, tell my father that my love grows each day even though we're apart.
My pride for who he was and what he gave would overflow the deepest blue ocean,
So tell him we share so much – especially our patriotic devotion.
Please take this message on your wings of gold to the man I speak of – my hero, my father,
I am so much of him, the woman who he would remember as only a toddler.
We'll meet again one glorious day, with smiles and laughter at Heaven's gate,
I love you, Dad, and anxiously wait to see you again, no matter how long the journey takes.

Maylinda McRae is a publications manager in Columbus.

He was a Soldier Once, My Father Forever

A Note from the Editor

When I first read Maylinda's story about her father in 2006, it seemed clear that the story wouldn't be complete until she visited the Vietnam Memorial. Thanks to the generosity of several businesses the trip became a reality. AirTran Airways contributed two first-class round trip tickets so that Maylinda and her 16-year-old daughter Lyndsey, who likewise hadn't visited the Wall, could fly to Washington, D.C. Lodging – also first class – was provided by Holiday Inn

Maylinda and daughter Lyndsey Paris Jones at the Vietnam Memorial in Washington, D.C.

Capitol, conveniently located a short walk from all the monuments on the Mall.

This promised to be a memorable event, so my wife, Lisa, and I decided to bring along our children. On a bitingly cold afternoon in early March, we picked up Maylinda and Lyndsey at Ronald Reagan National Airport. The next morning we found a handy parking space on Constitution Avenue and walked the short distance to the Vietnam Memorial.

Those of you familiar with the Wall know that it can be an overwhelming experience for any visitor. Its simple yet elegant design bears the names of the 58,253 Americans who died in Vietnam or are still missing in action. We quickly located the name of Maylinda's father, Paris Dale Dusch, on Panel 3E, Line 55.

That's when it became difficult for even the most seasoned stoic to keep moisture from his eyes. A kindly National Park Service volunteer who served three tours in Vietnam spent a good 45 minutes with Maylinda, sharing memories of her father and others who served. It was a special moment, one that I felt privileged to be a part of and which I'll always be glad my children experienced.

Just before we left the Memorial, Maylinda knelt and placed a photograph of her and her four children at the base of the Wall. Other visitors looked on in respectful silence, all of us movingly reminded of the great sacrifices made by so many of the men and women who have served our country.

A Message from Maylinda

On the morning of March 4, 2007 my daughter Lyndsey Paris Jones and I took off from Hartsfield-Jackson International Airport for Washington, D.C. This was no ordinary trip; it was to be the trip of a lifetime. Even during the flight, I never imagined how deeply this adventure would affect me.

When we walked down the sidewalk toward the Vietnam Memorial the next day, I felt as though this visit would reunite my father and me for the first time since I was a little girl. The anticipation made me shiver. Despite the biting cold outside, my hands were shaking and palms sweaty from being nervous, overwhelmingly sad, and elated all at once.

I was nearly overcome with emotion when I first glimpsed the beautiful black monument shining brightly in the late-winter sunlight. As I walked along the wall scanning the multitude of names, I was struck by the harsh reality of the lives each one represents – lives of those no longer able to hear the birds chirping or feel the cold wind on their faces.

Our steps slowed as we searched for the panel that bears the name of my father. There was a National Park Service volunteer nearby who immediately realized that we were looking for the name of a loved one. The kind, observant gentleman approached and asked for whom I was searching. My eyes filled with tears as I said, "Parris Dale Dusch." He looked at me knowingly and asked, "Was he your father?" I nodded and whispered, "Yes."

The volunteer pointed to a place on the wall. As I reached up to touch the inscription my love for my father poured out. I had known that this would be a very moving moment, but never could have realized how the feel of his name at this solemn place would ache and heal simultaneously. It was as though my finger was touching his for the first time since he left home four decades ago. He called me Snooks, and I could almost hear him saying, "It's okay Snooks; we never really lost each other. Now we have one another again. We are home."

The Last Flight of Paul Redfern

Robert Latimer Hurst

In the "Roaring '20s," daring aviation pioneers captivated the nation and the world as they competed to set new flight records. In one particularly memorable stretch, Charles "Lucky" Lindberg achieved everlasting fame when he flew solo from New York to Paris and, just three months later, Paul Redfern took off from a quiet Georgia beach. Redfern planned a crossing that would beat Lindberg's record by more than 1,000 miles, but rather than immortality his efforts achieved only enduring mystery.

For years, I listened to my mother's comments about her and Dad visiting St. Simons Island in 1927 on their honeymoon at the same time that aviator Paul Redfern entered history with his celebrated but ill-fated flight aimed for Brazil. Mom even had two pictures, somewhat faded by age, of the Port of Brunswick, Redfern's plane. During the latter part of her life, she enjoyed reminiscing about those all-too-short but happy days as a young wife caught up in the excitement of living in the 1920s.

Mom recalled that Paul Redfern was young and energetic, a perfect example of a dashing young ace out for adventure and fame. After

Dashing Aviator – Paul Redfern

all, the "War to End All Wars" had ended, and this era called for a thoroughly Bohemian way of life. Paul desperately wanted to beat Charles Lindbergh's flight record. If he could solo successfully to Rio de Janeiro, he would clock 4,600 miles, beating Lindbergh's three-month-old record of New York-to-Paris by 1000 miles. At 25 years of age, this young man was determined to challenge the "most popular man in the galaxy."

Sundays in Glynn County, Georgia, were quiet and one can't help but wonder why Redfern chose this location and time to launch his quest. In surveying the area, he evidently decided that the beach would be a better take-off point than the island's small airport, located close to the modern-day Redfern Village Shopping Center.

Today, Sea Island's posh Cloister Hotel overlooks the beach where Redfern took flight and there is a small marker detailing the pioneer pilot's efforts to make aviation history.

Paul Rinaldo Redfern's name preceded him even before he attempted to surpass Lindbergh's record. He was the first aviator to cross the Caribbean Sea solo, and perhaps it was this achievement that gave him the daredevil reputation and the confidence to try for Rio de Janeiro, Brazil.

Fledgling Years

At age 16, Redfern built a biplane glider near Columbia, South Carolina. This was a project for his industrial arts class at Columbia High School, and created such a sensation that the plane was soon displayed at the University of South Carolina. Because of his unusual expertise in the field of early flight, the boy gained permission from his parents to leave high school and sign on as an inspector for the Standard Aircraft Factory in Elizabeth, New Jersey. When the factory closed in 1919, the youngster returned home and resumed his high school studies.

As a senior, Redfern's growing interst in aeronautics led him to design and assemble a small biplane from spare parts and a used World War I aircraft engine. This feat led to his establishing Columbia's first commercial airfield, initially located in a cow pasture but later on the campus of Dreher High School. He soloed from this field in his homemade aircraft.

After his graduation from high school, Redfern began earning a living as an aviator. He acquired two more biplanes: a Curtiss Jenny JN-4 and a DeHavilland DH-4. He barnstormed across the country, visiting some 40 states, giving people their first airplane rides or just entertaining crowds by stunt flying. His flamboyant behavior landed him in jail in Texas when he "buzzed" a train and on South Carolina "for dropping a football dummy from 2,000 feet, an act which caused widespread fainting at an air show."

Described by those who remembered him as "genuine" and "full of sass and vinegar," Redfern remained true to his personality, a product of the 1920s and the budding aviation profession. In fact, his daring actions and popularity reportedly inspired MGM Studios to create *Too Hot Too Handle*, a 1938 film with Clark Gable as the pilot.

Go South Young Ma

In 1925, Redfern married Gertrude Hildebrand. He was employed as her father's personal pilot, but then took a job with the U.S. Customs Service in Savannah. It was from this port city that the young aviator, at 25 years of age, journeyed to nearby Brunswick, where the Chamber of Commerce agreed to pay him $25,000 to fly to Rio, the same sum Lindbergh had collected for his world-famous flight. Glynn County officials hoped that the publicity generated by his venture would repay the investment; indeed, Brunswick would bask in publicity created by the headlines that soon appeared in newspapers the world over, though hardly in the manner desired and expected.

For his flight, Redfern selected a Stinson Detroiter SM-1, "a high-wing monoplane with a Wright J-5 'Whirlwind' engine," the same type of motor found on Lindbergh's "Spirit of St. Louis." Redfern picked up the plane in Detroit and flew to Brunswick, averaging 86 miles an hour, with Eddie Stinson in the second seat. Stinson tried to talk his way onto the flight to Brazil, but Redfern refused, explaining that a "trip of this length is more than a man can stand."

A handsomely decorated green and yellow aircraft, the Stinson Detroiter carried the same colors as the Brazilian flag. On both sides of the fuselage just behind the engine were the words Port of Brunswick in bold white letters and, just behind the wing's

trailing edge, "Brunswick to Brazil." In large letters on the upper and lower wings was its registration number: NX773.

On August 25, 1927, Paul Redfern took off from the Sea Island beach while hundreds of spectators cheered. He never reached Brazil. Those gathered in Rio – including popular screen star Clara Bow and Brazil's president – realized that his fuel would have been exhausted by 4:30 p.m. on August 27. The festive atmosphere dissipated as it became clear that something was amiss.

Nothing was heard for two weeks, until September 8, 1927,

Paul Redfern and one of his sponsors stand beside the *Port of Brunswick*.

when the crew of the Norwegian steamship *Christian Krohg* docked in New Orleans and reported having an encounter "with Paul Redfern and his brightly colored airplane." The captain said that the pilot approached his ship from the north at a low altitude. "It was," he said, "near the island of Trinidad and some 165 miles off the coast from Venezuela." Redfern circled the ship, wrote a note on a piece of paper, placed it in a carton, and dropped it. The message requested directions toward land and a wave of a flag or handkerchief once for each 100 miles. The authenticity of Redfern's signature was later confirmed by his father.

Searches proved fruitless and neither Redfern nor the *Port of Brunswick* was ever found. Before he took off from the beach, he had told reporters "Do not worry about me if you do not hear from me for two or three years. I may walk out of the South American jungle someday with a swell story." Eighty years later, those who remember Paul Redfern still ponder his remark, but few hold out any hope for that "swell story."

The author is grateful to Ronald Shelton, Thomas Savage, Billy Rawl, Bill Foley, and Hank Rowland for their assistance in the preparation of this article.

Georgia's "Brag Dog"

W. Pate McMichael

Vereen Bell, a struggling young author from Cairo, Georgia, discovers that the road to fame and fortune leads into the heart of the Okefenokee Swamp.

Vereen McNeal Bell loved hunting dogs: how they would sniff out a covey of quail, learn to hold a point, tree a coon on a pitch-black South Georgia night, and track wounded deer deep into the Okefenokee Swamp. In high school everyone called him "Dog." He even looked a little like a pointer with a thin face, dusty blonde hair, and long, bony legs.

While growing up on the family farm in Cairo, Georgia, he submitted hunting-dog sketches to the *Atlanta Constitution* with a note that read: "Willing to accept any price reasonable if my cartoons are accepted." He hoped to be the next Bud Fisher, whose "Mutt and Jeff" was the first syndicated comic strip, but the Constitution declined to print his drawings.

Bell was born in 1911, the son of well-known Cairo lawyer Reason Chesnutt Bell and Jennie Vereen, a debutante from a prominent Thomasville family. With high hopes for Vereen's future, his parents sent him to Davidson College in North Carolina where he studied political science and played football. They hoped he would become a lawyer.

But young Vereen continued drawing and tinkering with writing. He eventually concluded that his real talent was for writing, so after his junior year he went to see Major John S. Cohen, president and editor of the *Atlanta Journal*, who offered Bell a job after graduation.

The following year, Vereen went back to Atlanta with degree in hand. But Cohen didn't have a job for him, most likely because of the growing hardships of the Great Depression. That left him without work. His only prospect - an unappealing one - was door-to-door sales of bluing (a dye) on commission.

Bell's parents still urged him to attend law school, but he didn't know what to do.

Swamp Water

Vereen Bell

Foreword by Vereen Bell, Jr.

The absorbing 1941 novel set in the Okefenokee Swamp

He found himself standing at bus stop in Atlanta one day —and at a crossroads. The bus was five minutes late when he bumped into his college roommate, Grier Martin. Martin had a proposition: Let's drive to Lake Charles, Louisiana, in your "pigs-eye-blue" (as Vereen dubbed it) 1928 Ford jalopy to visit another classmate.

Bell blushed, grinned, and quietly said, "all-rite." (I think I would change this to "All right." The southern vernacular just doesn't seem to come through with "all-rite."

Hard Times, Good Times

In Louisiana, the travelers met Charles Litten, a fiction writer who sold short stories to Sunday school magazines. Bell didn't have the courage to ask Litten for advice, but when he returned to Cairo he wrote Litten a note requesting an apprenticeship. Litten agreed, so Bell hopped in that ol' pig's-eye-blue jalopy once again and headed back to bayou country.

Vereen stayed with Litten only a few months, and in 1933 sold his first short story for $10. He moved back home and wrote in an upstairs room to make ends meet as a freelance writer. Each afternoon, he took his dogs quail and duck hunting all over South Georgia, or shark and bass fishing in the coastal waters of northern Florida. These trips generated more ideas for stories. In early 1934, Bell sold two in one day to a Sunday school magazine for the "princely" sum of $51.

He then drove to Thomasville, cashed the check for $51, and picked up his girl-friend, Flonnie Daniel. They drove to Tallahassee, ostensibly to see a few friends. The next day Reason Bell, by then a Georgia Supreme Court Justice, received a telegram from his son that read: "See letter in Encyclopedia Vol. 23."

Reason retrieved the book and inside found a letter advising: "Florence and I are going to get married. I did not tell you about it because I knew you would try to dissuade me, as my tangible possessions consist of only an old Ford car and $10 in money, but I know I will find a way to make a living for her."

During their honeymoon in Jacksonville, Florida, the newlyweds spent the $51 Vereen had received for his stories. When they returned to Cairo, the strapped young couple took up quarters in an old slave house on his father's farm. The living conditions left a lot to be desired. As a matter of fact, fleas were so bad they put meat on flypaper to attract and trap them.

And Bell continued to struggle as a writer when Flonnie soon became pregnant. So Bell took a job with the Federal Emergency Relief Administration and later bought a Thomasville ice-cream parlor, the Copper Kettle, to support his growing family. The Bells' first child, Vereen Jr., was born October 31, 1934.

Yet the urge to write continued to gnaw at Bell, so when it was his turn to play nursemaid, he tied a string to his foot to rock Vereen Jr.'s crib while hammering at the keys on his typewriter. Finally, a national magazine, The American Boy, bought one of his short stories. He submitted two more and they too were accepted.

He even took a job with the magazine in Detroit, but quickly grew disenchanted with Michigan's brief hunting season. When he sold "Field Trial" to *Colliers* magazine for $500 in 1937, he promptly quit his editing position and returned to Georgia to freelance.

Swamp Feve

Once back in Cairo, Bell settled into his familiar routine of writing and hunting. He fell in love with the culture and wildlife of the Okefenokee Swamp. He described his fascination with the area in a newspaper article: "The further you travel from cities, the more natural the people get to be. Down around the Okefenokee you won't find any pretense. If folks there have something to tell you, they say it, even if it hurts a little. And if they don't care to tell you, they just don't talk.

"Their politeness is not mere words or gestures. Fellows down that way have invited me to hunt birds with them. After the covey scattered they would insist that I shoot at the singles, claiming that they probably would miss anyway - when every darn one of them probably could shoot rings around me. I have had to argue to get them to take their half of the shots."

The Okefenokee became the setting for Bell's first novel, *Swamp Water*, which proved to be his big break. He wrote Grier Martin in the summer of 1940 and boasted that the serial publication rights were sold to The *Saturday Evening Post* for the unimaginable sum of $12,000. He told Martin that he anticipated receiving even more for the movie rights and publication of the book.

The novel appeared in serial form in the Post, the largest magazine in the country, in November and December 1940. Readers were enthralled by his fictional account of young Ben Ragan and his hunting dog Trouble; how they befriended Tom Keefer, a fugitive who lived in the mysterious Okefenokee; and Ben's journeys into the swamp to trap fur animals and hunt.

When the novel was published a year later, reviewers applauded the book. The London Times labeled it the best work of 1941, and the New Yorker and New York Times also sang its praises. *Swamp Water* became a national bestseller with a second printing less than a month after the first.

Twentieth Century-Fox bought the movie rights for $15,000 and hired noted French director Jean Renoir to shoot the epic story. Renoir fell under the spell of the Okefenokee himself and made the unprecedented decision to film part of the movie on location.

Regrettably, the screenwriter drastically changed Bell's story. The movie played up the dangers of the swamp and focused on the love story between Ben Ragan and Mabel McKenzie – a minor part of the book – instead of detailing the lessons young Ben learns during his adventures in the Okefenokee and through his friendship with Tom Keefer.

Swamp Water, starring Walter Brennan and Walter Houston, premiered in Waycross in 1941 with 28-cent matinee showings and 33-cent evening showings. Despite the alterations to the story line, it proved quite popular, and Governor Eugene Talmadge proclaimed October 23, 1941, as "Swamp Water Day" in Georgia.

To Live as a Man

Vereen Bell suddenly had riches and fame - both unimaginable just a short time before. He purchased a yacht, trained dozens of bird dogs, and hunted even more frequently. He was just 30 years old, but he had achieved great success as a writer.

So he went looking for new challenges and adventures.

That's when the dogs of war began barking. After the United States entered World War II, Bell spent the next year mulling his options. During this period he wrote a second novel – another entertaining hunting-dog story – that was serialized and eventually published in book form as Two of Kind.

Then one day he went back to Atlanta and found himself at another crossroads. He visited a friend – columnist Ralph McGill of the *Atlanta Constitution*. McGill later wrote in the Constitution:

"When the war came he came to see me and we talked about it. So, I know why he wanted to go, when he did not have to go. I know something of what he felt, about this being a time when we had to decide whether to live meanly or by compromise or as one believed a man should live."

In 1943, Bell enlisted in the U.S. Navy and shipped out for Quonset, Rhode Island. He could have served stateside as a gunnery instructor, but volunteered to serve in Naval Air Combat Intelligence. In this position, he helped select targets for Navy bombers and briefed pilots on their missions.

The Navy assigned Bell to VC-10, a squadron of Grumman TBF Avenger torpedo bombers assigned to the U.S.S. Gambier Bay, a brand-new escort carrier designed to

USS *Gambier Bay*

provide air cover for invasion task forces in the Pacific Theater. For a few weeks, the *Gambier Bay* and its crew trained off the coast near San Diego. Bell lived ashore with Flonnie for a while, but kissed her goodbye on April 30, 1944, and then walked up the gangplank, the last man to board the Gambier Bay. He carried his duffle bag to Stateroom 206 and took the upper bunk.

The enlisted men recognized Bell, and given his fame, assumed he would be snobbish (many servicemen had already received an armed forces edition of his writings, Brag Dog and Other Stories). Despite his notoriety, Bell soon won his comrades' friendship and respect. He had a dry sense of humor and subtle wit. He was self-effacing and downplayed his achievements and talent while encouraging and lauding others.

Bell buried himself in his work, learning the details of his job. He also volunteered for additional service as a technical observer. That meant he frequently went on bombing missions

In June 1944, Lieutenant Bell gave lectures over the squawk box to prepare the men of VC-10 for their role as air support for the invasion of Saipan. The squadron had already begun combat air patrols. One pilot even torpedoed and sank a Japanese submarine.

Bell's lectures included information about Saipan's topography and Japanese defenses. If shot down, he warned, the airmen could expect a hostile reception. He told the VC-10 pilots that the island's garrison included six-foot-tall Japanese marines.

On the third day of the invasion, the Gambier Bay endured its first enemy attack. At dusk on July 18, the Gambier Bay's sirens wailed. Japanese planes had penetrated the task force's combat air patrol cordon. The Gambier Bay's big 40-mm anti-aircraft guns began firing, and then, as the attackers drew closer, the 20-mm guns joined the fusillade. Bell watched as one of the Japanese dive bombers spun out of control into the water and exploded.

A bomb dropped by another Judy exploded close to the embattled escort carrier but caused little damage. A second bomb appeared to be right on target, but the ship's captain ordered evasive action, and at the last second the bomb missed.

Bell went on some missions as an observer during the Saipan invasion. "I flew some five-hour hops with the Skipper and we saw quite a lot," he later wrote. He also kept a journal, which he planned to publish after the war.

An End to the Story

By autumn, the *Gambier Bay* was a veteran of the Pacific war, having participated in the Allied invasions of Saipan, Tinian, Guam, Peleliu, and Ulithi Atoll. But there were also quiet times when the crew held races and put on amusing skits in makeshift costumes. The ship docked in port in Manus Harbor for two weeks in October, and Bell relished the rare opportunity to drink beer.

A week later, the *Gambier Bay* joined the massive armada assembling for the invasion of the Philippines. During the ensuing Battle of Leyte Gulf, the largest naval clash in modern history, the ship's aircraft flew combat air patrols for the immense Allied fleet, which included several task forces with a combined 35 aircraft carriers, 12 battleships, 24 cruisers, 141 destroyers, and more than 1,500 aircraft.

In a desperate effort to repulse the invasion, the Japanese hurled everything available - four aircraft carriers, nine battleships, 19 cruisers, 34 destroyers and other ships, and some 200 aircraft against the Allies. They also unleashed kamikazes for the first time.

Most of the Japanese fleet was annihilated over several days of action, but a powerful force of battleships and cruisers managed to cross the San Bernandino Strait and surprise part of the Allied fleet. The American commanders believed that only friendly ships were in the vicinity of the Strait and didn't take evasive action until it was too late.

The five escort carriers and accompanying destroyers in Admiral Clifton Sprague's

Task Unit 7.4.3 ("Taffy 3") were no match for the massive 18-inch guns of the famed Yamato battleship and three heavy cruisers. Sprague ordered Taffy 3 to steam toward cover in a squall line to the east, but the *Gambier Bay* brought up the rear and soon came under heavy fire from three cruisers which closed to point-blank range.

Vereen Bell was in the aircrew's "ready room" when a frantic VC-10 pilot entered and reported that orders had been given to launch all aircraft in a desperate attempt to strike the enemy ships. Without hesitation, Bell grabbed his flight harness, but the pilot told him he would have to remain aboard the *Gambier Bay* because of a shortage of aircraft.

At 8:11 a.m. on October 25, 1944, a shell landed on the aft end of the *Gambier Bay*'s flight deck, killing several sailors. Every few seconds thereafter, shells pounded the ship. Water flooded the lower decks and the lights began flickering.

Amidst this mayhem, Bell prepared the enlisted men to receive the "abandon ship" order. When the alarm finally rang, he walked calmly to his stateroom, grabbed a half-empty bottle of scotch, and raised a toast with two fellow officers. Then he returned to the flight deck, where he was wounded – but it is unclear today by what and how severely.

U.S. aircraft carriers seldom faced Japanese combat ships in direct combat, but on October 25, 1944, Japanese cruisers and a battleship sank the USS *Gambier Bay* (LEFT AND BELOW) in the Battle of Leyte Gulf. The *Gambier Bay* capsized just after 9 in the morning and sank four minutes later. More than 130 of her crew – including Vereen Bell – were lost with the ship and remain listed on active duty by the Navy. Nearly 800 survivors were rescued.

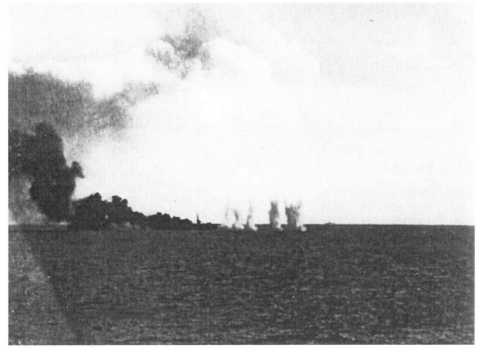

Despite his wounds, Bell jumped into the Pacific waters of Leyte Gulf, swam away from the vortex of the sinking ship, and made it to a life raft. There was no room aboard, so he and other survivors clung to ropes and bobbed in the water. From this vantage point, he watched the demise of the *Gambier Bay*. Fires raged on the crippled carrier and the ship was soon dead in the water. She capsized and sank at 9:07 a.m. on October 25, 1944. More than 800 *Gambier Bay* sailors and aircrew abandoned the ship, which settled into one of the world's deepest ocean rifts.

Bell struggled not to drink the seawater, which causes hallucinations, but there was no fresh water on any of the rafts. Fortunately it rained that afternoon, but the survivors still couldn't get enough to drink.

The ordeal was terrible ordeal. Survivors had to let the bodies of their dead shipmates go, and sharks preyed on both the dead and wounded. Many sailors simply vanished into the depths.

When hope seemed to run out, Vereen Bell put his nose to the wind, drank more seawater and began dogpaddling for the island of Samar – 50 miles away. At least twice, his shipmates had to rein Bell back in. Then when no one was looking, he sneaked away in the night for the third time. He simply vanished in one of the ocean's deepest seas at the age of 33.

Just days after the bloody Battle of Leyte Gulf, Vereen Bell's final short story, "Sis," appeared in *Colliers* magazine. He had written it aboard the *Gambier Bay*. Ironically, it's a story about a faithful hunting dog that belongs to a soldier who is missing in action and never comes home.

SOURCES:

In writing this article, the author reviewed scores of news stories and private letters in files maintained by the Davidson College Archives, consulted Edwin P. Hoyt's The Men of the Gambier Bay, and reviewed the Vereen Bell documents held by the Thomas County Public Library, Thomasville, Georgia, and the Hargrett Library at the University of Georgia.

The Lost Colony of Ayllón

ROBERT D. TEMPLE

ILLUSTRATIONS MICHAEL KIRTON

Decades before Europeans settled at Saint Augustine, Roanoke Island, and Jamestown, the Spanish established a tenuous outpost on Georgia's distant, unexplored coast.

Anxious passengers and crew crowded the decks of six ships as they sailed into the harbor and entered the mouth of a large river. They were six hundred Europeans and a few Africans: men, women, and children; priests and soldiers; and sailors who continuously cast lead lines to keep the ships off treacherous sand bars.

Every eye searched the shore, mostly marsh and low cedar islands. The coast – what in 200 years would become the colony of Georgia – was as alien, remote, and unexplored as a distant planet. Those in the leading ship, one of the lighter, faster caravels, first spotted high, forested land possibly suited to establishment of a village. These travelers had come to stay.

It was September 1526, just thirty-three years after Columbus carried the first reports of a New World to Europe.

Land of the Frog-Boy

By the 1520s, the Spanish were thoroughly exploiting the Greater Antilles – Hispaniola, Cuba, Puerto Rico, and Jamaica. The New World economy was in transition from mining for precious metals to the production of sugar, a lucrative industry but one increasingly plagued by labor shortages. The Arawak, Taíno, and Carib people, from whose sweat the money flowed, were rapidly declining, dying from introduced diseases, overwork, and hopelessness.

To find new sources of Native American slaves, Hispaniola businessmen commissioned exploratory voyages to the north, where maps showed only vast, empty spaces. Captains Pedro de Quejo and Francisco Gordillo sailed in 1521 but found the Bahamas already depopulated. Then they headed northwest, acting on rumors of other islands north of La Florida.

On June 24, 1521, nine days out of Great Abaco, Bahamas, the explorers reached land with a good harbor and a population of friendly Indians. After some days ashore as honored guests, the Spanish kidnapped sixty of their hosts to sell into slavery in Santo Domingo. The captives were Catawba people, and the harbor was Winyah Bay in what is now South Carolina.

One of the Catawbas became a domestic servant of one of the Hispaniola investors, Lucas Vásquez de Ayllón. The young Indian was bright, quickly learned Spanish, won acceptance as a member of Ayllón's household, and acquired the name Francisco el Chicorano. Chico-rano may have been a derogatory nickname at first – it might have meant something like "frog-boy" – but the name came to represent his distant homeland, and soon Chicora acquired an almost mythical significance.

Double-Cross

The businessmen formed a partnership and sent Ayllón to Spain to petition King Carlos for a license to explore and exploit Chicora. It took two years of negotiations, but eventually he won exclusive development and trade rights, valuable tax concessions, the position and salary of colonial governor, a large tract of land, and rights to one-fifth of any revenue the colony might generate.

To get these benefits, Ayllón had stretched the truth considerably, representing Chicora to the king as an Indian kingdom of great wealth, where grapes, olives, almonds, and fig trees grew in abundance. He also double-crossed his Hispaniola partners by negotiating in his name alone. He was already rich and important, but believed Chicora could be his ticket to the kind of astounding wealth that Hernán Cortés was taking from Mexico.

Lucas Vásquez de Ayllón was about 49 years old when he finished his work in Spain and returned to Hispaniola. The younger son of a distinguished family from Toledo, he had studied law at Salamanca and first arrived in Hispaniola in 1504, taking a judicial position. He built a reputation as a serious and learned man, skilled in politics, somewhat tyrannical, ambitious, and acquisitive. He married Ana de Bezerra, daughter of a rich mine owner, and added her dowry to the fortune he was building from

sugar, farming, and Indian slaves.

King Carlos had attached important conditions to his agreement with Ayllón, which set the course for development in Chicora. Under the requirements of a new decree, native people living under organized political leadership, peaceful, and open to trading – "civilized" according to European standards – were given legal rights. They were not to be enslaved or subjected to unprovoked armed conquest as long as they agreed to accept Christianity and submit to the King of Spain. The royal objective was to establish self-supporting Spanish colonial towns, whose inhabitants would bring the local Indians peacefully into the empire through good example, trade, and religious conversion.

Unimaginable Expense

When Ayllón returned to Hispaniola in mid-1524 with his exclusive royal license, his erstwhile partners sued him. Ayllón's lawyers stalled for time as he made preparations to establish a settlement in Chicora. The undertaking turned out to be unimaginably costly. Ayllón soon exhausted his cash reserves, ran up large debts against his estates, and spent his wife's dowry.

At considerable expense, he hired Pedro de Quejo to scout the coast of Chicora, since once the exaggeration and fantasy were stripped away, actual information was sketchy. In May 1525, Quejo returned to the harbor he had visited four years earlier. He made peace with the inhabitants by presenting gifts and bringing back a few of the captives taken during his first visit. He recruited volunteers to train as interpreters, named the large river near the harbor, which we now call the Santee, the Río Jordán, and cruised six hundred miles along previously unknown coast, south to La Florida and north to the Delaware and Chesapeake Bays.

Quejo returned to Santo Domingo by the end of July, bringing with him speakers of at least four different Indian languages. It was a dazzling achievement for only two month's sailing. The names he had given to landmarks would appear on maps for centuries to come.

Ayllón's biggest expense was the ships. The records are not entirely clear, but there were probably six. Four were of the type called naos, large cargo vessels some sixty feet long with 100-ton capacity, slow and clumsy, usually square rigged; two were caravelas, smaller, faster, and more maneuverable, carrying a combination of square and lateen-rigged sails on two or three masts. The naos were the flagship *Capitana*, *El Bretón Grande*, *El Bretón*, and *La Chorraca*; the caravels were the *Santa Catalina* and *La Trinidad*. (Since capitana simply means "flagship" in Spanish, the lead vessel's actual name is in question.)

Provisions for the journey included 300 tons of cassava bread, 1,000 bushels of corn, 4,000 gallons of olive oil, and unknown numbers of live cattle, sheep, and pigs for both food and breeding stock. Though they were scarce in the Caribbean, Ayllón had also managed to obtain one hundred horses.

The expedition included about one hundred seamen and five hundred settlers. Many were from Spain, bored adventure seekers and desperate men fleeing impoverished Estremadura and Andalucía. Others were refugees from failed settlements in Honduras and Panama or victims of Hispaniola's declining economy. While in Puerto Rico on legal business, Ayllón had recruited married men and their families, so women and children were aboard. There were also doctors, surgeons, pharmacists, priests, and Indian interpreters including Ayllón's servant, Francisco el Chicorano. The passengers included black slaves, personal servants to the wealthier travelers. These would be the first Africans to enter the land that would become the United States two-and-a-half centuries later.

Inhospitable Terrain

Despite his financial difficulties, and with the lawsuit stalled in court, Ayllón risked everything he had on the Chicora adventure. In mid-July of 1526, he sailed from Puerto Plata, Hispaniola, into the unknown with six heavily loaded ships and six hundred people. The expedition cruised east of the Bahamas, crossed the Gulf Stream, and made for the Río Jordán, a route well-known to Quejo and his crew.

The colonizers made land on Thursday, August 9, 1526, the church-calendar day of San Román, and in his honor named the cape at the north entrance to the bay (situated about twelve miles northeast of the place called Cape Romain today). As the vessels worked their way over the bar at the harbor entrance, the flagship Capitana went aground and was lost with its cargo, though the passengers and crew survived.

As soon as they were ashore, the Indians, including Francisco, whom Ayllón regarded as a good Christian and almost a son, vanished into the forest, demonstrating their opinion of European "civilization." Scouts found no sign of the expected Indian "kingdom," only a few small villages. The sandy, marshy, acidic soil was unsuited to agriculture and provided poor pasturage. No olive or fig trees were in evidence.

With guides and translators gone, few local people to provide trade, food, and religious conversions, supplies partly lost, and biting insects plaguing gentlemen, priests, and slaves alike, it was obvious this site would not do. Reality had caught up with the mythical Chicora.

Ayllón took decisive action. He sent out scouting parties in three vessels to explore the coast for a more suitable location. He organized a work crew to build another ship using local timber and pieces salvaged from the wreck. The new vessel was a small, crudely-built patache, a poor replacement for the lost flagship, but it did float, and the Spaniards named it La Gavarra.

One of the scouting parties reported finding an excellent harbor with powerful rivers, good land, and a high concentration of native people – perhaps everything Ayllón needed – only 40 to 45 marine leagues away (about 150 miles), an easy sail to the south. However, with the flagship gone, space for passengers and cargo was inadequate.

Ayllón came up with a surprising solution to this problem. He put the women, children, and the ill aboard the ships and, at the end of August, sent them south with the sailors. Then he led the able-bodied men, with horses and a few supplies, overland. The dense forests, swamps, and rivers of today's south Atlantic coast make the trek seem extraordinarily difficult, but conditions may have been better than we imagine. A well established Indian trail existed, roughly following the route of today's U.S. Highway 17A. Sea level was a bit lower than it is now, so the land may have been dryer. The longleaf pine forests were open and park-like in contrast to today's dense and thorny forests choked with undergrowth. Game was abundant, and foraging spared the dwindling food supplies.

Ayllón's gamble may seem remarkable, but even more astounding exploits by sixteenth-century Spanish adventurers, such as Hernando de Soto and Francisco Pizarro, are well documented. In this case, the travelers completed the journey in about three weeks and successfully reunited with the party sent by sea.

Disease and Death

The reunion took place beside what is now called the South Newport River, near Sapelo Sound: flat terrain covered by oak, chestnut, palmetto, and pine trees, and laced with rivers, creeks, and marshes. September 29, 1526 became the foundation date of the settlement, probably the date of the first observance of mass. It was the day of the feast of Saint Michael, and Ayllón named his town San Miguel de Gualdape. (Gualdape referred to the local Guale people, though its exact meaning is unknown.)

The Guale people spoke a Muskogean language and were cousins of the people later called Creeks. Living in villages loosely allied into chiefdoms, the Guale grew corn, beans, and squash; hunted game, caught fish, and collected shellfish; and gathered wild plants. They were untouched by slave raiders and cautiously welcomed the strange newcomers as guests.

The settlers built houses, a church, and perhaps some defensive works. Though hastily erected, the structures were more than mere temporary shelters. There would have been some log buildings and others made of wattle and daub – poles and interwoven sticks plastered with clay – with palm-thatched roofs. For water, Spanish practice was to construct barrel-lined wells. They dug holes to the water table and lined them with open-ended barrels stacked atop each other, forming a shallow, stave-lined shaft. Primitive hygiene practices made these water sources susceptible to contamination.

Food was an immediate and pressing problem. The cassava and corn supplies were exhausted, and the colonizers found few wild starches, fruits, or vegetables they recognized as edible. While game was abundant, many of the newcomers were too sick or weak to hunt and fish. They obtained some food from the Indians, but the Guale probably took the precaution of hiding most of their stores.

Disease set in quickly, including dysentery and typhoid fever from polluted water, and probably scurvy due to the inadequate diet. Smallpox had been epidemic throughout the Indies since 1520.

The settlers also began suffering severely from cold weather. The Julian calendar then in use meant that the foundation date of September 29 was the modern October 8, and temperatures might have fallen into the low 40s or even 30s (the record low for Savannah in October is 28°). To hungry, sick, poorly-clothed people used to the heat of the Greater Antilles, the Georgia coast felt very cold indeed.

Ayllón led a scouting party inland on an exhausting trek and returned weakened and seriously ill. On October 18, while preparing to send ships back to the Antilles for supplies, he died. Ironically, it was the feast day of Saint Luke, Lucas Vásquez de Ayllón's name day.

Chaos

The demoralized survivors of the colony soon split into factions. Loyalists, determined to stay the course, prepared to send a ship to Puerto Rico for supplies and to get instructions from Ayllón's designated successor, his nephew Juan Ramírez. Rebels, ready to seize the ships and abandon the settlement, captured the loyalist leaders.

A third group, disobeying the royal decree about Indians' rights, went in force to a large Indian town and demanded food. The town was about ten miles from San Miguel, the right distance for Pine Harbor, where archeologists now know a large village existed, perhaps the one called Tolomato by its inhabitants. The Indians treated the Spanish well for some days, then grew tired of their discourteous behavior and killed them all. This signaled the beginning of hostilities and sporadic attacks on the remaining settlers at San Miguel.

Adding to the turmoil, the African slaves set fire to several houses and, in the confusion, escaped into the interior. Sword-fighting between the Spanish factions broke out in the streets. Loyalists prevailed, arrested the rebel leaders, and executed at least one of them.

With starvation, epidemic, and exhaustion overwhelming them, relations with the native people in ruins, and the graveyard filling, the leaders decided to evacuate. They left during the first half of November 1526, although the precise date is unknown. Ayllón's model settlement in Georgia, San Miguel de Gualdape, had lasted only about six weeks.

Storms scattered the ships on the return voyage, and the defeated settlers endured great hardship. Cannibalism occurred on one vessel. *El Bretón* reached Puerto Plata in 21 days, while El Bretón Grande took as long as four months to reach safety in Puerto Rico, fifty of its original seventy passengers dying of hunger and thirst on the way. Of the 600 who set out from Hispaniola in July, only about 150 returned.

Legacies

Several of the Spanish survivors turn up in historical footnotes from Mexico, Peru, and Spain, where they doubtless had amazing stories to tell over a flowing bowl. Ayllón's widow, Ana Bezerra, not yet 30 at the time of his death, was left to raise five children under age 12 – Juan, Fernando, Pedro, Constanza, and Ynés – and deal with a mountain of debts. She went on to manage the sugar plantation, mill, and other business interests shrewdly and defended Ayllón's estate successfully against lawsuits and royal inquiries.

The Africans who remained in Georgia doubtless assimilated into the local population. Native Americans through the centuries were relatively free of racial prejudices, accepting many foreigners into their communities. African genes survive in several population groups known as "Southeastern Tri-racial Isolates," of which the Melungeons are perhaps best known.

The Guale people continued to live in the area near Sapelo Sound for another hundred years. They opposed Spanish advances north from Saint Augustine in the 1570s, then came under the influence of Spanish missions on Sapelo and Saint Catherines Islands. Their numbers reduced by imported diseases, all were pushed south of the Saint Marys River by the English and their Yamassee allies in the late 1600s. The survivors merged with other refugee groups under Spanish protection and were last noted in the Saint Augustine area around 1730.

As for the land itself, the Georgia-Carolina region was the "Land of Ayllón" on maps until the late 1500s. The legend of Chicora as a rich kingdom with olives and fig trees drew French and English adventurers to attempt settlements on the southeast coast: Jean Ribault in 1562 and 1565, and Sir Walter Raleigh in 1585 and 1587. Spain, discouraged by Ayllón's disaster, never effectively settled the region, and it remained a remote outpost of the empire, while great cities grew far to the south.

Beginning in the mid-1700s, cultivation obliterated the San Miguel site. Small farms owned by freedmen predominated after the Civil War. During World War II, the U.S. Army took possession and built an airfield for pilot training. The land went to the Fish and Wildlife Service in 1962 and now is managed as the Harris Neck National Wildlife Refuge. Miles of old roads and runways wind through mixed hardwood forests, live oaks draped with Spanish moss, palmettos, pines, and myrtle strung with greenbrier and grapevines, all bounded by miles of cordgrass marshes.

Modern archeologists have yet to find concrete evidence of the exact location of San Miguel de Gualdape. Even after nearly 500 years, traces of the settlement must remain – below-ground evidence of wells and buildings, distinctive ceramic and glass fragments, nails, horseshoes, and the bones of the many Spaniards who perished. Indeed, trade beads and a four-maravedí copper coin dating to the early 16th century have been found in Indian mounds on nearby Saint Simons Island, probably relics from San Miguel de Guadalupe.

Victors write history, and we English-speaking North Americans sometimes forget that the Spanish were here first, two hundred years before James Oglethorpe founded Savannah and long before Jamestown and Plymouth Colony. The history of European and African settlement in the land that would become the United States begins at the north end of Harris Neck in McIntosh County, Georgia.

Where was
San Miguel de Gualdape?

Scholars long studied and debated the location of San Miguel de Gualdape, proposing dozens of sites from Chesapeake Bay to Florida. Recent findings should end the speculation and controversy and add Harris Neck to the history books.

After carefully rereading the original source documents and discovering an important new one, historian Paul Hoffman convincingly pinned down Ayllón's 1526 settlement to the area of Sapelo Sound. The following summarizes his case:

Pedro de Quejo described a combination of rivers, capes, and a sound, which he found in 1521, revisited in 1525, and named Río Jordán. Descriptions and maps are entirely consistent with Río Jordán being the South Santee River, adjacent to Winyah Bay, in South Carolina. Quejo's companion Francisco Gordillo recorded the position as 33°30? north latitude, within twenty miles of the entrance to Winyah Bay, solid evidence given that his technology was accurate only to within half a degree. The Santee-Winyah features are the only ones near that latitude remotely resembling de Quejo's descriptions.

In their relocation in August-September 1526, the colonists sailed 40 to 45 leagues south along the coast from the Río Jordán to the San Miguel site. The mariners' handbook of Alonso de Chaves makes clear that the nautical league in

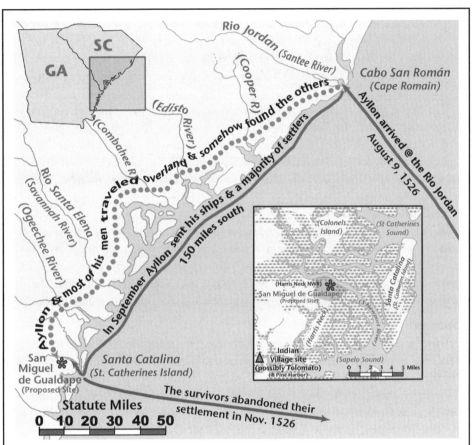

use at the time equaled 3.12 modern nautical miles or 3.59 statute miles, so the distance was 144 to 162 statute miles. The entrance to Sapelo Sound is 156 miles from the South Santee River.

The settlers sought an area of large native population. Archeological evidence shows dense Indian populations clustered around Sapelo and Saint Catherines Sounds in the early sixteenth century, with few or no settlements for some distance to the north and south.

Although modern archeologists have not found remains of San Miguel, a respected royal surveyor did report such evidence 150 years ago, in a publication uncovered by historian Louis De Vorsey, Jr. The site is on high ground now known as Harris Neck, then called Demetrius Island, lying on the south bank of the South Newport River about eight miles upstream from Sapelo Sound. In his official report to King George III, William Gerard De Brahm, Surveyor General of the British Southern District of North America, noted:

> ...the Author found in 1753 the Vestiga of an Intrenchment of a mile and a quarter in Length; as also many ruins of Ancient houses, by all Appearance

proving a settlement made there before, or in the Beginning of the 17th Century. For no Carolinan, much less Georgian can give any account of it, so that by the Author's Opinion, it has been a Settlement, which was neither favoured by the Spaniards nor left quiet by the Indians, and was at last extirpated or its inhabitants forced to leave the Place.

De Brahn was a native speaker of German, and his terminology in English is sometimes obscure; his "intrenchment" may have been the remains of a drainage ditch, defensive wall, raised roadway, or other earthworks. De Brahn goes on, in apparent puzzlement, to describe the location as entirely unsuitable for a military outpost and speculates vaguely that the residents may have been some unknown group of colonists.

Author's Note: *Existing records of Ayllón's expedition and efforts to colonize Chicora fall far short of modern standards for evidence, and many uncertainties exist about the events detailed in this article. I based my writing on what most likely happened, consistent with available information, without the burden of excessive qualifiers – the reader may insert as many "maybes" and "probablies" as desired. Recent studies do, however, allow us to identify the locations with considerable confidence.*

Sources

For the definitive recent scholarship on the Ayllón settlement and its location, see: Paul E. Hoffman, A New Andalusia and a Way to the Orient: The American Southeast During the Sixteenth Century (Baton Rouge: Louisiana State University Press, 1990); and Louis De Vorsey jr., "Early Maps and the Land of Ayllón," in Columbus and the Land of Ayllón: The Exploration and Settlement of the Southeast, Jennine Cook, editor. (Darien: Lower Altamaha Historical Society, 1992.) Hoffman's book also gives references to the original Spanish archival records, primarily works by Gonzalo Fernández de Oviedo, Pietro Martire d'Anghiera [Peter Martyr], and Alonso de Chaves.

For reliable general accounts, which place the Ayllón story in historical context, see: Charles Hudson and Carmen Chaves Tesser, eds., The Forgotten Centuries: Indians and Europeans in the American South, 1521-1704. (Athens: University of Georgia Press, 1994); and David J. Weber, The Spanish Frontier in North America (New Haven: Yale University Press, 1992).

For details about Indian rights, see Lewis Hanke, *The Spanish Struggle for Justice in the Conquest of America* (Philadelphia: University of Pennsylvania Press, 1949).

Sixteenth-century Spanish documents related to the Ayllón story appear in English translations in David B. Quinn, ed., *New American World: A Documentary History of North America to 1612*, volume 1, chapter 20 (New York: Arno Press, 1979).

The Lost Mission
of Santa Isabel de Utinahica

MARY ANN ANDERSON
ILLUSTRATIONS MICHAEL KIRTON

Archaeologists searching for a lost Spanish mission near the forks of the Oconee and Ocmulgee rivers may have discovered traces of it – one of Georgia's earliest European settlements – in Telfair County.

Way down in Telfair County, about 160 miles or so south of Atlanta, in a place so rural that 'possums and whitetail deer outnumber humans, the rolling hills are smothered by forests of impenetrable pine growing venerable and tall, where no one will ask you whether you want your iced tea "sweet or unsweet," there lies near the banks of the Ocmulgee River a site that may prove to be one of the most significant archaeological finds in Georgia's history.

This particular spot in the southernmost region of Telfair County, perched on a bluff near the tiny crossroads community of Jacksonville, is but a few miles as the crow flies from the "Forks," the name used by locals for the confluence of the Ocmulgee and Oconee Rivers, which merge to form the mighty Altamaha. Hidden away just underneath the surface of the earth, covered now by farm fields and brush and river swamp and deep woods, are the remnants of the early 17th century Spanish mission called Santa Isabel de Utinahica.

This mission, which purportedly existed from about 1610 until 1630 or so, was believed to be the most northerly and isolated of the missions established by the Spanish colonial government in Florida. Larger missions have been excavated at St. Augustine, near Lake City and

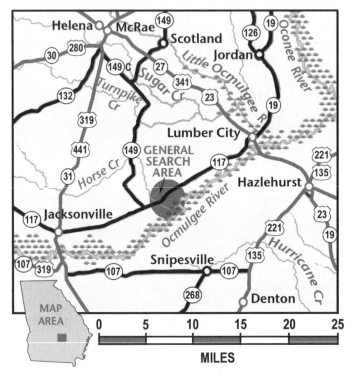

Tallahassee, and on Georgia's coast, including those at St. Catherine's Island, Cumberland Island, and Sapelo Island.

But as of today, there is very little concrete evidence that the Santa Isabel mission existed near the Forks – just a few artifacts like an iron tool resembling a hatchet blade and glass beads that were only made between 1520 and about 1560 in Venice, Italy – and which would interestingly enough predate the mission by about seventy-five years. Shards of both Indian and Spanish pottery have also been discovered here, as have a large marine shell bead, fragments of smoking pipes, and pieces of mussel shells and animal bones, especially those of deer – mealtime delicacies considered the "surf and turf" of the 17th century.

Even more exciting is evidence of dirt dauber nests found at the site - hardened now to an almost ceramic-like consistency. Since dirt daubers almost always assemble their nests on buildings, their presence here is evidence pointing to the existence and location of man-made structures.

But perhaps the best evidence of Santa Isabel de Utinahica comes from the journals of a Franciscan missionary who traveled through the area about 1616. For some two months that year, the friar ambled from St. Augustine to other missions throughout Florida and northward up to what is now Telfair County before he returned to the Georgia coast and then to St. Augustine. His mission was to explore the area and convert the Indians – mostly Creek, Cherokee, and Timucuan – to Catholicism.

Although the Franciscan kept a journal and wrote of Santa Isabel, after his return to St. Augustine, virtually nothing tangible was heard of the St. Isabel mission again until a few years ago when Fernbank Museum of Natural History agreed to conduct expeditions in the area in an attempt to pinpoint the church's exact location and to learn about early Spanish attempts to live amongst and convert the Native American population of the Georgia frontier.

Four hundred years of time have been Santa Isabel's enemy, and the assumption is that the missionaries more than likely abandoned the site after about 1630 – one can speculate that it was because of Indian attacks, the lack of civilization in the area, or simply that it was time to move on – but whatever was left of the mission probably fell into disrepair and eventually vanished with plenty of help from the natural elements, especially South Georgia's unremitting heat and humidity. Against the combination of occasional hurricanes, frequent and vicious summer thunderstorms, frosts and freezes, and even the rare snowstorm, 17th century wood and mud buildings had virtually no chance of survival.

Although the Santa Isabel de Utinahica mission has never "officially" been found, rumors of its existence have been swirling for centuries. These rumors were enough to bring Fernbank to Telfair County in search of the ruins. Fernbank's archaeological program, led by Dennis Blanton, curator of Native American archaeology, has brought an international spotlight to these back roads, previously known for not much more than being one-time home to the Talmadge clan and fodder for novels by southern literary great Brainard Cheney.

Typically, a Spanish mission was divided into several components, including the church and other buildings like a kitchen and the convent or friary where the friar lived. In his efforts to determine whether a mission actually existed here, Blanton is carefully searching for one critical indicator in particular. In the 17th century, it was

An assortment of objects collected on site.

a high honor to be buried beneath the floor of a church. Any mission that was in existence for several decades, as was Santa Isabel, is sure to have a grave or two, so finding evidence of one would be a momentous event for Blanton.

If Blanton and his team find solid evidence of Santa Isabel – the cemetery, pieces of a bell, a cross, other religious artifacts with distinct European influences, or even stonework or building foundations of some sort – that would lend credence to the notion that the Spanish probably settled in the area even before the mission was built (missions were generally built near settlements) and certainly long before John James Oglethorpe arrived in Georgia in 1733. With the mission's existence dating to the early 17th century, it's almost a foregone conclusion that someone else surely must have come along before the missionaries to settle the area. The question is who.

"The early settlers were led by Ayllón [Spanish explorer Lucas Vasquez de Ayllón], but no settlement has ever been found," Blanton explains the background behind the area's rich history. "But there were also probes by Hernando de Soto's 'special forces,' scouts for his expeditions. There almost had to be a settlement here, so the mission is sort of like chapter two of a book, and chapter one is Ayllón, de Soto, or someone else. My money is on de Soto."

So therein lies perhaps the single largest obstacle to finding the mission. The artifacts found on the archaeological site – the beadwork, the pottery, the bones – could have been left by someone merely passing through, like de Soto's scouts or Ayllon. Additionally, evidence of a permanent Spanish settlement can only be proved by the discovery of the church itself; otherwise it is possible that Georgia's first non-Indian guests, while more than likely the Spaniards, could also have come from as far away as the Mediterranean or even Eastern Europe since the origin of the beadwork found at the archaeological site is Italian.

Remember, too, that Santa Isabel, the "lost mission" in the heart of the homeland of the Creek and Cherokee, was at the time as far from civilization as it gets. Despite the area's incredible beauty, verdant, lush forests, and plentiful wildlife, unless other settlers or missionaries moved in, even the most solitary of friars would probably move on from this vast land of isolation and untamed Indians.

"This was in the 'boonies,'" Blanton reiterates of the mission's remoteness. "This was the frontier of the frontier of the time. This part of the state is under-appreciated, but it's very important to the history of the area. The find [of the mission] will prove the Spanish were the first in the area after the Indians. While we're not sure if we have found the mission, we are finding some very exciting, very important artifacts."

Blanton was also instrumental in uncovering the Santa Catalina de Guale mission in the Guale (pronounced "wally") chiefdom on St. Catherine's Island, one of Georgia's eight natural barrier islands. While it took years to uncover the remains of that particular mission – as could be the case with Santa Isabel de Utinahica mission – eventually millions of pieces of priceless artifacts were uncovered that shed considerable light on the vital relationship between the Native Americans and the Spanish missionaries. Since the St. Catherine's project was such a resounding success in unlocking the secrets of Georgia's Spanish and Indian history, Fernbank knew that excavation of the Santa Isabel site could provide additional data crucial to Georgia's colorful and mysterious past.

The South Georgia-raised Blanton (he graduated from Bacon County High School in Alma) and the Fernbank team came to Telfair County in search of Santa Isabel after Frankie Snow, a noted archaeologist from Douglas, found several Indian artifacts at the site. Snow realized that the place where he found the pieces could indeed be the most promising location of the mission. Now Blanton is using Snow's knowledge and

information, as well as the technology of magnetometers, contraptions that compare the intensity and direction of magnetic fields, and resistivity equipment, gizmos that measure the flow of electrical currents in the ground, to determine just what lies below the surface of the earth and whether it is indeed an area of interest. As a matter of fact, this same type of invaluable infrared technology was used to find the mission on St. Catherine's Island.

The archaeological project in Telfair

County, supported by the Georgia Department of Natural Resources and Land Management Associates in Eastman, draws public participation from all over North America. From places like Oklahoma, Tennessee, New York, Canada, and Atlanta, teams of high school and college students have visited, as have teachers, archaeology enthusiasts, Fernbank supporters, and local residents, many of them spending parts of the last two summers working side by side with Blanton and his assistants uncovering these wonders concealed just below the abundant mulch of the woods. To help offset expenses, applicants pay a fee of $100 per week for high school students and $200 per week for college students and other adults. By taking part in the project, participants are not only joining in a vital effort to link today's rural Georgia with the distant past, but also are using these learning opportunities to grasp the fascinating yet often tedious process of archaeology.

"Archaeology is a dirty job," Blanton recently told a group of school-age children during a talk at Telfair County's public library. "You get hot, and it's nasty, and here we have to swat at gnats all the time. At the same time, we have to excavate very carefully for artifacts. Artifacts are somebody else's trash, but we get excited over other people's garbage. Some artifacts are one of a kind, found nowhere else. Being an archaeologist is like being a detective. We're there to crack the case. But archaeologists would just as soon be lucky as good at their jobs."

The soil in South Georgia is, according to Blanton, "full of surprises," and the combination of archaeology, anthropology, geology, and the environment is the best way to dig into the region's early history. One way to look at it is to realize that discovering and learning about artifacts is akin to reading a treasure map of the past. And while Blanton and his team have been exceptionally fortunate so far in finding as many ancient "treasures" as they have, the Holy Grail of the project – the mission itself – lingers just out of reach. If he and his team find Santa Isabel, Blanton jokes, every historical marker in the area – like those noting that Jacksonville was settled in the early 1800s and incorporated in 1815 – will have to be "painted over" to reflect the new information.

"This year we recovered more and more artifacts," Blanton explained during the June 2007 excavations. "The bottom line is that Telfair County is the most fascinating place I've ever worked. And Fernbank is committed to this project. It's not a hit-and-run deal. We're not going to go away, and we plan to have programs every summer."

For more information about participating in the Santa Isabel project visit www.fernbank.edu or call 404-929-6300.

The Day German U-Boats
Sank The Jekyll Island Club

MARY ANN ANDERSON

In colonial days, much of Jekyll Island was a large plantation. In 1886, it became a huge playground for the likes of the Vanderbilts, Pulitzers, and Rockefellers, and for more than 50 years, their Victorian mansions and an impressive hotel dominated the island landscape. In 1942, however, with German U-Boats prowling the Georgia coast, everything changed forever.

Long before the legendary Jekyll Island Club was an exclusive hotel, the property was already remarkable for several reasons, the foremost probably being its prime location on one of the Golden Isles, part of the gently strung cluster of barrier islands on Georgia's coast. The impressive Victorian-style hotel on Jekyll was founded in 1886, and it served as a playground for an exclusive group of our nation's societal elite for half a century. Though much of the club's grandeur was lost over the years to weathering, neglect, and thieves, some of the opulent homes and other accommodations once inhabited by historic families from yesteryear may still be viewed at this site today.

Such notables as the Vanderbilts, Morgans, Pulitzers, and Rockefellers once journeyed to this pristine island of sand, surf, and natural beauty to relax, hunt, and, of

course, to escape the harsh winters of the North. For many years (1886-1942), they spent the winter months of each year and left their mark at the Jekyll Island Club.

The drive to this aged inn from yesteryear is a delightful experience in itself. The billowy marsh breezes provide just the right amount of salty scent, adding to the allure of the hotel's unique blend of isolation and privacy. Dazzling sunrises and sunsets await visitors to this uncommon place, which always seems cloaked in shards of sunlight steeped in every imaginable shade of gold.

The salt-tinged fragrance of the sea offers a splendid backdrop for quiet evenings spent on one of the many verandahs which enfold the hotel. The gentle coastal climate allows grass to flourish, nurturing it to a deep emerald hue, even during winter months. Spanish moss draped from scores of massive live oaks, the lively scent of sweet magnolias, and gently swaying palms complete this picture of serenity.

When I first began to scratch beneath the surface of the Jekyll Island Club, I realized there was more to this island paradise than just another grand resort hotel. Its distinctive history is unlike that of any other place in Georgia.

"The Jekyll Island Club sprang out of an idea of Newton Finney, a New York merchant," says John Hunter, who serves as chief curator and assistant director of operations and the museum of the Jekyll Island Authority. "Finney was the brother-in-law of John Eugene duBignon, a descendant of one of the early colonial landowners on the island."

Finney had links through his business associations to the Union Club in New York, one of the most exclusive clubs in the world at that time – a tradition continued today. In the 1880s, the membership roster of the club read like a "Who's Who" of business and industry in New York. It included the likes of William Rockefeller,

William K. Vanderbilt, J.P. Morgan, Joseph Pulitzer, Marshall Field, Frank Henry Goodyear, and many others.

In the 1880s, the railroad through Georgia terminated in Thomasville, so Florida was still relatively undiscovered and wild. Because of that, South Georgia had become the resort retreat of choice by wealthy Northerners bent on escaping the harsh winters. Jekyll Island became a natural progression of this seasonal migration.

"The idea was becoming very popular for the Union Club's members and their families to have hunting or winter retreats to which they would periodically travel," Hunter states. "This was not long after the Carnegies purchased Cumberland Island. Sapelo Island nearby was being purchased, and St. Simon's Island was starting to be a little bit of a resort area. After borrowing money to purchase Jekyll and develop it into a hunting club site, Finney and duBignon incorporated the Jekyll Island Club, and then sold shares for $600 apiece to members of the Union Club. The two men, in essence, sold the island to the club for $125,000, which in 1886 in South Georgia was a tremendous amount of money. In today's dollars, that's about $2.5 to $3 million."

Initially, there were a hundred members in the Jekyll Island Club, a number that remained fairly consistent throughout its history. Some of the first members of the club constituted not only the likes of Morgan, Vanderbilt, Rockefeller, Goodyear, Field, and Pulitzer, but also men such as Theodore Vail, president of AT&T and one of the early leaders of what is known today as the telecommunications industry.

Following their purchase of the acreage, the club members then invested more money to build a substantial clubhouse. Additionally, lots for exclusive private homes were laid out around the clubhouse property to be sold along with the memberships. The clubhouse, with its Queen Anne architecture, indoor plumbing, dozens of fire-

places, wraparound porches, and dramatic turret, was completed in time for the beginning of the winter season in January of 1888.

"The typical club season would begin – depending upon whether or not one had a cottage or stayed at the clubhouse – as early as Thanksgiving and last through mid-March," Hunter explains. "Those who had cottages would come down around Thanksgiving to mid-December. Most of the time, the other club members would come down just after New Year's and stay until February."

Between 1886 and 1928, other services were added to the club, including a dining room complete with Ionic columns, telephone service, and even an elevator. During this time, members also built lavish "cottages" that were reflective of their lifestyles during that period.

During the last years of the 19th century and the first few years of the 20th century, the club flourished in its stateliness and even contributed small slivers of modern history to the world. For instance, the framework for the Aldrich Act, which became the Federal Reserve Act, was drafted there in 1910, and the first transcontinental telephone call was made by Theodore Vail from the clubhouse in 1915.

"Vail was at the club because he had injured his leg," says Hunter. "He was supposed to be in Washington, D.C., with Woodrow Wilson for the first call, but he was in a wheelchair and couldn't make the trip. He had his engineers string and connect the lines, which they brought across the marsh and hooked up in the basement of the clubhouse. For the call, Vail was here, Woodrow Wilson was in Washington, Alexander Graham Bell was in New York, and Dr. Watson was in San Francisco."

By the 1920s, however, important and defining changes had gripped the country.

The jazz age was coming into vogue, and West Palm Beach and Miami were being opened up to tourism because of the railroad. South Florida had become a much more "happening" place with its Mediterranean styles and hot nightlife. Everything was all Hemingway, F. Scott Fitzgerald, and pink flamingoes. The Jekyll Island Club, with its old money blue-blood family ties and aging members, tried to keep pace with the times, but just couldn't.

To add to its woe, the club's isolation and its circumstances as a retreat from the hustle and bustle of the city became both a blessing and a curse. As the original club members who had joined in the 1880s grew older and began to die out, the club, says Hunter, wasn't seen as a family legacy, and [in many instances over time], the houses weren't handed down to family descendants. They were simply turned back in to the club, which then attempted to sell the property to new club members.

By the late 1930s, major conflicts in Europe were causing a ripple-effect in America, bringing with them a concern and anxiety about travel. In the spring of 1942, German U-Boats began prowling the east coast of the United States and sinking commercial vessels. A number of the craft were torpedoed and sunk within sight of the Georgia coast – some only a few miles from Jekyll. As a result, those remaining on the island were evacuated, and throughout the war years, the site remained essentially abandoned. The club became insolvent and was closed down and forgotten.

After World War II ended in 1945, efforts to revive the club were initiated by Frank Gould. He was the son of Edwin Gould, who was a club member, and the grandson of Jay Gould, a financier and railroad magnate. Frank's older brother, Edwin Jr., died on Jekyll Island in a hunting accident, and because of family connections to the island, he didn't want to give up on the old traditions.

Gould partnered with Bill Jones of the Sea Island Company to reinvigorate the club. The pair intended to model the club after The Cloister, an even more luxurious resort located on Sea Island a few miles to the north. Unfortunately, Gould – who was only in his mid-forties at the time – dropped dead after a massive heart attack one morning at his breakfast table. Jones and others in the investment group never recovered from the loss of their leader, and ultimately abandoned any further attempts to reopen the club.

Sue Andersson, who works in public relations and guest programs today at the Jekyll Island Club Hotel, says that when the old club members abandoned the club in the 1940s, the buildings and grounds were left with no maintenance for the ensuing years.

"By 1947, when virtually none of the members had returned, the mortgages, dues, and fees came due and were not paid," Andersson explains. "There was no money with which to continue maintenance or upkeep of the place."

That was when the State of Georgia stepped in. Under its direction, Jekyll Island was to be turned into a state park to make it accessible to all citizens. The state bought all outstanding shares of stock for $675,000.

For a while, it looked as if the state had a white elephant on its hands. "There was considerable concern about what would be done with Jekyll Island for the people of the state," Andersson continues. "They didn't have a loyalty to it. They didn't have fond memories of a childhood here because it had always been owned exclusively by club members from 1886 until 1942. No Georgia citizens [had been allowed to come] here because it was privately owned by the club members."

Eventually, the Jekyll Island Authority, an entity that continues to manage the island on the state's behalf today, was formed in 1950. The clubhouse was then opened as a sort of bed-and-breakfast, Andersson says, with some "minor politicians" being sent down to manage the property. But in the 1950s the only people who traveled to Jekyll Island were those who owned boats or had friends who owned boats, because the causeway had not yet been built that connected the island to the mainland. Certainly, then, tourists and their dollars were really very few and far between, and Jekyll Island continued to be difficult to both reach and maintain.

By the early 1970s, the clubhouse had been virtually shut down, because parts of it – including its once majestic verandahs – had deteriorated to the point of becoming unsafe. It was also during this period that many of the priceless furnishings, decorative items, and trappings – such as the solid silver window latches of the luxurious homes – were stolen by thieves and pilferers who carried the treasures by boat back to the mainland.

Sadly, the hotel continued to deteriorate until the 1980s, when a man named Barry Evans came to Jekyll to play golf. Evans, an architect, happened to drive past the old clubhouse and was intrigued by the site. He researched the property and found that it had been the exclusive hunting retreat for the likes of the Morgans, Astors, Vanderbilts, and the hundreds of others who once had enjoyed its unparalleled character.

"[Mr. Evans] thought how wonderful it would be to breathe life back into it," Ms. Andersson smiles. "He had made a career of seeking out properties that could be retrofitted to serve a contemporary, useful function. He and his partners transformed the Jekyll Island Club into a hotel and resort."

And that's where the Jekyll Island Club Hotel is today. From its richly appointed rooms to the intricate scrollwork to its manicured gardens, the hotel is once again a palatial resort. Its Victorian style – including that spectacular turret and the dozens of bay windows – reminds visitors of the good taste and grace of the "Gay 90s."

One legend surrounding the aged hotel maintains that the original members were required to dine in the clubhouse's dining room where they were often served sumptuous 10-course meals. Today's guests will find that the Grand Dining Room – its historic Ionic columns still in place – continues to offer a variety of specialty dishes like crusted grouper rolled in Georgia pecans; Grilled Pork Vidalia, which is a tangy pork loin topped with a Vidalia onion marmalade; or Plantation Shrimp, carefully prepared with Georgia white shrimp, all of which will tempt the palate of even the most distinguished guests.

Imprinting it in history, the hotel was recognized as a National Historic Landmark in 1978, and just recently was designated a Historic Hotel of American by the National Trust for Historic Preservation. Today, the Jekyll Island Authority owns all of the historic structures on the island, which includes anything built prior to 1947. The historic district, which is spread over 240 acres and comprised of 33 buildings including the hotel, cottages, and other structures such as stables and tennis courts, looks basically the same as it did during the island's heydays.

At the end of the day at the Jekyll Island Club, as I watched as shrimp boats navigating the slim channels of the Intracoastal Waterway, listened to the seagulls jabbering in the ocean air, tasted the saltiness of the endless acres of the peaceful marsh, and sensed the whisperings of ghosts of those who first came to the island, I realized that this place captures the heart and soul of Georgia's coast as can no other.

(The Jekyll Island Club is located at 371 Riverview Drive, Jekyll Island. The telephone number is (912) 635-2600 or toll-free (800) 535-9547. You may also visit the website at www.jekyllclub.com.)

Co-Editor R. Olin Jackson – A native of the north Georgia region, Olin Jackson is a graduate of Georgia State University (Bachelor of Arts in journalism) and North Georgia College & State University (Masters Degree in Education). In 1985, Olin founded Legacy Communications, Inc., the publisher of *Georgia Backroads* magazine (originally *North Georgia Journal*) and eight books devoted to Georgia history. Olin retired from the publishing world in 2005. He and his wife Judy reside in Roswell, Georgia. When Olin isn't singing in the choir at Mt. Pisgah United Methodist Church, he's usually working on his beloved cabin "on a peak in Polk" near Rockmart, Georgia.

Co-Editor Daniel M. Roper – A native of Miami, Florida, but happily residing in Georgia since 1979, Dan Roper is a graduate of the University of Georgia with degrees in forest resources and law. After practicing law in Rome for twenty years, Dan became the president of Legacy Communications, Inc. upon Olin Jackson's retirement in 2005. Dan and his wife Lisa reside in Armuchee, Georgia, with their three children Laura Anne, John, and Jackson.

Clifford Johnson is an Atlanta born, award-winning graphic designer of corporate and marketing print communications. Publications are a specialty and *Georgia Backroads* magazine is an example. He earned a fine arts degree at the University of Georgia at a time when the graphic arts were still largely executed by hand. Clifford Johnson Design was created in 1989 in Roswell, Georgia, where Clifford and his wife Lisa still live. Contact Clifford at cj.design@mindspring.com or 770-664-6433.